ANGLO-AMERICAN
UNDERSTANDING,
1898-1903

Anglo-American Understanding,

1898-1903

BY CHARLES S. CAMPBELL, JR.

BALTIMORE: The Johns Hopkins Press

Distributed in Great Britain by
Oxford University Press, London

Printed in the U. S. A.

Library of Congress Catalogue Card Number 57–9518

This book has been brought to publication with
the assistance of a grant from the Ford Foundation.

First printing, 1957
Second printing, 1965

Preface

IN RECENT years Great Britain and the United States have been thrown into close collaboration with each other. Although often disagreeing, sometimes seriously so, they have pursued the same basic objectives in their foreign policies. On the whole, a high degree of mutual trust and confidence has prevailed.

Even such limited collaboration is not easily achieved in the harsh and turbulent realm of international affairs. Diplomacy cannot accomplish everything, and it is sometimes maintained that it can accomplish nothing of consequence. But unremitting vigilance on the part of diplomats and others is essential if good relations are to exist between countries.

Throughout most of the years since American independence the United States and Great Britain, far from collaborating, worked at cross purposes, twice to the point of war, often to the point of angry recrimination and bellicose talk. Animosity, not friendship, was the rule. No doubt, strong underlying forces developed, as time passed, which helped drive the two perennial antagonists together; but certainly no ineluctable fate ordained that they should reach an understanding around the turn of the century. Persistent, patient diplomatic negotiations by the United States and Great Britain, with Canada sometimes participating, were necessary for that.

In this book I have examined the negotiations in some detail. Through them Britain and America, having come to realize that a comprehensive understanding was to the interest of each, took advantage of favorable circumstances and some luck in order to resolve serious controversies beclouding relations between the two countries, and even endangering the peace. Thereby they contributed to a notable, and so far a lasting, change in the climate of Anglo-American relations.

v

I am particularly grateful to Professor Samuel Flagg Bemis for having read my manuscript and for having made many helpful suggestions. I wish to thank the American Philosophical Society for a grant from its Penrose Fund in support of my work on this book.

Charles S. Campbell, Jr.

The Johns Hopkins University
Baltimore, March, 1957

FOOTNOTE ABBREVIATIONS

C. O. Colonial Office records, in Public Record Office
F. O. Foreign Office records, in Public Record Office

Contents

vii

ANGLO-AMERICAN
UNDERSTANDING,
1898-1903

CHAPTER 1

Preparation

IN THE spring of 1898 when the Spanish-American War started —that conflict that was to do much to bring about friendlier feelings between Britain and America—Great Britain and the United States had a long record of mutual hostility behind them. Two Anglo-American wars and a steady undercurrent of friction, often flaring up dangerously, had left a bitter legacy. Even as late as 1895 and 1896 a sharp clash over the Venezuelan boundary gave rise to much loud and bellicose talk in the United States. For many Americans Britain was *the* enemy: an implacable vindictive foe ever on the watch for an opportunity to strike down the impertinent republic that had once been British.

Yet a tremendous improvement in relations between the two countries took place in 1898, an improvement that facilitated, and was itself rendered more lasting by, a settlement of major controversies over the next five years. The effect of the war with Spain on Anglo-American relations will be examined in some detail in the next chapter. But it is desirable, first, to look into some of the obstacles to British-American friendship during the years following the Civil War, as well as into developments contributing to the settlement around the turn of the century.

For several years after the Civil War relations were critical, and a third Anglo-American war not impossible. The victorious North was convinced that the British, and the Canadians too for that matter, had had their hearts with the Confederacy, that their sympathy and material aid had prolonged the terrible

1

conflict, bringing untold suffering and expense to the nation. Particularly reprehensible was the building of Southern cruisers in Britain, the *Alabama*, the *Shenandoah*, the *Florida*. In a dramatic speech in April, 1869, the chairman of the Senate Committee on Foreign Relations, Charles Sumner, a man of immense prestige, put no less than half the total cost of the hostilities to British account; only through cession of Canada, he implied, could she absolve her heavy guilt. The immediate post-war crisis was eased by an agreement to appoint a Joint High Commission to settle outstanding grievances. Meeting in 1871, the commissioners drew up the famous treaty of Washington; it laid down final agreements, or procedures for reaching agreement, on most of the controversies. Under its provisions claims against Britain regarding the *Alabama* and other ships were settled in favor of the United States by the Geneva arbitration of 1872. A large part of the credit for this comprehensive settlement must go to the American Secretary of State, Hamilton Fish. Except for his wise and patient diplomacy another clash with Britain could easily have occurred. By avoiding such a catastrophe, and thereby giving the ugly Civil War passions time to subside, Secretary Fish made a momentous contribution to the rapprochement at the turn of the century.

But one potent source of ill-will was not removed, was not even considered indeed, by the Joint High Commission. It concerned too delicate a matter in American politics. During the same post-war years, when Anglo-American relations were bad enough as it was, thousands of determined Irish-Americans saw a heaven-sent opportunity to strike a blow for Ireland, then struggling for home rule. Could they but plunge their adopted country into war with detested Great Britain hopes would soar for the Irish cause. During the five or six years after the Civil War an organization of Irish-Americans, the Fenians, many of them veterans of the Union army, raided across the Canadian border on several occasions. Such was the power of the Irish vote that the federal authorities in Washington could not for some time muster up courage to suppress these outrageous activities. And when they did, naturalized Irishmen found another way to bait the British. Some of them returned to Britain or Ireland where they committed acts of terrorism; occasionally they courted arrest. Many of these revolutionists, the United States minister at London, James Russell Lowell, said, have "gone back to Ireland with the hope, and sometimes, I am justified in saying, with the deliberate intention, of disturbing the friendly relations between the U. S. and England." [1]

Quite apart from these more spectacular activities, the Irish had other means of embittering Anglo-American relations. Concentrated in large, politically important cities, their votes effectively marshalled by such organizations as Tammany Hall, Irishmen had an influence upon American elections out of all proportion to their numbers. All the more was this the case because the Republican and Democratic parties were so evenly divided that presidential elections in the 1870's, 1880's, and 1890's sometimes turned upon a handful of votes. No politician could afford to neglect the implacable prejudices of these rabidly anti-English and politically talented citizens from across the Atlantic.

Irish influence reached its peak during the first decade or so after the Civil War. As it began to taper off, another band of zealots stepped forward. These were the free-silverites. [2] The crusade for free and unlimited coinage of silver at a ratio of sixteen to one with gold acquired tremendous momentum and intensity in the late 1880's and the 1890's. For thousands and thousands of people on western farmlands, in silver-mining states, and in the still unreconstructed South, free silver became a formula to end their economic woes, even a creed to live by. But bimetallism could hardly succeed in the United States unless other financially important countries cooperated. The chief stumbling-block was Great Britain, citadel of the gold standard and controller of the immense silver hoards of India. By adhering to gold Britain could make the way hard indeed for silver. Consequently a dislike of Great Britain was an article of faith for any

[1] B. Willson, *America's Ambassadors to England (1785-1929)*, *a Narrative of Anglo-American Relations* (New York, 1929), p. 380.

[2] J. P. Nichols, "Silver Diplomacy," *Political Science Quarterly*, vol. 48 (1933), pp. 565-588.

true believer in free silver. Henry Cabot Lodge, senator from Massachusetts, called the money question the " deepest of all present causes " of antipathy toward England.[3] The greedy financial lords of British gold, to whom the United States and the rest of the world were in financial bondage, constituted the root evil; having succeeded, in collaboration with their Wall Street sycophants, in clamping their golden yoke upon the working masses of America, they could be dislodged by nothing short of force. " If it is claimed we must adopt for our money the metal England selects . . . ," a widely read book proclaimed,

> let us make the test and find out if it is true. . . . If it is true, let us attach England to the United States and blot her name out from among the nations of the earth. . . .
> A war with England would be the most popular ever waged on the face of the earth. . . . If it is true that she can dictate the money of the world, and thereby create world-wide misery, it would be the most just war ever waged by man.[4]

In addition to the pervasive influence of the Irish and the silverites certain specific controversies plagued relations between America and Britain. Some of the issues dealt with in the treaty of Washington became critical again as the years passed, and certain new controversies appeared for the first time. Most of these concerned the Dominion of Canada. The perennial debate, marked by occasional acts of violence, over fishing rights off Canada and Newfoundland; thorny problems associated with Canadian-American trade; clashes over Bering Sea seals—these matters, as we shall see in some detail in a later chapter,[5] led to much angry bickering during the 1880's and 1890's. In 1886 British gunboats were harrying American fishermen in the fishing grounds, and American revenue cutters were arresting Canadian sealers in the Bering Sea. Talk of war was not uncommon. Certainly Great Britain was not popular; and when her minister at

---

[3] B. E. C. Dugdale, *Arthur James Balfour, First Earl of Balfour, K. G., O. M., F. R. S., Etc.* (2 vols., New York, 1937), vol. 1, p. 166.

[4] W. H. Harvey, *Coin's Financial School* (Chicago, 1894), pp. 131-132. Happily the author decided that war was unnecessary.

[5] See ch. 3.

Washington, Sir Lionel Sackville-West, let himself be hoodwinked into expressing written preference for a Democratic victory in the election of 1888, he was ejected from the country by a Democratic administration indignant that it should be thought less hostile to Britain than the Republicans. Angry over this summary dismissal, Great Britain did not appoint a new minister for some months.

A few years later, at the end of 1895, came the sharpest clash of all.[6] For many years Great Britain and Venezuela had been at odds over the undetermined boundary between that South American country and British Guiana. President Grover Cleveland, during his second administration, resolved to bring the dispute to a head. His Secretary of State, Richard Olney, sent a note to Great Britain in July, 1895, demanding in effect that Britain arbitrate the dispute as one impinging upon the Monroe Doctrine. The reply several months later of Britain's Prime Minister and Foreign Secretary, Lord Salisbury, denying the Monroe Doctrine's relevance, seems to have infuriated the President. He sent an angry message to Congress—one may doubt, however, that he wrote it " sitting in his shirt sleeves, between two bottles of whiskey," as rumored at the time [7]—asking authority to appoint a commission to investigate the boundary. ". . . I am fully alive," he stated grimly, " to the responsibilities incurred and keenly realize all the consequences that may follow."

The immediate consequence was an explosion of anti-British feeling that resounded throughout the United States like a sudden clap of thunder. ". . . the note of war which he [Cleveland] sounded has produced in Congress and among the Public a condition of mind which can only be described as hysterical," Sir Julian Pauncefote, Sackville-West's successor, informed Prime Minister Salisbury.[8] For a moment it seemed as though long pent-up hatred of Britain of the most extreme character had suddenly been released and was now raging at large, quite out

---

[6] J. A. Sloan, " Anglo-American Relations and the Venezuelan Boundary Dispute," *Hispanic American Historical Review*, vol. 18 (1938) , pp. 486-506.
[7] Salisbury papers, Pauncefote to Salisbury, June 23, 1896.
[8] F. O. 80, 364, December 24, 1895.

of control. " It has been a most instructive thing for the dispassionate student of history," the American philosopher, William James, wrote a friend, " to see how near the surface in all of us the old fighting instinct lies, and how slight an appeal will wake it up. Once *really* waked, there is no retreat. . . . Cleveland in my opinion, by his explicit allusion to war, has committed the biggest political crime I have ever seen here." [9]

Fortunately, however, the instinct had not been " *really* waked." A strong reaction against war in both the United States and Great Britain flared up as quickly as the American clamor for war had done, with the result that the crisis blew over within a few days. Great Britain and Venezuela agreed to arbitrate; and a tribunal consisting of two American Supreme Court justices and one Russian and two British jurists returned an award favorable to Great Britain on October 3, 1899.

This extraordinary episode had an extraordinary sequel. Profoundly disturbed by the violence of the passions so suddenly awakened in America, people in both countries nervously searched for some means of preventing the dark abyss from ever again yawning beneath them. Seizing advantage of the mood, Olney and Pauncefote signed a general arbitration treaty on January 11, 1897. " The great Arbitration Treaty will take the wind out of the sails of the Jingoes as regards Great Britain, & the Eagle will have to screech at the other Powers, & let the British Lion nurse his tail," Pauncefote rejoiced.[10] But he rejoiced too soon; for the United States Senate, in a particularly jealous and petty mood, refused to ratify.[11]

Shortly before this disappointing and unexpected development the election of 1896 took place. It was fortunate that the Venezuelan crisis had finished by then, because excitement over free silver reached its peak during the election. Led by the indefatigable and eloquent William Jennings Bryan, silver forces cap-

[9] H. James, ed., *The Letters of William James, Edited by His Son Henry James* (2 vols., Boston, 1920) , vol. 2, p. 31.

[10] Salisbury papers, to Salisbury, January 1, 1897.

[11] N. M. Blake, " The Olney-Pauncefote Treaty of 1897," *American Historical Review*, vol. 50 (1945) , pp. 228-243.

tured the Democratic party and threw a scare into the bulwarks
of respectability from which they did not soon recover. It was
not only the orthodox of America who came under attack;
Britain, too, as the stronghold of gold, received a severe drubbing
from Bryan and his fellow spell-binders. Right in the Democratic
platform an article set the tone: " Gold monometallism is a
British policy and its adoption has brought other nations into
financial servitude to London. . . . We demand the free and
unlimited coinage of both silver and gold at the present legal ratio
of sixteen to one without waiting for the aid or consent of any
other nation." [12] If the Democrats had won, British investors in
the United States might have incurred heavy losses, and in any
event a period of heightened tension between the two countries
would have ensued. But with the victory of the Republicans
after a most exciting campaign, this particular threat disappeared.[13] Prosperity returned to the farm lands, and the cause of
silver lost its drive. Never again did it stir up thousands of
Americans to a state of righteous fury against the recalcitrant
British. " I have just returned from shaking hands for the last
time with President Cleveland," Sir Julian wrote Lord Salisbury.
" I hope the next administration will give us less trouble than
the two preceding ones during which, had you not been at the
helm at the stormiest periods, the good ship Peace would certainly
have foundered." [14]

Despite his high-tariff proclivities the new President, William
McKinley, turned out to be surprisingly well disposed toward
Great Britain. It was during his administration, in fact, that
a tremendous improvement in trans-Atlantic relations took place,
for which the President deserves much credit. McKinley was
himself a steady if not fervent proponent of closer ties with
Britain; and at the end of 1898 he made a notable contribution to
the better relations by the unusual choice as Secretary of State
of a man with no great political influence but a strong love

[12] J. F. Rhodes, *The McKinley and Roosevelt Administrations, 1897-1909*
(New York, 1922) , p. 18.
[13] Blake, " Olney-Pauncefote Treaty," p. 239.
[14] Salisbury papers, January 1, 1897.

for Britain, the American ambassador to the Court of St. James, John Hay. Backed by the President, Secretary Hay carried out a series of negotiations that reached a general settlement with the British and thereby contributed to and helped consolidate the friendlier sentiment. But for the basic causes of the change we must look further than the Republican triumph of 1896.

Since the early 1870's, when Hamilton Fish had succeeded in clearing away temporarily many of the accumulated issues with Great Britain, more than thirty years had elapsed. Difficulties, even sharp clashes threatening war, there had been; but war had been avoided, and the mere passage of time had had a stabilizing effect. It had softened the hoary picture of Britain as the colonial oppressor and inveterate enemy of independent America. The common language with Great Britain, the fact that after all a great many more Americans had come from there than from Ireland or any other country, the common legal and religious traditions, the similar concepts of government—such fundamental factors were bound to make themselves felt given a long enough period of peace. Time had softened even the Irish. By the end of the century a third generation had grown to manhood in its new land, men who had not experienced the terrible conditions which so embittered the "hunger immigrants" of the 1840's and their children. "The professional Irishman is losing his grip and the bulk of the Irish are becoming Americans," Theodore Roosevelt was pleased to find in early 1899.[15]

Since Civil War days when an aristocratic governing class in Britain welcomed what seemed to be the impending disintegration of upstart democracy, the social structure in both countries had changed. Now in 1898 not only was Lord Salisbury's government far more broadly based than Lord Palmerston's had been, but in the United States political power had come to a newly risen class of millionaires who liked to think of themselves as constituting, and in fact did constitute, a kind of American aristocracy. There was something in common between these American "aristocrats," with their country houses staffed with British

[15] S. Gwynn, *The Letters and Friendships of Sir Cecil Spring Rice* (2 vols., Boston and New York, 1929), vol. 1, p. 292.

servants and their daughters wedded to British noblemen, and the new governing classes in Britain.

It was indeed the age of trans-Atlantic marriages in high places. More than seventy Americans had married titled Britons by 1903; more than a hundred and thirty by 1914.[16] The glamorous wedding of the Duke of Marlborough and Consuelo Vanderbilt in 1895 had not only created the intended duchess for America and dollars for Blenheim Palace, but it had created an unintended tranquilizing effect on the contemporary Venezuelan affair by providing the American public with a far more fascinating spectacle even than the most provocative of Secretary Olney's notes.[17] Other Anglo-American marriages, though less spectacular, were more important politically. Lord Randolph Churchill had married the wealthy Jennie Jerome of New York, a union that by 1898 had already produced a famous Prime Minister of the future; George Curzon, whose career in 1898 lay mainly before him but who was already Under-Secretary for Foreign Affairs, had married Mary Leiter, daughter of a Chicago millionaire; Sir Michael Herbert, Pauncefote's successor as ambassador to the United States in 1902, had married another millionaire's daughter, Leila Wilson, thereby not only acquiring a fortune directly but becoming the brother-in-law of Mrs. Cornelius Vanderbilt and a comfortably close connection of John Jacob Astor's. Sir William Harcourt, leader of the Liberal party, and Joseph Chamberlain, Salisbury's Colonial Secretary, did not do so well financially. The former was the husband of Elizabeth Motley, daughter of the American historian; Chamberlain the husband of Mary Endicott, daughter of Cleveland's Secretary of War. Here was an extraordinary galaxy of American women married to British governmental leaders. One might almost stop with that in explaining the rise of friendly feelings between America and Britain.

America's phenomenal industrial growth after the Civil War,

[16] H. C. Allen, *Great Britain and the United States, A History of Anglo-American Relations (1783-1952)* (New York, 1955), p. 111.

[17] See Pauncefote's remarks to Salisbury in Salisbury papers, November 8, 1895.

which it might be thought would have fostered British resentment, served mainly to bring the countries together. As the century neared its close many Americans, their complacency shaken by the panic of 1893, were becoming worried about overproduction. Concerned lest the mounting industrial and agricultural output could not be consumed at home, they were searching for foreign markets to absorb the surplus.[18] From this point of view an easy transition led to the typical imperialistic, big-navy outlook on international affairs, the American variety of which was known as the Large Policy, with A. T. Mahan, Henry Cabot Lodge, and Theodore Roosevelt as leading exponents; it led also to admiration for and understanding of Great Britain as the imperialistic, big-navy nation *par excellence*,[19] a nation that held no menace for the United States if only because of the exposed position of Canada. At the same time America's overseas expansion, when it got well under way in 1898, directed itself mainly into areas where friction with Britain did not develop.

Other factors, too, may be mentioned. Returning prosperity in America after the panic of 1893 was undermining free-silver agitation with its anti-British overtones. Trans-Atlantic travel had reached a point where it increased international understanding, but not a point where some of the worst representatives of both countries were able to visit—and disillusion—the other. A fashionable cult of " race patriotism," emphasizing the allegedly superior virtues of Anglo-Saxons, made the subjects of John Bull and at least many citizens of Uncle Sam well pleased with each other. " Canada should annex the United States as Scotland annexed England," proclaimed Andrew Carnegie half jestingly, but half seriously, too. " I am a race patriot. I want the whole Anglo-Celtic race to get together." [20] Lord Salisbury's patient and conciliatory policy and Pauncefote's dignified bearing and

---

[18] Regarding these matters see C. S. Campbell, Jr., *Special Business Interests and the Open Door Policy* (New Haven, 1951), ch. 1.

[19] J. W. Pratt, *Expansionists of 1898, The Acquisition of Hawaii and the Spanish Islands* (Baltimore, 1936), gives the best account of the Large Policy.

[20] *The Times*, October 31, 1903.

solid competence were making inroads into traditional American suspicions.[21] So were the accumulating years of Queen Victoria, more and more an object of veneration in republican America. James Bryce pleased her with an account of the " great feeling " for her in that country which, he thought, " had much to do with the improved relations. . . ." [22] Bryce himself had contributed notably to the improvement by an unusually sympathetic portrayal of America in his widely read *The American Commonwealth*, first published in 1888.

All these were matters that had been exerting their influence over the years. Their influence was undoubtedly tremendous, though impossible to measure precisely. Had they not been steadily making themselves felt in the background, no rise in British-American friendship could have occurred around 1900. We must now turn from them, however, to a consideration of two other matters, more immediately and directly related to the Anglo-American settlement between 1898 and 1903—developments in China and threats to Britain's power elsewhere. These had a profound effect upon Anglo-American relations.

By the end of the nineteenth century the headstart in industrial development and international trade from which Great Britain had benefited for years was being rapidly cut down. Both the United States and Germany had developed their industries to a point where British manufacturing techniques were beginning to look old-fashioned; and France and Russia, though less advanced technically, were busy erecting massive tariff walls around

[21] In a debate in the House of Commons the Under-Secretary for Foreign Affairs, George Curzon, said: ". . . I have been under the impression that a great deal of that happy feeling [between Great Britain and the United States] was due not merely to the exigencies of the moment, or to the particular events now passing, but had been due to the consistently friendly and calm and dispassionate attitude assumed by the present Prime Minister in the discussions about difficult matters with America three years ago. . . . On all sides we see the temperate and courteous handling of these American disputes by Lord Salisbury three years ago bearing fruit, which we hope will produce peace in the future " (*The Times*, June 11, 1898).

[22] G. E. Buckle, ed., *The Letters of Queen Victoria, Third Series* (3 vols., New York, 1932), vol. 3, p. 305.

their growing empires. These were developments of gravest import to Britain, for whom flourishing commerce was a matter of life and death.

Of all foreign markets Great Britain pinned her chief hopes on the ancient Chinese empire. She had dominated China's trade for many years, and by the 1890's controlled over seventy percent of it. So great a lead did she have over her rivals as almost to preclude their ever catching up; so it seemed. Britain's trade with this one country alone had an annual value of around £33,000,000, one-sixth of her total international commerce. In addition, her ships carried three-fourths of China's foreign trade and over half of China's coastwise trade; and her great commercial houses, centered in Hongkong and the Yangtze valley, did business throughout the old empire. Not only was her current trade enormous but her hopes for the future were greater still. What could not be expected of a market with 400,000,000 consumers! In the 1890's Britain and other industrial countries were turning to China as a market potentially so immense as to be able to absorb any conceivable surplus. China, then, seemed to hold the answer for the delicately balanced British economy. Let the United States and Germany concentrate on technical improvements; let Russia and France concentrate on exclusive trading arrangements. Britain would outmaneuver them by developing that enormous potential market in the Far East. "China is the greatest potential customer in the world for certain classes of European goods—classes of goods in which we can hold our own against all rivals with a fair field"; so stated the London *Times*.[23]

". . . with a fair field," the *Times's* concluding phrase, was significant. Britain's success in China and her hopes for the future depended upon non-discriminatory treatment of imports into that country. Should her commercial rivals succeed in establishing preferential tariff areas in different parts of the country, Britain's exports would be hard hit. What she wanted, therefore, was simply the perpetuation of what she already had:

[23] January 6, 1898.

the chance to take on all comers throughout the length and breadth of China on a basis of non-discrimination. "Our interests there are not territorial; they are commercial," Arthur Balfour, leader of the House of Commons, said in early 1898; Great Britain demanded "equality of commercial opportunity," the policy of the open door.[24]

The United States saw pretty much eye to eye with Great Britain in this matter. True, Americans could boast of no such accomplishment as Britain's hold on seventy percent of China's trade; but their exports were increasing rapidly—more so than British exports—and in Manchuria they actually led the world. Moreover the vision of the potential market had fired the imaginations of many Americans who, obsessed with the spectre of overproduction, like the British looked to the 400,000,000 Chinese for salvation.[25] Naturally they viewed with pleasure an open door under which their businesses had prospered and which held high hopes for their future; naturally they sympathized with Great Britain, the champion of commercial equality, rather than with Russia, France, and Germany with their more exclusive systems.

Unfortunately, however, disquieting developments were taking place in the 1890's. Spheres of influence and leased territories were beginning to proliferate upon China's prostrate bulk; and it seemed all too likely that they would prove to be precursors of outright partition. Indeed, talk of partition was heard on all sides, and the belief was widespread that the great powers, having finished parcelling up Africa, would now turn to China, the last big area still unappropriated. Already their fleets and armed forces were frequenting the Chinese littoral. Not all these countries shared the British-American affection for the open door. Russia in particular, with her ally France not far behind, viewed it with the distaste natural to a country whose exporters needed protection. Even Germany, despite her efficient industries, seemed

---

[24] This statement was made January 10, 1898. For Hay's comments see State Department, Great Britain, Despatches, Hay to Sherman, January 11, 1898.

[25] Campbell, *Special Business Interests*, chs. I and II.

at times to share this point of view. In 1895 after the Sino-Japanese war she, Russia, and France collectively intervened to force Japan to disgorge a major part of her conquests—a move which aroused suspicions of a standing German-Russian-French agreement for common action in the Far East. Such an agreement would bode ill for Britain.

Far greater cause for concern came at the end of 1897. In November the precarious equipoise in the orient received a rude jolt when German troops debarked at Kiaochow in Shantung province, and a Russian fleet dropped anchor at Port Arthur.[26] At once a first-class crisis was precipitated. The long expected partition of China was surely at hand; even war seemed likely. Great Britain faced a terrible choice. Should she stand firm against Russia and Germany, and run a grave risk of conflict; or do nothing, and permit a serious weakening of the open door policy? One thing seemed certain: Britain would fight rather than be ousted from the oriental markets. Arthur Balfour gave solemn warning of the government's determination to uphold equal trading rights in China, " which is all they claim—but which they do claim." [27] And the Chancellor of the Exchequer, Sir Michael Hicks Beach, went further: " We do not regard China as a place for conquest or acquisition by any . . . power. We look upon it as the most hopeful place of the future for the commerce of our country and the commerce of the world at large, and the Government were absolutely determined, at whatever cost, even—and he wished to speak plainly—if necessary, at the cost of war that that door should not be shut." [28]

Confronted by these perils, Britain looked hopefully across the Atlantic. The American chargé d'affaires at London, Henry White, found that " the opinion is general in this country, that

---

[26] The details of these events are so well known that only the barest outline need be given here. The reader can find further information in P. Joseph, *Foreign Diplomacy in China, 1894-1900, A Study in Political and Economic Relations with China* (London, 1928), chs. ix, xi; and W. L. Langer, *The Diplomacy of Imperialism, 1890-1902* (2 vols., New York and London, 1935), vol. 2, ch. xiv.

[27] Speech at Manchester, January 10, 1898.

[28] *The Times*, January 18, 1898.

Her Majesty's Government . . . will have the sympathy and support of the people of the United States and not improbably of
our Government also." [29] And the London *Times* was "glad
to note that this country enjoys the powerful support of the
Government of the United States, as well as of the public opinion
of that portion of the American people which is not carried
away by blind jingo denunciations." [30] Such observations were
well taken. The news from the Far East did alarm Americans,
although they felt its impact far less than the British, who for
a moment stood face to face with war. The United States traditionally had held Russia in high regard, but the old friendship
had been shaken in recent years and it was to be shaken much
more as Russian expansion in the Far East directed itself squarely
at Manchuria, the one part of China where American exports
predominated. Germany had been in America's bad books for
some years; mainly because of her tactless diplomacy almost her
every move served only to confirm the prevailing American conception of the Fatherland as an overbearing and dangerous bully.
The United States would have to support Great Britain against
Germany and Russia, the *New York Herald* declared flatly, because the continental powers could be expected to set up discriminatory trading areas.[31] Hailing Britain as the "champion
of civilization," the *New York Times* affirmed: "Our interests
in the East are the same as hers." [32] And a senator of much
prestige, Senator Frye of Maine, declared publicly: "This country
is vitally interested in the situation in China. . . . Our interest
in the matter cannot be exaggerated. The injury to us resulting
from a partition of the Empire would be almost incalculable." [33]

[29] State Department, Great Britain, Despatches, White to Sherman, January
19, 1898.
[30] January 5, 1898.
[31] January 4, 1898.
[32] January 4, 1898. Not all newspapers agreed, of course. "There are jingo
papers," the American correspondent of the London *Times* admitted, "which
still write of 'England's game of grab,' and would write in the same vein
whatever England said or did"; he added, however, that "the best and
strongest American opinion is the other way" (*The Times*, January 5, 1898).
[33] *Philadelphia Press*, January 5, 1898. It is of interest to note that Nelson

Asked whether the United States would go to the aid of Great Britain in the event of war, Cushman Davis, chairman of the Senate Committee on Foreign Relations, made a surprisingly outspoken statement for that early date,' months before the Spanish War had brought the Stars and Stripes to the Philippines: " It is not to be expected that if our commercial interests were threatened abroad that [sic] we would sit with folded hands and make no sign. Under such circumstances this Government would be justified in departing from its time-honored policy and if necessity required seek a coalition with England or any other power in order to maintain those rights." [34]

Yet despite British threats and despite American talk Germany and Russia did not back down. They forced China to sign agreements in March, 1898, giving Germany exclusive rights in Shantung, and Russia in Port Arthur and Manchuria. With no ally to help, Great Britain had no choice but to decide against war. Notwithstanding assurances of the two continental powers that they would treat foreign imports into their respective spheres equally with their own, a heavy blow had been dealt the open door policy. The Chinese empire appeared to be on the brink of partition.

United Anglo-American action might yet preserve that empire for British and American commerce. In both countries there were influential people who had been giving thought to a common policy. Particularly was this so in Great Britain, where the crisis of 1898 gave ammunition to those who believed that in the Far East Britain could no longer hold her own single-handed. Ambassador Hay found officials in London contemplating the dark Far Eastern scene " with the utmost concern. They seem to think there is an understanding between Russia,

Dingley, chairman of the Ways and Means Committee, disagreed: " Were the powers to partition China the result would be no injury to this country. None in the least. China would be developed and our trade with the conquered provinces naturally increase. The governments in possession of the conquered provinces would be only too glad to encourage trade with the United States " (New York *Journal of Commerce and Commercial Bulletin,* June 18, 1898) .

[34] *Philadelphia Press,* January 4, 1898.

France and Germany to exclude, as far as possible, the trade of England and America from the Far East, and to divide and reduce China to a system of tributary provinces." [35] Lord Salisbury, though always an advocate of an independent policy, did not veto sounding out countries that might help. Some British leaders envisaged Germany as an ally. Japan, a formal ally in 1902, also had her champions. But in 1898 it was the United States that seemed most nearly to fit the specifications of an effective supporter of Britain's open door policy. "No power, except ourselves, is so deeply concerned in the future of China as is the United States," declared the London *Daily Chronicle* hopefully.

> In that matter, as in most, her real interests and ours are the same; and in that region, do what she will, she cannot long escape those entanglements which until now she has very properly avoided.
>
> We submit then for the consideration of all parties concerned, the question whether the present may not be a fitting time for the American Republic and the British Empire to consider their present and future relations and arrive at a definite understanding.[36]

After all, the *Chronicle*'s editor and others who thought like him may have reasoned, American isolationism had always directed itself mainly toward Europe rather than the Pacific and eastern Asia. The United States had taken the lead in opening Japan and Korea; had been quick to insist upon sharing privileges which European powers had extorted from China; and since 1889 had been engaged with Great Britain and Germany in a highly entangling condominium over the remote Samoan islands.

As a matter of fact, Great Britain had already approached the United States about a cooperative policy. Doubtless she had been encouraged to do this by a suggestion of Ambassador Hay's. Deeply perturbed over the Kiaochow and Port Arthur affairs, Hay in January, 1898, in effect offered his services to Salisbury

---

[35] State Department, Great Britain, Despatches, Hay to Sherman, March 25, 1898.

[36] April 15, 1898.

to enlist American aid.[37] But Britain had not then decided how to meet the challenge in China; and although later on the Prime Minister apparently made an offhand remark to Hay about an Anglo-German-American agreement in support of the open door policy,[38] his response in January was noncommittal: "if the commercial or other rights of the Treaty Powers were at all infringed, it would be necessary for the commercial nations most affected to take counsel together as to the language they should hold and the course they should adopt. In that case the United States would be the first country with which Her Majesty's Government would desire to communicate." [39]

Perhaps she had been encouraged, too, by a letter from a powerful senator, Henry Cabot Lodge, to Henry White, in charge at the American embassy in London while Hay was travelling in Egypt with his friend, Henry Adams. "If I had my way," Lodge wrote, "I should be glad to have the United States to say to England that we would stand by her in her declaration that the ports of China must be opened to all nations equally or to none, and if England takes that attitude firmly I am in hopes this may come about. . . ." [40] White read this letter to Arthur Balfour and to Joseph Chamberlain; [41] both were staunch friends of the United States, and it is a fact that Chamberlain, just about the time he saw the letter, urged the government to "approach the United States officially, and . . . ask an immediate reply from them to the question—Will you stand in with us in our Chinese policy?", and that both he and Balfour spoke to White of the

[37] F. O. 5, 2360, Salisbury to Pauncefote, January 12, 1898.

[38] C. S. Hay, ed., *Letters of John Hay and Extracts from Diary* (3 vols., Washington, 1908), vol. 3, p. 199. I have found no reference to such a remark in the British or American archives.

[39] F. O. 5, 2360, Salisbury to Pauncefote, January 12, 1898.

[40] A. Nevins, *Henry White, Thirty Years of American Diplomacy* (New York and London, 1930), p. 166; the letter was written about the beginning of 1898.

[41] N. M. Blake, "England and the United States, 1897-1899," in D. E. Lee and G. E. McReynolds, *Essays in Honor of George Hubbard Blakeslee* (Worcester, 1949), p. 263.

importance of Washington "taking some sort of action" to support British policy in China.[42]

On March 7, 1898, about six weeks before the outbreak of the war with Spain, the Foreign Office telegraphed Sir Julian Pauncefote to find out whether, " if the contingency should present itself," Great Britain " could count on the cooperation of the United States in opposing any action by foreign Powers which could tend to restrict the opening of China to the commerce of all nations." [43] Sir Julian, scenting high policy, dropped everything else and rushed off to tell the President his big news; his visit at the White House, at a time of crisis with Spain over Cuba, stirred up considerable press speculation. McKinley's reply through the State Department was as cautious as Salisbury's answer to Hay two months earlier. The President said that since he could discover no threat to the open door he did not see " any present reason for the departure of the United States from our traditional policy respecting foreign alliances. . . ." [44] The qualifying word " present " softened the blow somewhat, and Assistant Secretary of State William Day—the Secretary, John Sherman, was senile and about to retire—softened it more. Assuring the British envoy that McKinley sympathized wholeheartedly with Britain's Far Eastern policy, he implied that but for the rapidly developing Cuban situation and but for the constitutional requirement that Congress declare war, a more favorable reply might have been made.[45]

Some historians have read a good deal of significance into this curious overture by Great Britain. Almost certainly, however, the British government itself attached little importance to it. Nothing is known in the British archives to indicate that the

[42] Dugdale, *Balfour*, vol. 1, p. 185, Chamberlain to Balfour, February 3, 1898. Nevins, *White*, p. 162.

[43] F. O. 5, 2364.

[44] State Department, Great Britain, Instructions, Sherman to White, March 16, 1898; F. O. 5, 2361, Pauncefote to Salisbury, March 17, 1898. *Parliamentary Debates*, vol. 54, p. 1526, March 14, 1898.

[45] F. O. 5, 2361, Pauncefote to Salisbury, March 17, 1898; a Foreign Office minute on Pauncefote's despatch noted that it did not offer " much solid comfort."

step was considered in advance within the government. The instructions to Pauncefote were sent in the absence of Lord Salisbury because of illness; there is nothing to suggest that the Prime Minister approved. Moreover, if the Foreign Office was in fact considering basic policy, it is strange that it should have relied upon a short telegram with no covering despatch and that it should have dropped the whole matter forthwith on receipt of the unfavorable but not unfriendly American reply.[46] It is hard to reconcile such casual procedure with deep seriousness of purpose. Probably the approach to Washington represented no more than personal diplomacy by Arthur Balfour, in charge of the Foreign Office during Salisbury's absence; most likely he was encouraged by Joseph Chamberlain [47] and possibly by Henry White. Neither Balfour nor any other governmental official could have been sanguine about American acceptance; and when White conferred with him on March 12 about McKinley's answer, the American diplomat did not report that Balfour seemed at all distressed.[48]

But Ambassador Hay apparently did not consider some kind of agreement out of the question. Back in London in mid-March, 1898, he learned what had just happened. Having already urged the British to sound out America regarding collaboration in the Far East, he was of course disappointed at McKinley's response. Hay waited until the Spanish War had commenced and then, on June 30, wrote a personal letter to the President asking him to reconsider. That war was soon to change much American

[46] The statement of T. A. Bailey, *A Diplomatic History of the American People* (New York, 1955), p. 526, that the March "proposal was renewed on January 8, 1899 . . ." is misleading; Great Britain in 1899 asked only that the United States join with her in protesting "conjointly" against the extension of the French concession in Shanghai, whereas the proposal of 1898 had reference to "any action by foreign Powers" detrimental to the open door. For the British request see Hay papers, Pauncefote to Hay, January 8, 1899.

[47] G. F. Kennan, *American Diplomacy, 1900-1950* (Chicago, 1951), p. 26, suggests that the telegram to Pauncefote may have been a means of appeasing Chamberlain.

[48] White papers, White to Hay, March 12, 1898; Pauncefote had already sent a telegram about the interview with McKinley.

thinking on world affairs, but the ambassador had written a little too soon. Secretary of State Day—Sherman had retired on April 27—replied for the President that "while he fully appreciates the friendly attitude of the British Government, and the interest which our people have in this country's growing commerce in China, he does not feel that this is an opportune time for action in that direction"; Day ended with a significant prophecy: "The outcome of our struggle with Spain may develope [sic] the need of extending and strengthening our interests in the Asiatic Continent." [49]

Thus, however remote a formal alliance, the United States and Great Britain had much the same point of view as regards the open door policy and as regards the critical events endangering that policy in early 1898. To be sure, Britain's stake in China was far the greater. Nevertheless their common approach toward an area then at the center of international diplomacy created something of a bond between them. It furnished, moreover, a compelling reason for British support of America when that country went to war with Spain a month after China yielded Kiaochow and Port Arthur; and it helped keep them together during their difficult negotiations that, commencing with the war, continued through 1903.

Even had there been no Far Eastern crisis, however, other threats to Britain's international position would have driven her to the United States. In a well known passage in his *Education* Henry Adams ascribed her new friendship for America to the rise of German power: "the sudden appearance of Germany as the grizzly terror . . . frightened England into America's arms.

[49] Hay papers, Day to Hay, July 14, 1898. The connection between Cuba and China was noted by contemporary writers. "Diplomaticus" (Lucien Wolf) considered that Far Eastern and Cuban questions were really one, for the importance of Cuba was that it was a "blockhouse" on the future interoceanic canal which "will one day deepen the community of Anglo-American interests in the Open Door of the Far East"; see *Fortnightly Review*, vol. 70 (1898), p. 173. And the Madrid newspaper, *Imparcial*, reported bitterly that the intransigent American attitude resulted from confidence in British support made necessary by the grave situation in China (F.O. 115, 1075, Barclay to Salisbury, April 3, 1898).

. . ." [50] Although this observation oversimplifies a highly complicated situation, it was not without truth. Wherever the British turned they seemed to find a German hand trying all too successfully to undermine their long held positions. German goods burrowed into British markets; German diplomats snatched up unappropriated territory. Not only that, but the Kaiser was known to be working for a continental combine directed primarily at Great Britain—but useful also in countering the flood of American exports to Europe. In the autumn of 1897 following a trip to Russia he thought such a combine on the verge of realization. "The visit to Russia turned out far better than I expected," he exulted, "and in several exhaustive discussions I reached *complete agreement* with Nicky [Tsar Nicholas II] on all important political questions, so that together we have, so to say, disposed of the world. . . . The *Continental blockade* against America, and, *it may be*, England has been *decided* upon. Russia has *pledged* herself to bring France over to the idea *bon gré mal gré*." [51]

As a matter of fact the Kaiser was suffering from one of his periodic delusions. Continental animosities would not have permitted union even for so congenial a purpose as abasement of the haughty English; but Great Britain could not be sure of this and finding herself associated with the United States in the hostile view of the great continental powers, she naturally looked upon her kinsmen across the Atlantic with more sympathy than would perhaps otherwise have been the case.

United continental action might be a mirage; but German sea power was a very serious reality. In early 1898 when Spanish-American tension was rising, the famous German naval bill providing for a mammoth construction program was under debate in the Reichstag; on March 28, 1898, just before the outbreak of war with Spain, the measure passed. Unmistakable notice had thereby been served that Great Britain could never afford to

[50] Henry Adams, *The Education of Henry Adams, an Autobiography* (Boston and New York, 1918), pp. 362-363.
[51] Langer, *Diplomacy of Imperialism*, vol. 2, p. 447.

alienate the trans-Atlantic country likely to be the all important neutral in a coming conflagration.

Britain's relations were strained with other countries besides Germany. Already friction with the Boers in South Africa was developing dangerously. Imminent war with France, her traditional enemy, over disputed territory in the Niger river basin appeared not unlikely in February and March, 1898. This, however, was not the main area of friction. The British victory over the dervishes in the battle of the Atbara on April 8, 1898, brought up the immediate prospect of conflict with French forces under Marchand in the Sudan. The famous Fashoda crisis, soon to strain British diplomatic resources to the utmost, was already looming up in a most menacing fashion.

Since 1894 France had been allied with Russia. If Germany appeared as the deadly foe of the future, and France as the immediate danger of 1898, it was the colossal empire of the Tsars, ever pushing down from its frozen north, which threatened year in and year out to turn one British bastion after another all the way across Asia. The area under pressure in early 1898 was, as has appeared, north China and Manchuria, abutting upon cherished markets in the Yangtze valley for which Britain, just before the Spanish War, had threatened to fight.

Thus a complex and highly dangerous situation confronted Great Britain. The Colonial Secretary, Joseph Chamberlain, summarized the bleak outlook in a letter written in March, 1898, the month before fighting started in the Caribbean:

> We have in hand difficulties of the most serious character with France, Russia and Germany. We are engaged in an important expedition in the Soudan; and it is uncertain as yet whether the war on the North-west frontier of India has been finally concluded.
>
> We may emerge from all these troubles without a war, but I cannot conceal from myself that the prospect is more gloomy than it has ever been in my recollection.[52]

With dangers pressing from so many sides and war alarms filling

---

[52] J. L. Garvin, *The Life of Joseph Chamberlain* (3 vols., London, 1932-1934) , vol. 3, pp. 367-368.

the air, nothing could have been clearer than Britain's need of American friendship; the benevolent neutrality, at least, of the United States might prove essential in a major war. "The support of the United States may . . . be said to be vital to England, since, without it, if attacked by a Continental coalition, she would have to capitulate. Great Britain may . . . be not inaptly described as a fortified outpost of the Anglo-Saxon race, overlooking the eastern continent and resting upon America. . . ." So wrote Brooks Adams in 1898.[53] Many an Englishman must have noted with surprise this somewhat impertinent picture of the ruler of the seven seas, but some must have been in uneasy agreement; almost all must have appreciated Britain's need to cultivate a good understanding with the rising republic.

It will have been noted that these matters operated mainly in the direction of turning Great Britain toward the United States. Obviously the considerations of balance of power mentioned by Chamberlain operated altogether in that direction; and even the open door policy, though it did have some effect in disposing Americans more favorably toward Britain, was primarily a policy of British concern. We now come, however, to an occurrence of 1898 that worked in just the reverse direction, in the direction, that is, of turning America very decidedly to Britain. This was the Spanish-American War.

[53] B. Adams, "The Spanish War and the Equilibrium of the World," *The Forum*, vol. 25 (1898), p. 645.

CHAPTER 2

War and Friendship

IN EARLY 1898 the Cuban rebellion was in its third year. American sympathies were strongly with the rebels, and war between the United States and Spain seemed increasingly likely. Most of the great powers sided with Spain. Even Great Britain had strong, though not decisive, reasons for favoring that country. Would not the enormous trans-Atlantic republic, if allowed to continue its rapid rise, engulf Canada as well as Cuba? Did not its success endanger the aristocratic institutions of Great Britain herself? Did not the prodigious growth of its exports threaten to capture markets on which Britain depended for her very livelihood? Britain had important trading and shipping interests in Cuba, Puerto Rico, and the Philippines which she could hardly hope to retain should the United States take these Spanish islands and throw over them the exclusive mantle of its tariff and navigation laws.[1]

Furthermore, the courageous and dignified bearing of the Spanish Queen Regent attracted the sympathy of a people devoted to their own Queen. Victoria was the Queen Regent's aunt; she was naturally distressed by her niece's plight.[2] In any case her instinctive reaction must have been toward the ancient European monarchy rather than the upstart and truculent re-

[1] For a general account of British-American relations at the time see B. A. Reuter, *Anglo-American Relations During the Spanish-American War* (New York, 1924).

[2] G. E. Buckle, ed., *The Letters of Queen Victoria, Third Series* (3 vols., New York, 1932), vol. 3, pp. 236-7, 244.

25

public. As for Lord Salisbury, the Prime Minister and Foreign Secretary, this aristocratic descendant of the Burghleys and Cecils must surely have preferred the Spanish crown to business men across the Atlantic.[3]

Yet in actual fact it was the United States that the British government and people favored. No doubt the main reason for this is to be found in the dictates of Britain's delicate international position that have been mentioned—her anxieties as to the Chinese market, her involvements with France, her concern about Russia, her fear of Germany. Amidst such perils she could not afford to alienate America. In addition we must note that broad vein of humanitarian sentiment which so often has determined public opinion in Britain. As reports came week after week of a brutal and seemingly endless conflict prostrating Cuba and decimating her population, ordinary British people recoiled in horror. True, brutalities were not confined to one side; but belief in Spanish cruelty and Spanish corruption and misgovernment had become so firmly engrained in the popular mind ever since the Armada as to leave no doubt as to which contestant was responsible. It was Spain, the traditional oppressor, not the Cubans struggling to be free. ". . . this Committee," declared a characteristic resolution, " heartily sympathises with the American People in their humane efforts to deliver the Cubans from the horrors they have so long endured, and appeals to her Majesty's Ministers to put moral pressure on the Spanish Government to recognize the justice of the Cuban claims." [4] Three years previously the British had been stirred to their depths by the terrible Armenian massacres. It was all too easy to see Cuba as another Armenia with " Butcher " Weyler, the Spanish general, in place of the Bloody Sultan. Harking back to the emotions of 1895, the *Times* found it natural to draw the parallel:

[3] É. Halevy, *A History of the English People in the Nineteenth Century* (6 vols., New York, 1949-1952), vol. 5, p. 43, makes this observation.

[4] State Department, Great Britain, Despatches, Hay to Sherman, March 29, 1898; the resolution was adopted by an organization known as the Liberal Forwards.

We know how, in this country, public opinion has been more than once profoundly stirred by atrocities perpetrated in the Turkish Empire and how these spasms of popular emotion, often heedless equally of fact and reason, have deflected international policy and disturbed international relations. We do not, therefore, reproach the American people, in the least, with their interest in the Cuban sufferers by Spanish misgovernment, or with their impatience at the continuance of evils that are a discredit to the civilization of Spain as well as a nuisance to the neighbours of her unhappy colony.[5]

It was for these main reasons that the predominant British reaction to the various Spanish-American incidents leading up to war was one of understanding and sympathy for the United States. This was illustrated in February, 1898, when the American press published a letter written by the Spanish minister at Washington, Dupuy de Lome, to a friend in Cuba. Stolen by the rebels and held back from publication until an opportune moment, the letter described McKinley as " weak and a bidder for the favor of the crowd." That a Spaniard had dared write of an American President in mildly derogatory terms, even were they true, stirred the American people to fury; and newspapers, disregarding the letter's private character and the dubious circumstances of its publication, broke forth in shrill and insistent cries for blood. De Lome did not wait for Washington to demand his recall; he resigned at once.

It might seem hard to condone this violent American reaction. After all, the letter was private. Could it reasonably be contended that a diplomat must never in personal correspondence be uncomplimentary about the government to which he is accredited? With but few exceptions the British press maintained that such was indeed the case, and insisted that de Lome had behaved badly. " No doubt," the London *Daily Telegraph* said, " the letter . . . was a private one; but a public man in a foreign capital must often deny himself the luxury of making even per-

[5] *The Times*, April 15, 1898. *Economist*, vol. 56 (April 16, 1898), p. 579: " it was only yesterday that all Europe was asked to destroy Turkey . . . because the Sovereign of Turkey had massacred fewer persons than have perished in misery from the misgovernment of Cuba."

sonal communications to a friend." [6] And the *Times* agreed:
" if it be an indiscretion to do what knavery or treachery can
employ to end such usefulness, then the late Spanish Minister
was very indiscreet." [7] Such opinions presented a suggestive contrast to Britain's defence of Sackville-West ten years earlier.

A few days later a mysterious explosion destroyed the United
States warship, *Maine*, in Havana harbor with the loss of two
hundred and sixty lives. Again the British rallied strongly to
the American side. No sooner had the ship disappeared beneath
the blue Caribbean waters than numerous messages of con-
dolence began to arrive at the American embassy in London.
The Queen, the Prince and Princess of Wales, the Duke and
Duchess of York, the Duke of Connaught, the First Lord of the
Admiralty, the Lord Mayor of London, and many others expressed their horror. Englishmen certainly did not believe that
Spain had sunk the *Maine* deliberately, but their sense of an
almost shared loss with the United States is plain. Of the dozens
of newspaper comments the following is typical:

> Whatever our disagreements with the United States may be
> from time to time, and however apt we are on both sides of
> the Atlantic to use sharp words about each other's short-
> comings, at bottom we all regard America as—to use the phrase-
> ology of sport—" our side " in the great game of the world. It
> is no exaggeration, therefore, to say that the sorrow and sym-
> pathy felt by us on this occasion is but little less vivid than if
> the appalling calamity had overtaken one of our own ships.[8]

For some weeks after the disaster tension abated somewhat.
An American naval commission went to Havana to investigate the
explosion, and people seemed to be suspending judgment until
its report appeared. Although certainly deploring the possibility

---

[6] February 11, 1898.

[7] *The Times*, February 11, 1898. See also the London *Standard*, February
11, 1898, and the *Spectator*, February 12, 1898. The *New York Tribune*,
February 14, 1898, said: " Nearly every [British] journal describes the letter
as an unpardonable outrage "; see Reuter, *Anglo-American Relations*, p. 68.

[8] London *Daily Chronicle*, February 17, 1898. See State Department, Great
Britain, Despatches, February and March, 1898, for numerous despatches
from the American embassy, London, citing British expressions of good will.

of war, British opinion in general continued to back the United States. "Nearly all the leading journals of London," reported Ambassador Hay on March 26, "have articles this morning on the relations of the United States and Spain; most of them are in a sense favorable to us"; [9] they recognized "the correct and loyal conduct of the United States, and the intolerable features of the situation in Cuba." [10] A few days later there appeared in the *Times* a poem by the poet laureate, Alfred Austin, which concluded with an emotional plea for Anglo-American solidarity in a dangerous world:

> Yes, this is the voice of the bluff March gale;
>   We severed have been too long;
> But now we have done with a worn-out tale—
>   The tale of an ancient wrong—
> And our friendship shall last as love doth last
> and be stronger than death is strong.[11]

And a widely read newspaper, the *Daily Chronicle*, went so far as to advocate a 'demonstration" at Havana by the British North American squadron and the sale of British warships to the cousins across the ocean.[12] It was no wonder that Hay thought British friendship and sympathy "beyond question. I find it wherever I go—not only in the press, but in private conversation. For the first time in my life I find the 'drawing-room' sentiment

[9] State Department, Great Britain, Despatches, Hay to Sherman, March 26, 1898.

[10] *Ibid.*, Hay to Sherman, March 28, 1898.

[11] *The Times*, March 29, 1898. Not all Englishmen agreed with this effusion. The May, 1898, issue of the British *Review of Reviews* contained the following parody:

> Yes, this is the voice of the bluff March gale;
>   We've squabbled and sniggered too long,
> But now we'll tell quite another tale
>   And on 'Change sing another song.
> We'll smoke our pipes together,
>   Long as our baccy'll hold,
> And face the dirty weather
>   Safe in each other's gold.

[12] April 7, 1898.

altogether with us." [13] And it was no wonder that Spain confidently expected Britain to be the only great power standing with America in the event of war.[14]

When the naval commission on March 21, 1898, reported an external explosion as being the cause of the sinking, Americans in general accepted this as confirmation of Spain's guilt. An intemperate outburst swept across the country, making war all but inevitable. Some of the great powers began to consider mediation in the hope of averting even at that late hour a conflict which could be expected to result in the humiliation of a sister monarchy. A few of them toyed with the idea of collective intervention. Mainly, it would seem, because the Queen Regent of Spain was related to the Austro-Hungarian royal family but also because the Austro-Hungarian Foreign Minister, Count Goluchowski, disliked the United States and feared the effect of American competition on Europe's economy, the government at Vienna, more than any other outside Madrid, would have welcomed such intervention.[15] The French government, too, in-

[13] W. R. Thayer, *The Life and Letters of John Hay* (2 vols., Boston and New York, 1915), vol. 2, p. 165, Hay to Lodge, April 5, 1898. In this letter Hay said: "we could have the practical assistance of the British Navy" in the event of war, a remark that has been cited by two or three writers—for example, G. L. Beer, *The English-Speaking Peoples, Their Future Relations and Joint International Obligations* (New York, 1917), p. 102; H. C. Allen, *Great Britain and the United States, a History of Anglo-American Relations (1783-1952)* (New York, 1955), p. 557—apparently with no trace of scepticism. But no evidence exists to support the remarkable assertion except an alleged suggestion by Earl Grey, who was not in the government, that America borrow the fleet (Beer, *English-Speaking Peoples*, p. 102); and on general grounds it is impossible to believe that the British, however friendly, would have permitted meaningful "practical assistance" of the Royal Navy. Indeed, the Under-Secretary of State for War, St. John Brodrick, denied any such intention (*Parliamentary Debates*, vol. 54, p. 1526, March 14, 1898).

[14] F. O. 115, 1075, Barclay to Salisbury, March 23, 1898.

[15] For a revealing account of Goluchowski's attitude, which was not unlike that of many of his class in Europe, see F. O. 115, 1076, Villiers to Pauncefote, July 1, 1898, enclosing Rumbold to Salisbury, Vienna, June 11, 1898: ". . . Count Goluchowski again expressed his reprobation of the manner in which the quarrel had been fastened on Spain by the United States Government.

fluenced by large French investments in Spain, favored collective action.[16] Near the end of March, 1898, it sounded out Great Britain, but received a discouraging reply.[17] As for Germany, although governmental leaders and the Kaiser himself sympathized strongly with Spain and her Queen Regent and considered America "overbearing, indeed brutal,"[18] they had far too lively an appreciation of their country's material interests to risk affronting the powerful republic. Foreign Minister Bülow avowed frankly that Germany, however anxious to maintain the monarchical principle in Spain, could not neglect her "vast commercial interests" in the United States.[19]

It is the attitude of Great Britain that particularly concerns us. When rumors of intervention began to be heard, the Foreign Office gave explicit instructions to Ambassador Pauncefote to be guided by the wishes of the American government before associating himself with any collective action by the foreign envoys in Washington.[20] About two weeks before the outbreak of hos-

He considered that Government to have been so utterly in the wrong in the manner in which they had forced on the war that he could not sufficiently regret the Powers not having adopted a very different attitude towards them. Events had clearly shown how utterly incapable the American Government were to offer resistance to any strong and united pressure from Europe. But the opportunity had been allowed to pass away, and the result was that henceforward Europe must be prepared to deal with a Power which would soon become as formidable as it was unscrupulous and overbearing. We shall all of us soon learn this to our cost, and more especially as regards our economic relations with the New World. This, I may observe, is a favourite theme of Count Goluchowski." See also F. O. 115, 1075, Rumbold to Salisbury, April 12, 1898, where Goluchowski denounced American syndicates allegedly fomenting war.

[16] Count Eulenberg, German ambassador to Austria-Hungary, discussed with H. Rumbold, the British ambassador, the activity of France in working for European intervention, which activity, he said, "was easily accounted for by the very large stake held in France in Spanish securities" (F. O. 115, 1075, Rumbold to Salisbury, March 29, 1898).

[17] Ibid., Villiers to Pauncefote, March 31, 1898.

[18] Ibid., Rumbold to Salisbury, March 29, 1898, quoting Eulenberg.

[19] Ibid., Lascelles to Salisbury, Berlin, April 1, 1898.

[20] State Department, Great Britain, Despatches, Hay to Sherman, April 6, 1898. This is what Lord Salisbury told Hay; I have not found any such instructions in the British archives, but they were perhaps given verbally.

tilities the representatives of Austria-Hungary, France, Germany, Russia, and Italy met with Sir Julian (April 6, 1898) to consider whether they could help arrest the rapid drift to war. They decided to submit collective representations to the United States, and drew up a draft note. In accordance with his instructions Sir Julian got the consent of his colleagues to discuss the draft with the Assistant Secretary of State, William Day; and he incorporated Day's suggestions in an amended version which the six diplomats delivered to President McKinley on April 7. The note expressed hope that the United States would conduct itself with moderation and with due regard for the best interests of humanity at large. " My Colleagues share with me," Pauncefote reported to London, " the view that the delivery of the Collective Note will be of use at the present juncture in reminding the people of this country that the eyes of the whole civilized world are upon them, and it is hoped that it will thus exercise a moderating influence over all classes of the community whose feelings have been strung up to an extraordinary pitch of blind resentment by the deplorable catastrophe of the ' Maine ' explosion." [21]

But McKinley replied noncommittally that if the United States intervened, it would indeed do so for humanity's best interests; and the diplomats' hopes of exerting a " moderating influence " were not realised. " The action of the European Legations has, in fact, contributed . . . to strengthen rather than to weaken the war party in the United States and to hamper the President's policy of moderation and reserve," the London *Times* commented sadly.[22] Be that as it may, Great Britain could hardly have been more considerate of American sensibilities.

Her attitude was equally considerate when another move for mediation was made a week later. In a memorandum dated April 10, 1898, Spain announced that reconcentration was suspended and an armistice declared, thus accepting virtually all the demands the United States had made. But unfortunately President McKinley in a special message to Congress the next day did not give these major concessions the prominence they undoubtedly

[21] F. O. 5, 2517, Pauncefote to Salisbury, April 8, 1898.
[22] April 8, 1898.

deserved; and Congress proceeded to give vent to violent declamations that brought war very near. In this inflammable situation the six European envoys once again met together, this time on April 14, 1898, at the British embassy, that place being chosen by virtue of Sir Julian's position as dean of the diplomatic corps.

At the meeting Pauncefote submitted a draft statement recommending a collective expression of hope by the six powers that the United States would give favorable consideration to the Spanish concessions, which, they felt, made armed intervention unjustifiable.[23] But the envoys decided that it would be more effective in the heightened emergency for their governments to address identical representations to the American envoy in each of the six capitals; such a striking gesture, they thought, might correct the complacent American persuasion that the whole civilized world would approve the use of force against Spain. The French ambassador, Jules Cambon, was asked to draw up a telegram, based on Pauncefote's draft and written in French as the language of diplomacy, counselling such representations. All

[23] On April 11, 1898, the Foreign Office telegraphed Pauncefote that Spain had agreed to suspend hostilities and had asked Britain to persuade America to stop helping the rebels and to pay just compensation to Spain; it told Pauncefote: "We must leave any action on this request to your discretion"; see R. G. Neale, " British-American Relations During the Spanish-American War: Some Problems," *Historical Studies, Australia and New Zealand*, vol. 6 (1953), p. 79. For Pauncefote's draft see F. O. 115, 1239, Lansdowne to Pauncefote, April 9, 1902: " The attitude of Congress, and the Resolution of the House of Representatives passed yesterday by a large majority, leaves but little hope for peace, and it is popularly believed that the warlike measures advocated have the approval of the Great Powers. The Memorandum of the Spanish Minister delivered on Sunday appears to me and my colleagues to remove all legitimate cause of war. If that view should be shared by the Great Powers, the time has arrived to remove the erroneous impression which prevails that the armed intervention of the United States in Cuba commands, in the words of the Message, the support and approval of the civilized world. It is suggested by the foreign Representatives that this might be done by a collective expression from the Great Powers of the hope that the United States Government will give a favourable consideration to the Memorandum of the Spanish Minister of the 10th instant, as offering a reasonable basis of amicable solution, and removing any grounds for hostile intervention which may have previously existed."

the envoys approved Cambon's text, even though it went considerably beyond Pauncefote's draft in vigor of expression, particularly in the flat assertion that armed intervention in Cuba would not be justified in view of Spain's concessions.[24] Each of the six envoys telegraphed the Cambon text to his government, but we need concern ourselves only with the telegram sent by Sir Julian.

When it reached the Foreign Office on April 15, 1898, Arthur Balfour, leader of the House of Commons, was in temporary charge, Lord Salisbury being in France recuperating from ill-

[24] F. O. 115, 1079, Pauncefote to Salisbury, April 15, 1898. The Cambon draft was as follows: " L'attitude du Congrès ainsi que la résolution que la Chambre des Représentants a votée hier à une grande majorité ne laissent plus que peu d'espoir de paix, et l'opinion générale est que les mesures de guerre proposées ont reçu l'approbation des Grandes Puissances. Le memorandum du Ministre d'Espagne présenté Dimanche dernier paraît offrir une base raisonnable d'arrangement et supprimer toute cause légitime de guerre. Si cette manière de voir est partagée par les Grandes Puissances, le moment serait arrivé de dissiper le sentiment erroné qui prévaut ici que l'intervention armée des États-Unis à Cuba dans le but d'y créer un État indépendant a, selon les termes du message, l'appui et l'approbation du monde civilisé.

" Dans ces conditions, les Représentants des Grandes Puissances à Washington estiment que leurs Gouvernements respectifs pourraient utilement appeler l'attention du Gouvernement des États-Unis sur le memorandum pré-cité du Ministre d'Espagne et faire connaître que leur approbation ne saurait être donnée à une intervention armée qui ne leur paraît point justifiée.

" Les observations des Puissances pourraient revêtir la forme d'une note déposée par leurs Représentants à Washington entre les mains du Secrétaire d'État, mais il paraîtrait préférable à ces derniers qu'une note identique fût remise le plus tôt possible par chacun des ministres des Affaires Étrangères des Six Grandes Puissances au Représentant des États-Unis accrédité près d'Elles. L'impression morale qui en résulterait serait plus grande aux yeux de l'Europe et du Peuple Américain, et donnerait à cette intervention des Six Puissances un caractère qui n'exposerait pas les Ambassadeurs à paraître renouveler leurs premières démarches que le message du Président a passées sous silence.

" Il est dans la pensée des Représentants des Grandes Puissances que la plus grande publicité devrait être donnée à cette Note pour dégager la responsabilité morale du monde civilisé d'une agression à l'appui de laquelle on invoque son autorité."

ness.[25] Balfour himself was in Wiltshire, when a messenger from London arrived with the urgent message. " I confess to be in great perplexity," he wrote to Joseph Chamberlain, the Colonial Secretary, on reading it. " The Representatives of the Powers at Washington . . . appear to wish us to give the United States a lecture on international morality. If Pauncefote had not associated himself with this policy I confess I should have rejected it at once; but he knows our views, he is on the spot, and he is a man of solid judgment. It seems a strong order to reject his advice." [26] But reject it he did. Making a quick decision (" The whole thing had to be done in a quarter of an hour or 20 minutes . . .") he telegraphed Sir Julian the same day that although Great Britain would join the other powers in representations in favor of peace, " it seems very doubtful whether we ought to commit ourselves to a judgment adverse to the United States, and whether in the interests of peace such a step would be desirable." [27] Two days later, influenced perhaps by Chamberlain's enthusiastic endorsement of his action,[28] Balfour warned Pauncefote against even mild representations:

> I gather that President is most anxious to avoid if possible a rupture with Spain. In these circumstances advice to United States of America by other Powers can only be useful if it strengthens his hands, and of this he must be the best judge. Considering our present ignorance as to his views, and extreme improbability that unsought advice will do any good, and the inexpediency of adopting any course which may suggest that

[25] B. E. C. Dugdale, *Arthur James Balfour, First Earl of Balfour, K. G., O. M., F. R. S., Etc.* (2 vols., New York, 1937) , vol. 1, p. 188.

[26] *Ibid.*, p. 192, April 16, 1898.

[27] F. O. 5, 2517, Balfour to Pauncefote, April 15, 1898. Pauncefote did not argue but telegraphed Balfour: " It appears to me that if it should be decided to take any further action, an [intimation ?] to United States Representatives at Capitals of the six Great Powers, in sense indicated by you namely that the Powers, while expressing no judgment on the merits of controversy, think suspension of hostilities by Spain offers an opportunity for peaceful settlement, and hope that that view may yet prevail, would suffice to rebut the assumption of Congress that any of the Powers approve of its violent policy " (*ibid.*, Pauncefote to Foreign Office, April 16, 1898) .

[28] Dugdale, *Balfour*, vol. 1, p. 193.

we take sides in the controversy we shall, at least for the moment, do nothing. Please keep us informed of fresh developments.[29]

With Britain standing firm against intervention, the proposal of the Washington envoys fell through. No identic representations or representations of any kind were made, and within a few days the United States was at war with Spain.

By rejecting the ambassador's advice Balfour performed an important service to Anglo-American friendship, not to mention saving Pauncefote from perhaps the most grievous mistake of his career. On the verge of going to war for what they believed to be the loftiest motives the American people, it is safe to say, would have bitterly resented any European aspersions upon their contemplated move. Deep-rooted suspicions of Great Britain, somewhat allayed by Britain's recent sympathy, would have strongly revived; and any fundamental amelioration of relations would have been postponed. And certainly the diplomatic expostulation contemplated by the Washington envoys would not have averted hostilities; on the contrary it would have encouraged Spain and infuriated America to a point where war would have been more likely even than before.

It is difficult to understand how a cautious, level-headed diplomat like Sir Julian, who had labored for nearly ten years to win American friendship and who had been specifically warned by his government not to offend that country, could have accepted the Cambon text. Four years later Pauncefote was accused by Germany of being the prime mover in the affair.[30] Because his role became the subject of a famous international controversy in 1902 that held its dangers for Anglo-American relations, it is

[29] F. O. 5, 2517, Balfour to Pauncefote, April 17, 1898. Compare with this the following telegram from Chamberlain to Balfour, April 16, 1898: " Am convinced message will do no good and will be bitterly resented. Americans insist Spain should leave Cuba. Nothing less will satisfy them. Spain will rather fight. Message practically takes part with Spain at critical juncture, and will be so understood both in America and this country " (Dugdale, *Balfour*, vol. 1, p. 193) .

[30] See pp. 244-252.

desirable to look with some care into his position at the meeting of April 14, 1898.

There is no doubt that he was indignant at the cavalier treatment accorded by McKinley and Congress to the Spanish concessions. He wrote accusingly to Salisbury:

> The President only gave publicity [in his message to Congress] to that part of the [Spanish] Memorandum which refers to the suspension of hostilities, and did not as specifically requested enlighten public opinion on the other important facts which it recalls to his memory.
>
> It is to be regretted that the Memorandum was not appended in extenso to the Message, as though communicated by the Spanish Minister to certain Journals it has been ignored as much as possible by the Press.[31]

Nor is there any doubt that Pauncefote welcomed the second meeting; and he himself admitted that he "strongly advocated at the meeting an identic telegram to our Governments counselling action based on Spanish memorandum in the hope of averting war. . . ."[32] But this does not necessarily mean that he must bear *primary* responsibility for the telegram, as Germany contended. (He must of course, along with the other representatives, bear some of the responsibility.) The final Cambon version differed markedly from Sir Julian's.[33] Apart from this consideration, we have documentary evidence strongly suggesting that the prime mover was not Sir Julian but the minister at Washington of Austria-Hungary, Baron Hengelmüller von Hengervár.

[31] F. O. 115, 1079, April 12, 1898. But Pauncefote thought that "war is certainly less imminent since the delivery of the President's Message, which is said to have gravely disappointed the War Party."

[32] F. O. 5, 2517, Pauncefote to Foreign Office, February 13, 1902.

[33] The London *Daily Telegraph*, January 12, 1903, cited a high American official to the effect that Pauncefote's draft of April 14 was actually prepared in the State Department; F. W. Holls stated that it was "in all essential particulars drafted by President McKinley himself who at that time was very anxious to avoid the war" (Holls papers, to von Halle, April 16, 1902; see also his letter to Lange, February 14, 1902). Most likely, however, the writers had confused the note of April 14 with that of April 7. I have

On April 15, 1898, the day after the second Washington meeting, Count Deym, the Austro-Hungarian ambassador to Great Britain, called at the Foreign Office with a telegram from Hengelmüller; he had been instructed by his Foreign Minister, Count Goluchowski, to discuss it with the British and to ask whether they would be disposed to make collective representations which, as now urged by Hengelmüller, would be " no longer . . . simply a friendly appeal but which should express disapprobation of the aggressive attitude assumed at Washington." [34] This proposal, it will be noted, was to the same effect as that made by the six diplomats on April 14. Now the significant point is this: the despatch of Hengelmüller's telegram must have antedated the Washington meeting, for a telegram sent from Washington on April 14 could hardly have reached Vienna—the British government did not believe that it had in fact done so [35]—in time to furnish the basis of instructions sent from Vienna and acted upon in London early [36] on April 15. Thus since we know that

not found anything in the British or American archives to show an American origin of the later note.

[34] F. O. 115, 1075, Sanderson to Rumbold, April 16, 1898; and F. O. 115, 1239, Lansdowne to Pauncefote, April 9, 1902. In the former reference we find that: " The Austro-Hungarian Ambassador was informed in reply that Her Majesty's Government would be ready to join in any representation agreed upon by the other Powers in favour of the maintenance of peace and to express their earnest hope that the declaration of an armistice by Spain may appear to the President—as it appears to them—to afford an opportunity for a peaceful settlement. But they think it very doubtful whether it would be wise to express any judgment on the attitude of the United States, or whether such a step would be conducive to the interests of peace." It will be noted that this was much the same message as the one, cited above, p. 35, sent by Balfour to Pauncefote the day before.

[35] See Appendix 1, Lansdowne to Pauncefote, April 9, 1902, where it is stated with reference to Hengelmüller's telegram that it was " written apparently before the meeting . . ."; and that " the Austro-Hungarian Government had received an independent suggestion from their Representative at Washington, recommending strongly the course proposed in the identic telegram. . . ."

[36] Count Deym left Hengelmüller's telegram at the Foreign Office early enough on April 15 for the Foreign Office messenger to be able to deliver it to Arthur Balfour in Wiltshire on the same day. See Dugdale, *Balfour*, vol. 1, p. 192.

prior to April 14 Hengelmüller had urged just the sort of collective step which he and the other European diplomats agreed upon at their conference on April 14, is it not highly probable that he rather than the discreet Pauncefote was the person primarily responsible both for convening the conference and for persuading the envoys to adopt the stronger Cambon text? The probability becomes greater when we consider also the Vienna government's undisguised sympathy for Spain.[37]

In any event, the decisive consideration is not the attitude of Ambassador Pauncefote but the attitude of Her Majesty's government in London. And with regard to the mediation proposal of April 14, as with the collective note of April 7, the government, as has appeared, displayed utmost consideration for the United States.

Although the prevailing tone in Great Britain was sympathetic with America, it must not be supposed that there were no dissenters. America's blatant behavior, especially during the last two or three weeks before hostilities commenced, gave its friends a number of extremely unpleasant pills to swallow. The extravagant reaction to the *Maine* report was disturbing. More disturbing was the aggressive temper of Congress after President McKinley's message of February 11, and the frenzied determina-

[37] Evidence that the Vienna government, following the Spanish concessions, was trying to avert hostilities is to be found in F. O. 115, 1075, Rumbold to Salisbury, April 11, 1898, where there is a report from the British ambassador at Vienna to the effect that Austria-Hungary was about to request the United States to remove its warships from proximity to Cuba in return for the Spanish concessions. *Amtliche Aktenstücke zur Geschichte der Europäischen Politik, 1885-1914 (Die Belgischen Dokumente zur Vorgeschichte des Weltkrieges)* (5 vols., Berlin, 1925), vol. 2, p. 129, and H. Leusser, " Ein Jahrzehnt Deutsch-Amerikanischer Politik (1897-1906)," *Historische Zeitschrift*, Beiheft 13 (1928), p. 17, defend Hengelmüller but give no evidence to support their position. See also L. B. Shippee, "Germany and the Spanish-American War," *American Historical Review*, vol. 30 (1925), pp. 754-777; A. Vagts, *Deutschland und die Vereinigten Staaten in der Weltpolitik* (2 vols., New York, 1935), vol. 2, pp. 1400-1410; O. Ferrara, *The Last Spanish War: Revelations in " Diplomacy "* (New York, 1937), pp. 141, 148; Neale, "British-American Relations During the Spanish-American War," p. 83.

tion of the legislators to rush into war despite Spain's sweeping concessions. " Much of the declamation upon humanitarian grounds seems decidedly belated," the *Times* commented sourly. " Indignation would have been much more in place before the Spaniards granted autonomy, which has never been allowed a chance of working, before they abandoned their ruinous concentration of the peasants in the towns, before they recalled General Weyler, and before they offered the armistice which General Blanco is now striving to render effective and to which the rebels refuse to agree." ". . . the representatives of the American people are engaged in spoiling a case which has so far commanded a considerable amount of sympathy." [38] Such observations doubtless reflected widely held opinions. Yet Congressional and other extravagances, however extreme, could not offset the cumulative effect of weeks of pro-American orientation, nor could they sway a people who well understood their national interests. It is clear that many well informed persons felt uneasy about associating with noisy Yankees, but when war came on April 21 no one could doubt which side the British government and people favored.

Thereafter it became easier to suppress lingering doubts. Instead of unpleasant senators, romantic figures like Theodore Roosevelt and his Rough Riders filled the headlines. And no longer did some American newspaper magnates need to resort to unscrupulous sensationalism in order to keep up circulation; the war did that for them. Such changes made it easier for Britons to see the war as Americans saw it: a heroic struggle for the liberation of Cuba from Spanish tyranny.

An unexpected and dramatic event occurring a few days after the outbreak of hostilities furnished a new and strong reason for British support of America. This was Commodore Dewey's destruction of the Spanish fleet at Manila Bay on May 1, 1898, a victory that at once brought up the prospect of American annexation of the Philippines. It is true, as we shall see,[39] that some British trading and shipping interests disliked American

[38] *The Times*, April 14 and 15, 1898.
[39] See pp. 58-62.

expansion into the Philippines and other Spanish islands, commercial preserves of their own; but these were minority interests; on the whole people in Britain welcomed this new imperialism. To appreciate the significance of the battle of Manila Bay one must consider it against the background of the German and Russian moves at Kiaochow and Port Arthur, which it will be remembered had been settled less than two months before with a resulting intensified threat to the Chinese empire and to Britain's open door policy. The sudden appearance of American power in the Far East at this crucial juncture must have seemed providential to the harassed British. For would not the United States, ensconced in the Philippines just off the Chinese coast, be bound in its own defense to participate in the momentous events just then shaping the fate of the ancient empire? Would it not at long last join Britain in defense of non-discriminatory commercial policies in China? The *Times* expressed a widespread opinion in saying hopefully: " if the United States are to become one of the dominant . . . forces in . . . the Pacific, it is obvious that the policy of open trade, to which our transatlantic kinsmen are as much bound as we are in the Far East, will be enormously strengthened." [40]

Great Britain encouraged the United States to follow up Dewey's victory by annexing the whole Philippine archipelago. The government would be disappointed, Ambassador Hay notified the Secretary of State, and the President a few days later, if America did not keep the islands.[41] It might be thought that

---

[40] *The Times*, May 9, 1898. Some of the pre-war irritation with the United States still lingered, however; the *Literary Digest*, vol. 16 (May 7, 1898), p. 562, reported much British criticism of America's noisy diplomacy. " The sudden effusion of friendliness towards England during the past fortnight, so far from being grateful to us, fills us rather with a sense of indecent humbug . . . ," said the *Saturday Review*, vol. 85 (April 30, 1898), p. 582.

[41] A. L. P. Dennis, *Adventures in American Diplomacy, 1896-1906* (New York, 1928), p. 100, Hay to Day, July 28, 1898; C. S. Olcott, *The Life of William McKinley* (2 vols., Boston and New York, 1916), vol. 2, p. 135, Hay to McKinley, August 2, 1898. J. K. Eyre, Jr., " Russia and the American Acquisition of the Philippines," *Mississippi Valley Historical Review*, vol. 28 (1942), p. 546.

Britain would have wanted them herself, especially as a promising road to annexation presented itself when Spain invited her to occupy Manila. But Lord Salisbury wisely refused: a mere extension of territory under the Union Jack, even had the United States been agreeable, would by no means have had the same value as planting the Stars and Stripes close to the cherished but shaky market in China. And when a rumor spread of German pressure to enlist British help in opposing American annexation of the Philippines, Lord Salisbury hastened to assure Hay that the rumor was false. Germany, he said, would never have dreamed of making such a proposal, so well known was Britain's friendship for the United States.[42] Similarly the British encouraged America to annex the Hawaiian islands, no doubt with the thought that one long step out into the Pacific ocean would provoke the still longer one to the Philippines.[43]

As a consequence of these developments, raising the welcome prospect of Cuban liberation and Far Eastern easement, articulate British sentiment rallied strongly to the conquering republic. " Whether the struggle be brief or protracted, there can be as little doubt of the result as there is of the direction in which lie the sympathy and the hopes of the English people," declared the

[42] State Department, Great Britain, Despatches, Hay to Day, June 15, 1898.

[43] Reuter, *Anglo-American Relations*, pp. 172-173. As regards Hawaii Germany did apparently propose to Great Britain in 1897 resistance to annexation by the United States, but Salisbury did not accept; see *Die Grosse Politik der Europäischen Kabinette, 1871-1914* (40 vols., Berlin, 1924-1927), vol. 13, pp. 3409 ff. The two letters of Cecil Spring Rice, then at the British embassy in Berlin, to John Hay (April 30 and May 7, 1898), arguing that the United States should annex Hawaii quickly lest Germany demand compensation in Samoa, are well known. There is, however, no evidence that Spring Rice was acting under instructions except the general consideration that it would have been extraordinary for a trained diplomat to take such action entirely on his own initiative. Regarding these letters see: S. Gwynn, *The Life and Friendships of Sir Cecil Spring Rice* (2 vols., Boston and New York, 1929), vol. 1, pp. 246-247, 248; State Department, Great Britain, Despatches, Hay to Day, May 3, 1898; C. S. Hay, ed., *Letters of John Hay and Extracts from Diary* (3 vols., Washington, 1908), vol. 3, p. 128, Hay to Lodge, July 27, 1898.

Times.[44] Typical of the general reaction was a resolution of the South Saint Pancras Liberal and Radical Association, adopted unanimously " amidst cheers ":

> That this meeting deeply sympathises with the Cubans in their attempt to cast off the intolerable yoke of Spain and achieve their independence, and expresses its hope that our American Kinsmen will succeed in their war with Spain, and will successfully bring about freedom and peace in Cuba.
>
> This meeting trusts that this great act of international justice and the response which it awakens in this country may be the means of a closer sympathy and co-operation among the great English speaking peoples.[45]

So many Britons sought to enlist in the American forces that the embassy in London had to publicize a statement discouraging applications.[46] On the fourth of July it was " barely an exaggeration " to say that only the Stars and Stripes flew in London; and a great meeting proclaimed the essential unity of the English-speaking world, a meeting which would apparently have taken the form of a national demonstration in the Albert Hall had that been thought consistent with neutrality.[47] Always on the alert for a struggle for freedom, the non-conformist religious bodies issued messages of encouragement to the gallant crusaders. Letters to the American embassy from the Men's Sunday Union, the Baptist Union of Great Britain and Ireland, the Congregational Union of England and Wales, and a group of so-called Liberal Churchmen came close to depicting the placid, portly William McKinley as another William the Silent struggling valiantly against great odds to liberate a downtrodden people.[48] Perhaps more significant were distinct signs of approval from the sedate Church of England. Four bishops publicly expressed their hopes of an American victory, and one of them, the Bishop of

[44] *The Times*, April 21, 1898.
[45] State Department, Great Britain, Despatches, Hay to Sherman, April 30, 1898.
[46] *The Times*, April 23, 1898.
[47] London *Daily Chronicle*, July 5, 1898.
[48] State Department, Great Britain, Despatches, Hay to Day, May 4, 5, 14, 19, 1898.

Ripon, gave a "most enthusiastic" speech at an Anglo-American dinner in London.[49]

Not only religious leaders but men distinguished in other walks of life hastened to record their benevolent feelings for America. Much of the June, 1898, issue of the English *Review of Reviews* consisted of propaganda for what its well known editor, W. T. Stead, termed "an informal Association of Friendly Fellowship" for promoting common action throughout the English-speaking world. Some seventy of the most prominent men in the country contributed statements advocating Anglo-American "reunion," such men as William Gladstone, Arthur Balfour, Joseph Chamberlain, Sir William Harcourt, Sir Henry Campbell-Bannerman, James Bryce, John Morley, Henry Asquith, Sir Edward Grey, the Duke of Argyll, the Duke of Sutherland, the Duke of Westminster, Cecil Rhodes, Lord Charles Beresford, Sir Stafford Northcote, Sir Frederick Pollock, Cardinal Vaughan, the Master of Harrow, Herbert Spencer, Henry Irving, Sir Rider Haggard, Conan Doyle, Holman Hunt, and many others.[50] Although the Association of Friendly Fellowship never materialized, the substantial unanimity of so many distinguished contributors was indicative of sentiment throughout the country. "The state of feeling here is the best I have ever known," Ambassador Hay reported enthusiastically. "From every quarter, the evidences of it come to me."[51]

Among political leaders Hay noticed "a somewhat eager desire that 'the other fellows' shall not seem the more friendly."[52] The leader of the opposition, Sir William Harcourt, asserted: "Ever since I have had anything to do with public life my . . . foremost object has been the cultivation of good relations with the United States."[53] A former Prime Minister and Foreign Secretary, the Earl of Rosebery, presiding at a lecture on "The

[49] J. Ralph, "Anglo-Saxon Affinities," *Harper's New Monthly Magazine*, vol. 98 (1899), p. 388.

[50] *Review of Reviews*, vol. 17 (1898), pp. 599-613.

[51] Thayer, *Hay*, vol. 2, p. 168, Hay to Lodge, May 25, 1898.

[52] *Ibid.*, p. 169.

[53] *The Times*, June 11, 1898.

English-Speaking Brotherhood," spoke in glowing terms of the need for Anglo-American friendship; he was, however, a trifle indiscreet in adding that " we may once more call the New World into existence in order to redress the balance of the Old." [54] In an address that Hay thought " one of the most important and striking expressions of English good will," the Marquess of Dufferin and Ava, a man who had occupied many important posts, decried cynics prophesying dissipation of the new friendship with the end of the war; on the contrary, he declared, the United States would ever be grateful for Britain's stand against continental intervention.[55] And in a speech at the Guildhall Prime Minister Salisbury hailed " the mighty force of the American Republic " as conducive to British interests.[56]

There would be little point in piling up further indications of British friendship, but mention should be made of two episodes because of their prominence in British national ritual: the " March Past " on Salisbury plain and the Lord Mayor's parade. On the former occasion, in the presence of the commander-in-chief of the army, the Secretary of State for War, the foreign military attachés, and several members of the royal family, the Stars and Stripes alone of foreign flags was flown on the principal marquee at the saluting point, side by side with the Royal Standard, the Union Jack, and the White Naval Ensign.[57] As for the Lord Mayor's parade, it was carefully arranged to stress fraternal feelings between the two countries. To that end it centered attention on an allegorical float in the form of a ship representing " Sea Power " and flying British and American flags. On the prow appeared the legend " E Pluribus Unum "; on one side " Defence, not defiance "; on the other

[54] *Ibid.*, July 8, 1898.

[55] State Department, Great Britain, Despatches, Hay to Day, September 7, 1898; *The Times*, September 7, 1898.

[56] State Department, Great Britain, Despatches, White to Hay, November 10, 1898.

[57] *Ibid.*, Hay to Day, September 13, 1898. This was Hay's last despatch before becoming Secretary of State.

side " Blood is thicker than water "; standing on the deck, Britannia extended her hand in friendship to Columbia.[58]

Speeches and processions did not satisfy some zealous spirits who hoped to consolidate and perpetuate the mood of the moment by giving it institutional expression. Already since the first month of the war a small committee in London had been working for better relations with America and opposing interference by the continental powers.[59] Soon the need for an organization not limited to wartime exigencies became felt; and beginning in June a number of prominent men, including the Archbishops of Canterbury and York, Henry Asquith, James Bryce, Sir Stafford Northcote, Rudyard Kipling, and many members of Parliament, joined an informal group, apparently an outgrowth of the earlier committee, with the hope of its becoming a permanent organization devoted to fostering Anglo-American friendship. Meeting at Stafford House in London on July 13 under the presidency of the Duke of Sutherland, this group assumed the name Anglo-American League and drew up a statement of purpose:

Considering that the peoples of the British Empire and the United States are closely allied by blood, inherit the same literature and laws, hold the same principles of self-government, recognize the same ideas of freedom and humanity in the guidance of their National policy and are drawn together by strong common interests in many parts of the world, this meeting is of opinion that every effort should be made in the interests of civilization and peace to secure the most cordial and constant coöperation on the part of the two nations.[60]

[58] London *Daily Telegraph*, November 8, 1898; see State Department, Great Britain, Despatches, White to Hay, November 11, 1898, for a letter from the person in charge of arrangements for the parade referring to the intention to emphasize " with more than usual force the fraternal feeling existing between our two countries."

[59] State Department, Great Britain, Despatches, Hay to Day, May 6, 1898.

[60] *An American Response to Expressions of English Sympathy* (New York, printed for the Anglo-American Committee, 1899). Regarding the assertion of common interests Carl Schurz, although on the whole very sympathetic with the League, wrote: " It is much wiser frankly to recognize the fact that while the Americans and the English are of kin in many important

The League's General Committee included several hundred well known individuals from many walks of life; its honorary officers were James Bryce, the Duke of Sutherland, T. Lee Roberts, R. C. Maxwell, and Sir Frederick Pollock.[61]

So marked was the Anglo-American rapprochement that many informed people suspected a secret alliance had been concluded. Speculation was intensified by the famous Birmingham speech, May 13, 1898, of the Colonial Secretary, Joseph Chamberlain. "What is our next duty?" Chamberlain asked.

It is to establish and to maintain bonds of a permanent amity with our kinsmen across the Atlantic. They are a powerful and a generous nation. They speak our language, they are bred of our race. Their laws, their literature, their standpoint upon every question are the same as ours; their feeling, their interest in the cause of humanity and the peaceful development of the world are identical with ours. I do not know what the future has in store for us. I do not know what arrangements may be possible with us, but this I know and feel,—that the closer, the more cordial, the fuller, and the more definite those arrangements are, with the consent of both peoples, the better it will be for both and for the world. And I even go so far as to say that, terrible as war may be, even war itself would be cheaply purchased if in a great and noble cause the Stars and Stripes and the Union Jack should wave together over an Anglo-Saxon Alliance.[62]

respects, and while they can and should do much in harmonious concurrence for the advancement of human civilization, their spheres of action are not the same." See *The Atlantic Monthly*, vol. 82 (1898), p. 438. The League became inactive after 1900.

[61] Reuter, *Anglo-American Relations*, p. 159, mentions the League; State Department, Great Britain, Despatches, Hay to Day, June 7, 1898, gives a few details of its founding; *The Times*, June 7, 1898, has a list of its members as of that date.

[62] In a debate on this speech in the House of Commons, June 10, 1898, there was, Hay reported, "agreement of all the speakers, of every shade of opinion, as to the desirability of an intimate and cordial understanding between England and the United States" (State Department, Great Britain, Despatches, Hay to Day, June 11, 1898). Chamberlain again expressed desire for "union between England and America" in a speech at Leicester, November 30, 1899. See also his article, "Recent Developments of Policy in the United States and Their Relation to an Anglo-American Alliance," *Scribner's*

This forthright declaration by one of the two most important men in the British government was widely interpreted to mean that an alliance, if not already signed, was just about inevitable. In Spain, which for long had seen in America's confident policy a strong indication of support by Great Britain, the Foreign Minister asked the British ambassador point blank whether an alliance existed. The ambassador replied in the negative.[63] Even in England a person described as a leading politician twice a holder of Cabinet rank could assert that an alliance was, "if not already concluded, certain of being so." [64] And the Kaiser in later years believed that the Fatherland had been encircled since 1897 by a secret Anglo-American understanding.[65] "*Anglo-saxonia contra mundum* is for the moment the watchword," the Paris *Temps* stated disgruntledly.[66] In New York the watchful Irish organized an Anti-British Alliance Association of the United States.[67]

Magazine, vol. 24 (1898), p. 675. Even as early as two months before the Birmingham speech a question was asked in the House of Commons as to whether an alliance existed; the government replied noncommitally (*Parliamentary Debates*, vol. 54, p. 1526, March 14, 1898).

[63] F. O. 115, 1077, Drummond to Salisbury, July 29, 1898; F. O. 115, 1238, Durand to Lansdowne, December 14, 1901.

[64] *The Times*, May 16, 1898.

[65] L. M. Gelber, *The Rise of Anglo-American Friendship, a Study in World Politics, 1898-1906* (London, 1938), p. 18. The Kaiser entertained this belief despite a letter to him from Tsar "Nicky," December 14, 1898: "I don't think there is much chance for England to form a real alliance with the United States, against Europe in general, and Russia in particular—as there are so many divergent interests—Canada or the growing question of the Nicaragua canal. Of course they (I mean the English) would like to push the Americans against us in China. This neither frightens me, because we sit firmly on land at Port Arthur—and above everything—Russia's borders touch the Afghan frontier!" See Prince von Bülow, *Memoirs* (4 vols., Boston, 1931-1932), vol. 1, p. 267. With regard to suspicions of an alliance in France it may be mentioned that the famous Paris correspondent of *The Times*, de Blowitz, said that he was as sure that one had been concluded "as any man can be of a thing which he has not actually seen . . ." (F. O. 115, 1077, Monson to Salisbury, August 15, 1898).

[66] April 20, 1898.

[67] *The Irish World* (New York), February 5, 1898; see F. O. 5, 2361, Pauncefote to Salisbury, January 24, February 1 and 5, 1898, for accounts of Irish hostility.

Despite the rumors, however, no alliance had been concluded or even seriously considered in diplomatic exchanges. Neither in Great Britain, Joseph Chamberlain notwithstanding, nor in the United States would one have been possible. Lord Salisbury believed as strongly as ever in isolation (or as his nephew has preferred to call it, independence) [68] for his country; [69] and no American government, it hardly needs saying, would have contemplated for a moment such a flagrant departure from the deep-rooted tradition against European entanglements. But the mere fact that many people in touch with international affairs gave credence to so impossible a thing as an Anglo-American alliance at the turn of the century shows how strong the signs of friendship were. The rapprochement was not close enough for an alliance to be feasible, but it was close enough for erroneous deductions to abound.

We have seen some of the many evidences of the friendly feeling for the United States that existed in Great Britain. To what extent did Americans reciprocate it? On this point the opinion of the British ambassador at Washington, Sir Julian Pauncefote, a most sober reporter, is good evidence. In a private letter to Lord Salisbury he wrote on May 26, 1898, shortly after the outbreak of the Spanish War: " The most astonishing feature of the present time is the sudden transition in this country from Anglophobia to the most exuberant affection for England & ' Britishers ' in general. I am overwhelmed with addresses in prose & verse or in the form of music or drawing or illustrated buttons with Flags intertwined, commemorative of the supposed Anglo-American ' Alliance '." [70]

Further confirming the " exuberant affection " is a memorandum prepared by Reginald Tower, second secretary and Pauncefote's right-hand man at the Washington embassy, de-

---

[68] A. Cecil, *Queen Victoria and Her Prime Ministers* (London, 1953), p. 333.

[69] In his " Dying Nations Speech," May 4, 1898, the Prime Minister said: " But we know that we shall maintain against all comers that which we possess, and we know, in spite of all the jargon about isolation, that we are amply competent to do so."

[70] Salisbury papers, Pauncefote to Salisbury, May 26, 1898.

scribing American opinion in early 1898. Tower reported that a "most remarkable change has taken place within the last few weeks in the feelings of the American people towards England . . ."; that "unanimous, or almost unanimous friendliness to England is now manifested by the Press through the length and breadth of the country, and the 'Union of Hearts' sentiments of today bid fair to pass the bound of moderation in as great degree as the dislike and distrust of yesterday." The memorandum was written shortly after Chamberlain's Birmingham speech. Even the proposal of an alliance, Tower said, met with "hardly a dissentient voice"; he cited as recent advocates of an alliance or a close understanding the *New York Herald*; the *New York Tribune*; D. A. Munro, editor of the *North American Review*; the chaplain of the Senate; Lyman Abbott, a well known clergyman; and Richard Olney, Secretary of State in Cleveland's second administration, a man remembered for his brusque handling of Britain in the Venezuelan boundary controversy of 1895. Particularly remarkable, Tower thought, was an article by Olney arguing that Washington's Farewell Address was outworn and that henceforth the United States should cooperate with Great Britain, " our best friend." [71]

Another point that struck the Englishman was the American celebration of Queen Victoria's seventy-ninth birthday, " the occasion for a fresh outburst of enthusiasm in favour of England "; and he noted with satisfaction that on that day in Tampa, the headquarters of the American army, " the Union Jack and the Stars and Stripes hung side by side." [72] Tower had in mind the situation early in the war. Had he written some months later he could have adduced other instances of friendliness for Britain: a banquet in Portland, Oregon, in honor of Victoria's accession to the throne; [73] the " remarkable enthusiasm " that McKinley evoked everywhere during his trip to Omaha in the autumn of

[71] R. Olney, "International Isolation of the United States," *The Atlantic Monthly*, vol. 81 (1898), p. 5.

[72] F. O. 5, 2362, Pauncefote to Salisbury, May 27, 1898.

[73] F. O. 115, 1080, Pauncefote to Salisbury, July 1, 1898; the banquet, Pauncefote said, reflected " the warmth of the feeling which has sprung up towards Great Britain in that part of the country."

1898 at references to American and British flags flying together; [74] the annual dinner of the influential New York chamber of commerce at which closer union between Great Britain and the United States was the theme.[75]

These judgments of the British diplomats were confirmed by other people. " Good will to England was never so marked or so general as to-day," wrote the famous American correspondent of the London *Times*, George Washburn Smalley. " Listen to those cheers in the New York theatres—loud, long-repeated, and universal—when ' God save the Queen ' is played next after the American National Anthem. They are echoed throughout the United States; they are themselves but the echo of a deep and genuine feeling. . . ." [76] And Henry White, home from London on a short visit just before the war, found the change in temper " astounding." [77] Nor was the British embassy alone in noting Queen Victoria's immense popularity in republican America.

> Year by year [reported the *New York Tribune*] the Queen's birthday is more and more celebrated in the United States. The celebrations of it increase in number, in the largeness and importance of the attendance, and in cordiality of sentiment. Men of American birth and American parentage are glad to join in these tributes of affection and admiration to the revered woman who has for more than half a century been the unwavering friend of this Republic and often its great benefactor, and who now, far more than any other living person, is the head and crown of the entire English-speaking world. She is a Queen of our own race and blood, head of a sister nation, titular ruler of the elder half of our own people, who are one with us in spirit, in sympathy, in ambition, and in destiny.[78]

[74] F. O. 5, 2363, Pauncefote to Salisbury, November 17, 1898.

[75] *New York Tribune*, November 16, 1898; see also F. O. 5, 2363, Pauncefote to Salisbury, November 17, 1898, where the ambassador cited the dinner as " proof of the cordial relations between the two countries."

[76] *The Times*, March 16, 1898.

[77] *Ibid.*, April 22, 1898; see A. Nevins, *Henry White, Thirty Years of American Diplomacy* (New York and London, 1930), p. 133, for White's discovery of " a complete change of sentiment here [America] with regard to England; particularly in Congress, where they seem really to appreciate England's action in refusing to mediate or to join other Powers in mediating."

[78] May 26, 1898.

The United States, it is true, had no real equivalent of the London Anglo-American League, although it did have an Anglo-American Committee founded in New York on July 27, 1898. The Committee, however, represented mainly a small number of people who felt that establishment of so impressive a body as the League called for something substantial in return. Twenty-six public figures, including Whitelaw Reid, William C. Whitney, Daniel Lamont, John G. Carlisle, Carl Schurz, and Benjamin F. Tracy, comprised the original Committee, which drew up the following " Address ":

> We, citizens of the United States of America, desire to express our most hearty appreciation of the recent demonstrations of sympathy and fellowship with this country on the part of citizens of the various countries comprised in the British Empire. We earnestly reciprocate these sentiments, recognizing as we do that the same language and the same principles of ordered liberty should form the basis of an intimate and enduring friendship between these kindred peoples,—a friendship destined to hasten the day of peace and good-will among all the nations of the earth.

The Address, which it will be noted was rather more reserved than the League's Statement of Purpose, was signed by over 1000 well known Americans.[79]

The reasons for the revolution in American sentiment noted by Pauncefote, Tower, and others are not far to seek. Some of the background reasons have been mentioned—the softening of memories with the passage of time, the birth of a new generation of Irish, the dwindling of the free-silver controversy. But the immediate cause, and a most important one, was the war with Spain. A contemporary article describing opinion on the Continent informed Americans that " In newspapers, in clubs, in society, even in the street, the dislike of Americans, the wish that they might be defeated, the desire, if it were only safe, to give

---

[79] For a brief account of the Committee and a complete list of members and signers of the Address, see *An American Response to Expressions of English Sympathy*.

them some savage snub, is unmistakable." [80] What a contrast such feelings presented to the friendly sentiments we have noted in Britain! Alone among the great powers Britain stood, in reality and in appearance, with the United States; and her press and people agreed that the time had come to put a stop to Spanish misrule in Cuba. The appearance became more marked following the mediation discussions of early April, 1898, when the legend arose of a new concert of Europe restrained from intervening in the New World only by British opposition, directed in Washington by Sir Julian Pauncefote.[81] During the war Great Britain took charge of American interests in Spain and Spanish possessions; and several of her diplomatic and consular officers performed conspicuous acts of service to Americans.[82]

The story of the fleets which assembled at Manila Bay after Dewey's victory is well known. On several occasions a German squadron there, so it was believed in the United States, maneuvered threateningly, and once it was prevented from overt interference with the American ships only by timely action on the part of a British squadron, fortunately also on the scene. As a matter of fact, although the commander, Vice-Admiral von Diederichs, did irritate Dewey he had no unfriendly intent.[83] Nevertheless, the story of German hostility at Manila died hard;

[80] "The Continental Dislike of Americans," *The Spectator*, vol. 81 (July 16, 1898), p. 76; see also Ferrera, *Last Spanish War*, p. 97.

[81] For a typical opinion see C. A. Gardiner, "The Proposed Anglo-American Alliance," *Journal of Social Science*, no. 36 (1898), p. 158: "Great Britain alone averted the active interference of Europe in our late war. She refused to join the European concert, and her suggestion of an Anglo-American alliance sobered every European power."

[82] One of them, F. W. Ramsden, was so helpful to American naval prisoners at Santiago that after the war the United States Navy Department placed a tablet on his house in that city (F. O. 5, 2460, Hay to Pauncefote, March 26, 1901). Reuter, *Anglo-American Relations*, pp. 99-101.

[83] T. A. Bailey, "Dewey and the Germans at Manila Bay," *American Historical Review*, vol. 45 (1939), pp. 59-81; von Bülow, *Memoirs*, vol. 1, p. 216; von Diederichs, "A Statement of Events in Manila, May-October, 1898," *The Journal of the Royal United Service Institute*, vol. 59 (1914), p. 446, quotes a letter from Dewey, April 16, 1899, stating: ". . . I rejoice that our differences have been of newspaper manufacture."

and even five years later one of Dewey's officers could win applause by declaring dramatically in a public address in New York: "When the German fleet threatened us the English fleet silently changed its anchorage into line with the American, and we did not need to ask which side they were going to take. We knew." [84]

British encouragement of American expansion has been referred to. Here the effect on public opinion in the United States was probably small, for not only was America itself profoundly divided on the issue but some of the country's best friends in England warned that its true interests did not lie in the direction of acquiring colonies. Nevertheless, proponents of expansion, such men as Henry Cabot Lodge, Theodore Roosevelt, A. T. Mahan, could not help but contrast Britain's understanding attitude with the grudging spirit of other powers which would have liked the Spanish islands for themselves.

Britain as the friend and champion of the United States—this was a new concept for Americans who habitually had thought of her as the deadly foe always on the watch for a favorable opening to attack. Far from taking advantage of the country's involvement with Spain, Great Britain had now gone out of her way to warn off the malevolent continental powers—so Americans began to believe. "Then came the Spanish war," Carl Schurz wrote in a magazine in 1898, "and the demonstrative display of British sympathy with the United States. Even the most inveterate Anglophobist was bound to admit that if Great Britain had been watching for an opportunity to hurt this republic, her time to take advantage of its embarrassment had come, and that if, under such circumstances, she proved herself not only not hostile, but positively friendly, the old cries could not be sustained." [85] So instructed by their leaders, many Americans changed their minds about the traditional foe. Naturally they appreciated the sympathy shown by British statesmen and the British press. For the first time they were leaving their snug continental borders

[84] *The Times*, April 25, 1903.
[85] Carl Schurz, "The Anglo-American Friendship," *The Atlantic Monthly*, vol. 82 (1898), p. 434.

and venturing forth into the bleak, harsh domain of international strife; feeling lonely and somewhat apprehensive they turned eagerly to the one country befriending them.

About that time a new stock character joined vaudeville companies touring the country: a British naval officer, the guardian angel of a virtuous American sailor lad in distress.[86] The valiant officer fitted in well with the new American conception of Great Britain. We may be sure that he was applauded heartily as night after night he raised his strong right arm against the powers of evil.

[86] *The Times*, January 17, 1899.

CHAPTER 3

The Issues

THE SUDDEN appearance of almost extravagantly friendly feelings between the United States and Great Britain afforded a golden opportunity not likely soon to recur for negotiating on outstanding issues. If the two countries could take advantage of the hot-house growth of trans-Atlantic affection in order to arrive at a broad agreement the basis for a lasting betterment of relations might be established. Both countries found themselves in a dangerous and exposed position in 1898 that made a rapprochement particularly desirable just then. Involved in a war whose repercussions they could not foresee, and conscious of hostility from all the great powers except Britain, Americans could not but appreciate the advantages of closer ties with the powerful empire befriending them. As for Britain, if she could use her new association with America in order to buttress hard-pressed positions all over the world and particularly in the Far East, that would be a signal triumph indeed. " How long the fit [of the " most exuberant affection for England "] will last," Ambassador Pauncefote advised Salisbury, " no wise man would venture to predict, but it will certainly have an excellent effect on the future relations of the two countries, & we must seize this opportune moment to ' straighten out,' as they call it, all our . . . difficulties." [1]

As Sir Julian implied, lasting improvement in relations could not be based upon the pro-British emotionalism that had swept over America; it could come only from settling specific disputes

[1] Salisbury papers, Pauncefote to Salisbury, May 26, 1898.

through hard, persistent negotiations. What were these disputes? They centered on two main areas, one to the south of the United States where at the end of 1898 Americans turned with a sudden violent impulse to clear the way for an American canal by sweeping aside the restrictions of an old treaty with Great Britain— the Clayton-Bulwer treaty of 1850; the other to the north, where several issues involved the Dominion of Canada. Of the Canadian issues three were quite capable of undermining the still precarious Anglo-American harmony: those regarding the Alaska boundary, Newfoundland fisheries, and Bering Sea fur seals. Another, the question of commercial reciprocity, although less dangerous, was so important to Canada that it, too, needs careful attention. Several others may be passed over as being of little significance.[2]

Much the most urgent of all these issues were those concerning the Clayton-Bulwer treaty and the Alaska boundary. These constituted the principal material of British-American negotiations through 1903; and until the former was abrogated at the end of 1901 they were closely associated together in the sense that Great Britain steadily refused to abandon the treaty unless the United States modified its position regarding the boundary. Both were extremely complicated, and both struck deep emotions, particularly in Canada and the United States.

Realizing that the Canadian questions, all of them dating back over many years, could not safely be allowed to drag on much longer, America and Britain agreed to submit them for settlement to a Joint High Commission which convened in August, 1898, the month of the Spanish War armistice. The decision to negotiate on the Clayton-Bulwer treaty was not taken until some weeks later.

Before describing these Canadian and canal controversies— the main stumbling-blocks to a broad settlement—we must turn

---

[2] For general accounts of the Canadian issues see: A Canadian Liberal, " The Anglo-American Joint High Commission," *North American Review*, vol. 167 (1898), pp. 165-175; J. G. Bourinot, " Canada's Relations with the United States, and Her Influence in Imperial Councils," *The Forum*, vol. 25 (1898), pp. 329-340; E. Farrer, " The Anglo-American Commission," *ibid.*, pp. 652-663.

first to another matter which, although not constituting a principal subject matter of Anglo-American negotiations, nevertheless formed an important part of the general situation between the two countries that should not be passed over in silence. It concerned complications arising from American overseas expansion.

Although American expansion in the Pacific and the Caribbean was on the whole welcomed by Great Britain, as we have seen, it created certain problems for her, and also for Canada and other British colonies. As the Spanish-American War drew to its close, British shipping and trading firms dealing with Cuba, Puerto Rico, Hawaii, and the Philippines began to wonder uneasily how their fortunes would be affected if the United States, an ultra high-tariff country, annexed these islands. Would it impose its navigation laws on them? Would it erect discriminatory tariff systems? If so, British interests would suffer. The London *Times* expressed the apprehension:

> In this country, no jealousy has been provoked by the natural desire of the United States, an advancing and expanding Power, to acquire points of vantage, outside the limits of the American continent, as naval stations and as openings for trade. At the same time, we have assumed that in taking up such a position the Washington Government would be actuated by the principles which are laid down, in relation to the spheres of European influence in China, by President McKinley in his Message to Congress. The absence of " exclusive treatment " is the foundation of our own commercial policy in the colonies and dependencies of the British Crown, and we have a right to look for reciprocity of conditions from the United States as a colonial Power.[3]

But hopes of equal treatment appeared dubious when on December 6, 1898, the Secretary of the Treasury, Lyman Gage, in his annual report recommended extending American navigation laws to Puerto Rico and Hawaii.[4] Incorporation of these and other

---

[3] *The Times*, December 10, 1898; see also *ibid.*, November 12, 1898.
[4] See *ibid.*, December 8, 1898, for a caustic comment on Gage's assertion that his recommendation followed British practice.

Spanish islands into an exclusive commercial system now began to seem inevitable.

Hawaii and Puerto Rico were not of prime concern to Great Britain; but Cuba, as Lord Salisbury said, furnished a market of "magnitude and importance. . . ." [5] As for the Philippines, British ships carried part of the commerce between those islands and the United States, generally in the course of the longer voyage between England and the Far East. Consequently Britain was disappointed when an early report that Washington had decided on the open door for that large archipelago proved mistaken; [6] and she was further disappointed when the State Department refused to accept her contention that American trade with the Philippines, not being coastal, fell outside the scope of the navigation laws.[7]

As the United States began to impose discriminatory commercial and shipping regulations in its new acquisitions, British commercial interests besieged London with appeals for help. Unless the United States changed its policy, the Iron Trade Association wrote Prime Minister Salisbury in 1899, British trade with Cuba and Puerto Rico faced "virtual ruin." [8] "We shall feel it very much if a prohibitive Tariff . . . is put into force," Glasgow exporters of machinery to Hawaii told their member of Parliament.[9] Speaking for shipping interests, the Chamber of Shipping of the United Kingdom unanimously resolved to ask Salisbury to warn the United States government of "the serious injury which British Shipping would sustain should that Government confine to vessels carrying the American Flag the carrying trade with Cuba, Porto Rico, and the Philippine

[5] F. O. 5, 2367, Salisbury to Pauncefote, November 25, 1898.
[6] State Department, Great Britain, Despatches, White to Hay, November 23, 1898.
[7] F. O. 5, 2367, Herschell to Salisbury, August 29, 1898; F. O. 5, 2399, Hay to Pauncefote, November 23, 1899.
[8] F. O. 5, 2412, British Iron Trade Association to Salisbury, letter undated but sent in the spring of 1899.
[9] F. O. 5, 2449, Watson, Laidlaw and Co. to A. C. Corbett, June 13, 1900; see F. O. 5, 2505, for a letter from Smith, Wood and Co., April 16, 1900, complaining of American policy in the Philippines.

Islands." [10] Numerous other such protests expressed the alarm felt in commercial circles.[11]

In view of the outcries, it is no wonder that the Foreign Office warned Henry White, chargé d'affaires at the American embassy, that discrimination would undermine the " present good understanding between both countries "; [12] and that Lord Salisbury instructed Pauncefote to warn the United States of the considerable apprehension felt in Britain.[13] But the ambassador could only report " no hope of any present concession. . . ." [14]

In addition to Britain herself, some British colonies were injured by the discriminatory practices. Australian and New Zealand ships trading with North America were largely pre-

[10] F. O. 115, 1113, Chamber of Shipping of the United Kingdom to Salisbury, March 21, 1899.

[11] For other protests see: F. O. 5, 2412, North Staffordshire Chamber of Commerce to Salisbury, January 19, 1899; ibid., T. H. Davies and Co. to Foreign Office, undated; F. O. 5, 2433, Pauncefote to Salisbury, April 23, 1900; F. O. 5, 2499, Ommaney to Sanderson, October 22, 1900; F. O. 5, 2434, Pauncefote to Sanderson, November 12, 1900; F. O. 5, 2449, The St. John's Gas Co., Ltd., to Lansdowne, December 4, 1900; F. O. 5, 2476, A. W. Wills and Son to Stone, March 11, 1901; ibid., Council of the Walsall and District Incorporated Chamber of Commerce to Lansdowne, April 12, 1901; ibid., Gosselin to Wolverhampton, Birmingham, and Sheffield Chambers of Commerce (three letters), April 15, 1901; ibid., Manchester Chamber of Commerce to Lansdowne, April 20, 1901; ibid., London Chamber of Commerce to Lansdowne, April 26, 1901; F. O. 5, 2462, Pauncefote to Lansdowne, May 2, 1901; F. O. 5, 2461, Lansdowne to Pauncefote, December ,17, 1901; F. O. 5, 2505, Foreign Office memorandum by Villiers, about May 1, 1902; F. O. 5, 2493, Raikes to Lansdowne, June 14, 1902.

[12] State Department, Great Britain, Despatches, White to Hay, November 23 and 26, 1898. For other such warnings see A. Nevins, Henry White, Thirty Years of American Diplomacy (New York and London, 1930), pp. 165-166, White to Hay, November, 1898; and F. O. 5, 2367, Herschell to Salisbury, August 29, 1898; The Standard (London), September 12, 1898.

[13] F. O. 5, 2367, Salisbury to Pauncefote, November 25, 1898; Pauncefote had already expressed " gravest apprehension " (Hay papers, to Hay, November 16, 1898).

[14] F. O. 5, 2400, Pauncefote to Salisbury, February 6, 1899. Cartwright had already expressed the opinion that " we shall not succeed in getting the clause about the carrying trade " (F. O. 5, 2421, Cartwright to Campbell, December 23, 1898).

vented from carrying goods between Hawaii and the United States. New Zealand, concerned over disruption of a valued business, appealed to Great Britain in a memorandum signed by the Premier himself to intercede at Washington.[15] Although Pauncefote did plead the cause of the anxious colonials he did not succeed in regaining the Hawaiian carrying trade for them.[16]

Canada, too, suffered; and her grievance had a cumulative effect upon her other grievances with the United States. From early days Canadian schooners, mostly from New Brunswick and Nova Scotia, had carried cargoes of fish to Puerto Rico, reloaded with molasses and rum for New York and other east coast ports, and there taken on goods for Canada. Now after the Spanish War, American navigation laws and protective duties lay heavy upon this customary course of trade. At the Joint High Commission the British commissioner, Lord Herschell, broached the subject of Puerto Rico, hoping to persuade Washington to hold open its commerce in partial compensation for a British retreat on the fur seals question.[17] He did not succeed. When the commission adjourned, Canada urged Britain not to meet American wishes regarding the Clayton-Bulwer treaty unless America first satisfied Canada as to her Puerto Rican trade, and also as to her demands regarding the Alaska boundary.[18] Such an approach had already been discussed in the Foreign Office [19] and had gained the powerful support of Joseph Chamberlain and the Colonial Office; [20] but given American determination to have a national canal, it was doomed to failure. The utmost Britain could hope for, Pauncefote advised—and he was not sanguine about even

[15] F. O. 5, 2476, memorandum signed by R. J. Seddon and dated December 13, 1900.

[16] F. O. 5, 2462, Pauncefote to Lansdowne, March 20, 1901.

[17] F. O. 5, 2421, Cartwright to Campbell, December 16, 1898; *ibid.*, Herschell to Salisbury, December 22, 1898. See also F. O. 5, 2367, Herschell to Salisbury, August 29, 1898; and F. O. 5, 2417, memorandum by Herschell, December 30, 1898.

[18] F. O. 5, 2416, telegram from Minto received April 10, 1899.

[19] F. O. 5, 2412, memorandum to Salisbury from "St. J. B." (St. John Brodrick), February 1, 1899.

[20] F. O. 5, 2416, Colonial Office to Foreign Office, May 13, 1899.

that—was an assurance that the President would try to persuade Congress to be lenient with British commerce in return for concessions in Central America.[21] But no such assurance was forthcoming.

Thus Canada lost out as regards her traditional Puerto Rican commerce. Not only that, but she had to stand by and watch the two English-speaking countries, between which she was so uncomfortably wedged, sign a number of reciprocity treaties relating to the British West Indies which, although not ratified as it turned out, threatened to increase American commercial predominance in the Caribbean still further.

No more need be said about this particular aspect of American expansion. British protests notwithstanding, the United States did not relax discrimination in its new possessions; and British and Canadian commercial interests had to reconcile themselves to seeing much of their business slip away to Americans.

We may now return to the far more serious and difficult controversies regarding the Dominion of Canada and to the Clayton-Bulwer treaty. We shall consider first the controversy over the treaty.

The disputes over Canadian matters, particularly those relating to the fisheries and the Alaska boundary, and to a less extent that relating to the seals, were dangerous partly because of their intrinsic importance but even more because large numbers of aggressive persons of two nationalities were thrown together under circumstances where they might easily have clashed. This was not the case as regards the dispute over the Clayton-Bulwer treaty. This dispute, however, concerned an issue—construction and control of an isthmian waterway—which was one of the most far-reaching of the time. A canal would transform prevailing patterns of world commerce, would modify military and naval strategy, and would profoundly affect the whole international balance of power. The immense repercussions of a new interoceanic waterway would be felt by all countries, but par-

[21] F. O. 5, 2400, Pauncefote to Foreign Office, February 6, 1899; F. O. 5, 2416, Colonial Office to Foreign Office, May 6, 1899.

ticularly by the United States as the great power in closest proximity to Central America, and by Great Britain as the leading naval and commercial power. Canada, too, which like the United States needed a canal for quicker communication between her two coasts, had a direct interest in the matter.[22]

Like the Alaska boundary question, the canal question came into prominence at the time of the Spanish-American War; it did not, however, become critical until after the war. American interest in a canal was not new, of course. From early days of New World settlement people had envisaged binding together the Atlantic and Pacific oceans by a waterway across the narrow isthmus, and had taken pretty much for granted that someday this would be done. After the acquisition of Oregon in 1846 and of California two years later, thousands of Americans travelled between the east and west coasts by way of Central America, thereby avoiding the dangers and hardships of travel in unsettled areas of the United States. Inevitably the uncomfortable need to interrupt an easy sea trip in order to proceed overland across the isthmus directed attention to a canal's convenience. Of much the same effect was the contemporary opening of oriental markets, from which owners of American factories, situated mainly in eastern states, hoped to oust their European rivals once a new interoceanic waterway provided a shorter route to the Far East.

Because of the heightened interest in such a waterway the United States and Great Britain took steps to gain control of possible sites, and the consequent maneuverings of their agents in Central America gave rise to considerable tension in the late 1840's. But sanity prevailed, and the two countries negotiated the Clayton-Bulwer treaty of 1850. The terms of this treaty, which constituted one of the principal subjects of British-American negotiation until its termination in 1901, should be carefully

[22] For the canal question see M. P. DuVal, *Cadiz to Cathay: The Story of the Long Diplomatic Struggle for the Panama Canal* (Stanford, 1940); G. Mack, *The Land Divided* (New York, 1944); D. C. Miner, *The Fight for the Panama Route: The Story of the Spooner Act and the Hay-Herrán Treaty* (New York, 1940).

noted. They stipulated that neither country would ever "obtain or maintain for itself any exclusive control" over a Central American canal, or fortify such a canal; that neither would colonize any part of Central America; that both would guarantee the neutrality of the canal, which would forever be open and free to all countries on equal terms; and that in entering into the convention both desired not only to lay the ground for a canal but to establish "a general principle" of joint protection and neutrality for any interoceanic waterway across Central America. Like two other old treaties, which we shall consider below—the Anglo-American treaty of 1818 regarding the fisheries, and the Anglo-Russian treaty of 1825 regarding the Alaska boundary—the Clayton-Bulwer treaty, after having largely slipped from notice for some years, reemerged after the war with Spain to disturb relations between the United States and Great Britain.

During that conflict the dramatic race of the warship *Oregon* from the west coast all the way around Cape Horn in order to engage the Spanish fleet in the Caribbean drove home as could nothing else the enormous significance of a shorter route between the two American oceans. More fundamental in its influence upon American thinking, though less dramatic, was the acquisition of overseas territory. Just as settlement of the west coast a half century earlier had turned thoughts to the isthmus, so now did expansion into the Caribbean and the Pacific. As a result of the war the United States acquired Guam, Puerto Rico, and the Philippines; about the same time it annexed Hawaii and part of Samoa. With possessions on both sides of the isthmus, responsibilities in the Far East, and the increased prestige of a victorious nation and a growing naval power, the United States had suddenly arrived at a situation where national interests called in unmistakable terms for a canal. And the American people, flushed with pride and full of confidence after their easy conquests, were determined to acquire not just an international canal as specified by the Clayton-Bulwer treaty but an exclusively national canal, the only kind they thought worthy of their new glory. Even before the war ended, in fact, they had come to the conclusion that construction of such a canal must not be postponed much longer.

As full of peril for Anglo-American relations, at least in the short run, was the controversy over the boundary between Alaska and Canada.[23] Of all the Canadian controversies it was by far the most explosive; determination of the remote and nebulous boundary was therefore the most urgent and important matter before the Joint High Commission. It was also the most complicated and difficult one, too complicated and difficult, in fact, for the commissioners to solve. This was unfortunate, because it proved to be the key issue around which all major Anglo-American negotiations turned for a number of years. It held up negotiations with Great Britain over other Canadian matters and over the Clayton-Bulwer treaty; for Canada would settle nothing at all until the boundary was agreed upon, and Great Britain for some time was unwilling to terminate the canal treaty until the Canadian issues had been disposed of. Because of this controversy's crucial importance it requires particular consideration.

What made the boundary's delineation pressing in 1898 was the fact that the famous gold rush had commenced a year or two earlier and was then close to its height. Lured by reports of fabulous gold strikes, thousands of rough and ready prospectors from all over the world, but mainly from the United States—of the 50,000 persons in the gold country in July, 1898, about three-fourths were Americans—were stampeding to the far northwest of the Dominion, to the region of the Klondike river, close to Alaska. Almost overnight towns like Circle City, Dawson City, Bonanza, and El Dorado were springing up from a wilderness hitherto unknown to habitation. "It is doubtful if, in rapidity, size, and intensity," an authority says, "the Klondike gold rush has ever been equalled in the whole range of economic expansion."[24] The transformation in the Canadian northwest and in Alaska, especially in the southern coastal strip (the so-called panhandle) across which the main stream of prospectors

[23] L. B. Shippee, *Canadian-American Relations, 1849-1874* (New Haven, 1939); C. C. Tansill, *Canadian-American Relations, 1875-1911* (New Haven, 1943).

[24] H. A. Innis, *Settlement and the Mining Frontier* (Toronto, 1936), p. 183.

journeyed, imparted a sense of urgency to what had been till then a leisurely consideration of the boundary's true course.

In order to understand this protracted and bitter dispute, not finally settled until 1903, a clear picture of the geographical setting is necessary. It was next to impossible to travel overland from southern Canada to the Klondike, more than a thousand miles from the nearest settled part of the Dominion. Most prospectors boarded ship at one of the western ports of the United States, usually Seattle or Tacoma; a few embarked at Vancouver in British Columbia. Some sailed along the coast far northward to St. Michael, a small town at the mouth of the Yukon, and proceeded up that river to the gold fields. But the great majority, after going up the coast a thousand miles or so, turned eastward through the island screen off the Alaska mainland and entered the Lynn Canal, a fjord some two or three miles wide on the average and a hundred miles long that penetrated deep into the welter of forbidding mountains guarding the continent's frozen interior.

Near its northern end this so-called canal divides into two branches: the Chilkat Inlet and the Chilkoot Inlet. On the former was a landing-place known as Pyramid Harbor; on the latter two little towns had just sprung up to a bustling, chaotic, lawless existence: Dyea and Skagway. As late as July, 1897, Skagway consisted of nothing but a log house and a tent; less than a month later it had a population of 2,000, and this figure had doubled by 1898. Dyea, close by, was smaller. Above Pyramid Harbor the Dalton Trail leads into the interior. Although low and easy to follow it does not reach navigable inland water, so that the weary gold hunter of 1898, at length coming to its end, still faced a long and difficult trip overland. The Chilkoot Pass above Dyea, twenty-three miles long, and the White Pass above Skagway, thirty-five miles long, run parallel through the mountains to the head of inland navigation. Each was used more than the Dalton Trail; of the two the White Pass was the more popular, especially after a railway was built through it to the flatter country beyond the mountains. Already by February, 1899, this railway had been constructed twenty-one miles, from Skag-

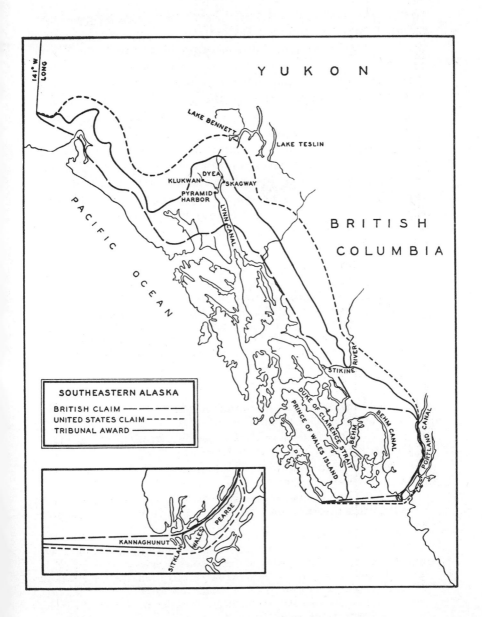

SOUTHEASTERN ALASKA
BRITISH CLAIM — — —
UNITED STATES CLAIM — — — — —
TRIBUNAL AWARD ————

way to the summit of the pass.[25] Forty miles from Skagway, east of the White Pass, lies Lake Bennett, the first of a series of waterways through which river boats could go all the way to the Yukon in warm weather. Thus the Lynn Canal, Skagway, the White Pass, Lake Bennett, and subsequent waterways formed a chain connecting the high seas with the Canadian northwest. The canal was the key link; the nation controlling its headwaters would dominate the gold country.

The boundary controversy centered upon the ambiguities of an old treaty, the Anglo-Russian treaty of 1825. Part of this treaty had been incorporated into the Russo-American treaty of 1867, by which the United States acquired Alaska, to define the territory's eastern boundary, that is, the line between Alaska and Canada. This section of the 1825 treaty must be quoted:

> Commencing from the southernmost point of the island called Prince of Wales Island, which point lies in the parallel of 54 degrees 40 minutes north latitude, and between the 131st and the 133d degree of west longitude, (meridian of Greenwich,) the said line shall ascend to the north along the channel called Portland channel, as far as the point of the continent where it strikes the 56th degree of north latitude; from this last-mentioned point, the line of demarcation shall follow the summit of the mountains situated parallel to the coast as far as the point of intersection of the 141st degree of west longitude, (of the same meridian;) and finally, from the said point of intersection, the said meridian line of the 141st degree, in its prolongation as far as the Frozen ocean.
>
> IV. With reference to the line of demarcation laid down in the preceding article, it is understood—
>
> 1st. That the island called Prince of Wales Island shall belong wholly to Russia,
>
> 2nd. That whenever the summit of the mountains which extend in a direction parallel to the coast from the 56th degree

---

[25] *Ibid.*, p. 213, describes the amazing progress of construction. " On April 10th, 1898, the chief engineer arrived at Skagway, on May 28th, construction was begun, on July 21st, four miles of track were completed, on August 25th, Heney Station or Mile 13 was reached, on February 18th, 1899, the Summit or Mile 21, and on July 6th, Lake Bennett. A year later, July 30th, 1900, through trains ran from Skagway to White Horse at the foot of the rapids to connect with steamboats to Dawson."

of north latitude to the point of intersection of the 141st degree of west longitude shall prove to be at the distance of more than ten marine leagues from the ocean, the limit between the British possessions and the line of coast which is to belong to Russia as above mentioned (that is to say, the limit to the possessions ceded by this convention) shall be formed by a line parallel to the winding of the coast, and which shall never exceed the distance of ten marine leagues therefrom.

No controversy existed as to the line north of the intersection of the mountains and the 141st degree, delimitation of which was simply a matter of accurate surveying. But by 1898 two serious points of contention had emerged with regard to the southern portion of the line, that is to say, the coastal strip.

First, what was Portland channel? Here the problem was to decide whether the body of water usually known as Portland Canal in the 1890's was the "Portland channel" mentioned in the treaty of 1825. The treaty refers to Portland channel as being to the *north* of the southern tip of Prince of Wales Island and as striking the 56th degree, whereas the Portland Canal familiar to people of 1898 is *east* of the tip and does not extend as far north as that degree. The United States contended that Portland channel was obviously Portland Canal; Canada, probably with little conviction, and Great Britain, with none—". . . I regard the [Canadian] contention as hopelessly untenable," Lord Herschell, the British representative on the Joint High Commission declared [26]—held out for Duke of Clarence Strait or just possibly Behm Canal, which do fit the specifications of the treaty.[27] Ownership of many square miles at the coastal strip's southern end hinged upon the identity of Portland channel.

Second, did the boundary curve around the heads of the inlets, particularly of the Lynn Canal, or cut across them? On this question's answer hung the ownership of the canal's headwaters and control of communications with the Klondike. Unfortunately

[26] F. O. 5, 2421, Herschell to Salisbury, September 2, 1898.
[27] A. Begg, *History of British Columbia from its Earlier Discovery to the Present Time* (Toronto, 1894), p. 559, was probably the first to put forward the Behm Canal theory. See pp. 104-105.

various uncertainties—some geographical, some pertaining to the treaty's wording—clouded the issue.

For one thing, did a mountain range parallel to the coast exist? The United States insisted that there was no such range; Canada, on the other hand, claimed knowledge of a coastal range less than ten marine leagues (about thirty-five miles) from salt water; if she was right, the canal's headwaters would be British.

Another point concerned the meaning of the word "ocean." Did the ocean include, as the United States contended, waters inside the archipelago bordering the continent, and also waters of such inlets as the Lynn Canal—all salt water in other words? Or did it include only the high seas outside the archipelago, as Great Britain contended? If no coastal range existed, much would depend on the answer; for a line measured inland from the ocean as defined by Great Britain (but not as defined by the United States) would cut across the Lynn Canal, and its headwaters would be British.

Finally, what did the phrase "winding of the coast" mean? Here again the two countries stood apart. The United States insisted that the boundary must twist and turn ten marine leagues inland, following all the coastal sinuosities—including the deep penetration made by the Lynn Canal. Great Britain rejoined that in the first place the phrase had no relevance since a coastal range did exist and therefore determined the boundary; but that in any event it referred to the coast's general trend. A line parallel to the general trend would cross the canal some thirty-five miles from its mouth; and, again, its headwaters, and control of the Klondike trade, would be in British hands.

The United States had effective possession of the whole Lynn Canal, and this created a problem for Canada and Great Britain. Apart from the annoyance of being dependent upon a foreign country for communication with an integral part of her own domain, the Dominion resented American control for specific economic and military reasons. For one thing, such control facilitated discrimination against Canadian goods. At first American officials at Dyea and Skagway would not allow British vessels even to land their cargoes; but after vehement protests the United

States made the two towns sub-ports of entry. Canadian goods then became subject to American import duties or other irritating charges. Importers could escape duties by paying six dollars a day, plus three dollars a day for subsistence, for having their imports convoyed across the contested strip.[28] For a while the convoys were controlled by an outlaw known as Soapy Smith; and after the importer had paid tribute to this unsavory person, he must often have wished that he had paid the duty instead. Yet the duty, too, could be onerous. Canadians believed that many of the customs inspectors were bribed to divert business to American hands. Businessmen in Vancouver and elsewhere felt exasperated over this ruinous grip on intra-Canadian commerce. "Can nothing be done with the government at Washington to put a stop to these impositions?" asked a Canadian official angrily;[29] and rumors were heard of closing the Lynn Canal passes to Americans.[30] Partly due to British protests the United States in March, 1898, exempted merchandise in transit across the coastal strip from duties and other levies.[31] But by then some ninety percent of all commerce with the northwest was in American hands.

Canada also resented American control for military reasons. The possibility of trouble with the prospectors, most of them Americans, haunted people's thoughts; and the Dominion feared that if a clash should occur, the United States would not permit her to send troops up the canal.[32] Law and order might collapse; even a full-scale rebellion might break out; all too quickly a self-proclaimed republic—another Texas—might be applying for admission to the union. In that event a third Anglo-American war could be close at hand.

For these reasons Great Britain and Canada were determined to shake off the cramping stranglehold at the Lynn Canal. Their

[28] *Sessional Papers, Volume 12, Fourth Session of the Eighth Parliament of the Dominion of Canada*, 62 Victoria, no. 15, A. 1899, part III, p. 112.

[29] J. W. Dafoe, *Clifford Sifton in Relation to His Times* (Toronto, 1931), p. 164, Walsh to Sifton, January 22, 1898.

[30] *The Times*, January 26, 1898.

[31] Dafoe, *Sifton*, p. 164.

[32] F. O. 5, 2384, memorandum by Sifton, February 28, 1898.

main effort was directed to the Joint High Commission; but for several months before it met, Canada considered opening another route to the gold country, a route that would by-pass the Lynn Canal. After examining various possibilities the government decided in early 1898 to sponsor a railway from Telegraph Creek, some distance up the Stikine river, to Lake Teslin, near Lake Bennett; in time it could be extended south to a Canadian port and north to Dawson City on the Yukon.[33]

There were difficulties, however. Who would build it? The government would not; in fact it would not even give a cash subsidy. And a private company would find it hard to finance so speculative a venture as a railway to the bleak frozen north country when the gold rush, however booming, might soon peter out and when a shorter American line starting at a more northerly point might soon be in operation. Already talk was heard of such a line from Skagway; and construction actually began in March, 1898. Because they did not believe the projected Canadian railway could meet such competition, Mackenzie and Mann, the concern contemplating building the Stikine-Teslin line, demanded a guarantee that the Skagway railway would not be extended into Canada.[34] This the Canadian Cabinet was willing to give; it consequently introduced appropriate legislation in Parliament. Without waiting for Parliament to act, Mackenzie and Mann signed a contract on January 26, 1898, to construct a wagon road in six weeks and a railway by September 1, 1898, from Telegraph Creek to Lake Teslin; the government for its part agreed not to permit any railway to cross from Alaska into Canada and to grant the company 25,000 acres of land for every mile of construction.[35]

A more serious difficulty now appeared. Angered by the discrimination against the Skagway line, the United States Congress was devising a move to bring pressure on Canada. It took the form of a bill introduced by Senator Frye of Maine banning transhipment except under most onerous conditions at Fort

[33] The Times, January 27, 1898.
[34] F. O. 5, 2384, memorandum by Sifton, February 28, 1898.
[35] Innis, Mining Frontier, p. 196; Dafoe, Sifton, p. 165.

Wrangel, a tiny American town at the mouth of the Stikine river. Since ocean-going vessels could not navigate the Stikine and since only at Fort Wrangel was transhipment practicable, the Frye bill if enacted would block Canada's project.[36] Not only that, but the bill's real purpose, a senator told Ambassador Pauncefote, was to oblige Ottawa to remove the ban on extending railways from Alaska into Canada, a consideration that makes one wonder if American railway interests, perhaps the promoters of the Skagway line, had not been busy prodding Senator Frye.[37]

The bill dismayed and angered Ottawa. Of what avail to escape the stranglehold at Dyea and Skagway only to fall into another at Fort Wrangel? By the treaty of Washington of 1871 Britain and Canada could freely navigate the Stikine; and they maintained that it would be illegal to nullify the right by banning transhipment.[38] Sir Julian Pauncefote gave formal warning of Britain's intent to demand full observance of the treaty.[39]

Probably more effective in dampening enthusiasm for the Frye bill was a growing realization in Washington of the danger of pushing the Dominion too hard. Already Ottawa was under pressure to exclude Americans from the gold fields as long as American mines were closed to Canadians.[40] In any event, agitation for the Frye bill dwindled when the railway bill failed in the Dominion Senate.[41]

When the Joint High Commission met at Quebec four months later, bitterness still lingered between Canada and the United States over this affair. Moreover hope in Canada of an alternative to the Lynn Canal route had been dimmed and she and Britain had the more reason to turn with redoubled determination to the boundary question: Canada must acquire at least a foothold

[36] *The Times*, February 25, 1898.

[37] F. O. 5, 2384, Colonial Office to Aberdeen, March 31, 1898.

[38] See *ibid*., for an opinion written by the Minister of Justice, dated February 27, 1898, and appended to a memorandum written by Sifton, February 28, 1898. See also F. O. 5, 2378, for a Colonial Office memorandum expressing the same point of view.

[39] F. O. 115, 1079, Pauncefote to Salisbury, April 9, 1898.

[40] *The Times*, February 7 and 16, 1898.

[41] *Ibid*., February 11 and March 17, 1898.

on the canal's headwaters. "The acquisition of a port on the Lynn Canal," Clifford Sifton, Minister of the Interior, wrote to Sir Wilfrid Laurier, the new Prime Minister, then attending the Joint High Commission, " is the only method we have of getting back the trade of the Yukon district, which has been entirely lost owing to the failure of our railway policy of last session." [42]

Quite apart from Canadian aspirations, there were other reasons why a boundary settlement could hardly be postponed much longer. Thousands of individuals under the spell of gold were thronging into the coastal strip nearly every month, most of them going on to the Klondike but not a few remaining within the area claimed by the United States. This human flood reminded people forcibly that the boundary between Alaska and Canada was unknown. The canal area was itself auriferous. At Juneau near the canal's mouth the Alaska Treadwell Mining Company had been operating for several years; farther inland in a region claimed by both the United States and Great Britain, large numbers of prospectors were frantically searching for the metal along the Chilkoot and White passes.[43] Full of rough, turbulent men, this disputed zone, particularly the parts near the passes where no country had clear-cut responsibility for law and order, constituted the area of greatest danger. At any moment important gold strikes might occur; and the question of ownership would then become acute.

In early 1898 conflicting assertions of jurisdiction were already arising. Hearing a rumor of an American military expedition about to embark at Portland, Oregon, preparatory to occupying territory between Skagway and Lake Bennett, Canada in January, 1898, hastily despatched some forty mounted policemen to the summits of the Chilkoot and White passes, both of which she believed to lie well to the east of any reasonable American claim.[44] Soon customs officials arrived and, to the annoyance of the

[42] Dafoe, *Sifton*, p. 171.

[43] F. O. 5, 2383, Colonial Office to Foreign Office, February 21, 1898; F. O. 115, 1077, instructions from Salisbury to the British and Canadian delegation to the Joint High Commission, July 19, 1898, p. 5.

[44] Dafoe, *Sifton*, p. 214.

streams of men thronging the passes, began to collect duties—
clear evidence that Canada claimed title at least to those points.[45]
Indignant American officials in Alaska retaliated by putting in
a claim to territory east of the passes, thereby indirectly challenging the Canadians. This was the area just south of Lake
Bennett, forty miles from Skagway, where for a short while the
Stars and Stripes flew and newly arrived miners produced documents signed by United States officials at Sitka purporting to
prove the region American.[46] Fortunately, however, Washington
did not back this extravagant pretension. Not long afterwards,
on March 26, 1898, the ranking official at Dyea asked the
Canadians to withdraw from the passes and also from Lake
Lindemann, still further inland though not as far as Lake
Bennett.[47] Although once again Washington declined to support
the local action, it was clear that the boundary's delineation was
becoming urgent. "A large influx of United States miners is
beginning now," the Governor-General of Canada, Lord Aberdeen, telegraphed Joseph Chamberlain in early 1898, "and questions of disputed jurisdiction will increase the difficulty of
maintaining Canadian authority. The entire boundary line is
unsettled; and probably a concession at one point would be the
signal for similar unfounded claims all along the boundary."[48]

Fearing serious trouble in the event of gold discoveries near
the Lynn Canal, Great Britain on February 23, 1898, just when
her chorus of sympathy over the *Maine* disaster was being heard
with lively appreciation in the United States, proposed putting
the boundary question before three jurists, one to be appointed
by each country and the third by a neutral country.[49] But the
United States refused, unwilling to submit the disposition of
Dyea and Skagway, settled on the unchallenged assumption of

[45] F. O. 5, 2383, Aberdeen to Chamberlain, received January 30, 1898.
[46] *The Times*, January 15, 1898.
[47] F. O. 115, 1075, Foreign Office to Pauncefote, April 8, 1898.
[48] F. O. 5, 2383, Aberdeen to Chamberlain, received January 30, 1898.
[49] *Ibid.*, Salisbury to Pauncefote, February 18, 1898; the draft telegram is
in Salisbury's handwriting, an indication of the importance he attached to
a boundary settlement. See also *ibid.*; State Department, Alaskan Boundary
Convention; Pauncefote to Sherman, February 23, 1898.

being American, to a foreign arbitrator; as an alternative it suggested appointing British and American commissioners in equal numbers, a majority to decide.[50] This reply, along with the British proposal, accurately foreshadowed the positions which the two countries, and Canada, were to take throughout the protracted controversy until Great Britain yielded in early 1903, with a consequential delimitation of the boundary much as the United States desired.

It is unnecessary to follow subsequent modifications of these opening moves. Agreement in principle was finally reached in the summer of 1898 by which Canada and the United States directed their troops stationed at the head of the Lynn Canal not to advance further, and agreed to submit the boundary controversy to the Joint High Commission due to convene the next month.[51]

We now come to the last three major controversies involving the Dominion of Canada—those concerning reciprocity, fisheries, and fur seals. Although not comparable as immediate threats to Anglo-American understanding with the Clayton-Bulwer treaty or the Alaska boundary question, and although not settled until several years after both these more serious controversies had been disposed of, all of them had been fomenting ill will for many years and all of them occupied much time and attention in London, Ottawa, and Washington while the canal and boundary settlements were being reached.

Canada's desire for reciprocal trade relations with the United States was of long standing.[52] To many Canadians it seemed only sensible to develop a network of north-south trading routes with

[50] F. O. 5, 2384, Pauncefote to Salisbury, March 2, 1898.

[51] State Department, Alaskan Boundary Convention, British embassy memorandum, April 18, 1898; Day to Pauncefote, May 9, 1898; Pauncefote to Secretary of State, July 20, 1898. F. O. 5, 2384, Pauncefote to Salisbury, May 10, 1898.

[52] Shippee, *Canadian-American Relations*; Tansill, *Canadian-American Relations*; D. C. Masters, *The Reciprocity Treaty of 1854* (London, 1937); J. W. Longley, " Reciprocity between the United States and Canada," *North American Review*, vol. 176 (1903) , pp. 401-409.

the wealthy republic across the border instead of relying upon their own ridiculously protracted east-west route. Particularly zealous in advocating reciprocity, and not overly fearful of commercial union with the United States, for all its dangers of eventual political union, was the Liberal party.

As for Great Britain, she steadily backed Canadian-American reciprocity, and indeed at times regarded even commercial union calmly, taking pretty much for granted Canada's eventual absorption by the United States. But toward the end of the century her attitude toward losing Canada changed; she now envisaged the Dominion as an integral part of an empire that could stand close-knit against the whole non-British world. Britain continued to support reciprocity, however, as a means of consolidating Canadian prosperity.

In the United States little pressure for reciprocity existed. Most Americans saw not the slightest reason to lower their high tariffs for the benefit of standoffish Canadians. On the contrary, many Americans, especially in the Republican party, deliberately opposed helping the Dominion in the belief that depression would prove good medicine for fomenting sentiment for annexation.

The election of 1896 brought the Liberals to power in Ottawa, the party that had traditionally championed reciprocity; but it brought better times also. Within a year or so came the great gold rush, and Canada began to envisage herself, not as a struggling colony, but as a thriving nation with a brilliant future. Although still ardent proponents of reciprocity, the Liberals came to realize that commendable alternatives existed. To American chagrin the new government in 1898 granted Britain a 25 percent tariff preference, which it increased in 1900 to $33\frac{1}{3}$ percent. Not only was Canada no longer moving toward the American orbit; she was moving away from it.[53]

[53] J. S. Willison, *Sir Wilfrid Laurier and the Liberal Party* (2 vols., London, 1903), vol. 2, pp. 291, 308; Sir Charles Tupper, *Recollections of Sixty Years* (London, 1914), pp. 254-255; E. M. Saunders, ed., *The Life and Letters of the Rt. Hon. Sir Charles Tupper, Bart., K. C. M. G.* (2 vols., London, 1916), vol. 2, p. 260.

But when the Joint High Commission met in 1898, the Liberals still wanted a commercial agreement; in fact they probably regarded reciprocity as the agenda's key item. Constantly accused by Conservatives of partiality for America, they viewed tariff reductions on several articles, notably, lumber, fish, and agricultural products, as politically imperative.[54] Without that, they could not allow modification of two long-held, stoutly defended, and explosive tenets: the right to engage in pelagic sealing in the Bering Sea and the right to exclude American fishermen from Canadian and Newfoundland ports. Thus the question of commercial reciprocity, while not dangerous itself, affected the disposition of other issues that were dangerous.

Off Canada's east coast, and off the coasts of Britain's colony, Newfoundland, lay the great fishing-grounds of the north Atlantic. A dispute over rights in those waters was the oldest of any between Great Britain and the United States; like the disputes over the Clayton-Bulwer treaty and the Alaska boundary, it seemed potentially dangerous enough in 1898 to jeopardize the new Anglo-American friendship.[55]

By an old Anglo-American treaty, the treaty of 1818, the United States had acquired the liberty to fish within the three-mile limit off certain uninhabited coasts of Canada and Newfoundland, and to dry fish on those coasts; but it had renounced forever any right to fish or to dry fish on other coasts. American fishermen did not in general deny Canada's right to reserve her inshore fisheries. But they did most strenuously challenge her measurement of the three-mile line. The United States contended that the line ran parallel to twists and turns of the shore, so that parts of bays with entrances over six miles wide would be open to its fishermen. Great Britain on the other hand contended that it ran three miles offshore parallel to a line drawn from headland to headland, thus shutting off the bays.

[54] F. O. 5, 2422, Herschell to Salisbury, February 7, 1899.
[55] For the controversy see 61st Congress, 3rd session, Senate document 870, *North Atlantic Coast Fisheries Arbitration* (12 vols., Washington, 1912-1913); H. L. Keenleyside, *Canada and the United States* (New York, 1929); Shippee, *Canadian-American Relations*; Tansill, *Canadian-American Relations*.

A matter of greater moment concerned the right of entry of American fishermen into ports along the restricted coasts. The treaty permitted entry for getting shelter, repairs, wood, and water, and " for no other purpose whatever." Was this sweeping prohibition to be taken literally? Notably, did it preclude purchasing bait? Americans naturally claimed a right to purchase; Great Britain, pressed by Canada, denied it. In a time when bait could not be kept fresh throughout a long sea voyage, American fishermen, if unable to buy in those northern ports, would be tremendously handicapped as compared with their Canadian and Newfoundland competitors. By a British-American *modus vivendi* of February 15, 1888, American fishing vessels could get permits, at a charge of $1.50 per ship ton, to buy bait and other supplies in Canadian and Newfoundland harbors. When the *modus* expired in 1890 Great Britain wisely and generously renewed it. She was still observing it in 1898.[56] Thus the dispute was comparatively quiescent at the time of the Spanish War.

It was far from having been settled, however, and could have flared up at any moment. The lull was deceptive, depending as it did on the gratuitous observance by Great Britain of an agreement that had expired eight years before. By 1898 the American fishing industry had been operating under the *modus vivendi* for ten years, and in conformity therewith had acquired a structure that could not easily be altered; the industry could be counted upon to fight tooth and nail to retain privileges by now taken for granted. At the same time a considerable body of opinion in Canada and Newfoundland insisted that appeasement was getting nowhere, that Americans understood nothing but toughness, and that consequently the treaty of 1818 should be rigidly enforced. This was the delicate state of affairs confronting the Joint High Commission when it met at Quebec in August, 1898.

Far away, off the Dominion's west coast, lived the great fur seal herds of the north Pacific.[57] Since the controversy regarding

[56] F. O. 5, 2422, memorandum by Cartwright, March 25, 1899.
[57] For the controversy over the seals see *Fur Seal Arbitration* (16 vols., Washington, 1892) ; Tansill, *Canadian-American Relations*.

them furnished the immediate occasion for convening the Joint High Commission, it must be described in some detail.

As part of the Alaska purchase of 1867 the United States acquired the Bering Sea islands of St. George and St. Paul, which together constitute the Pribilof Islands. This was valuable property, the most valuable in all Alaska at that time, because during the warmer months it was frequented by the seals. In 1870 the United States Treasury leased to an American company, the Alaska Commercial Company, monopoly rights on the islands for twenty years. The company was authorized to kill 100,000 seals annually under regulations designed to safeguard the herd. Between 1870 and 1893 the Treasury received over $11,000,000 from royalties paid for the rights and from duties on manufactured skins,[58] thus developing a pecuniary interest of its own in the islands.

All went well for some years. But after a while Canadian fishermen, seeing no reason why Americans only should benefit, began to use boats for hunting seals outside the three-mile limit, a practice known as pelagic sealing. This ate into profits of the Alaska Commercial Company, not to mention receipts of the Treasury Department. Both the company and the Treasury came to view pelagic sealers with extreme displeasure.

President Cleveland's Secretary of the Treasury, Daniel Manning, resolved to put a stop to these inconvenient interlopers.[59] In 1886 an American revenue cutter, the *Corwin*, arrested three Canadian sealers in the Bering Sea sixty miles or more from land.

[58] F. O. 5, 2421, Herschell to Salisbury, September 2, 1898, citing information supplied by John Foster.

[59] Former Secretary of State John Foster denied that the United States government was responsible for the resulting seizures. They were, he asserted, engineered by the Alaska Commercial Company. See J. W. Foster, *Diplomatic Memoirs* (2 vols., Boston and New York, 1909), vol. 2, pp. 26-27. *The Nation*, vol. 52 (April 2, 1891), p. 277, agreed; it charged regarding the seizures of 1886 that: "The Alaska Commercial Company really usurped executive power in the affair, using government revenue cutters and Alaska courts for company purposes." Foster and *The Nation* may have been correct as regards the 1886 incidents, but it is hard to believe that the company could have brought about seizures and condemnations over four years without governmental backing.

A federal court in Alaska condemned the ships and sentenced the officers to fines and imprisonment. Within a year five more ships had been condemned; and further seizures were made in 1889. Altogether about fourteen vessels were condemned, many others ordered to leave the Bering Sea, and still more frightened away from their customary pursuits.[60]

Great Britain strongly protested these disgraceful proceedings, branding the seizures illegal as having occurred outside the three-mile limit. An angry altercation ensued. The United States replied that pelagic sailing was morally wrong; that it had a property right in the seals and therefore a right to protect them wherever they might roam; and that pelagic sealers were destroying such excessive numbers of seals as to menace the herd's very existence. Although these contentions could not be sustained in law, the wastefulness of pelagic sealing did lend strength to the American position. "The Canadians have the strict law on their side: the Americans have a moral basis for their contention which it is impossible to ignore. If both sides push their pretensions to an extreme, a collision is inevitable."[61] This was Lord Salisbury's accurate summary of the controversy.

Following a *modus vivendi* of 1891, the United States and Great Britain signed a treaty of arbitration in February, 1892. Meeting in Paris in August, 1893, the arbitrators found against the United States and assessed damages. But they also laid down regulations designed to preserve the seals, banning pelagic sealing within an area sixty miles around the Pribilof Islands at all times and providing for an annual close season from May 1 to July 31.

Unfortunately this did not terminate the dispute. The United States deeply resented the decision. Spurred on by an indignant Commercial Company, which insisted that the regulations were inadequate to preserve the species, Washington did its best, short of further seizures, to harass pelagic sealers. ". . . we cannot much longer," they were driven to admit, "continue the struggle under existing restrictions and against the hostile efforts

[60] *Fur Seal Arbitration*, vol. 3, pp. 188 and 292.
[61] Salisbury papers, Salisbury to Pauncefote, March 28, 1890.

of a powerful Company backed by the adverse influence and legislation of a foreign Government who are determined by any means and at any cost to drive us out of the industry." [62] And the Collector of Customs at Victoria reported that considerable anxiety had arisen as to the sealers' future.[63]

A notable development had occurred in 1890 when the Alaska Commercial Company's lease expired and a new lease was awarded another American concern, the North American Commercial Company. At least two of this company's five shareholders were men of considerable influence.[64] D. O. Mills had made a huge fortune in California and was the father-in-law of Whitelaw Reid (editor of the *New York Tribune* and a prominent Republican) ; Senator Stephen B. Elkins, Secretary of War in President Harrison's administration, was a well known politician. Eager to make the most of its opportunities on the Pribilof Islands, the North American Commercial Company undoubtedly used its official connections in order to spin out the debate with Great Britain to the utmost.

When President McKinley's Republican administration took office in March, 1897, the company had for some time been raising its influential voice against pelagic sealers, who were so inconsiderately cutting into its profits. No doubt its pleas were more pressing because it had recently been sued by Cleveland's less friendly Democratic administration for back taxes and rentals, and a judgment, at the moment under appeal, had been rendered for over a million dollars.[65] An opportunity for the company to strengthen its position existed in a stipulation of the Paris award to the effect that every five years Great Britain and the United States should review the sealing regulations with a view to determining whether modifications were needed. The first

---

[62] C. O. 42, 857, memorandum dated February 16, 1898.

[63] C. O. 42, 856, Milne to Gourdeau, January 5, 1898.

[64] Salisbury papers, Pauncefote to Salisbury, April 16, 1897; *New York World*, April 12, 1897.

[65] *New York World*, April 12, 1897. The *World* implied that the company was planning to disregard the governmental regulations and slaughter all the seals it could, in an all-out effort to recoup its fortunes. The more pelagic sealing was restricted, the greater success it could anticipate.

five-year period would end in August, 1898, the month of the
armistice with Spain and the convening of the Joint High Commission. Mobilizing its resources, the company was able to secure
the favorable appointment of two special commissioners for fur
seal negotiations: C. S. Hamblin, former Assistant Secretary of
the Treasury, and John W. Foster, Blaine's successor as Secretary
of State.[66] Since Hamblin dropped out of the picture almost at
once, it was Foster who shortly assumed charge of fur seal negotiations, and to a slighter degree of all negotiations concerning
Canada. As a key figure in these matters, and therefore, in
British-American relations, he deserves particular notice.[67]

In a private letter to Prime Minister Salisbury, Sir Julian
Pauncefote cited the *New York World* to the effect that Foster
was secretly in the North American Commercial Company's pay
as its legal adviser.[68] The *World* gave an account of a dinner in
Washington at which J. Stanley Brown, a paid agent of Senator
Elkins', who it will be remembered was one of the company's
principal shareholders, persuaded Secretary of the Treasury Lyman Gage to appoint Foster special commissioner. Although the
story of the Washington dinner appears to be true, no confirmation of Foster's alleged link with the company has been found.
It is a fact, however, that he consistently took a line favorable
to its interests. A stubborn unyielding negotiator who haggled
over every detail, Foster had made himself unrivaled master of
the two controversies of particular concern to the west coast:
those regarding fur seals and the Alaska boundary. Admirably
suited as an expert behind-the-scenes adviser, he was unfortunately cast in the role of negotiator, a role in which his utter
conviction of being always right, made all the stronger by the
fact that he did know more details than anyone else, rendered
nearly impossible any large compromise. It was this man who,
in anticipation of a conference to amend the Paris regulations,

[66] Salisbury papers, Pauncefote to Salisbury, April 16, 1897.
[67] Foster was related to two later Secretaries of State; he was the father-
in-law of Robert Lansing and the grandfather of John Foster Dulles.
[68] Salisbury papers, April 16, 1897; Pauncefote had reference to the *World*
of April 12, 1897.

now embarked upon a crusade to abolish pelagic sealing.[69] He did not succeed, but the unexpected upshot was the convening of the Joint High Commission.

Shortly after taking office the McKinley administration on Foster's advice invited Great Britain—and also Russia and Japan, two other countries interested in the north Pacific seals—to confer at Washington over the regulations of 1893. Russia and Japan accepted; Great Britain declined, fearful of finding herself alone in supporting pelagic sealers.[70] At the subsequent meeting the United States, Russia, and Japan, declaring that the seals were "threatened with extinction," agreed to refrain from pelagic sealing for a year, provided Great Britain did the same. But Britain refused on the ground that the herds were not in fact endangered and that anyway it was unfair to penalize Canadian sealers without similarly restricting the North American Commercial Company.[71]

Although Great Britain shied off from the larger meeting, she was agreeable to a conference limited to her own, Canadian, and American experts, the purpose of which should be, not to propose new regulations, but to study the operation of the existing ones. Such a conference did meet in Washington; it contradicted the American, Russian, and Japanese experts by finding that although the herds had decreased in number, their extinction need not be feared.[72]

Neither conference being to Foster's liking, since neither restricted pelagic sealing, he now launched out on a new course. While the American-Russian-Japanese conference was still in session Foster, to Ambassador Pauncefote's indignation over

[69] Salisbury papers, Pauncefote to Salisbury, April 16, 1897.

[70] F. O. 115, 1071, Adam to Sherman, October 15, 1897.

[71] State Department, Great Britain, Despatches, Salisbury to Pauncefote, January 12, 1898, enclosed in Hay to Sherman, January 16, 1898; F. O. 5, 2385, Salisbury to Pauncefote, January 12, 1898. The three countries signed a convention dated November 6, 1897.

[72] For their report, dated November 16, 1897, see the British White Paper, *United States, No. 2 (1898)*. *Joint Statement of Conclusions Signed by the British, Canadian, and United States' Delegates Respecting the Fur-Seal Herd Frequenting the Pribyloff Islands in Behring Sea.* Cd. 8703.

such efforts to by-pass his government, was able to "allure" to Washington Sir Wilfrid Laurier, Canada's Prime Minister, and Sir Louis Davies, her Minister of Marine and Fisheries.[73] There on November 16, 1897, and subsequently in private correspondence, he tried hard to persuade them that even if Canada would not adhere to the convention she should at least agree to suspend pelagic sealing in return for an American guarantee to suspend sealing on the Pribilof Islands and also to convene an international commission for settling all Canadian-American issues.[74]

Although they would have welcomed such a commission, Laurier and Davies were unwilling to terminate pelagic sealing even for a limited period. Sir Wilfrid cited the recent British-American-Canadian report to show the needlessness of such a course.[75] Besides, Foster's apparently fair offer had a fatal defect: the pelagic sealing industry, already in a serious plight, could not have survived a suspension of operations. Indicative of this was the sealers' alarmed reaction on hearing rumors of a suspension; it would, they declared, "result disastrously to the sealing interests of British Columbia . . . inasmuch as interruption for the period referred to would break up established commercial arrangements and cause the dispersion of sealing crews, which in effect, would mean the disruption of the industry as it at present exists."[76]

Foster now tried his hand with the British. Calling on Sir Julian Pauncefote, he warned that Congress, in a bitter mood, was preparing more trials for the sealers; that it had already passed legislation prohibiting imports of foreign seal skins (as a result of which several Canadian sealing vessels were considering not putting to sea in 1898);[77] and that unless the two countries acted quickly, they could not devise new sealing regu-

[73] The quoted word is Pauncefote's; see his despatch to Salisbury, January 21, 1898, F. O. 5, 2385.

[74] On this matter see State Department, Great Britain, Despatches, Hay to Sherman, January 16, 1898; F. O. 5, 2385, Hay to Salisbury, January 17, 1898, and Salisbury to White, February 11, 1898.

[75] C. O. 42, 861, Laurier to Foster, November 24, 1897.

[76] C. O. 42, 856, report of the committee of the executive council, November 27, 1897.

[77] Ibid., Milne to Gourdeau, January 5, 1898.

lations by August, 1898. Could not the impasse be broken by naming a board of three naturalists whose decisions on amending the regulations would be binding? If Great Britain agreed, Foster promised, the United States would help establish a Joint High Commission that would wipe the slate clean of Canadian-American issues.[78]

The British government, which for some time had been under pressure from the sealers [79] and which suspected Foster of maneuvering to abolish pelagic sealing to benefit, not the seals, but the North American Commercial Company,[80] viewed this plausible suggestion with considerable reserve. " We shall not arrive at a settlement," Pauncefote cautioned Lord Salisbury, " so long as General Foster continues to be charged with the negotiations. . . . He is a tricky lawyer, & is playing into the hands of the [North American Commercial] company." [81] The government declined to accept the proposal except on the condition that new regulations should be approved by all three naturalists and also by the proposed commission.[82] The condition was of course unacceptable to Foster.[83]

By that time the Spanish-American War was near; and the United States, about to embark on its great adventure, was responding eagerly to British expressions of friendship. The atmosphere was favorable to a settlement; both countries, with their dangerous international involvements, wanted one. Even the cantankerous congressional mood described by Foster was beginning to dissipate under the mellow glow of " hands across the sea " sentiments. Five years after the Paris award of 1893

[78] F. O. 115, 1078, Pauncefote to Salisbury, January 14, 1898.

[79] See F. O. 5, 2387, for a letter dated February 16, 1898, to the Foreign Office from the agents of fifteen British Columbian schooners; see C. O. 42, 856 and 857 for further representations from sealers.

[80] F. O. 5, 2385, Colonial Office to Foreign Office, February 7, 1898.

[81] Ibid., Pauncefote to Salisbury, January 21, 1898. It is interesting to find Pauncefote stating that the simplest solution would be for America to pay Canada a percentage of its annual earnings from the seals, in return for the suspension of pelagic sealing. This was the arrangement finally adopted thirteen years later, in 1911.

[82] Ibid., Colonial Office to Foreign Office, February 18, 1898.

[83] F. O. 115, 1078, Pauncefote to Salisbury, March 1, 1898.

Henry Cabot Lodge introduced a bill in the Senate on April 18, 1898, to pay the $472,151.26 recently agreed upon as compensation to the Canadian sealers; and two months later, to nearly universal Anglo-Saxon applause,[84] Congress unanimously voted the appropriation.

The break in the sealing negotiations came suddenly. During a visit with President McKinley on March 10, 1898, Sir Julian Pauncefote spoke of his trials with the argumentative Foster. The President was sympathetic; he was, he said, anxious for a settlement. If it seemed impossible at the moment to agree about the seals would it not be advisable to temporize, and to set up a Joint High Commission anyway? This sensible suggestion proved immediately acceptable to Great Britain and Canada.[85]

Accordingly a series of meetings, delayed somewhat by the outbreak of the Spanish War, was held in Washington at the end of May during which Davies, Pauncefote, Foster, and John A. Kasson, the State Department's expert on commercial negotiations, agreed upon the agenda for a Joint High Commission.[86] Included on the list were all the Canadian controversies, that is to say, those concerning fur seals, fisheries, reciprocity, the Alaska boundary, and other less important matters.[87] The Joint High Commission thus provided for met in Quebec in August, 1898, as the Spanish-American War, which had done so much to make it possible, was drawing to a close.

[84] A notable exception was the consistently hostile *Saturday Review* which, vol. 85 (April 30, 1898), p. 582, characterized the payment as a bribe.

[85] F. O. 115, 1078, Pauncefote to Salisbury, March 10 and April 1, 1898.

[86] State Department, Alaskan Boundary Convention, " Anglo-American Protocol of May, 1898," signed May 30; F. O. 115, 1080, Pauncefote to Salisbury, May 31, 1898. A brief flurry of excitement occurred when the Senate, disgruntled by the applause for the executive, asserted itself by refusing to make an appropriation for expenses of the American delegation to the commission. An outcry from all over the country, but particularly from New York commercial circles, and pressure from the administration induced the senators, their dignity upheld, to change their minds. See the press, June 29-July 4, 1898, for this absurd little affair.

[87] The other matters on the agenda were: transit of merchandise, alien labor laws, mining rights, naval vessels on the Great Lakes, delineation of certain parts of the Canadian-American boundary, conveyance of criminals, wrecking and salvage.

CHAPTER 4

The Joint High Commission

THE American members of the Joint High Commission were Senator Charles W. Fairbanks, head of the delegation; Representative Nelson Dingley, chairman of the Ways and Means Committee; Senator George Gray; John W. Foster; John A. Kasson, the reciprocity expert; and T. Jefferson Coolidge, former minister to France. Gray, who soon resigned to go to Paris on the delegation making peace with Spain, was replaced by Senator Charles J. Faulkner. Dingley died on January 13, 1899; Representative Sereno Payne succeeded him two or three weeks before the Commission disbanded.

Meeting with the five Americans were one Englishman, four Canadians, and Sir James Winter, Attorney General of Newfoundland. The Englishman, who headed the delegation, was Lord Herschell, Lord High Chancellor of England; the Canadians were Sir Wilfrid Laurier, Prime Minister; Sir Louis H. Davies, Minister of Marine and Fisheries; Sir Richard J. Cartwright, member of Parliament; and John Charlton, another member of Parliament. "A very weak commission," commented John (later Sir John) Anderson, the British Colonial Office official in charge of Canadian affairs. "Cartwright is an able but wrong-headed uncontrollable person. Sir L. Davies and Sir W. Laurier very amicable, but neither very practical nor very strong & Mr. Charlton is a violent partizan of everything American, & is popularly known in Canada as the 'member from Michigan.'" But the Colonial Secretary, Joseph Chamberlain,

88

thought otherwise, and for a reason of some interest: "I do not quite agree with Mr. Anderson. Hitherto the fault of Canada has been its 'irreconcilability' in dealing with the U. S." [1]

The Joint High Commission held its first meeting in the provincial Parliament building at Quebec on August 23, 1898.[2] After appointing Lord Herschell as chairman, W. C. Cartwright (a British Foreign Office official) and Henri Bourassa (member of the Canadian Parliament) as secretaries of the British-Canadian-Newfoundland delegation, and Chandler P. Anderson (a State Department official) as secretary of the American delegation, the commissioners proceeded to the Chamber of the Legislative Assembly, where members of the provincial government, the city council, and leading citizens of Quebec were assembled to greet them. The mayor of Quebec read an address of welcome, and Senator Fairbanks and Lord Herschell replied with felicitous references to Anglo-American amity. All seemed well, but observers might have recorded another, less auspicious meeting that same day. Hardly had the two delegations left the Chamber, their ears ringing with the exuberant oratory, when representatives of the Michigan lumber industry called upon the American commissioners and delivered stern injunctions against concessions. Special economic interests, the lumber industry not the least of them, were to prove major obstacles to agreement.

The commission got down to business on August 24 and thereafter met regularly until September 2 when it adjourned so that Dingley could go to Maine for the mid-term elections. Reconvening on September 20, it worked intensively until October 10. It then moved to Washington, where new sessions began

[1] C. O. 42, 857, minutes by Anderson and Chamberlain, dated June 20, 1898.

[2] The best source of information about the commission is the British Foreign Office archives; much material is also in State Department, Alaskan Boundary Convention, and State Department, Miscellaneous Archives, Alaskan Boundary, 1899-1903. The commission's protocols are in State Department, Reciprocity Treaties, 1898-1907, Canada, John A. Kasson papers. C. C. Tansill, *Canadian-American Relations, 1875-1911* (New Haven, 1943), *passim*, has useful material about the commission.

November 9. These terminated on February 20, 1899, when the commission met for the last time.

It is important to bear in mind the diplomatic and political situation during the six months that the Joint High Commission was in session. Despite much hard work at Quebec little was accomplished there because of the imminent American elections in November, 1898; Senator Faulkner said flatly that the American delegation would not commit itself on any major point until the returns were in.[3] More inauspicious for the commission's success, after as well as before the elections, was the fact that about two weeks before its first meeting the Spanish-American armistice was signed. Although still grateful for British friendship, the United States no longer felt the compulsions of an uncertain military and diplomatic position; it had recovered full freedom of action and its mood of strident nationalism and overweening confidence was not conducive to concessions.

As for Great Britain, although perhaps less endangered in the autumn of 1898 than in the spring, when war cries had resounded over the Port Arthur crisis, she was still in an exposed international position, still anxious to have the conqueror of the Philippines at her side. But that is not to suggest that she felt obliged to meet every American demand; and even had she wanted to, she could not have run the risk of alienating Canadian affections. Gone were the days when Britain could manage her colony's affairs according to her own whims. Among Canadians the belief was deeply engrained that the mother country had not scrupled in the past and would not scruple in the future to sacrifice them in order to appease the inexorable Americans.[4] Britain could not allow that belief to flourish. It will have been noted that the Canadian members on the Joint High Commission outnumbered the British four to one. The division of membership represented a significant change from the commission of 1871 with its four Britons and one Canadian, and from the commission of 1887 with two Britons and one Canadian. The change

[3] F. O. 5, 2421, Herschell to Salisbury, October 11, 1898.
[4] A. G. Dewey, *The Dominions and Diplomacy, the Canadian Contribution* (2 vols., London, 1929), vol. 1, p. 188.

reflected the rise in Canadian power, a rise that brought with it a heightened nationalism that no government in London could disregard no matter how unreasonable it sometimes thought the colonials.

Canada, too, had certain hesitations about the commission. However eager to settle outstanding issues, the Liberal government, in office after years of Conservative rule and bitterly accused by the Conservative leader, the redoubtable Sir Charles Tupper, of grovelling before the United States (to which alleged posture Sir Charles later attributed the Joint High Commission's failure),[5] had to be most careful not to give the opposition an opportunity to convict it before the electorate of abandoning Canadian rights. Political suicide lay in that direction.

Negotiations over fur seals, which, as has appeared, had been proceeding actively for some years before the commission met, were not complicated and almost succeeded in reaching agreement. A slight hitch occurred at the outset when the British and Canadian delegates on the committee dealing with seals (Fairbanks, Foster, Davies, and Herschell), discovering that they knew much less than Foster, asked for an adjournment so that their experts could go to Victoria to inform themselves.[6] From the beginning Britain and Canada accepted the demand made by the United States since the dispute started over a decade earlier: that pelagic sealing be abolished. The reason for their capitulation is not altogether clear; but presumably they simply decided that the diminished sealing industry was not worth the constant friction it engendered; they may also have been impressed with the experts' report the previous November that pelagic sealing, even if not likely to destroy the herds, had in fact caused them to decrease. Whatever the reason, there is no doubt that the Liberals, who less than a year earlier had called abolition out of the question, were taking a big chance politically; and news of the reversal spread consternation throughout the

---

[5] *The Times*, February 18, 1899; Canada, *Debates of the House of Commons*, 1899, vol. 2, pp. 4265-4267, June 5, 1899.

[6] F. O. 5, 2421, Cartwright to Campbell, October 10, 1898.

sealing industry. The Attorney General of British Columbia rushed to Quebec with vigorous protests;[7] and the sealers addressed a "Humble Petition" to Queen Victoria denouncing "the practical expropriation of their business for the sake of preserving peaceful relations with the United States of America."[8]

In return for their offer the British expected a substantial *quid pro quo*. If the sealers discontinued a legal calling, they ought to receive liberal compensation from the United States, to whose advantage the absence of competition would redound; and if Britain renounced a national right, approved by an international tribunal in 1893, and incurred the expense of enforcing a prohibition of sealing, all for the benefit of Americans, she, too, should be compensated.[9] These were reasonable demands as the American commissioners recognized; and an agreement in principle was easily reached. But when it came to filling in the details, to deciding just what the compensation should amount to, the commissioners ran into trouble.

The trouble stemmed from difference of opinion over prospects of the pelagic sealing industry. If on its last legs already, it did not deserve much compensation. The Americans contended that the sealers had undermined their own livelihood by decimating the herds.[10] Herschell disagreed. Although admitting that the herds had diminished, he argued that the sealing fleet, too, had been sufficiently reduced so that seal births and deaths were tending to equilibrium and pelagic sealing could continue indefinitely. He and his colleagues were exasperated by the bland American disregard, as it seemed to them, both of the industry's claims and of the British concession's magnitude. Referring to the simultaneous fisheries negotiations, Herschell said rather tartly to Fairbanks that the pelagic sealers "may be wrong in the views which they entertain, but they have surely as much

---

[7] *The Times*, September 30, 1898.

[8] F. O. 5, 2387; the petition is undated but was received by the Foreign Office October 26, 1898.

[9] F. O. 5, 2417; State Department, Alaskan Boundary Convention; Herschell to Fairbanks, December 21, 1898.

[10] F. O. 5, 2422; State Department, Alaskan Boundary Convention; Fairbanks to Herschell, December 24, 1898.

right to entertain those views as the Gloucester [Massachusetts] fishermen have to entertain theirs. . . . The views of the Gloucester fishermen have practically closed the negotiations. . . .[11]

Yet the commissioners stood on the verge of a satisfactory compromise when the Joint High Commission broke up. After hard bargaining the United States offered to pay Canadian sealers $500,000, as against the British demand of $600,000, and to pay Canada annually a percentage of earnings on the Pribilof Islands.[12] It may be noted that these were the essential features of the convention of 1911 which at length concluded the controversy.

In the fisheries dispute the country dissatisfied with the existing situation and therefore taking the initiative in making proposals was Canada, with Newfoundland giving close support. Canada resented a *modus vivendi* whose main purpose was to coax the United States into final agreement when year after year the United States, quite satisfied with things as they were, showed no sign of being coaxed.[13] Consequently, Canada and Newfoundland lost no time in suggesting to the committee on fisheries (Faulkner, Coolidge, Davies, and Winter, with Herschell often sitting in) [14] that the perennial controversy be settled on the basis that had seemed near success in 1888, namely, renunciation of restrictions set by the treaty of 1818 in return for removing the American tariff of half a cent per pound on fresh fish. It seemed not at all impossible that Washington would accept an arrangement so similar to the one the administration had agreed to in 1888 when the country was considerably less friendly toward Great Britain.[15] For the poor fishermen of the Maritime Provinces

[11] F. O. 5, 2417; State Department, Alaskan Boundary Convention; Herschell to Fairbanks, December 21, 1898.
[12] F. O. 5, 2421, Cartwright to Campbell, December 23, 1898; F. O. 5, 2422, memorandum by Cartwright, March 25, 1899.
[13] F. O. 5, 2421, Herschell to Salisbury, September 2, 1898; F. O. 5, 2422, memorandum by Cartwright, March 25, 1899.
[14] F. O. 5, 2421, Herschell to Salisbury, September 2, 1898.
[15] *Ibid.*, Herschell to Salibury, November 25, 1898.

and Newfoundland the formula of free fish for free fishing would have meant a quick end to their economic woes. Their disappointment was the greater, therefore, when the United States, far from being more favorably disposed than ten years before, showed itself unalterably opposed to the proposal.

What blocked an understanding was America's radical disagreement with Britain as to the status of the treaty of 1818. Since America contended that the treaty restrictions had not properly been in force since 1830 when Britain opened Canadian and Newfoundland ports to foreign ships, it could not logically interpret a modification of the restrictions as a concession.[16] The United States, indeed, went so far as to insist that continuing observance of the *modus vivendi* demonstrated good will, not by Britain, but by itself, because in purchasing licenses Americans were paying for a right already legally theirs.[17] So why bargain for abolition of illegal restrictions? Why lower the tariff to get fishing privileges already rightfully possessed, and as a matter of fact already being enjoyed? Even had it been inclined to do so, the Republican majority in Congress in 1898 could not without embarrassment have accepted substantially the same terms as those the party—in some cases the same individuals—had denounced ten years before.[18] As with bargaining over the seals, the American commissioners simply refused to give the British credit for their offer: abolition of pelagic sealing would count for little because the industry was almost dead anyhow; removal of fishing restrictions would count for less because they were in fact illegal.

In addition to this legalistic argument, a highly practical political consideration stood in the way of agreement. New England fishing interests, centered upon Gloucester, Massachusetts, resolutely opposed any tariff modification enabling Canadian and Newfoundland fish to compete more effectively on the

[16] *Ibid.*, Herschell to Salisbury, October 11, 1898.

[17] F. O. 5, 2422; State Department, Alaskan Boundary Convention; Fairbanks to Herschell, December 24, 1898.

[18] The British were quite aware of this political difficulty; see F. O. 5, 2421, Herschell to Salisbury, October 11, 1898.

home market; and they were zealously championed by two of the most influential members of Congress: Henry Cabot Lodge and George F. Hoar, senators from Massachusetts. These men had the desire and the power to block any proposal not acceptable to Gloucester fishermen. A leader in rejecting the treaty of 1888, Hoar could be counted upon not to spoil one of the triumphs of his career by changing front in 1898; and Lodge, although in 1898 a believer in the British connection and anxious to settle difficulties with Canada, was even more solicitous of the wishes of Gloucester, soon to be represented in Congress by his son-in-law and already cherished by the senator as a breeding-ground of sailors.[19] To dispel any shadow of doubt as to their desires, a deputation of New England fishing interests went to Quebec, where it expressed itself frequently and cogently.[20]

Gloucester furnished an excellent example of the influence relatively small interests, strategically placed, have often had over large matters of American policy. Puzzled at the deference shown this little town, Lord Herschell thought it well to speak privately to Senator Fairbanks. " I said," he wrote the Prime Minister,

> that . . . the opposition [to a treaty] . . . emanated chiefly from the fishing town of Gloucester, Massachusetts, and that it seemed strange that it should be regarded as more important to conciliate a single town in one of the States than at the risk of giving offence to the inhabitants of that town to ensure a satisfactory settlement with Great Britain. I added that it was not what I had been led to expect when assured of the very strong amicable sentiment which now animated the people of the United States.[21]

As long as the United States refused to recognize Britain's right of exclusion under the treaty of 1818, and as long as Gloucester held an effective veto over a tariff reduction, it is hard to see

---

[19] Tansill, *Canadian-American Relations*, p. 91, to White, January 7, 1899. Lodge induced Paul Dana, editor of the New York *Sun*, to print an article insisting on protection for American fishermen, and then sent copies of the article to all the commissioners; see J. A. Garraty, *Henry Cabot Lodge, a Biography* (New York, 1953), pp. 235-236.

[20] *The Times*, September 2 and 24, 1898.

[21] F. O. 5, 2421, Herschell to Salisbury, November 25, 1898.

how any solution involving removal of the duty on fish could have been attained. Certainly a suggestion of the federated boards of trade of eastern Canada had no chance whatever of acceptance, namely, that the United States admit Canadian goods into Puerto Rico and Cuba on the same terms as its own goods, in return for inshore privileges.[22]

At length realizing the impossibility of tampering with a duty championed by such stalwarts as Hoar and Lodge, Great Britain offered to renounce the contested restrictions on three conditions: that the question of the bays be settled; that the United States recognize British right as a sovereign power—not, be it noted, because of rights claimed under the treaty of 1818—to control sales of bait; and that the United States grant substantial tariff concessions of benefit to the Maritime Provinces and Newfoundland on products other than fish.[23] The American commissioners were agreeable to Canada and Newfoundland reserving almost any bays they wished; and were apparently not disposed to make trouble about sales of bait, realizing that Britain was contending for a principle, not proposing action. But although the reciprocity committee was prepared to recommend duty reductions on minerals important to Newfoundland, it arrived at no decision on products of interest to Nova Scotia and New Brunswick.[24] Britain's second proposal, therefore, like her first, came to grief against the unyielding rock of the American tariff.

Britain gave her colony a free hand in the reciprocity negotiations, on the understanding that it would not yield the right to grant tariff preferences within the empire.[25] American commercial circles naturally resented the new Canadian discrimination against themselves; and some of them hoped to get it abolished by persuading Washington to make an extension of

[22] *The Times*, August 23, 1898.
[23] F. O. 5, 2422, Herschell to Salisbury, February 7, 1899; the original despatch is dated 1898, but 1899 is of course correct.
[24] *Ibid.*, memorandum by Cartwright, March 25, 1899.
[25] F. O. 115, 1077, Salisbury to the British and Canadian commissioners, July 19, 1898; F. O. 5, 2422, memorandum by Cartwright, March 25, 1899.

the preferential rates to the United States a condition of tariff reduction. Canada, however, was not disposed to comply; and her attitude undoubtedly hardened American policy and impeded a settlement.

The most important concessions considered by the committee on reciprocity (Fairbanks, Dingley, Kasson, Cartwright, Davies, Charlton) related to fish, coal, and lumber. As has appeared, abolition or even reduction of the fish duty proved impossible before the determined opposition of Gloucester fishermen. Nothing could have been more evident than the benefit from free trade in coal. Mines existed in Nova Scotia and British Columbia, in Ohio and Pennsylvania, so that except for the tariff wall bisecting the continent both American seaboards would have imported from Canada, whereas interior regions of the Dominion would have imported from the United States. Millions would have had cheaper coal. The commissioners actually reached agreement for progressive reductions in the duty on bituminous coal until, after three years, coal would be on the free list; [26] but mine owners of Nova Scotia, fearing to lose more from American competition at Montreal than they would gain from easier access to New England, raised strong objections.[27] Unable to resist their pressure, the Canadian commissioners reconsidered and refused to touch the duty. Special interests, it is apparent, operated on both sides of the border.

As for lumber, the controversy over the duty on boards stirred up more anger than that over any other commodity. The Dingley tariff act of 1897 had strengthened the position of American sawmills as against Canadian sawmills by imposing a charge on imports of boards and planks of two dollars per 1,000 feet, while admitting logs free. Canadian lumber interests hotly demanded retaliation, with the result that in 1898 Ontario, where Americans, mainly from Michigan, held extensive leases of timber land, passed an act designed to force Congress to repeal the duty on sawn lumber. It prohibited American lessees of Ontario timber

[26] State Department, Kasson papers, Fairbanks to McKinley, February 3, 1899.

[27] F. O. 5, 2422, memorandum by Cartwright, March 25, 1899.

land from exporting logs as long as the United States refused to put boards on the free list. Spurred on by outraged American lumber interests the State Department formally protested to Great Britain, charging that the Ontario act if applied to existing leaseholders amounted to confiscation of vested interests; [28] and Michigan lumbermen filed claims against Britain amounting to some $400,000.[29] But although the federal Canadian authorities, like London, had doubts as to the wisdom of the provincial action, they did not seek to change it. It was in the ugly atmosphere occasioned by these maneuverings that the negotiators turned to the lumber duty.

The Canadian commissioners made a determined stand for free lumber, which they seem to have regarded about as desirable as free fish; certainly lumber and fish were the products on which they displayed the greatest anxiety to obtain tariff reductions. They were confronted by equally determined opposition of the powerful American lumber industry, backed by a combination of paper makers with an enormous capital. Although the great newspapers, especially in eastern and central states where lumbermen were less in evidence, campaigned strongly for free paper and pulp and, as associated with these, free lumber, it soon became evident that free lumber was just as impossible as free fish.[30] Delegations from lumber and paper industries, as from Gloucester, gathered at Quebec " in great numbers," where they kept a sharp eye open for the slightest tampering with their duty. During the entire sitting Congressman Tawney of Minnesota was also there, hard at work for his constituents.[31] And the adamant refusal of Ontario, whose Premier Hardy also haunted the conference rooms, to rescind its recent legislation only made Americans the more stubborn.[32] After the Joint High Commis-

[28] *The Times*, August 23, 1898.

[29] *Ibid.*, September 30, 1898.

[30] F. O. 5, 2422, Herschell to Salisbury, February 7, 1899. See State Department, Kasson papers, for many petitions against reducing the lumber duty.

[31] *The Times*, September 24, 1898.

[32] *Ibid.*, September 23, 1898. See F. O. 5, 2422, Herschell to Salisbury, February 7, 1899; the original despatch is dated 1898, but 1899 is of course correct.

sion adjourned to Washington, lumber and paper agents from all over the country converged upon the capital, resolved to fight for lumber whatever became of reciprocity or anything else.[33] They had little to fear; no matter what the Joint High Commission might have decided, the Senate Foreign Relations Committee, weighed down with senators from timber states, would doubtless have rejected any treaty tinkering with the lumber duty.

One small ray of hope for free lumber existed in the person of Nelson Dingley, the influential chairman of the Ways and Means Committee, who, although from the timber state of Maine and a high tariff man *par excellence*, surprisingly did not oppose removing the duty. But Dingley's unfortunate death in early 1899 not only threw all reciprocity negotiations into confusion pending appointment of his successor, Sereno Payne, but destroyed whatever possibility may have existed of a meaningful concession on lumber.[34] At one point during the negotiations, it is true, the American commissioners did propose a sizable duty reduction. The Canadians asserted, however, that even the lower duty would have been prohibitive; and in any case as time passed the firmness of the offer became increasingly doubtful.[35]

Although fish, coal, and lumber were the main products considered, they were not the only ones. Canada wanted concessions on agricultural products and on lime in order to compensate Nova Scotia and New Brunswick for their proposed sacrifices in the fisheries; Newfoundland wanted concessions on minerals. But the only agreement in sight regarded minerals and some agricultural products not of particular concern to the Maritime Provinces.[36] As for concessions sought by the United States, here,

---

[33] *Ibid.*, February 17, 1899.

[34] F. O. 5, 2421, Cartwright to Campbell, December 16, 1898. The appointment of Dingley's successor was delayed because McKinley wanted to name on the Commission the new chairman of the Ways and Means Committee. Payne's powers were not presented to the Commission until 18 days before its adjournment.

[35] F. O. 5, 2422, memorandum by Cartwright, March 25, 1899; State Department, Kasson papers, Fairbanks to McKinley, February 3, 1899.

[36] F. O. 5, 2422, memorandum by Cartwright, March 25, 1899.

too, only a meagre outcome could be anticipated in the face of opposition from Canadian furniture, bicycle, agricultural implements, shoe, typewriter, sewing machine, and other interests, which, terrified lest they be exposed to the full blast of American competition, bombarded Ottawa with demands for continued protection.[37] And apart from such protests, it must be remembered that Lord Herschell and the Canadian commissioners never envisaged equal concessions on both sides; on the contrary, they expected the United States to make far greater concessions to balance their own major concessions regarding seals and fisheries.

Thus after months of study the reciprocity committee had accomplished next to nothing. Dingley's death had been a heavy blow, but more than anything else the pitiful result demonstrated the power of pressure groups in both countries. Herschell wrote to Salisbury:

> Whenever it has been rumoured that a concession was about to be made by a modification of the Tariff affecting any particular article, whether a natural production or manufactured, the United States' or the Canadian Commissioners, and sometimes both, have been almost overwhelmed by protests and deputations. The utmost to be hoped for is . . . that some small step may be taken towards a freer interchange of commodities, and that the way may be paved for further progress in that direction in the future.[38]

To be sure, not all American special interests followed the fish and lumber industries in opposing reciprocity; on the contrary some of them supported it strongly. The Cleveland chamber of commerce petitioned the commission for a reciprocal trade agreement.[39] The Boston chamber, which claimed to be the mouthpiece of United States commercial interests in general, and the American Home Market Club sent deputations to Quebec; both

[37] Tansill, *Canadian-American Relations*, p. 450; J. M. V. Foster, " Reciprocity and the Joint High Commission of 1898-1899," *Report of the Canadian Historical Association, 1939*, pp. 91-93.

[38] F. O. 5, 2421, October 11, 1898.

[39] *Ibid.*, Herschell to Salisbury, November 25, 1898.

appealed for a comprehensive treaty.[40] And American importers of Canadian raw materials—brewers,[41] fertilizer makers, nickel and leather workers, and others—were keen advocates of lower duties.[42] But when the commissioners turned to articles produced in the United States as well as in Canada—and these were the products of main concern to Canada—they encountered vociferous objection. Everyone was delighted with concessions for someone else, but not for himself; and the delicately poised political situation in both countries set definite limits to the risks either government could take in alienating supporters.

Was there no escape from the barren haggling apparently inevitable to this commodity-by-commodity approach? Dingley is reported to have suggested a radical one. According to W. C. Cartwright, secretary of the British delegation,

> He has actually suggested to Laurier to make a complete Zollverein between the U. S. & Canada and has guaranteed to carry such a measure through Congress. . . . We should not like that at all. Canada would be closed to us as well as the U. S.
>
> I am sure my namesake [Richard Cartwright, member of the Canadian delegation] believes, and no doubt rightly, that this would be the best thing for Canada, but fortunately Canada, and Toronto especially, would not hear of it. Still the fact that such a proposal was made by Dingley, who is perhaps the most influential man in Congress at the present time, is well worth noting. It would be a step to annexation! [43]

Here was the old idea of a North American commercial union, a first step, as Cartwright observed, to political union. A decade or so earlier, had the Liberals been in office, the suggestion might

---

[40] *The Times*, September 2, 3, and 23, 1898. Demand in Massachusetts for reciprocity continued very strong; see State Department, Miscellaneous Letters, January 23, 1902, for an enormous petition signed by thousands of Massachusetts business men and by some in New Hampshire and Maine, asking for a treaty with Canada.

[41] Brewers of northern New York asked that Canadian barley, excluded from the United States the preceding eight years, be admitted duty free (*The Times*, October 4, 1898).

[42] For appeals from such sources see State Department, Kasson papers.

[43] F. O. 5, 2421, Cartwright to Campbell, October 10, 1898.

have borne fruit; but in 1899, after the improvement in her fortunes, there was little or no chance that, however great the benefit to lumber, fish, and many other interests, Canada would have cast in her lot to that extent with her great neighbor. And, of course, despite Dingley's reported confidence, acceptance by the American Congress of so drastic a transformation of the economy as commercial union would have engendered, was anything but certain or even likely.[44]

The commissioners did not expect the Alaska boundary question to prove difficult; on the contrary they were confident of settling it, and believed their greatest problems to lie elsewhere. Perhaps they should not have been optimistic, for as has appeared big stakes were involved in the ownership of the Lynn Canal; and strong forces, especially in the American northwest, were determined that no British flag should float over that vital waterway.[45] What were those forces?

There were first of all the west coast shipping interests. American navigation laws did not permit foreign vessels to participate in the coastal trade. A British ship, for example, could not carry between the United States and Skagway. On the other hand American vessels could carry between Vancouver or some other Canadian port and Alaska. But if Canada should acquire a foothold, say Pyramid Harbor, on the Lynn Canal the situation would be reversed: British ships could then carry between the United States and Pyramid Harbor but American ships could not carry between Canada and Pyramid Harbor. Of all west coast cities Seattle was the most deeply involved in the Yukon

[44] Looking back on the negotiations Laurier seemed surprisingly, even unduly, charitable: " On the whole, with reference to the reciprocity question, I am quite satisfied with the progress which we made, barring the sole article of lumber, and we can at any moment make a very fair treaty "; see Foster, " Reciprocity and the Joint High Commission of 1898-1899," p. 93.

[45] But see a curious undated petition signed by some 152 American residents of Dyea and addressed to the Joint High Commission, asking that Dyea be ceded to Canada and that Canada be given " free access to Lynn canal equally with americans [sic] . . ." (State Department, Alaskan Boundary Convention).

trade. Throughout 1898 a ship a day on the average left there for Alaska, a traffic that benefited the city and indeed the whole state enormously. These ships carried north nearly 15,000 persons in the first three months alone.[46] " It is the best thing which has happened for the prosperity of Seattle for some time," a newspaper stated in August, 1897. " The hotels are full of people, stores are doing a rushing business, and everyone is on the jump." [47] Other Pacific coast ports, too, notably Tacoma, likewise prospered. No wonder, therefore, that owners of the 250 steamers engaged in the Alaskan trade in 1898 were resolved at all costs to keep the lucrative business in their own hands—and that meant preserving the status quo in the coastal strip.[48] They constituted a powerful interest group opposed to concessions.

Besides the shippers, exporters to the Canadian northwest had a vested interest in American possession of the canal. Vancouver suppliers of mining equipment writhed in indignant frustration as they watched profitable business with another part of their own country being monopolized by rivals just across the border. If only Canada could acquire a port on the Lynn Canal they would be rid of exasperating American controls.

Seeing eye to eye with shippers and exporters was the North American Commercial Company. Already vexed by pelagic sealers operating from Victoria, the company dreaded the appearance of another Canadian port even nearer the sealing waters.

Besides these special interests a less tangible but even more formidable obstacle existed to any agreement acceptable to Canada. It arose from the fact that over the years Great Britain had never challenged American pretensions regarding the boundary.[49] As late as 1897, when Americans almost ostentatiously

[46] State Department, Miscellaneous Letters, January 15, 1900, from A. G. Foster.

[47] Vancouver *News-Advertiser*, August 11, 1897; quoted by F. W. Howay, W. N. Sage, H. F. Angus, *British Columbia and the United States, the North Pacific Slope from Fur Trade to Aviation* (Toronto, 1942), p. 338.

[48] For the figure of 250 see State Department, Miscellaneous Letters, January 15, 1900, from A. G. Foster.

[49] A possible but doubtful exception to this statement, sometimes cited by Great Britain, related to an incident of June, 1888, when the British heard

started to build Dyea and Skagway, no one in Britain or Canada seems to have considered protesting. United States ownership was simply taken for granted. " We ought to have protested when the Americans occupied Dyea and Skagway . . . ," Cartwright, the British delegation's secretary, admitted. Canada's silence resulted from lack of confidence in her own case. Not until 1898 did Lord Herschell bring a " windfall . . . in the shape of a sound argument " showing the Canadians that their case was not as hollow as they had supposed. " The fact is," wrote Cartwright,

> that, whatever irresponsible writers may have said, the Canadian officials and Govt. never realized till now that there was any back-bone in their contention. They vaguely asked for a great deal more than they were entitled to, but they did not believe in their right to the Lynn Canal. It is even now difficult to persuade some of their men here [in connection with the Joint High Commission] that they have a good claim there, although the balance of the Cabinet at Ottawa . . . are clamouring for absolute sovereignty at Pyramid Harbor—or a rupture of negotiations.[50]

If the Dominion as late as 1898 was only partially persuaded of the validity of its contentions, the British government in London was still less persuaded. " I do not think," wrote John Anderson, the Colonial Office official, " that any person who knows anything of the boundary question has asserted that Canada has a good claim to the Lynn Canal. It has certainly never been put forward either by the Dominion Govt. or H. M. G. hitherto. . . . An old gentleman named Begg who died lately started the Lynn Canal

a rumor that the United States had granted a charter for laying a trail from the Lynn Canal through the White Pass. Sir Lionel Sackville-West, British minister at Washington, wrote the State Department that " The territory in question is part of Her Majesty's dominions," but he did not specify any location and dropped the matter altogether (to the annoyance of Canada ten years later) when Secretary of State Bayard denied the existence of any such charter. See James White, *Boundary Disputes and Treaties* (Toronto, 1914), pp. 932-933.

[50] F. O. 5, 2422, Cartwright to Campbell, February 16, 1899.

doctrine a yr or two ago, but I am surprised to hear the Canadians who have got all the corrdce. pretending to take it seriously." [51]

This compliance with American assumptions over three decades provided the most persuasive argument in favor of the United States. How could anyone take seriously a claim suddenly put forward in 1898 when for so long Great Britain had acquiesced in acts which, had the claim been well founded, should have been resolutely challenged? Due in large measure simply to the abrupt way in which the British advanced their claim, few Americans doubted it was trumped up because of gold discoveries; that it was a "manufactured case," as Henry Cabot Lodge contended.[52] "We are absolutely driven to the conclusion that Lord Herschell put forward a claim that he had no belief or confidence in, for the mere purpose of trading it off for something substantial," Secretary of State John Hay, a true friend of Britain's, believed.[53] Angered by what it thought dishonest tactics, the United States became the more set in its determination not to yield. Yet its interpretation was wrong. Britain's case was not manufactured; it had been neglected simply because it related to one of the least critical and most remote parts of the world prior to the gold rush.

If the United States found it difficult to compromise on the boundary line, so did Canada. For one thing, she came increasingly to believe in her case. But in addition the new Liberal government, in none too strong a position politically, and constantly sniped at by the relentless Sir Charles Tupper, felt compelled, as John Hay perceived, to appear "in the attitude of stout defenders of Canadian rights and interests." [54] For political reasons, if for no others, the Canadian commission had to demand a substantial American retreat at the Lynn Canal.

[51] C. O. 42, 856, memorandum dated January 31, 1898. For the opinions of the "old gentleman" cited by Anderson see Alexander Begg, "Review of the Alaskan Boundary Question," *British Columbia Mining Record*, vol. 7 (1900), pp. 216-222, 254-259, 310-314.

[52] Nevins, *White*, pp. 189-190, to White, January 7, 1899.

[53] W. R. Thayer, *The Life and Letters of John Hay* (2 vols., Boston and New York, 1915), vol. 2, p. 205, to White, January 3, 1899.

[54] Tansill, *Canadian-American Relations*, p. 187.

The committee dealing with the boundary consisted of Herschell, Laurier, Fairbanks, and Foster. Most of the negotiating was done by Herschell and Fairbanks (though apparently Foster dominated the senator).[55] Herschell had mastered the essentials of the question, but he did not possess Foster's detailed knowledge. The only person on the British and Canadian side who could hope to rival the American was W. F. King, co-author of a voluminous boundary report of 1895; but he unfortunately was "addicted to whisky and has no power of speech."[56]

Secretary of State John Hay attributed the Joint High Commission's failure partly to what he called Herschell's legalistic temper of mind. ". . . by far the worst member of the Commission to deal with," he declared, "is Lord Herschell, who is more cantankerous than any of the Canadians, raises more petty points, and is harder than any of the Canadians to get along with. In fact, he is the principal obstacle to a favorable arrangement."[57] Judging by the written record this seems an unfair verdict. Herschell stood up resolutely for British rights and showed himself a keen bargainer; but he was always polite and ready to compromise. In forming an estimate of the Englishman, one must bear in mind his difficult position as chairman of a delegation otherwise composed of Canadians and a Newfoundlander. With their inveterate suspicion of British proneness to sacrifice them to curry American favor, Canadians were all too ready to jump to unwarranted conclusions over the slightest sign of leniency displayed by Lord Salisbury's envoy. A cartoon in the *Toronto World* depicted him on a bicycle the front wheel of which was labelled "Herschell's personal ambition," and the

[55] . . . he [Foster] has instigated all the arguments used by Fairbanks . . . . he seems to dominate their councils . . ." (F. O. 5, 2422, Cartwright to Campbell, February 16, 1899).

[56] F. O. 5, 2421, Cartwright to Campbell, October 10, 1898.

[57] White papers, to White, December 3, 1898; C. S. Hay, ed., *Letters of John Hay and Extracts from Diary* (3 vols., Washington, 1908), vol. 3, pp. 142-143, Hay to White, February 14, 1899. American historians who have criticized Herschell are Tansill, *Canadian-American Relations*, pp. 173-174, 457; Nevins, *White*, p. 187; T. Dennett, *John Hay, from Poetry to Politics* (New York, 1933), p. 228.

back wheel " English desire for settlement (any kind) "; **the** bicycle, which was following a pointer marked " To treaty **at** any cost," had in tow a cart (" Canadian case ") carrying Richard Cartwright and Sir Wilfrid Laurier; terrified at the pace, Laurier was saying, " We'd—better let go—now—Dickey before it's—too late! " [58] The cartoon was typical of Canadian sentiment.

From the outset negotiations turned on the Lynn Canal, recognized by both sides as " the only part of any grave importance. . . ." [59] To be sure, at an early session Lord Herschell, from loyalty to Canada, made a routine stand for Duke of Clarence Strait as being Portland channel; but he did not press the pretension, which he considered untenable.[60] Herschell raised two serious arguments against the American claim to own the canal's headwaters. First, he made the point that the word " *océan* " had been expressly inserted in the treaty of 1825 to replace the word " *mer* " (which might apply to salt water generally) ; the substitution, he contended, must have been made to exclude from the treaty's scope such inlets as the Lynn Canal, which might be parts of a " *mer* " but not of an " *océan*." Second, he maintained that because " it would be absurd and even impossible to draw a line inland, corresponding with all the indentations," the term " winding of the coast " necessarily referred to the coast's general trend.[61] A boundary drawn on the basis of either of these contentions would have cut across the canal and left the United States, as John Hay indignantly noted, " only a few jutting promontories without communication with each other." [62] Herschell's points were well taken and they gave the American commissioners, who had assumed nothing could be said for the other side, a nasty jolt. After studying the Englishman's argument, Senator Gray admitted confidentially that it had much validity; [63]

[58] December 22, 1898.
[59] F. O. 5, 2417; State Department, Alaskan Boundary Convention; Herschell to Fairbanks, December 21, 1898.
[60] F. O. 5, 2421, Herschell to Salisbury, September 2, 1898.
[61] *Ibid.*
[62] Thayer, *Life and Letters*, vol. 2, p. 205, to White, January 3, 1899.
[63] F. O. 5, 2422, memorandum by Cartwright, March 27, 1899.

and even the disputatious Foster was described as being " rather stumped "—a most unusual state of mind for him.[64]

However impressed, the American commissioners did not of course renounce the United States claim. On the contrary, quite unruffled on the surface, they maintained their stand unaltered, continuing to insist that the boundary ran ten marine leagues inland measured from salt water. In fact they blandly disregarded Herschell's whole argument—just as they were simultaneously discounting Britain's offer to abandon pelagic sealing and her claims under the fisheries treaty of 1818. Fairbanks countered with an offer which took for granted American ownership of the entire Lynn Canal. Let British ships, he suggested, be accorded access to the canal equally with American ships, and let merchandise in transit across Alaska be exempted from duty.[65] Doubtless annoyed by the cavalier disregard of his careful exposition, Lord Herschell retorted that Canada had no interest in being offered the free use of her own ports.[66]

If nothing else, Fairbanks's proposal made clear his utter refusal to settle for the " few jutting promontories." That much having been demonstrated, bargaining now proceeded between the two sides in terms offering some hope of success. Herschell made the first move. He proposed settling the dispute in either of two ways: Great Britain would cede all she claimed except Pyramid Harbor and a strip of territory from it to the Dalton Trail; or she would agree to the delimitation of the boundary by experts on the understanding that no matter what the decision Dyea and Skagway would be American and Pyramid Harbor Canadian.[67] But he was still asking too much. Fairbanks was not going to hand over Pyramid Harbor; and as for arbitration, Herschell's own secretary, Cartwright, confessed that " after all that has

[64] F. O. 5, 2421, Cartwright to Campbell, October 11, 1898.

[65] F. O. 5, 2417, draft article regarding harbors of the Lynn Canal received from Fairbanks December 14, 1898. The second part of the offer would not seem to go beyond the privileges already enjoyed by Canada since March, 1898.

[66] Ibid., memorandum respecting the Lynn Canal given to Fairbanks December 16, 1898.

[67] Ibid.

passed it is illusory to suppose that the United States Government would place itself in the position of being obliged to admit Canadian jurisdiction at Pyramid Harbour even if the Arbitrator decided that the whole of the Lynn Canal belonged to the United States." [68] Besides, the United States, still suffering from the shock of the Paris sealing award of 1893, viewed arbitration in general with deep suspicion, except indeed for others; and it had already refused to submit the fate of Dyea and Skagway to a neutral arbitrator.[69]

Fairbanks replied with an offer, not of a cession, but of a fifty-year transfer of Pyramid Harbor to exclusive Canadian jurisdiction (except that the area could not be fortified), the United States retaining nothing but nominal sovereignty and the right to equal treatment with British vessels.[70] Although this offer represented a sincere attempt to reach an accord it did not, any more than his first offer, come to grips with Herschell's argument; nor did it sanction the least deviation from the boundary claimed by the United States. Lord Herschell of course recognized this. " Here again," he wrote the senator, " it seems to me with deference that you decide in your own favour the question as to the territory in dispute, treating the British claim to it as absolutely without foundation, and practically ask me to do the same." [71] Nevertheless, the offer did interest the Englishman and his Canadian colleagues.[72] Indeed, after some further discussion,

[68] F. O. 5, 2422, memorandum by Cartwright, March 27, 1899.

[69] Henry Cabot Lodge had another reason for opposing arbitration of the boundary: he feared any procedure that would risk giving Britain another naval base on the west coast; see Nevins, *White*, p. 189, Lodge to White, January 7, 1899. F. W. Seward, son of the purchaser of Alaska, foresaw another Gibraltar " in the heart of an American territory"; see his letter to the *New York Tribune*, November 14, 1902, cited by T. W. Balch, *The Alaska Frontier* (Philadelphia, 1903), pp. 175-177.

[70] F. O. 5, 2422; State Department, Alaskan Boundary Convention; Fairbanks to Herschell, December 24, 1898. F. O. 5, 2422, Herschell to Salisbury, February 7, 1899; the original despatch is dated 1898, but 1899 is of course correct.

[71] F. O. 5, 2422, Herschell to Fairbanks, December 31, 1898.

[72] Cartwright, however, believed that the first offer was more advantageous and should have been accepted. ". . . Pyramid Harbor," he said, with much

they believed it would prove acceptable. If so, the Joint High Commission's success would have been assured; [73] and in all probability the Clayton-Bulwer treaty would, as a result, have been modified at an early date.

But this bright prospect, alas, was not to be realized. News of the proposed transfer leaked out; it gave rise to violent agitation in the West, which envisaged its profitable business with Alaska being disrupted by a British lodgment at Pyramid Harbor. A memorial adopted by the Washington state legislature on February 16, 1899, declared in no uncertain terms:

> The cession of . . . any . . . Alaskan port will transfer from the United States to a foreign power the sole and absolute control of intercourse with the great interior, in which is involved a traffic of enormous proportions and of great wealth. Such cession will injure every citizen of the United States from San Diego to Sitka, and will humiliate the country from ocean to ocean and end to end. For the first time in our history our flag will be hauled down and the land over which it has long floated will be given away, sold or surrendered, this, too, without considering the wishes, wants or rights of the people most affected; and this, too, for either no consideration or for a consideration of trifling character.[74]

President McKinley received about a hundred telegrams from the Pacific coast, a few of which actually threatened secession by the three coastal states if Canada was allowed to ensconce herself on the canal.[75] Although secession was of course out of the question, the threats indicated very strong feelings which the government would disregard at its peril.

pertinence, "would be a white elephant to the Canadians. It would be a one-horse place and a useless expense, and it would, if developed, only compete with the [Skagway] railway, now nearly completed . . ." (*ibid.*, to Campbell, February 16, 1899). The London *Times* (May 29, 1899) agreed: a railway from Pyramid Harbor, it thought, would be so impracticable as compared with other Lynn Canal railways that it would not even have been considered except for the influence of contractors.

[73] F. O. 5, 2422, Cartwright to Campbell, January 6, 1899.

[74] State Department, Miscellaneous Letters, January 15, 1900, from A. G. Foster.

[75] F. O. 5, 2422, Cartwright to Campbell, February 16, 1899.

Another indication came from the shipping interests. Aroused over the threat to their prosperity, they warned the State Department on February 2, 1899, that the states of Washington, Oregon, and California were "very much exercised over a report that the Joint High Commission has conceded to Canada a . . . Port on Lynn Canal," and that the step would be "highly detrimental" to their interests.[76] The American commissioners could not resist the pressure. It was probably a coincidence, however, that the very next day after the telegram was sent, a "fatal complication" threatened the negotiations, up to then proceeding auspiciously. The Americans on February 3 made the embarrassing admission of having overlooked the fact that by the terms of their offer British vessels would be entitled to carry between American ports, thereby contravening United States navigation laws; and accordingly they gave notice that they would have to withdraw the offer unless the navigation laws were understood to apply to Pyramid Harbor.[77] Whether a coincidence or not, this condition met the shippers' objections by maintaining the American shipping monopoly between the west coast and the Lynn Canal.

The unexpected change of front knocked out an essential part of the arrangement that had seemed so near. "Of course this right [to use Pyramid Harbor as a British port] ought to be conceded to us; it is one of the chief advantages of getting the port," Cartwright declared.[78] The British and Canadians resented the new proviso all the more because in their opinion the United States was not meeting them halfway on other issues—those concerning Atlantic fisheries, Bering Sea seals, and com-

[76] State Department, Alaskan Boundary Convention, to Senator G. C. Perkins, February 2, 1899. Perkins sent a copy of the communication to the State Department.

[77] F. O. 5, 2422, Cartwright to Campbell, February 5, 1899. See State Department, Miscellaneous Archives, Alaskan Boundary, 1899-1903, for an undated, unsigned memorandum (probably written by Adee): "nor should a lease be made upon such conditions as will change the state of the commerce of Alaska to the great injury of the Pacific States."

[78] F. O. 5, 2422, Cartwright to Campbell, February 5, 1899.

mercial reciprocity.[79] But Fairbanks and his colleagues by then appreciated too keenly the perils for the Republican party implicit in the hue and cry from western states to back down. An apparently " insuperable difficulty " in the way of agreement had thus appeared in the shape of United States navigation laws as they affected special interests on the west coast.[80]

The negotiation's were at a crisis. Herschell telegraphed despondently to Salisbury that " owing we believe to pressure from interests on Pacific Coast," success seemed remote. He asked for authority—which he was given—to adjourn the Joint High Commission if the United States would not arbitrate the boundary dispute.[81]

During the Commission's final two weeks a strong effort was made to put the dispute to arbitration. " What then is to be done," Herschell asked Fairbanks, " when two friendly nations differ as to the construction of a Treaty or as to matters of fact, or their legal effect, which are alleged to have modified the rights which it originally created? We know of nothing except to obtain the opinion of a capable Tribunal, both independent and impartial." [82] An arbitral agreement, he suggested, could be patterned on the Venezuelan boundary agreement of February 2, 1897, with the understanding—intended to safeguard Dyea and Skagway for the United States—that " the whole question should be adjusted with a full regard to what justice and the equities of the case required." [83]

Not the slightest chance existed of this suggestion being accepted; twice already the United States had refused to consider arbitrating, unless perchance half the arbitrators were American. Yet the appeal to the Venezuelan dispute could not be rejected out of hand; for not only did it relate to a boundary, but its arbitration had been sponsored by the United States. Now with

[79] *Ibid.*, Herschell to Salisbury, February 7, 1899.

[80] *Ibid.*, memorandum by Cartwright, March 25, 1899.

[81] *Ibid.*, to Salisbury, February 12, 1899.

[82] F. O. 5, 2417; State Department, Alaskan Boundary Convention; Herschell to Fairbanks, February 15, 1899.

[83] F. O. 5, 2422, Herschell to Salisbury, February 24, 1899. See p. 6.

the situation reversed, how could the United States refuse to apply to itself virtually the same procedure it had recently foisted upon Great Britain? [84] Embarrassed, Senator Fairbanks hedged. He agreed first to arbitrate everything—except the one thing that mattered most, the Lynn Canal.[85] But such selective arbitration could not be defended, as President McKinley himself had previously admitted; [86] and Fairbanks soon felt constrained to talk in terms of arbitrating the whole line. For a moment the clouds seemed to be lifting, and Herschell at once submitted a draft modelled on the Venezuelan treaty. His hopes soared higher because that very day, February 16, 1899, John Foster was obliged by illness to leave for Palm Beach. " It may be hoped," the Englishman wrote, " that, in his absence, matters will proceed more smoothly, if we take into account the strong disinclination which he has always shown to . . . arbitration." [87]

Herschell should have known better. Political requirements relating to the western states were too plain to permit any arrangement rendering possible an award against the United States. " Apparently American Commissioners dare not compromise in face of agitation on Pacific Coast," Ambassador Pauncefote telegraphed sadly.[88] Fairbanks made two counter-proposals, both of which in the circumstances amounted to rejection of meaningful arbitration: first, that the odd-numbered arbitrator be selected from a Latin-American country (Herschell insisted that he come from Europe) ; second, that there be an even-numbered board,

[84] " We are not informed of the reasons which have induced the representatives of the United States to reject the precedent that was established in the case of Venezuela at the instance of the American Government," the *Times* remarked (February 23, 1899). See also London *Daily News*, February 23, 1899, and London *Daily Telegraph*, February 23, 1899.

[85] F. O. 5, 2417; State Department, Alaskan Boundary Convention; Fairbanks to Herschell, February 14, 1899. ". . . our proposal provides for the submission to arbitration of all questions and of all points which have been the subject of correspondence between the two Governments up to the time of the assembling of the Joint High Commission." Such was the senator's ingenious terminology to exclude the Lynn Canal question.

[86] F. O. 5, 2421, Herschell to Salisbury, December 22, 1898.

[87] F. O. 5, 2422, Herschell to Salisbury, February 17, 1899.

[88] Salisbury papers, to Salisbury, February 19, 1899.

three arbitrators on each side, a majority to decide, with Dyea and Skagway reserved to the United States.[89] Pauncefote seems to have supported this second proposal, which as a matter of fact foreshadowed the arrangement by which the controversy was resolved in 1903. John Hay so stated; [90] and bearing him out is the fact that Sir Julian had already recommended arbitration by a board of six, three on a side, with Dyea and Skagway guaranteed to the United States and access to the Lynn Canal guaranteed to Canada.[91] Hay stated further that Lord Salisbury as well supported the second proposal.[92] This is altogether possible, though no other indication of the Prime Minister's attitude is known. But whatever the opinion of Pauncefote and Salisbury, Herschell rejected the proposal outright. To the Prime Minister he defended himself on the ground that an even-numbered board might fail to reach a majority decision, and that " although some boundary disputes might be left undetermined even for a long period without danger, the speedy delimitation of this boundary was, under existing circumstances, of urgent importance." [93]

Neither side made additional proposals. Having failed to agree upon a compromise arrangement, the commissioners had

[89] F. O. 5, 2422, Herschell to Salisbury, February 21 and 24, 1899. See also State Department, Great Britain, Despatches, Hay to White, February 18, 1899: " American Commissioners have offered arbitration: three jurists on each side, a majority to determine. Hope to avoid intervention of a foreign umpire, though that may be kept in view as a last resort." It is not clear whether Hay was thinking of a Latin American umpire or whether he was prepared to accept a European umpire if necessary. If the latter, acceptance of valid arbitration by the United States was not hopeless.

[90] Hay, Letters and Diary, vol. 3, p. 145, to White, February 21, 1899.

[91] F. O. 5, 2400, Pauncefote to Foreign Office, February 6, 1900. See also Salisbury papers, Pauncefote to Salisbury, February 19, 1899: " Privately I gather from Mr. Hay that the objection to a foreign umpire is as great as it was during negotiation of the [Anglo-American 1897] general arbitration Treaty but I think there is a disposition to agree to an arbitration of three eminent jurists (no politicians) on either side who shall decide by a majority of four to two. . . ."

[92] Hay, Letters and Diary, vol. 3, p. 145, to White, February 21, 1899.

[93] F. O. 5, 2422, February 24, 1899.

now failed to provide for arbitration. Further discussion appeared hopeless. Six months had elapsed since the first meeting, and the negotiators were at a complete impasse. The Joint High Commission, soon to break up, debated the Alaska boundary question no more.

When the difficulty of determining the boundary became evident, the normal expectation would have been, not disruption of the whole commission, but continued negotiation to secure agreement on as many as possible of the remaining eleven items on the agenda. As a matter of fact agreement in principle had been reached on a number of them—conveyance of prisoners, alien labor laws, Pacific coast and inland fisheries, wrecking and salvage [94]—and seemed reasonably promising in the case of them all—Pauncefote had just informed London to that effect [95]—despite the serious difficulties in the reciprocity and fisheries negotiations. Senator Fairbanks did suggest proceeding with the other questions. " They are well advanced; in fact, nothing but formal assent is necessary to dispose of several of them," he said. " The differences with respect to others have been reduced to a very small number, and in the main do not seem insuperable." [96]

He may have been surprised, though probably he was not, when Lord Herschell refused to negotiate on anything once the boundary deadlock had been reached.[97] The manner in which he and his associates " would be prepared to adjust some of the other important matters under consideration," Herschell ex-

[94] *Ibid.*, Cartwright to Campbell, February 24, 1899.

[95] F. O. 5, 2400, to Foreign Office, February 6, 1899. See also State Department, Alaskan Boundary Convention, undated memorandum initialed " J. A. K." (John A. Kasson) ; State Department, Kasson papers, Fairbanks to McKinley, February 3, 1899.

[96] F. O. 5, 2417; State Department, Alaskan Boundary Convention; Fairbanks to Herschell, February 11, 1899.

[97] In this position Herschell was supported and to some extent instigated by Canada. In the Dominion House of Commons Laurier stated, May 26, 1899, that matters before the commission stood in a fair way of settlement until Canada took the position that the Alaska boundary question must be settled before she would agree to the settlement of any other question (*The Times*, May 27, 1899) .

plained, " must depend . . . upon whether it is possible to arrive at a settlement of all the questions which might at any time occasion acute controversy, and even conflict. Of these the Alaska boundary question . . . stands in the forefront." [98] Indignant at the rebuff, Fairbanks retorted that no excuse could be found for making settlement of any one question depend on " wholly unrelated questions." [99] Nevertheless the British and Canadians did not yield: if the boundary dispute was not settled, nothing would be.

Accordingly, on February 20, 1899, the Joint High Commission announced suspension of negotiations until August 2, when it would reassemble at Quebec.[100] Despite the date set, however, people generally understood that in fact it had failed completely and would never meet again. This expectation was realized; the session of February 20, 1899, was the last ever held.

On the surface the commissioners " parted on friendly terms " (as Herschell told Salisbury),[101] but a more frank description was given by Cartwright:

> " We parted on friendly terms "—Yes; but Laurier was burning with suppressed fury; Kasson was rather nasty, though very pleasant unofficially; Lord Herschell and Foster were absent so they could not quarrel, but they will never meet again on business, I am sure.
>
> The last discussion was a ticklish job, and it was extremely difficult to agree on a Protocol. We should never have got through if Foster had been there. Faulkner behaved very well and helped to bring us together; Davies also did something in smoothing Laurier.[102]

Meeting at a time when relations between the United States and Great Britain were supposedly at their best, the Joint High Commission of 1898-1899 was the first such body that had ever disbanded in apparently unmitigated failure.

[98] F. O. 5, 2422, Herschell to Salisbury, February 24, 1899; see also Herschell's telegram to Salisbury, February 21, 1899 (ibid.).

[99] F. O. 5, 2417; State Department, Alaskan Boundary Convention; Fairbanks to Herschell, February 11, 1899.

[100] F. O. 5, 2422, Herschell to Salisbury, February 21, 1899.

[101] Ibid.

[102] Ibid., Cartwright to Campbell, February 24, 1899.

It would be difficult to find a better example than these proceedings of the Joint High Commission of the influence of special interests upon foreign policy. Shippers and exporters in northwestern states, coal and lumber industries in Canada and the United States, the fishing town of Gloucester, pelagic sealers, the North American Commercial Company—these and several other such interests made their wishes very evident to the politicians and diplomats. Vital national interests may have pointed in one direction, but these smaller, special interests were not concerned with that: they had themselves to think about. Without constant awareness of their pressure upon Washington, London, and Ottawa, sometimes harmful, usually strong and steady, no one can understand the difficulties of reaching an Anglo-American settlement around the turn of the century.

There was another factor. As so often in human affairs, chance played a leading role. A consideration of this point takes us back to Lord Herschell's disruption of the Joint High Commission. How can his action be accounted for? Why should so clever a man have put Great Britain in a position where in future years she could be accused with every show of plausibility of having refused to settle anything unless she could settle everything? His explanation to Fairbanks, although undoubtedly valid for some of the matters under discussion, for example, armaments on the Great Lakes and transit privileges, had little or no force in relation to such other matters as wrecking, salvage, cattle branding, conveyance of prisoners, alien labor laws, minor boundary rectifications, and perhaps even fur seals and fisheries. Surely agreement could have been reached on many or all of these without prejudice to British prospects in a hypothetical war with the United States. The real explanation of Herschell's behavior lies elsewhere.

The winter of 1899 was a severe one in Washington. The famous Cuban general, Garcia, caught a chill there and died. A vandal smashed windows in the British embassy; flying glass injured one of the ambassador's daughters, and icy blasts sweeping through the drawing rooms disturbed the composure of poor Lady Pauncefote and spread confusion among her guests at a large tea party. The death of Nelson Dingley and the ill health of John Foster have been mentioned. (The Joint High Commission was hard on its members.) In the middle of February Lord Herschell fell on a slippery street. Although forced to take to bed, he at first appeared to have sustained only a minor injury; but complications ensued, and in early March he died.

It is in this unfortunate accident that the true explanation of the commission's disruption is to be found. Its most obvious effect was to remove the one person on the British and Canadian side who held all threads of the negotiations. "Laurier could not have carried on without him . . . ," Cartwright thought.[103] Combined with Foster's illness, which left Fairbanks stranded (although he could fall back on the State Department), Herschell's death deprived the commission of its two mainstays. But the accident had another, more significant effect. When it occurred, Herschell anticipated a period of physical inactivity that, while keeping him in Washington longer than he had expected, would not incapacitate him for hard mental work. He planned to take advantage of his unexpected residence there to carry negotiations to a successful conclusion. Lord Herschell gave his real reasons for terminating the Joint High Commission, not to Senator Fairbanks, but to Lord Salisbury:

> Americans were very anxious that there should be no rupture in the negotiations but only an adjournment. I think they entertain a hope that by diplomatic negotiations a solution of this difficulty [the Alaskan boundary] might be found after which the other matters could probably without serious difficulty be adjusted. I should have been prepared to continue negotiations and still press for a settlement but for the following reasons: no settlement could be expected but after considerable delay, and the return of my Canadian Colleagues to Ottawa had become imperatively necessary; moreover I thought a more favourable result was to be hoped for outside rather than through the Commission. My accident which proves a serious one will detain me here many weeks. I shall endeavour if Your Lordship approves to utilize this detention by direct personal negotiations to which I have reason to believe the United States Government might not object.[104]

---

[103] F. O. 5, 2422, Cartwright to Campbell, February 24, 1899.
[104] *Ibid.*, Herschell to Salisbury, February 21, 1899.

This statement puts quite a different light on the commission's break-up. Far from refusing to settle anything unless he could settle everything, Herschell in actuality had no intention of declining to negotiate; rather, he saw a splendid opportunity both to shock the Americans into a more conciliatory attitude by terminating the commission, and at the same time, by taking advantage of his accident, to continue negotiations under fresh conditions. Lord Salisbury agreed to this scheme, and Secretary Hay gave assurances that he was " most anxious to negotiate with Lord Herschell." [105] Thus it was the Englishman's totally unexpected death that spoiled a clever and hopeful plan. This is not to imply that general agreement would have been reached had he lived; but probably, even assuming continued failure on the boundary question, agreement would have been possible on many or even all the remaining issues.

In view of these circumstances it is apparent that Canadian-American relations, though no doubt bad enough and though no doubt an obstacle to Anglo-American friendship, were not so bad as the collapse of the Joint High Commission would suggest. The commission did of course come to an end, and with a fair amount of acrimony; but unknown to the public, arrangements had been made for continuing negotiations. The long delay that ensued before the Canadian questions were finally adjusted, in some instances not until over a decade later, was perhaps due not so much to their intrinsic difficulties, great as they were, as to Lord Herschell's tragic accident one wintry day in Washington.

CHAPTER 5

Breakdown

AUGUST, 1898, is a noteworthy date in the history of Anglo-American relations. It was then that the armistice was signed, terminating hostilities in the war that did so much to improve mutual sentiment in the two English-speaking countries; it was then that the Joint High Commission convened at Quebec; and it was also then that the American government made its first move toward persuading Great Britain to modify the Clayton-Bulwer treaty.

On the 16th of that month F. W. Holls, who was a fairly prominent figure in the Republican party—he had been Roosevelt's legal adviser when Roosevelt was governor of New York—and who occasionally performed special missions for the State Department, called on Arthur Balfour in London. Claiming to be speaking with authority from Washington, he told Balfour that Germany had requested one of the Philippines, but that Washington had refused to act without getting British approval. Could not Britain, he suggested, use this bargaining point to make a deal with Germany? Specifically, could she not agree to use good offices at Washington in order to get Germany a suitable island provided Germany agreed to cooperate with Britain and America in China? Russia also had approached the United States, Holls added, offering to secure for it preferential tariff rates in China in exchange for American collaboration in the Far East.[1]

[1] F. O. 5, 2378, memorandum by Balfour, August 16, 1898.

Balfour heard these surprising and far-reaching remarks with much interest. They indicated, as he noted, " the most friendly feeling towards this country and may prove most useful." [2] But what did the United States want in return? Holls now made this plain. The United States, he said, had made up its mind to build a Central American canal as a great national project, the canal to cut through a strip forty miles wide of what would be American territory. Such a project ran counter to the Clayton-Bulwer treaty, and Washington therefore intended to ask Britain to modify or terminate that treaty. In fact, President McKinley would probably broach the subject in his annual message to Congress in December. Holls asked Balfour to prepare the British government for a quick and favorable response to the coming request.

The American support in the Far East envisaged by Holls would of course be helpful to Britain, already hard pressed in her struggle to retain her lucrative markets there. Balfour must have been reminded of the British suggestion for cooperation in China put forward in March, 1898, to a preoccupied government in Washington.[3] Perhaps he reflected that now, five months later, with the Spanish War won and American troops occupying Manila, events seemed to have dictated a change of mind across the Atlantic. Perhaps, too, he thought of the opportunities that Anglo-German-American cooperation in the Far East might provide for the rapprochement with Germany and the alignment with her and the United States that were intriguing Joseph Chamberlain and other British officials just then. Yet Balfour did not, of course, have authority to give Holls immediate assurances. Any such comprehensive proposal could be accepted, if at all, only after most careful consideration. " I contented myself with observing in general terms," he therefore stated, " that a canal across the Isthmus in the hands of a strong neutral and peaceful Power would be a blessing to mankind, but I frankly told him that the danger, and the only danger which I foresaw was that in the very improbable event of hostilities between our two countries, such a canal would be an immense strategic ad-

---

[2] *Ibid.*   [3] See p. 19.

vantage to the United States." [4] After all, perils still lurked in the unsettled controversies involving Canada; and it was then too early to know whether the Joint High Commission would succeed.

Although no immediate bargain was struck—or expected—the British leaders now had precise knowledge of America's canal aspirations. Doubtless this stimulated them to clarify their thoughts and doubtless it prepared them for the somewhat untactful remarks in McKinley's message to Congress four months later.

It is difficult to be sure of the correct interpretation of this curious interview. In effect Holls offered Great Britain a veto over German expansion in the Philippines and a road to possible understanding with Germany, in exchange for Britain relinquishing her canal veto; and he added the encouragement of a mild hint that if she did not accept, the United States might turn to Russia, Britain's arch-rival throughout Asia. If Balfour concluded that the United States was determined to build a canal, the Clayton-Bulwer treaty notwithstanding, that the McKinley administration was well disposed toward Great Britain, and that it was beginning to pluck up courage for hesitant steps in the Far East, he got a correct impression. But if he concluded that the administration was prepared to win release from the treaty by throwing in its lot with Britain in eastern Asia, he was certainly wrong. However strongly it desired to get rid of the old treaty, Washington was not ready in 1898 to take sides in the developing struggle over the moribund Chinese empire.

More puzzling than the meaning of Holls's proposal is the question of its authenticity. Why was it not advanced through regular diplomatic channels? Three years later he had another interview with Balfour about canal matters; and on that occasion Secretary Hay carefully warned the American embassy at London against his pretension to speak officially.[5] Whatever his credentials in 1898, Holls had no power, of course, to commit the United States and probably overstated the possibilities of Ameri-

---

[4] F. O. 5, 2378, memorandum by Balfour, August 16, 1898.
[5] Choate papers, Choate to Hay, July 26, 1901. See p. 231.

can action. No doubt he was a man who loved to dabble in high policy and was apt to magnify his own importance. " Such beings as Holls drive me frantic by their overweening egotismus . . . ," Alvey Adee, Assistant Secretary of State, confessed.[6] It seems unlikely, however, that Holls misrepresented his official status in 1898. The government had confidence in him at least through the summer of 1899, when he served on the American delegation to the Hague peace conference. Furthermore, his predictions to Balfour as to future canal moves were perfectly correct: the United States did embark upon a national canal project, and McKinley did raise the matter in his annual message. And following a talk with McKinley on his return to America, Holls wrote to Balfour in terms confirming the President's support:

> . . . I have nothing to modify as respects the statement made to you.
> The feeling that nothing should be done by this country in the Far East, except after a full understanding on every point with the Government of Great Britain, is surely stronger than ever, and I am confident that no other policy will be *even considered* by this Administration. Germany can gain nothing whatever, *except* through the good offices of Great Britain. . . . the basis is afforded of a favor from Great Britain which should lay Germany under deep and lasting obligations, and which should thus indirectly contribute to that informal alliance or good understanding between the three great Anglo-Saxon Protestant Powers which seems so very desirable.[7]

In any event, the British government for a long time refused to meet American wishes as regards a canal without receiving a

[6] Hay papers, to Hay, September 16, 1899.

[7] F. O. 5, 2378, Balfour to Sanderson, September 20, 1898, enclosing a letter from Holls. See also Holls papers, Holls to Porter (McKinley's secretary) , August 25, 1898, asking for an early appointment with the President: " I have some extremely important messages to the President from Mr. White in Berlin and Mr. Balfour in London, supplementing reports which I have hitherto made on the international situation "; *ibid.*, Holls to Strachey, September 1, 1898: " Personally, I have no doubt whatever that the British Government will meet our own Government here in an amicable settlement of all questions connected with the Nicaragua Canal, according to American ideas."

substantial concession; certainly it never considered abandoning the bargaining power represented by the Clayton-Bulwer treaty because of vague proposals through irregular diplomatic channels of possible American cooperation in the orient.

Considering the various incidents converging in August, 1898, as the Spanish-American War drew to its close, one can see the broad lines along which the McKinley administration was moving. A comprehensive settlement with Great Britain, the one friendly power during the war crisis, was indispensable. It was to be reached by two parallel and simultaneous, but entirely separate, sets of negotiations which would clear the slate of outstanding controversies: one dealing with Canadian matters, the other with the Clayton-Bulwer treaty. Ample scope existed for bargaining on the former but not on the treaty, where the United States wanted everything and had nothing to offer except the general advantage to Britain of another canal. This explains why the United States tried to keep the negotiations separate, and, conversely, why Great Britain tried to combine them; for if all issues were lumped together, it would be awkward for the United States to avoid yielding much in the north in order to get its way in Central America. Seals, fisheries, gold fields— these and more might have to be abandoned to escape the hold of the detested Clayton-Bulwer treaty.

As regards these Canadian and Central American questions, the administration had a clear-cut policy toward Great Britain. In addition it was beginning to feel its way toward a Far Eastern policy that might include a measure of cooperation with the British. However, the main impulse for such a policy came, despite what Holls said in London, not from diplomats anxious to compensate the British for withdrawing in Central America, but from American military and naval strategists and even more from American business men interested in eastern Asia.

President McKinley could have named no Secretary of State better suited to reach an understanding with Great Britain than John Hay.[8] Having been Lincoln's private secretary as a young

---

[8] For a sympathetic study see T. Dennett, *John Hay, from Poetry to Politics* (New York, 1933).

man and in later years a person of moderate influence in inner circles of the Republican party, he well understood, even if he did not always observe, the political necessities which any successful Secretary of State must heed. As secretary of the American legation at Madrid in 1870, Assistant Secretary of State from 1879 to 1881, and ambassador to the Court of St. James from 1897 to 1898, he had diplomatic training unusual to Secretaries of State in the Gilded Age. A frequent visitor to Great Britain, he knew the country and many of its statesmen well; and his familiarity with British letters—he was a literary figure of some distinction himself—gave him further insight into the country. Of equal if not greater importance was his real love for Britain. Both for this reason and because he believed American interests lay parallel to British interests, the main ambition of his last years was to work for close understanding between the two English-speaking countries. At the Lord Mayor's Easter banquet at the Mansion House on April 21, 1898, he gave an address significantly entitled "A Partnership in Beneficence." "The reasons of a good understanding between us," he said,

> lie deeper than any considerations of mere expediency. All of us who think cannot but see that there is a sanction like that of religion which binds us to a sort of partnership in the beneficent work of the world. Whether we will it or not, we are associated in that work by the very nature of things, and no man and no group of men can prevent it. We are bound by a tie which we did not forge and which we cannot break; we are joint ministers of the same sacred mission of liberty and progress, charged with duties which we cannot evade by the imposition of irresistible hands.[9]

The "Partnership in Beneficence" came close to being a sacred quest for the new Secretary.

For all his fine qualities, however, Secretary Hay had certain serious weaknesses. Conscious of his own intellectual and moral superiority, he was something of an aristocrat who had nothing

[9] John Hay, *Addresses of John Hay* (New York, 1906), pp. 78-79. Hay delivered his speech only after consultation with top British officials (State Department, Great Britain, Despatches, Hay to Sherman, April 21, 1898).

in common with the ordinary man. He detested United States senators. He took his frequent battles with them much too hard. These battles sapped his nervous energy and wore him down physically and mentally. " It is rather sad . . . ," Whitelaw Reid thought, " to see how completely he got the Senate on the brain in his later years." [10] Impatient and petulant, he had little stamina or repose.

Working closely with Hay and sharing his aspirations for British-American friendship, was Her Majesty's Ambassador at Washington, Sir Julian Pauncefote (he became Lord Pauncefote in 1899) .[11] Although each of these men faithfully represented the interests of his own country, in a real sense they formed a team working harmoniously to promote the common welfare of Britain and America. " For the moment," Henry Adams, Hay's close friend, believed, " Hay had no ally, abroad or at home, except Pauncefote, and . . . Pauncefote alone pulled him through." [12]

Before his American appointment Pauncefote had had a distinguished career. He practised law in Hongkong, was Chief Justice of the Leeward Islands, and served in the Foreign Office where he became Permanent Under-Secretary of State in 1882. He first came to Washington at a difficult time, succeeding Sackville-West as minister when that unfortunate man was declared *persona non grata* by President Cleveland in 1888. So well did he perform his mission of rescuing Anglo-American relations from the morass into which they had fallen because of the dismissal of Sackville-West and because of the Bering Sea and fisheries controversies, both of which were then critical, that he was named first British ambassador to the United States in 1893.

Of the many eminent British representatives at Washington no one has done more, perhaps not as much, as Pauncefote to improve relations between the two countries. Yet his personality

[10] J. A. Garraty, *Henry Cabot Lodge, a Biography* (New York, 1953) , p. 212.
[11] R. B. Mowat, *The Life of Lord Pauncefote, First Ambassador to the United States* (Boston and New York, 1929) .
[12] H. Adams, *The Education of Henry Adams, an Autobiography* (Boston and New York, 1918) , p. 374.

was not one to attract Americans. Almost painfully dignified, unbending, and formal, he was the epitome of Victorian stability and solidity. He was a stickler for form. He surprised a well-intentioned host in Washington by refusing to accept a dinner invitation unless advised where he would sit at the table; he declined an invitation from the Mayor of New York to be present at the dedication of Grant's monument until he learned that the President and members of the Cabinet were to be there; then he quickly solicited and accepted a renewed invitation.[13] Scrupulously avoiding publicity, even refusing to make public speeches, he held himself aloof from the crowd.

This eminently proper Britisher came to be very fond of the country in which he spent the last years of his life. When due to retire in 1900 he wrote Lord Salisbury that " my ten years of service here have been full of interest & my relations with the people, officially & socially, have been most agreeable even in the dark days." [14] " The dearest political wish of my heart," he told Hay, is " the lasting fraternity of our respective countries." [15] It was to the credit of Americans that they could appreciate the solid worth and good sense of this upright old Englishman who refused to make any concessions to the more egalitarian society in which he found himself. He was respected rather than popular. But when he died at his post on May 24, 1902, a colleague at the embassy noted that " All sections of the American Press have in a remarkable manner united in testifying to the real affection and the universal esteem in which Lord Pauncefote was held in this country and to the value of his services to the United States as well as to his own country." [16] Secretary Hay and President Roosevelt called at the embassy, flags on the White House and other government buildings were put at half mast,

[13] F. O. 115, 1070, Pauncefote to Sherman, April 3, 1897; New York *Evening Post*, May 24, 1902.

[14] Salisbury papers, January 19, 1900. His retirement was postponed.

[15] Hay papers, June 25, 1900.

[16] F. O. 5, 2486, Raikes to Lansdowne, May 27, 1902; see an editorial in the *New York Tribune*, May 25, 1902.

and Pauncefote's body was carried to Great Britain on the U. S. S. *Brooklyn*.[17]

When John Hay became Secretary of State in September, 1898, the Canadian questions had just gone before the Joint High Commission at Quebec, F. W. Holls had just discussed America's canal aspirations with Arthur Balfour, and the Spanish War armistice had just been declared. Hay was of course resolved to carry through to a successful conclusion the negotiations thus launched. With discussion of the Canadian issues under way, the immediate need was to modify the Clayton-Bulwer treaty. The Secretary and Sir Julian fully appreciated the urgency of taking precautions against an American flare-up over that awkward treaty. Accordingly Hay asked Pauncefote, who had represented Great Britain at the Suez Canal conference in Paris in 1885 and who was a leading authority on questions of international law relating to canals, to draw up unofficially a convention omitting objectionable features of the Clayton-Bulwer treaty. Pauncefote was agreeable; without informing his government until almost three years later he quickly prepared a draft convention which, with a few minor non-substantive changes, Hay accepted.[18] It was this Pauncefote draft, with Hay's slight alterations, that the two governments had before them at the beginning of 1899 and that, as shall appear, they signed early the following year. Had the senators known, when they debated its ratification in 1900, that it had been composed in all essentials by the British ambassador, they doubtless would have scrutinized it even more closely than they did.

Thus when President McKinley delivered his annual message to Congress on December 5, 1898, both the British government in London through Holls, and the British ambassador in Washington [19] had received ample notice of America's canal intentions.

[17] F. O. 5, 2486, Raikes to Lansdowne, May 24 and June 18, 1902; F. O. 5, 2484, July 29, 1902.

[18] F. O. 55, 406, Pauncefote to Lansdowne, April 11, 1901.

[19] It is not certain that Hay asked Pauncefote to prepare a draft before McKinley's message was delivered but Pauncefote implied that Hay so requested soon after taking office as Secretary of State in September, 1898 (F. O. 55, 406, Pauncefote to Lansdowne, April 11, 1901).

The President's statement could have been no surprise to them, though its blunt wording may have been. The key sentences were the following:

All these circumstances suggest the urgency of some definite action by the Congress at this session if the labors of the past are to be utilized and the linking of the Atlantic and Pacific oceans by a practical waterway is to be realized. That the construction of such a maritime highway is now more than ever indispensable to that intimate and ready intercommunication between our eastern and western seaboards demanded by the annexation of the Hawaiian Islands and the prospective expansion of our influence and commerce in the Pacific, and that our national policy now more imperatively than ever calls for its control by this Government, are propositions which I doubt not the Congress will duly appreciate and wisely act upon.[20]

McKinley's failure to mention that his recommendations ran squarely against the Clayton-Bulwer treaty led to a little flurry of indignation in the British press. Nobody reading the message, the *Daily Chronicle* observed rather tartly for so pro-American a journal, " would imagine for a moment that the United States is bound by a solemn treaty with this country to refrain from securing or attempting to secure any such exclusive control over the . . . Canal as is here declared by the President . . . to be indispensable." [21] But concern was short-lived. Government officials in Britain, if not the press, well understood how to interpret McKinley's words. Assured " most emphatically " by Hay that the country would not ignore the Clayton-Bulwer treaty,[22] Pauncefote told Salisbury that " the attitude of the

[20] *Foreign Relations of the United States, 1898*, pp. lxxi-lxxii.

[21] *Daily Chronicle*, December 6, 1898. Many other papers were in general agreement; but the *Morning Post*, December 6, 1898, recalling Bismarck's dictum that when a country has made a treaty contrary to national interests it cannot observe it indefinitely, said: " That is the American attitude towards the Treaty of 1850. It seems to us quite intelligible." See also *Literary Digest*, vol. 18 (January 7, 1899) , p. 22.

[22] F. O. 115, 1080, Pauncefote to Salisbury, December 8, 1898.

President at present is quite satisfactory—more so than the language of his Message."[23]

As for Americans, the tide of friendly sentiment toward Britain was still running strong. "The British Lion's tail has had a long respite & indeed the alliance sentiment is as fervid as ever . . . ," Pauncefote wrote a few days after the controversial message. He added that although he favored letting the United States build the canal under proper conditions, he doubted if Congress would pass the necessary legislation in view of the risks, enormous cost, and opposition of transcontinental railways.[24] Thus the general atmosphere in both countries was favorable to negotiations. Hay instructed Henry White to sound out the Prime Minister; and on December 21, 1898, Salisbury authorized Pauncefote to do what in fact he had already done, namely, confer with Hay about modifying the Clayton-Bulwer treaty; Salisbury revealed his own hesitation, however, by telling the ambassador not to hurry negotiations.[25]

By January 11, 1899, the two men had put the finishing touches on what may be termed the Pauncefote convention; it modified the Clayton-Bulwer treaty by allowing the United States to construct a Central American canal. But it at once became apparent that Washington and London were going to assume markedly different attitudes as regards the urgency of concluding the new treaty. This was only to be expected; for Americans were impatient to have their canal whereas the British were happy enough with the existing state of affairs. Soon after the presidential message, on January 21, 1899, a bill sponsored by Senator Morgan of Alabama providing for construction and control of a canal by the United States government and not citing the obligations of the Clayton-Bulwer treaty passed the Senate 48 to 6; a similar bill had been introduced in the House by Representative Hepburn the preceding December 12.[26] It was becoming

[23] Salisbury papers, Pauncefote to Salisbury, December 9, 1898.

[24] *Ibid.*

[25] State Department, Great Britain, Instructions, Hay to White, December 7, 1898; *ibid.*, Despatches, White to Hay, December 22, 1898. Salisbury papers, Pauncefote to Salisbury, December 23, 1898.

[26] *Congressional Record*, vol. 32, p. 133; see also *ibid.*, pp. 97-112, 320-321,

clear that an alarming number of Congressmen were prepared to trample roughshod over solemn national obligations unless the treaty should be quickly amended to suit them.

But the British showed no sign of haste. With the State Department prodding it to make up its mind, the Foreign Office proceeded at a leisurely pace, deliberately gathering opinions from other governmental departments as well as from the Dominion of Canada about the draft treaty. So far-reaching a project as an interoceanic canal required most careful consideration of a wide range of imperial interests. The government's caution was perhaps greater because of the hesitation of shipping and commercial interests which might have been expected to welcome a new waterway. The Chamber of Shipping of the United Kingdom urged the government " to maintain the terms of the Clayton-Bulwer treaty . . . unless and until satisfactory guarantees be obtained from the Government of the United States providing for the absolute neutrality of the proposed . . . Canal, and also securing that no preferential rates shall be granted to the vessels of any one nation over those of any other nation." [27] The Board of Trade, too, though approving the draft in general, considered that " the Maritime Powers chiefly interested in a canal of this kind should, so far as possible, have some say as regards dues." [28] Furthermore, the Military Intelligence Division had just submitted a report recommending a staggering list of conditions for meeting American wishes: conclusion of an arbitration treaty, formal American acceptance of the open door policy, settlement of Canadian and other outstanding questions, special consideration for West Indian commercial problems, provision of facilities for Canada on the Alaska coast, and readjustment of the boundary in the San Juan Straits between Vancouver Island and the

356, 674, 887-911, 2605, for similar bills and related matter. See *ibid.*, vol. 31, pp. 4923-4924, for a resolution introduced by Morgan as early as May 16, 1898.

[27] F. O. 55, 392, to Salisbury, January 11, 1899.

[28] *Ibid.*, letter to Foreign Office, February 2, 1899; for the letter see Appendix 2.

mainland.[29] Considered advice of the Military Intelligence Division could not be taken lightly, but if Great Britain was to insist upon even one of these conditions, protracted negotiations loomed ahead, with success doubtful.

In transmitting the convention to London, Pauncefote warned that Hay had asked for a reply " at the earliest date, and, if possible, by telegram "; [30] later he cautioned that " Public feeling has been so aroused throughout the country in favour of the construction of the canal *by the nation* that if the [Morgan] Canal Bill passes, the project will be carried out at whatever risk & cost & in defiance of the Clayton Bulwer Treaty." [31] But Salisbury, never a man to be rushed into an important decision, refused to be intimidated; instead of hastening to accept the convention, he ordered still further consultation with Canada.[32]

This deliberate bringing into the picture of the perhaps overly sensitive Dominion had the effect, as it turned out, of throwing discussions wide open and deferring a conclusion for nearly three years. Canada felt entitled to full consideration because, quite apart from the fact that her commerce as well as American commerce, would be affected by a canal, the canal negotiations had a direct bearing on the other negotiations then occupying her. In early 1899 prospects of the Joint High Commission were far from bright. The United States was persisting in an attitude unacceptable to Sir Wilfrid Laurier and his colleagues. Should the mother country give way in Central America, the Dominion would have little or no chance of gaining her objectives with respect to the Alaska boundary, fur seals, fisheries, and reciprocity. Fully realizing this, the Privy Council in Ottawa cautioned Joseph Chamberlain to insist upon referring the boundary question to arbitration " on terms of Venezuelan reference, before Her Majesty's Government agree to the modification of the

---

[29] *Ibid.*, memorandum by Sir John Ardagh, December 9, 1898. See Appendix 3 for the memorandum.

[30] *Ibid.*, Pauncefote to Salisbury, January 12, 1899.

[31] Salisbury papers, Pauncefote to Salisbury, February 7, 1899.

[32] F. O. 55, 392, minute by Salisbury on Pauncefote to Salisbury, January 12, 1899.

Clayton-Bulwer treaty, and also that the injury done to Canadian trade with Porto Rico by American coasting laws should be urged while that Treaty is being considered." [33] This position, to which Canada stubbornly adhered until driven by British pressure several months later to abandon it,[34] proved an insuperable barrier to the quick action the United States wanted.

Thus when Henry White called on Lord Salisbury at the Foreign Office on January 26, 1899, to urge prompt acceptance of the new treaty, the Prime Minister made the pointed rejoinder that he " could not help connecting the precarious prospects and slowness of the negotiations which were being conducted by Lord Herschell with this proposed rapidity of decision," and that he did not believe it politically possible for Great Britain to give way completely on one set of issues unless she got far more than then appeared likely on the other.[35] He promised, however, to submit the whole matter to the Cabinet. When he did so, on February 1, 1899, his colleagues supported him. Since a canal would double the strength of the United States navy, so they agreed, Great Britain could not permit construction unless outstanding issues dangerous to peace were first resolved. Specifically, if the United States (and here the Cabinet followed the recommendations of the Canadian Privy Council) would give suitable assurances as to navigation laws applicable to Puerto Rico, Cuba, and the Philippines, and if it would come to terms on the Alaska boundary, Britain could afford to view more favorably the modification or even the termination of the Clayton-Bulwer treaty.[36]

Although considerably more moderate than the recommendations of the Intelligence Division, these conditions were still too harsh for American acceptance. Notified of the Cabinet's de-

[33] F. O. 5, 2416, Minto to Chamberlain, telegram received April 10, 1899.

[34] See p. 192.

[35] F. O. 55, 392, Salisbury to Pauncefote, January 26, 1899. See also State Department, Great Britain, Despatches, White to Hay, January 26, 1899; A. Nevins, *Henry White, Thirty Years of American Diplomacy* (New York and London, 1930), p. 147, citing a remark by Joseph Chamberlain to somewhat the same effect.

[36] F. O. 55, 392, Salisbury to Pauncefote, February 2, 1899.

cision, Ambassador Pauncefote telegraphed pessimistically: "It is all they [the McKinley administration] can do to maintain 'general principle' [of the Clayton-Bulwer treaty for the neutrality of a Central American canal] against the extremists who would vehemently oppose any reciprocal concession appearing on treaty. Any such concession could be obtained if at all separately in recognition of our friendly policy." [37] The extremists, in other words, and they were not a negligible quantity, were taking the position that it was absurd for Britain to demand payment for permitting the United States to build a canal at its own expense that would enrich Britain herself and the whole world.

Meanwhile negotiations before the Joint High Commission had been going from bad to worse. By the date of the Cabinet's meeting on the Pauncefote draft, failure seemed imminent. In what was probably a last-minute attempt to save the commission, together with the canal negotiations, Salisbury summoned Henry White to the Foreign Office. "I saw Mr. White to-day," he wrote Pauncefote on February 15, 1899,

> and informed him that Lord Herschell had intimated his fear that it might be necessary to break off the negotiations of which he had hitherto had charge. The United States' Government declined to adopt his views with respect to the Alaska boundary, and, which was more serious, declined even to refer the proposals he made to arbitration. If they adhered to this policy, he did not see that it was possible that any agreement could be arrived at. I told him that this telegram from Lord Herschell had been laid before the Cabinet, and had received their unanimous assent. I further said that under those circumstances I did not see how we could sign any treaty with respect to the Clayton-Bulwer arrangement, as the opinion of this country would scarcely support us in making a concession which would be wholly to the benefit of the United States at a time when they appeared to be so little inclined to come to a satisfactory settlement in regard to the Alaska frontier.[38]

[37] F. O. 5, 2400, Pauncefote to Foreign Office, February 6, 1899.

[38] F. O. 55, 392, Salisbury to Pauncefote, February 15, 1899. See *ibid.*, Colonial Office to Foreign Office, April 17, 1899: "Mr. Chamberlain is strongly of opinion that until the United States Government are prepared

We have seen that Lord Herschell's fears were justified: the Joint High Commission did break up, holding its final meeting on February 20, 1899. With negotiations on Canadian questions at a standstill Britain stood fast in her resolve not to yield on the canal treaty.

In the final analysis the Alaska boundary was the crucial factor. As has been noted, the Dominion would not settle any issue considered by the Joint High Commission unless the United States would agree on the controversial boundary, and she now cast her veto against further discussion of canal matters as long as those issues remained unresolved. A canal settlement depended on a Canadian settlement, which in turn depended on a boundary settlement; and all Anglo-American negotiations ground to full stop against the formidable obstacle raised by the perplexing Alaskan question. Although not rejecting Pauncefote's draft the Foreign Office simply left it in the files unsigned. Yet it was unwilling to slam the door irrevocably against further discussion. Two days after the Prime Minister's interview with White calling off negotiations Francis Villiers, Assistant Under-Secretary of State in the Foreign Office, told the American " that we shall give way in any case on that subject (i. e., modification of the Clayton-Bulwer treaty), but if the Washington [Joint High] Commission fails we must adhere to diplomatic forms and allow a certain time . . . before doing so." [89] There was evidently a limit to the distance the government would go in currying favor with Canada, if that meant alienating American goodwill.

In August, 1898, the United States and Great Britain, taking advantage of their dramatically improved relations, embarked upon a comprehensive discussion of issues dividing them. Six months later, in February, 1899, the Joint High Commission adjourned without having reached final agreement on a single point, and at the same time the new canal treaty was relegated

to agree to a reasonable arrangement for settling the Alaska Boundary question, Her Majesty's Government should defer proceeding with the discussion of the proposed modification of the Clayton-Bulwer treaty."

[89] White papers, White to Hay, February 17, 1899.

to a quiescence barely distinguishable from death. The high hopes of August, 1898, had been replaced by the dismal failure of February, 1899.

It might well be thought that the breakdown would have given a severe, perhaps fatal, shock to the still budding British-American friendship. Yet it seems to have had little or no such effect. The new friendship had not waned, the London *Times* observed in April, finding its judgment confirmed in " the truly remarkable demonstration of American as of English feeling during those sad days when Mr. [Rudyard] Kipling's life was in danger." [40] The truth is that both the American government and the American people blamed not Great Britain but the Dominion of Canada, which thus performed the useful function of absorbing wrath that otherwise might have hurtled back and forth across the Atlantic.[41] As for the British, the failure of early 1899 did not come home to them directly enough to cause resentment. No one in Britain could work up anger over a delay in building a canal of main advantage to another country; and although governmental leaders saw the need to settle the more dangerous of the Canadian controversies, the average Englishman viewed such matters as the Alaska boundary and Bering Sea seals with the utmost detachment.

The collapse of negotiations did not reflect nor did it portend a deterioration in Anglo-American relations. It resulted in part from the bad luck of Lord Herschell's death and in part from attempting to accomplish far too much far too quickly. Overoptimism, not hostility, caused the collapse. The two countries had hoped to take advantage of better trans-Atlantic feeling in order to rush through a settlement before American public opinion cooled off and before (with respect to the Clayton-Bulwer treaty) Congress got out of hand. But they had undertaken more than they could handle. The truth of the matter is that the diplomats were dealing with issues not only extremely

[40] April 6, 1899.

[41] In that negative sense Canada already served as a coupling pin, as she was later called, in Anglo-American relations; see S. F. Bemis, *A Diplomatic History of the United States* (New York, 1955) , ch. XL.

complicated in themselves but affecting solidly entrenched interests far too powerful to be rushed in short order into a novel situation detrimental and in some instances ruinous to themselves. Human beings and situations were too intractable for all-out diplomacy.

Once the excessive optimism of 1898 had ended, the United States and Great Britain, now better informed as to the complex nature of the issues dividing them, turned to a more modest, step-by-step procedure. For the remainder of 1899, in fact, the natural let-down following the disillusion of February, 1899, made almost hopeless further efforts to reach a definitive settlement of the Canadian and Central American questions. Instead of a frontal attack on all outstanding issues the two countries therefore turned their energies toward creating a measure of stability in the area of greatest peril—along the disputed Alaska boundary. Throughout that year, moreover, both countries became involved in controversies with third countries. The fact that more often than not they found themselves acting together reflected a basic similarity of national interests that helped prepare the way for renewed negotiations on their common problems. In time these brought success.

CHAPTER 6

Modus Vivendi

WHEN NEWS reached Canada of the Joint High Commission's breakdown in February, 1899, the press broke forth in angry abuse of the United States. Newspapers of all opinions implored the government to stand up to the aggressive Yankees; and some urged it to impose duties on natural products essential to major American industries. It was particularly through their enormous timber reserves that many Canadians saw a means of bringing Americans to terms. "Cotton . . . was once called king, but King Cotton is a lesser potentate than King Timber must soon become"; such, the London *Times* reported, was the belief in the Dominion.[1] At a big meeting in Toronto in February Sir Charles Tupper, always an outspoken nationalist, urged retaliation: if the United States imposed harsh lumber, mining, and labor regulations upon Canadian subjects and unfair navigation laws upon Canadian ships, let Canada do likewise; there was a limit to human endurance, he asserted, and the only way to get justice from the United States was to treat it roughly;[2] its attitude regarding Alaska was, he proclaimed later, "the most unreasonable . . . that it was possible for any government to assume on a question of that kind."[3]

Indignation and desire for retaliation were not confined to one side of the border, however. Michigan lessees of Ontario

[1] March 17, 1899.
[2] *The Times*, February 24, 1899.
[3] Canada, *Debates of the House of Commons*, 1899, vol. 3, pp. 8153-8154, July 22, 1899.

timber lands, already disappointed by the Joint High Commission's failure to help them, were outraged over a recent ruling by the Ontario Attorney General postponing for at least two years a decision as to the legality of the provincial law banning exports of manufactured logs; angrily they asked the United States government to prohibit imports of lumber from the entire Dominion.[4] Senator McMillan of Michigan, a state already at odds with Canada over lumber matters, supported their demands.[5]

More dangerous both immediately and in the long run were conditions among prospectors in the gold fields. Although peace reigned in the Yukon territory, disturbing rumors were rife in the Lynn Canal area and in another mining center, the Atlin gold fields of British Columbia, east of Skagway. Aggrieved over what they interpreted as the provincial government's deliberate failure to record their claims, American miners in the Atlin country petitioned President McKinley for help. ". . . the business of the country has been prostrated, and the property of the citizens of the United States has become almost valueless; all improvements in Atlin City and other places have been suspended; and large numbers of people are leaving the country. . . ."[6] Further British Columbian legislation excluding aliens from the Atlin mines served notice on an estimated 10,000 Americans planning to go to the district in 1899 to change their minds.[7]

In another place, too, lay cause for concern. Along Porcupine creek near the Dalton Trail above Pyramid Harbor, where the boundary was entirely undefined, "great excitement" held sway among approximately 2,500 Americans, some of them refugees from the Atlin, who were searching for gold in rivalry with

[4] *The Times*, May 18, 1899.

[5] *Ibid.*, May 31, 1899.

[6] F. O. 5, 2416, J. C. Miller et al to McKinley, February 10, 1899. Joseph Chamberlain wrote Lord Minto, Governor-General of Canada, that he hoped that Ottawa would persuade British Columbia to amend its laws (*ibid.*, Chamberlain to Minto, April 27, 1899). See also State Department, Great Britain, Notes, Tower to Hay, May 8, 1899.

[7] *The Times*, February 27, 1899.

Canadians.[8] Press rumors of armed clashes, and alarmist reports from the governor of Alaska worried the British and United States governments; [9] and an American decision—abandoned after protest from London—to establish a military post at Pyramid Harbor added to the confusion.[10]

Washington and London of course recognized the danger latent in the nebulous boundary. Secretary Hay described President McKinley as " so anxious for a settlement " that he would agree to arbitrate "even at the risk of possible objection from Congress "; and he urged Britain to persuade British Columbia to suspend the discriminatory laws meanwhile.[11] Ottawa, too, was concerned. Laurier feared " dangerous friction " [12] in the gold districts; but since the slightest concession to the United States could be expected to inflame that formidable figure, Sir Charles Tupper, the government's freedom of maneuver was severely cramped. Nevertheless it was willing enough to arbitrate provided the controversy was submitted to an odd-numbered tribunal and on numerous occasions it urged the relevance to Alaska of the treaty of February 2, 1897, under which the protracted Venezuelan boundary dispute was soon to be concluded. As for the recent legislation in Ontario and British Columbia, although Laurier and his colleagues disapproved of it they could not help but see in it a useful bargaining weapon. Together with the

[8] State Department, Great Britain, Despatches, Hay to Choate, June 27, 1899.

[9] F. O. 5, 2416, Pauncefote to Salisbury, March 21, 1899; Pauncefote to Foreign Office, April 23, 1899. A telegram from the Governor-General of Canada minimized the incidents, however (*ibid.*, Minto to Colonial Office, April 25, 1899).

[10] Regarding the affair see *ibid.*, Tower to Salisbury, May 5, 1899, and Foreign Office to Tower, May 11, 1899; State Department, Great Britain, Notes, Tower to Hay, May 12, 1899; F. O. 5, 2416, Tower to Salisbury, May 17, 1899.

[11] F. O. 5, 2416, Pauncefote to Foreign Office, April 23, 1899; Tower to Salisbury, May 4, 1899.

[12] *Ibid.*, Minto to Chamberlain, May 5, 1899. But Salisbury told Choate, July 12, 1899, that he was not worried about Alaska at the moment (State Department, Miscellaneous Archives, Alaskan Boundary, 1899-1903, Choate to Hay, July 15, 1899).

Clayton-Bulwer treaty—if Britain would only proceed slowly in modifying it—this legislation might furnish the means of winning concessions regarding the coasting laws and Alaska; and Sir Wilfred let it be known in London that it would disappear overnight once the United States yielded on the boundary question.[13]

Thus an awkward and potentially dangerous state of affairs confronted Great Britain and the United States in the spring of 1899. Their high hopes of an inclusive settlement had come to grief with the collapse of the Joint High Commission and the canal negotiations; and the collapse itself, together with tension in the Atlin and Porcupine districts, had given rise to an uneasy situation that could have deteriorated rapidly. Forced to abandon the spectacular, all-out, and perhaps ill-advised methods of the Joint High Commission, they now proceeded by means of the routine, humdrum, but on the whole more trustworthy methods of normal diplomacy to attack the crucial problem of the Alaska boundary along two lines: one looking to a definitive settlement, as had the Joint High Commission; the other—undertaken in case no such settlement could be made—looking simply to a *modus vivendi*. Recourse to a *modus vivendi* had already been had in recent years in the fisheries and sealing disputes, in both instances with success. Now in early 1899, as reports came of trouble in the Atlin district and clashes along the Porcupine, John Hay and Sir Julian Pauncefote (until the latter's departure for the Hague conference on armaments in the spring of 1899) and then Hay and Reginald Tower, chargé d'affaires at the British embassy, set themselves to the laborious task of working out a provisional line that, while reserving their countries' full rights as to the boundary's final course, would provide sufficient stability to tide things over in the disputed areas for the time being.

Before giving an account of the *modus* mention should be made of the concurrent negotiations for a definitive demarcation of the line; because although they did not succeed they marked another step on the way to eventual settlement in 1903

[13] F. O. 5, 2416, Minto to Pauncefote, April 25, 1899; Tower to Salisbury, April 28, 1899.

and they throw light on attitudes taken in Washington, London, and Ottawa toward this key boundary issue. When Sir Julian went to London in May, 1899, en route to The Hague he took along "something like an understanding" at which he and Hay had arrived; [14] and there he continued negotiations with Ambassador Joseph Choate, a prominent New York lawyer who had succeeded Hay at the embassy and who was to prove one of the most successful representatives in Britain the United States has ever had. By the middle of May the two men had completed a plan for settling the dispute once and for all, a plan that Choate thought "practicable and fair" [15] and that gave promise of accomplishing the unprecedented feat of meeting Canada's demand for an odd-numbered tribunal while allaying American fears for Dyea and Skagway. Based on the essential features of the Venezuelan treaty (an odd-numbered tribunal, and settled areas confirmed to the occupying country), it provided for arbitration of the whole boundary by seven jurists, with Dyea and Skagway (as the only settled areas involved) specifically reserved to the United States.[16]

At first, adoption of this ingenious scheme seemed likely. It was "undoubtedly approved by Lord Salisbury" and officials in Washington were reported to have "made up their minds" to accept it.[17] But Pauncefote and Choate had overlooked a decisive factor: Canadian party politics. The Laurier government would have none of the proposal, not because it was intrinsically unacceptable but because it opened the way for Tupper and the Conservatives to accuse the Liberals of handing over Dyea and Skagway without an equivalent concession.[18] "No more monstrous, no more insulting proposition could be made"—so

[14] State Department, Great Britain, Notes, unsigned memorandum dated May 18, 1899.

[15] State Department, Great Britain, Despatches, Choate to Hay, May 12, 1899.

[16] *Ibid.*; F. O. 5, 2416, Chamberlain to Minto, May 12, 1899.

[17] State Department, Great Britain, Despatches, Choate to Hay, May 19, 1899; Choate papers, Choate to Pauncefote, May 20, 1899; F. O. 5, 2416, Hay to Tower, May 19, 1899.

[18] F. O. 5, 2416, memorandum by Pauncefote, June 5, 1899.

thundered Sir Charles. " The result of many years' close acquaintance with British statesmen had impressed him forcibly with
their great unwillingness to allow any circumstance whatever
even to threaten collision with the United States. . . . If England
had treated France [in the Fashoda affair] as she was treating
the United States to-day the Nile would not now have been in the
possession of Great Britain." [19] With such denunciations reverberating through Parliament and spreading out through the
length and breadth of the land, statements emanating from an
experienced leader with a wide following, it is no wonder that
the Liberals found it embarrassing to admit publicly a known
fact: that Dyea and Skagway would never be Canadian. " It only
shows how difficult it is to satisfy Politicians whose tenure of
office is at stake," Pauncefote wrote in disgust to Choate.[20]

For these reasons Canada would not accept the proposal unless
she, too, were guaranteed something—and she named Pyramid
Harbor.[21] The United States instantly repudiated this condition;
its insistence on Dyea and Skagway had been based, Choate
pointed out indignantly, on the " obvious and impregnable
ground " (if the Venezuelan agreement was the model) that they
had been established and settled by Americans, without protest;
Pyramid Harbor, on the other hand, was an uninhabited landing
place that by no stretch of the imagination could be brought
under Venezuelan terms.[22] Thus a deadlock had been reached.
No American government would agree to an arbitration it could
lose (that is, to an odd-numbered board) unless assured as a

---

[19] *The Times*, July 24, 1899. In a speech in the Canadian House of Commons a few months earlier Sir Charles had devoted no less than four hours
to berating the Liberals' supineness toward the United States; see *ibid.*,
March 22, 1899; Canada, *Debates of the House of Commons*, 1899, vol. 1,
p. 40 ff., March 20, 1899.

[20] State Department, Great Britain, Despatches, May 22, 1899. Later Pauncefote submitted to the Foreign Office a draft article which he thought would
get around Laurier's objection by in effect guaranteeing Dyea and Skagway
to the United States without naming them (F. O. 5, 2416, memorandum by
Pauncefote, June 5, 1899). But nothing came of this clever suggestion.

[21] F. O. 5, 2416, Minto to Chamberlain, May 14, 1899.

[22] State Department, Great Britain, Despatches, Choate to Salisbury, May
19, 1899.

minimum of Dyea and Skagway; the Laurier government, although fully aware that by Venezuelan terms, whose applicability to Alaska it had been urging, it could never get Dyea and Skagway, would not risk political defeat by so stating publicly; [23] and the British, even if most dubious about Canada's case,[24] felt obliged to back her because they dared not strengthen the deep-rooted belief in British proneness to sacrifice the Dominion whenever the United States lifted an admonitory finger. And so to Hay's refusal to put Pyramid Harbor, devoid of inhabitants, on a par with settled towns like Dyea and Skagway, Lord Salisbury simply replied: ". . . Canada is, and always has been perfectly willing to submit the whole question to arbitration unconditionally. . . ."[25] This of course was correct, but it left the dispute as far up in the air as ever.

One other effort to determine the boundary was made prior to conclusion of the *modus vivendi*. By agreement with Portugal Great Britain held a perpetual lease at the Chinde mouth of the Zambesi river in Mozambique. Could not this arrangement be adapted to the somewhat similar case of Alaska? Could not

[23] *Ibid.*, Pauncefote to Choate, May 22, 1899.

[24] There is plenty of evidence to show that British officials thought Canada's claim to Dyea and Skagway very weak. See for example the following minute by John Anderson of the Colonial Office, on which Joseph Chamberlain wrote, "I agree.": "Their [Canadian] argument as to their not having protested against the [American] occupation & settlement of Dyea & Skagway is idle. It is quite possible that the occupation began before they knew or could have known of it, but they knew of it for certain more than two years ago, and yet until the Confce met the Americans were not told officially that their claim was questioned. The real reason why they did not protest was, I believe, that at the time their technical advisers considered that there was no question that the whole of the Lynn Canal was in U. S. territory. That was told me in confidence by Mr. Klotz of the [Canadian] Dept. of the Interior . . ." (C. O. 42, 868, minute by Anderson, May 15, 1899). See also: F. O. 5, 2416, Colonial Office draft to Minto, undated but about May 28, 1899; *ibid.*, memorandum by Pauncefote, June 5, 1899; *ibid.*, Chamberlain to Minto, June 16, 1899; State Department, Great Britain, Despatches, Choate to Hay, June 16, 1899; F. O. 5, 2415, memorandum by Villiers, July 21, 1899; *ibid.*, Chamberlain to Minto, July 21, 1899; *ibid.*, memorandum by Villiers, August 1, 1899.

[25] State Department, Great Britain, Notes, Tower to Hay, June 11, 1899.

Canada be persuaded to abandon the Lynn Canal to the United States if she were awarded a lease of half a square mile on the canal, with the liberty to build a railway from there to the Yukon territory? Such was the proposition advanced by Great Britain in July, 1899, with the approval of Canada's Minister of Public Works, J. I. Tarte, who happened to be in London.[26] Once again, however, a plausible suggestion came to grief against a Canadian condition, a condition which the Foreign Office itself admitted was an impossible one.[27] Canada would not accept unless the proposed lease (unlike the Chinde lease, which did not convey jurisdiction) included a harbor under her jurisdiction.[28] This of course raised the same difficulty as to navigation laws that the Joint High Commission had found insuperable. A port removed from American control would offer advantages to Canadian ships over American ships in the carrying trade against which the west coast shipping interests, whose power had already been demonstrated, would be certain to throw their weight.

British officials were exasperated with the Dominion's attitude, which they believed to be completely unrealistic. They understood, as Canadians presumably did not, that it could only result in Canada getting nothing at all. In a minute approved by Joseph Chamberlain, John Anderson, the Colonial Office official in charge of Canadian relations, had just observed:

> The Canadians do not appear to realize how much a prolongation of the existing state of things is in favour of the U. S. as the party in possession.
>
> The U. S. except for the sake of getting other matters out of the way have no reason to be dissatisfied with the existing state of things, and in regard to the other questions, none of them really pinch them seriously.
>
> Behring Sea, lumber, Atlantic Fisheries, miners' rights in the Atlin district, are all questions that do not seriously concern any but a small fraction of the people of the U. S. . . .

[26] F. O. 5, 2415, Salisbury to Tower, July 12, 1899; Salisbury to Choate, July 18, 1899.

[27] *Ibid.*, memorandum by Villiers, July 21, 1899.

[28] *Ibid.*, Minto to Chamberlain, July 19, 1899.

The only question that they do attach great and immediate importance to is probably the amendment of the Clayton Bulwer Treaty, and we can hardly postpone a settlement of that indefinitely in order to gain concessions for Canada in Alaska, which but for their own supineness they would not have required.[29]

Faced by the Dominion's rejection of a proposal directly sponsored by the Cabinet, the Colonial Office and the Foreign Office together concocted a carefully considered reply addressed to Lord Minto, Aberdeen's successor as Governor-General; it is of great importance as showing the hostility of the highest British officials including the Prime Minister, who initialed it, to Canada's main position:

We desire to impress upon your [Minto's] Ministers that whatever arguments may be based on letter of Treaty of 1825, *careful examination of United States case for possession of shores of Canal based on continuous uninterrupted jurisdiction since date of Treaty, and admissions of Hudson [sic] Bay Company, Imperial and Dominion Governments, shews that it is unassailable.*

Delay in settlement highly prejudicial to Canadian interests, and we cannot but think that your Ministers will not wish to sacrifice only chance of obtaining an all British route to Yukon, and will acquiesce in action of Her Majesty's Government which was only taken after discussion with Mr. Tarte in full belief that it would be acceptable to Dominion Government.[30]

Even this rebuff did not shake the Canadians from their reckless disregard of realities. Courageously perhaps, but foolishly certainly, they adhered to their position: no lease without jurisdiction.[31]

Thus, caught up in an inextricable tangle of various pressures —economic interests in the state of Washington, the self-righteous

[29] C. O. 42, 868, May 15, 1899.
[30] F. O. 5, 2415, Chamberlain to Minto, July 21, 1899; italics inserted.
[31] *Ibid.*, Minto to Chamberlain, July 25, 1899. In response to a British suggestion, Canada announced that a special envoy was going to London to try to concert procedures. Sir Louis Davies, Minister of Marine and Fisheries, was the person selected.

American refusal to jeopardise Dyea and Skagway, Canadian politics, and Britain's reluctance to push her sensitive colony too hard—ordinary methods of diplomacy had made no more headway toward a final demarcation of the Alaska boundary than had the more open and ambitious procedures of the Joint High Commission. By July, 1899, the futility of seeking an early demarcation, and the wise foresight of Hay and Pauncefote in insuring against such a contingency by simultaneous negotiations for a *modus vivendi*, had become patent. On March 20, 1899, exactly a month after the Joint High Commission disbanded, the Secretary of State had proposed to Pauncefote a temporary boundary acceptable to the United States: a line drawn " at the watershed on the summit of White and Chilkoot passes, and at a point 30 marine miles from Pyramid Harbor on the Chilkat Pass and otherwise known as the Dalton Trail. . . ." [32]

His suggestion as to the first two passes proved quickly acceptable, but a protracted argument ensued with regard to the boundary near the Dalton Trail. The United States did not insist on a line just thirty marine miles from Pyramid Harbor but it did insist on full consideration for the two or three thousand American miners around Porcupine creek; and however great the good will of Hay, Pauncefote, and Tower its insistence was not easily reconciled with equally stubborn Canadian demands. Britain felt obliged to refer every detail of the discussions to Canada—a frustrating and time-consuming process; and the McKinley administration had to step warily lest it alienate voters in the Far West. On the Pacific coast the shipping, trading, and lumber interests, whose close ties with Alaska and the Canadian northwest had been so manifest during the sessions of the Joint High Commission, were naturally concerned about the new diplomatic activities of 1899. Learning of Hay's negotiations the Seattle chamber of commerce wrote to the Secretary of State in some perturbation:

> The people of the North Pacific Coast, and particularly those of Washington and Alaska, are much exercised over the

[32] *Foreign Relations of the United States, 1899*, pp. 321-322; F. O. 5, 2416, Hay to Pauncefote, March 20, 1899.

proposed modus vivendi, and are apprehensive of personal
and national loss in the deal said to be contemplated. The
latest trouble is that in which the American miners in the
Porcupine district are involved. . . . Seeing that it was a valuable and desirable country, the Canadians have fixed their
attention upon it, and, as in other parts of the North Pacific
coast are determined to acquire it, if possible. They have set
up a claim to it, have advanced their lines, and are now proposing through the modus vivendi to secure it.

Against such claim and against such acquisition by Canada
our people unitedly and strongly protest. . . . There is not an
inch of Alaska . . . that our country can afford to part with,
and the Administration that does part with any portion of it
will be condemned in positive terms forever.[33]

It would not be wise for a business administration a year before
a presidential election to disregard this plainly worded statement;
nor would it be wise, even though Americans in the Lynn Canal
area did not vote, to be heedless of the strong feelings displayed
by the Skagway chamber of commerce in protesting " against
a settlement of the boundary dispute . . . upon any such
terms. . . ." [34]
Nevertheless there is no evidence that Secretary Hay stiffened
his attitude because of such protests. On the contrary, when
negotiations threatened to bog down he retreated from his thirty-
mile line; he telegraphed Choate: " Some *modus vivendi* imperatively required. Suggest to Lord Salisbury as provisional
boundary, without prejudice, summit of White and Chilkoot
Passes, and on Dalton Trail a line passing north of Indian village
of Klukwan." [35] This was essentially the line of the *modus vivendi*
as finally concluded, but nearly five months of hard and occasionally acrimonious bargaining were required before its acceptance. For a time indeed, in July, just when negotiations for a

---

[33] State Department, Miscellaneous Letters, July 14, 1899. A committee of
the Seattle Chamber of Commerce visited Alaska in August, 1899; on its
return it issued a report stressing the importance of Alaska to the American
northwest (*The Seattle Post-Intelligencer*, September 10, 1899).

[34] C. C. Tansill, *Canadian-American Relations, 1875-1911* (New Haven,
1943), p. 208; the resolution was dated October 13, 1899.

[35] F. O. 5, 2416, May 27, 1899.

definitive settlement collapsed, negotiations for a *modus* likewise seemed on the verge of failure. Misinterpreting a point raised by Hay, Great Britain threatened, over hastily it would appear and doubtless in the absence of Lord Salisbury who, preoccupied by his wife's serious illness, could not give much attention to the Foreign Office,[36] to break off negotiations: " unless the Government of the United States are prepared to second the efforts of that of Her Majesty to find a ' via media,' it would appear to be impossible to make any further attempt to determine a provisional Boundary Line." [37] Fortunately the misunderstanding was cleared up; and from then on negotiations proceeded smoothly with eventual success never in serious doubt.

It is unnecessary to follow the subsequent bargaining. The *modus vivendi* became operative with an exchange of notes between Hay and Tower on October 20, 1899; it laid down provisional lines at the summits of the Chilkoot and White passes and at a point near the Dalton Trail about fifteen miles from tidewater.[38] Since most American miners in the Porcupine creek district were thereby brought under United States jurisdiction, the greatest danger of a clash was removed; and responsibilities of government were clearly defined in the three main disputed areas where American and Canadian miners were in juxtaposition. As far as the Alaska boundary was concerned, limited diplomacy had accomplished more than the Joint High Commission had been able to do. If a comprehensive settlement could not be attained, at least a partial temporary one could be; and the way of wisdom was obviously to accept a small alleviation, even if far short of the ideal.

Nevertheless the *modus* did not really satisfy anyone. Perhaps it was Great Britain that was most dissatisfied; and her determination to push ahead to a lasting agreement was considerably enhanced by two other occurrences of October, 1899: outbreak of the Boer War, which at once vastly increased the need for American friendship; and rendition of the arbitral award termi-

[36] Choate papers, Choate to Hay, July 15, 1899.
[37] State Department, Great Britain, Notes, Tower to Hay, July 29, 1899.
[38] *Foreign Relations, 1899*, pp. 328-331.

nating the Venezuelan boundary controversy, which raised hopes for a similar settlement regarding Alaska. Consequently, less than a week after concluding the *modus* London again implored Canada to come down to earth and agree to arbitrate on terms giving Dyea and Skagway to the United States.[39] Four years, however, were to pass before arbitration took place; and then, under conditions almost certainly less favorable than she could have had in 1899, the Dominion lost not only those two little towns but a good deal more besides.

No doubt the *modus* introduced a welcome measure of stability along the frontier and softened fears of clashes in a no-man's land, but it probably had little effect in offsetting the unfortunate impression created among the British, American, and Canadian peoples by the ostentatious breakdown of the Joint High Commission in February, 1899, and by the termination of the canal negotiations at the same time. The *modus*, after all, represented a rather dismal anti-climax to all the earlier hopes of a broad Anglo-American settlement; and in any case it was not the sort of agreement to attract much notice in the press. Far more noticeable, and therefore more effective in healing the wounds of February and restoring a popular conviction of essential harmony between Britain and America, were various other episodes occurring in 1899. These were not episodes pertaining to the dull details of a temporary boundary delineation but episodes suffused with the drama of international diplomacy and the magic of distant lands; and in them the United States and Great Britain, for the moment rid of petty Canadian matters, seemed to stand together once again as in Spanish War days against other, non-English-speaking powers.

[39] F. O. 5, 2417, Colonial Office to Foreign Office, October 25, 1899.

CHAPTER 7

"Partnership in Beneficence"

IN AUGUST, 1898, that eventful month for Anglo-American relations, the king of the remote Samoan islands, Malietoa Laupepa, died; and this occurrence far across the world gave rise to a train of developments during which, as four months previously when the war with Spain was about to commence, Great Britain and the United States gave every appearance of close collaboration.

Since 1889 the Samoan islands had been neutralized under a nominally independent native government but in fact ruled jointly by the United States, Great Britain, and Germany under a condominium established by the Berlin Act of that year.[1] Real authority was vested in five foreigners: the Chief Justice, who in 1898 was an American named Chambers; the President of the Municipal Council, a German named Raffel; and the consuls of the three powers, of whom the most notorious was the German, Rose. Although the condominium had preserved peace for several years, enough friction had developed among the occupying countries so that by the time of Malietoa's death consideration was being given to partitioning the islands. Germany in particular was dissatisfied, and hardly had the island monarch died when her Foreign Minister, Count von Bülow, instructed the ambassador at London, Count Hatzfeldt, to sound out Britain as to partition.

[1] For American relations with Samoa see G. H. Ryden, *The Foreign Policy of the United States in Relation to Samoa* (New Haven, 1933).

Further complicating the situation was a struggle over the Samoan succession. Following Malietoa's death a considerable body of chieftains in due conformity with local custom elected a certain Mataafa king; and they so proclaimed on November 12. Two days later another faction elected Malietoa's son, Malietoa Tanu. Thus there were two claimants to the throne, each with a powerful backing. It shortly became evident that disagreement among the natives extended to the foreigners in Samoa: Germans backed Mataafa, British and Americans Malietoa Tanu. The Berlin Act provided for a disputed election to be decided by the Samoan Supreme Court. Accordingly on the last day of 1898 Chief Justice Chambers named Malietoa Tanu the rightful monarch. Immediately civil war broke out between the two pretenders. Malietoa was defeated; with some of his followers and Chambers he took refuge on a British warship. The government thus disrupted, the three consuls on January 4, 1899, set up a provisional government dominated by Mataafa and Raffel. But the Chief Justice refused to recognize it. Raffel then closed the Supreme Court on the ground of Chambers's flight, only to have it forcibly reopened on January 7 by the British and American consuls and the commander of the British warship. A period of anarchy ensued during which the German consul, Rose, supported Mataafa, while the American and British consuls backed Malietoa.

These disturbing events aroused violent passions among natives and foreigners alike. Britons and Americans in Samoa were furious with the Germans, Rose and Raffel, whom they charged with abetting Mataafa in complete disregard of the Chief Justice. On the other hand, Germans feared a British-American plot to seize the islands. Repercussions of the chaotic situation spread far beyond the little archipelago, to Washington, London, and Berlin. " I have requested the American Ambassador here," Bülow informed the German ambassador at Washington, " to press for the early recall of Chambers, the Chief Justice, seeing that the statement . . . of this official who is shared by all three Governments, betrays that his aim is to drive Germany out of

Samoa. . . ." [2] The argument proceeded mainly between Great Britain and Germany, each of which suspected the other of maneuvering to oust it from the islands; the two English-speaking countries, on the other hand, sided together, with the natural result of still more resentment being aroused in Germany. As for the United States, it found itself in the fortunate position of being wooed by both its partners in the condominium and of having its continued occupation of Tutuila, one of the three main islands, seemingly beyond dispute.

Early in March the American Admiral Kautz arrived at Apia, the capital, located on Upolu, the principal island. He took vigorous steps to end the disorder. Declaring the provisional government deposed, he ordered American and British marines to land. In the process their ships bombarded points held by Mataafa, including parts of Apia. Besides destroying native property, the gunfire, probably that of the American ship, damaged the German consulate. Violent indignation surged up in Germany. ". . . the bombardment . . . would seem to give some colour to the suspicion that England and America were trying to override that [Berlin] Act and drive Germany out of Samoa," Bülow asserted.[3] Malietoa Tanu was now officially crowned. But his position was not secure; and on April 1, 1899, Easter Sunday, Mataafa defeated his army and ambushed a British-American force, killing several marines. Fighting continued to rage through April, with British and American warships aiding the new monarch. Obviously a dangerous situation existed which could not be allowed to prolong itself.

German public opinion, quick to take offense in matters touch-

[2] E. T. S. Dugdale, ed., *German Diplomatic Documents, 1871-1914* (4 vols., London, 1928-1931) , vol. 3, pp. 46-47, to Holleben, February 20, 1899.

[3] G. P. Gooch and H. Temperley, eds., *British Documents on the Origins of the War, 1898-1914* (11 vols., London, 1926-1938) , vol. 1, p.. 113, Lascelles to Salisbury, April 6, 1899. See also Dugdale, *German Diplomatic Documents*, vol. 3, p. 54, Hatzfeldt to Foreign Office, March 25, 1899; Hatzfeldt complained to Chamberlain that he could only conclude that " the American Admiral in Samoa had been instructed to carry out majority decisions, i. e. decisions on which the British and American Consuls [but not the German consul] were agreed."

ing Samoa, scene of the Fatherland's first colonial activities and graveyard of many a true patriot, was outraged at what it considered an intolerable plot to push Germany right into the South Seas. "The Emperor . . . ," reported the British ambassador at Berlin, Sir Frank Lascelles, "was greatly agitated by the news from Samoa, and was indignant that, in what seemed like a conflict between the German and United States authorities in Samoa, the English should have taken the part of the latter . . . . the news that the English have sided with the Americans against the Germans in Samoa will cause an outcry in the German press. . . ." [4]

Yet Germany did not blame the United States; it was the sinister hand of Great Britain in the person of the detested Lord Salisbury that she saw raised against her. "I can not escape the impression," Bülow told the Kaiser, "that in the recent events in Samoa, it was England who drove and America who was driven. It looks as if the British meant to use the Americans to push us out of Samoa." [5] The Kaiser agreed, going so far indeed as to accuse Great Britain of bribing the American press to attack Germany.[6] No doubt Germany had solid grounds for resentment over the damage to her consulate, but Britain, too, had cause for concern. Rose and Raffel had behaved stupidly, as Holstein, the important Foreign Office official, admitted; [7] and Lord Salisbury was justified in retorting stiffly: "an impression exists both in Samoa and England that Germany has been attempting to force America and England out of Samoa. . . ." [8] Thus each side was persuaded of the other's ill will. In Germany angry and protracted outbursts against Britain went to such lengths that

[4] Gooch and Temperley, British Documents, vol. 1, p. 112, Lascelles to Salisbury, March 31, 1899.

[5] Dugdale, German Diplomatic Documents, vol. 3, p. 56, Bülow to Foreign Office, April 1, 1899.

[6] Gooch and Temperley, British Documents, vol. 1, p. 118, Lascelles to Salisbury, May 26, 1899.

[7] Dugdale, German Diplomatic Documents, vol. 3, p. 45, Holstein to Hatzfeldt, January 20, 1899.

[8] Gooch and Temperley, British Documents, vol. 1, p. 115, Salisbury to Lascelles, April 4, 1899.

at one moment the Foreign Minister actually considered breaking off diplomatic relations.[9]

Fortunately good sense prevailed. The three countries agreed in mid-April to send a special commission to the distracted islands with full powers to enforce an armistice and to recommend basic changes in the government. The commission which reached Apia on May 13 had three members: Bartlett Tripp, an American lawyer and diplomat; C. N. E. Eliot, second secretary of the British embassy in Washington; and Speck von Sternburg, counselor of the German legation in Washington. An ugly state of affairs confronted it. Open fighting had stopped, but Mataafa's forces still dominated the countryside around the capital. Defending the city was Malietoa's small army, commanded by American and British officers, armed with American and British rifles, and reinforced by American and British marines.[10] The Germans in Samoa, although still favoring Mataafa, could do little without troops. Assuming authority as another provisional government, the commission succeeded in disarming both sides. It then upheld Justice Chambers's decision; but it decreed the office of king forever abolished and it persuaded Malietoa Tanu to abdicate. Peace was now restored. Protracted negotiations, mainly between Great Britain and Germany, reached a conclusion favorable to the latter only after the onset of the Boer War in the autumn of 1899 had weakened Britain's bargaining position.

It would be easy to attach too much significance to this British-American collaboration. Although the two countries did cooperate, especially during the fighting in the spring of 1899, and although Germans strongly suspected collusion, in point of fact the cooperation was not so intimate as it appeared. No secret understanding existed and the concerted action in Samoa resulted more from decisions taken by local officials than from decisions

[9] See J. L. Garvin, *The Life of Joseph Chamberlain* (3 vols., London, 1932-1934), vol. 3, pp. 328-329, for reference to a telegram from Bülow to Hatzfeldt, April 11, 1899.

[10] *Foreign Relations of the United States, 1899*, p. 616, Tripp to Hay, May 18, 1899.

of the home governments. As a matter of fact, once the joint commission took charge the United States seems to have worked more closely with Germany than with Great Britain. Even John Hay, who disliked Germans almost as much as he liked Englishmen, had to admit this: " Our relations with Germany are perfectly civil and courteous. . . . It was rather the English Commissioner who was offish." [11]

But the commission's plodding work captured neither the headlines nor the imagination. Much more stimulating were the exciting skirmishes in Samoa. Who could fail to be moved by the dramatic news a month after the collapse of the Canadian negotiations and the shelving of Pauncefote's canal treaty that Americans and Englishmen fighting side by side were meeting death at the hands of a common enemy on a distant South Sea island? Whatever bitterness may have arisen in February was mitigated by the fraternization in March.[12] And every German step served only to enhance the general impression of British-American solidarity. It was a dreadful dilemma for the Fatherland; and Bülow bewailed " the undoubted rapprochement which has taken place between England and the United States, even if it has not yet reached the stage of a binding alliance. Every disturbance of our relations with these two States would be succeeded unfailingly by a rapprochement between them, in spite of any differences, such as those which arose lately over the Nicaragua Canal question and the Canadian question." [13] Canada had already provided a convenient scapegoat which Americans could blame for British delinquencies, and now, with the Spanish War no longer serving its former useful purpose, Germany all too unwillingly stepped into the role of a *bête-noire* eminently suitable for tightening slightly ruffled trans-Atlantic friendships.

[11] W. R. Thayer, *The Life and Letters of John Hay* (2 vols., Boston and New York, 1915) , vol. 2, p. 220, to White, September 9, 1899.

[12] In 1902 a memorial was erected in the Mare Island dockyard chapel to American and British officers, seamen, and marines killed in Samoa in 1899; see F. O. 5, 2484, Foreign Office to Raikes, September 26, 1902.

[13] Dugdale, *German Diplomatic Documents*, vol. 3, p. 53, memorandum by Bülow, March 14, 1899.

Somewhat the same British-American alignment reappeared a month or so later at the Hague peace conference. This famous assembly, in response to a call of the Russian Tsar on August 24, 1898, twelve days after the Spanish-American armistice, met at The Hague from May 18 to July 29, 1899, to discuss limitation of armaments. Because of his experience in negotiating two recent arbitration treaties—the treaty of 1897 regarding the Venezuelan boundary and the abortive Olney-Pauncefote treaty of the same year—Sir Julian Pauncefote was summoned from Washington to serve on the British delegation.[14] Andrew D. White, United States ambassador to Germany, headed the American delegation. F. W. Holls was its secretary.

British, Americans, and Russians all had plans for an arbitral tribunal to settle minor international controversies. From the American point of view the Russian plan had the drawback of providing for compulsory arbitration of disputes over river navigation and international canals; " this," Andrew D. White noted in his diary, " in view of our present difficulties in Alaska and in the matter of the Isthmus Canal, we can hardly agree to." [15] However, numerous conferences between White and Pauncefote, sometimes attended by de Staal, the chief Russian delegate, produced a compromise plan for a court of arbitration that the conference subsequently adopted.[16]

Although neither the British nor the American government put much stock in the proposed court, Pauncefote and White were proud of their creation and their governments gave it full backing as something which could at least do no harm and which had a great deal of humanitarian sentiment behind it in both countries. Accordingly when Germany, interpreting the arbitration move as nothing but a trick designed to counter her ability to mobilize more quickly than any other country, announced

[14] Gooch and Temperley, *British Documents*, vol. 1, pp. 225-226, Salisbury to Pauncefote, May 16, 1899. See p. 6.

[15] A. D. White, *Autobiography of Andrew Dickson White* (2 vols., New York, 1905), vol. 2, p. 280; See also F. W. Holls, *The Peace Conference at The Hague* (Boston, 1900).

[16] White, *Autobiography*, vol. 2, p. 274.

firm opposition to any such scheme, Great Britain and the United States hastened to the rescue of their arbitral court. Germany's stand must, indeed, be viewed as another example of her tactless diplomacy, for the tribunal could hardly have been more innocuous. Lord Salisbury told Count Hatzfeldt that he " considered it absolutely out of the question " for it to deal with any important political issue; [17] and he also tried to reassure Germany's ally, Austria-Hungary.[18]

It was the American delegation at The Hague, however, which seems to have been most effective in inducing Germany to back down. Andrew D. White in particular was distressed at her opposition to the court, by which he set great store. Moreover, as a firm believer in better German-American relations he feared that the intransigence of the Kaiser's government would further alienate American opinion, already exasperated over current Samoan affairs. The ambassador now took an unusual step. Without consulting Washington he wrote a long letter to Bülow, dated June 16, 1899, pointing to the hostility certain to arise in the United States if Germany persisted in her stand. He also wrote privately to the Kaiser. These letters he entrusted to F. W. Holls, who departed forthwith for Berlin. The Kaiser was out of reach on his yacht; but on June 19, 1899, Holls had a long interview with several high German officials, including Hohenlohe (the Chancellor), Holstein, and possibly Bülow.[19] Two days later the Foreign Minister advised the Kaiser that after all Germany should not turn down the tribunal. To reject it, he argued, would offend both Russia and the United States; whereas to accept it " will make a fresh leaning of the Americans towards England difficult, and the United States will rather turn towards us." [20] The possibility of attaining this cardinal goal of policy

[17] Dugdale, *German Diplomatic Documents*, vol. 3, p. 78, Hatzfeldt to German Foreign Office, June 14, 1899.

[18] Gooch and Temperley, *British Documents*, vol. 1, p. 227, Salisbury to Rumbold, June 12, 1899.

[19] For the Holls mission see White, *Autobiography*, vol. 2, pp. 308-318; Dugdale, *German Diplomatic Documents*, vol. 3, p. 80. White wrote that Holls talked with Bülow, but this is not certain.

[20] Dugdale, *German Diplomatic Documents*, vol. 3, p. 81, Bülow to the Kaiser, June 21, 1899.

could not be ignored, and Germany withdrew her opposition to voluntary arbitration and the tribunal.

Despite the essential agreement of Britain and America over the arbitral court, it would be incorrect to view the conference as illustrating a common policy. Great Britain firmly opposed what was perhaps America's pet project, a project, moreover, which some delegates thought was aimed squarely at Britain.[21] This was the traditional American proposition that private property at sea be declared immune from capture. Although Pauncefote was reported to be personally somewhat sympathetic,[22] his government resolutely opposed a proposal that would offset the advantage of Britain's maritime supremacy.[23]

On balance, the Hague conference did not constitute a particular significant development for Anglo-American relations. About the most one can conclude is that Andrew D. White and Pauncefote cooperated amicably (" had a very interesting talk on conference matters with Sir Julian Pauncefote, finding that in most things we shall be able to stand together as the crisis approaches," White observed with pleasure) ; [24] that their governments had pretty much the same general attitude toward most subjects discussed; and that the conference probably had some slight effect in bringing about friendlier feelings between the peoples of the two countries, especially among those who saw in the court of arbitration a long step toward abolishing war.

In a report from the conference the British military attaché at The Hague mentioned a conversation with A. T. Mahan, the famous expounder of the influence of sea power on history, and

[21] *Ibid.*, vol. 3, p. 79, report by Siegel, German naval delegate at The Hague.
[22] *Ibid.*, vol. 3, p. 77, Münster, chief German delegate, to the Chancellor, June 12, 1899.
[23] White noted sadly in his diary that Fisher, the British naval delegate, used the same arguments regarding sea warfare as Münster had used regarding land warfare (White, *Autobiography*, vol. 2, p. 268) . See Gooch and Temperley, *British Documents*, vol. 1, p. 231, " Note on the Limitation of Armaments," July 29, 1899, for a report of the British military attaché at The Hague sneering at the proposal.
[24] White, *Autobiography*, vol. 2, p. 336; the notation was made on July 19, 1899, ten days before the conference adjourned.

United States naval delegate at the conference: " Captain Mahan has . . . informed me that he considers that the vital interests of America now lie East and West, and no longer North and South; that the great question of the immediate future is China, and that the United States will be compelled, by facts if not by settled policy, to take a leading part in the struggle for Chinese markets. . . ." [25] We may be sure that this prediction deeply interested the British government, for the Far Eastern scene had continued to darken following the disconcerting developments at Kiaochow and Port Arthur the preceding year. The prediction, moreover, foreshadowed an episode which, far more than the establishment of an arbitral tribunal, more even than British-American military collaboration in the distant Samoan islands, had the effect of associating Great Britain and the United States together in the popular mind. This was the dramatic American diplomatic intervention in the struggle over China when, five weeks after the curtain rang down on the Hague conference, Secretary Hay dispatched the first of his open door notes.

It will be recalled that Hay, when still ambassador, had written President McKinley shortly after the Spanish-American War commenced, urging joint support with Great Britain of the open door. The war would soon incline many Americans to such thoughts. Thus the New York *Journal of Commerce* could hardly wait for the last dilapidated Spanish warship to be destroyed by Commodore Dewey at Manila Bay before it began to instruct its readers in imperial responsibilities:

> We have allowed Great Britain to fight our battle for an open market in China: with our flag floating within 500 miles of Hong Kong we shall be able to give that policy something more than a merely moral support in the future. . . . We stand in the Far East for the policy pursued by England and Japan, and with our adhesion, there is no possible combination of Powers that could resist its enforcement.[26]

The armistice of August 12, 1898, providing for American

---

[25] Gooch and Temperley, *British Documents*, vol. 1, p. 231, Charles À Court, " Note on the Limitation of Armaments," July 29, 1899.

[26] *Journal of Commerce and Commercial Bulletin*, May 4, 1898.

occupation of Manila pending final disposition of the Philippines, pushed the country another notch or two toward a stronger policy in China. With American forces established just off the Asiatic mainland the fate of the tottering oriental empire began to concern a growing number of Americans. We have seen that within a few days of the armistice F. W. Holls was in London holding out hopes of cooperation with Britain to strengthen the open door policy. Although his proposal was contingent upon British concessions in the Caribbean it nonetheless presented a suggestive contrast to American policy before the war had opened dazzling Far Eastern vistas. Britain welcomed the occupation of Manila: there would be less danger of one of her European rivals succeeding Spain in that strategic place. In an article in *Scribner's* magazine, which must have been written about the time of the armistice, Joseph Chamberlain, who at least since February had been urging an understanding with the United States on Far Eastern matters, did his part to spur on America's rapidly evolving mood:

> The recent collapse of China has opened up one of the greatest questions of our time. Is this vast country, with untold mineral and other resources, and with a population of four hundred millions of frugal, industrious people, to be partitioned among European nations? Is the greatest potential market of the world to be permanently closed to general trade, or is it to remain open, with its incalculable possibilities, to all nations on equal terms? The interest of the United States in the decision is the same as that of Great Britain. If it should ever be necessary to enter into negotiations, in order to secure to all the world an equal opportunity in regard to this commerce, it cannot be doubted that they would be infinitely more influential if backed by the joint action of the United States and Great Britain, than if either of these Powers held aloof.[27]

Three days after the armistice, on August 15, President McKinley revealed the tenor of his own thinking by asking Ambassador John Hay to succeed William Day as Secretary of State. Hay

---

[27] J. Chamberlain, " Recent Developments of Policy in the United States and Their Relation to an Anglo-American Alliance," *Scribner's*, vol. 24 (1898) , p. 678.

was known not only as an Anglophile but also as an advocate of a vigorous Far Eastern policy; and it is impossible to believe that McKinley, two months after Hay had gone out of his way to urge cooperation with Britain in China, would have summoned the ambassador to the State Department unless the President himself, now that he was thinking of annexing the Philippines, had come to sympathize with his views. " It may or may not be a significant fact," the Baltimore *News* speculated on learning of Hay's appointment, " that just at the time England and the United States are getting closer together than ever before, and when there is a certain amount of talk about their acting in concert in the far east, our ambassador to England, who happens to be on the very best of terms with the English people, is selected for the post of secretary of state. Mr. Hay will come back thoroughly acquainted with England's fight for the ' open door ' in China." [28]

With John Hay presiding over the State Department and American forces occupying Manila, the stage was set for major developments. But the Secretary had to proceed with utmost circumspection. However fervent his own belief that the United States should support the open door, he had to be careful about associating himself and the Republican party with a British policy. No doubt the American public did entertain more friendly feelings toward Great Britain; no doubt they were more favorable to a positive role in China; no doubt the Secretary of State, and also the President, were prejudiced in favor of the country that had been so uniquely friendly during the Spanish War. Nevertheless no miraculous transformation of deep-rooted traditions and predilections had occurred. When McKinley rejected the British suggestion of March, 1898, for a common policy in China, Assistant Secretary Day reminded Pauncefote of the continuing force of George Washington's warning against foreign involvements; [29] he could have reminded him, too, that—as Sir Julian well understood—another customary American attitude,

---

[28] Quoted in *Public Opinion*, vol. 25 (August 25, 1898), p. 235; see pp. 232-233 for other such conjectures. See also *The Times*, August 24, 1898.

[29] F. O. 5, 2361, Pauncefote to Salisbury, March 17, 1898. See p. 19.

namely, distrust of British wiles, also persisted, notwithstanding recent encouraging tendencies.

Fortunately for his aspirations Hay soon found self-interested support at home. From about the beginning of 1898 certain important business interests had become convinced that something must be done to preserve the collapsing Chinese market. During the Spanish-American War they established a propaganda agency named the American Asiatic Association; it had headquarters in New York, branches in Shanghai, Tokyo, and Kobe, and a most impressive membership list.[30] No Republican administration could afford to overlook the recommendations of prominent businessmen. Business wealth had contributed heavily to McKinley's exciting victory over the " dangerous " William Jennings Bryan in 1896 and would be needed again in 1900. Apart from the President, John Hay by personal sympathy and through his wife's great fortune had close ties with the business and financial world.

But we are here not so much concerned with business pressure as such as with its British orientation. Like the new Secretary of State American business in its higher circles was pro-British on the whole and like him it favored steps to safeguard the great market across the Pacific. ". . . *what American and British merchants require*," stated the president of the American Asiatic Association, " *for the maintenance of their trade with China are open ports*, under their treaties, *without any outside restrictions or interference. It is in this direction that we have to devote our energies. . . .*"[31] Although intense competition held sway among American and British traders and concession hunters actually in China, something like an Anglo-American business entente was being developed in Great Britain and the United States by the many men who felt they must present a common front against the machinations of Germany, Russia, and France.

Indicative of the trend was an agreement to cooperate in acquiring railway concessions in China concluded in 1899 be-

[30] C. S. Campbell, Jr., *Special Business Interests and the Open Door Policy* (New Haven, 1951) , chs. iv, v, and vi.

[31] *Ibid.*, p. 42, speech delivered by Everett Frazar, October 31, 1898.

tween the American-China Development Company, an American concern composed of some of the most important business interests in the country, and the British and Chinese Corporation, a British syndicate composed of prominent firms and financiers in Great Britain.[32] Another indication was the triumphal American tour of Lord Charles Beresford, a member of Parliament and former admiral, following a visit to China in behalf of the Associated Chambers of Commerce of Great Britain. An enthusiastic proponent of British-American collaboration to preserve commercial freedom in China, Beresford had known Hay in England and had kept up the acquaintance after Hay went to the State Department. ". . . it is imperative for American interests as well as our own," he wrote the new Secretary in November, 1898, " that the policy of the ' open door ' should be maintained. I have every hope that in the near future the suggested commercial alliance between Great Britain and America with reference to the ' open door ' in China, may become an absolute fact." [33] In a series of speeches in February, 1899, he hammered home this thesis to business organizations throughout the United States. Everywhere the dynamic Englishman was accorded a sympathetic hearing. At a banquet given for him at Delmonico's in New York by the American Asiatic Association he was greeted with " hearty cheers " and his address aroused " prolonged applause." [34] He also visited Washington where he was

[32] For the members of the two companies see *ibid.*, pp. 21-22 and p. 39. Pauncefote reported to London that the American-China Development Company was " very powerful," with " representatives of some of the greatest business interests in the United States . . ." (F.O. 5, 2363, Pauncefote to Salisbury, September 20, 1898).

[33] A. L. P. Dennis, *Adventures in American Diplomacy, 1896-1906* (New York, 1928), p. 186, Beresford to Hay, November 29, 1898. See also C. Beresford, *The Break-Up of China* (New York and London, 1899). Beresford thought it wise to play down his British background; interviewed as he was about to sail for England he told the press: " You must not think that I came to this country in the capacity of an authorized agent for my country. . . . I simply came here on my own responsibility . . ." (New York *Journal of Commerce and Commercial Bulletin*, March 2, 1899).

[34] New York *Journal of Commerce and Commercial Bulletin*, February 24, 1899.

the guest of honor at a dinner given by the Secretary of State.[35] Already favorably disposed to his message, many people seem to have found in Beresford just the catalyst needed to crystallize their thoughts.

Even in early 1899, when the Canadian and canal negotiations stood on the brink of failure, so cautious a diplomat as Sir Julian Pauncefote could acclaim " the special community of interest [between Britain and America] . . . in China "; [36] and by the autumn, when Hay despatched the first open door notes, the two countries had fought side by side in Samoa, upheld the righteous cause of arbitration at The Hague, and were associated together in popular thinking as stalwart defenders of commercial equality against the intrigues of cynical continental powers.

On various dates beginning September 6 and ending November 21, 1899, the Secretary sent notes to Great Britain, Germany, Russia, France, Italy, and Japan, asking each to agree that within any sphere of influence or leased territory it might possess in China it would not interfere with treaty ports or vested interests, would not prevent the Chinese tariff from being applied to imports, and would not levy discriminatory harbor dues or railroad charges. To these requests the powers replied with varying degrees of consent. At last the United States had stepped forth to lend a helping hand to the country which had befriended it throughout the perils of war and which for long had borne unaided the responsibility of maintaining the open door—such was the general impression in Britain and perhaps America as well.

Some writers have seen much significance in the fact that the draft notes—they were drafted by Hay's adviser, W. W. Rockhill —paraphrased and in places copied memoranda written by Alfred Hippisley, an Englishman.[37] This, they imply, shows that Great

[35] *Ibid.*, February 23, 1899.

[36] T. Dennett, *John Hay, from Poetry to Politics* (New York, 1933) , p. 288, to Hay, January 8, 1899.

[37] See A. W. Griswold, *The Far Eastern Policy of the United States* (New York, 1938) , ch. II.

Britain through Hippisley enticed the United States to sponsor a British policy.[38] But the implication is highly conjectural. Indeed the whole theory of a British origin of Hay's notes has been overdone, and no material is known to exist in the British archives to support it. In all likelihood Hippisley's role was simply that of the minor official, well known in government offices, whose well turned memoranda are taken over by busy policy-makers already persuaded as to the views expressed. The disquiet of the British government on receipt of Hay's note, a disquiet very evident in the Foreign Office's several draft replies,[39] is sufficient to establish its non-British origin. John Hay, as we have seen, had long been persuaded of the need to act in support of the open door; it is unnecessary to look even to his adviser Rockhill, let alone Hippisley, in order to explain Hay's adherence to his own belief. And by the autumn of 1899 he and the President had evidence from business organizations and other sources of substantial desire for diplomatic intervention in China—enough evidence to make their move politically expedient.[40]

It has also been suggested that the open door notes constituted one part of a tacit international bargain on the grand scale by which America moved to Britain's side in eastern Asia in return for Britain's withdrawal from the Caribbean—somewhat the same bargain that F. W. Holls broached to Balfour in 1898.[41]

[38] T. A. Bailey, *A Diplomatic History of the American People* (New York, 1955), p. 527, concludes a paragraph about Hippisley by stating: "Thus the British succeeded in committing the United States to a policy favorable to their Chinese interests." S. F. Bemis, *A Diplomatic History of the United States* (New York, 1955), p. 484, says only: "It would be interesting to know if Mr. Hippisley had any connection, direct of indirect, with the British Embassy, in Washington, or with the Foreign Office." The present writer has found no evidence of such connection in the British archives. P. A. Varg, *Open Door Diplomat, The Life of W. W. Rockhill* (Urbana, 1952), p. 29, is undoubtedly correct in believing that "Hippisley was not, in any sense, an emissary of the British government."

[39] See F. O. 5, 2408, for various draft replies to Choate's letter of September 22, 1899, enclosing Hay's open door note of September 6.

[40] Campbell, *Special Business Interests*, ch. vii.

[41] T. Dennett, "The Open Door Policy as Intervention," *American Academy*

By this theory the notes amounted to advance payment for Britain's consent to modify the Clayton-Bulwer treaty in early 1900. This is an ingenious supposition but there is nothing to support it except the fact that one event did follow hard upon the other. Holls's vague proposals, which in any case Balfour rejected, certainly cannot be cited in evidence. And just as a Hippisley is not required to account for John Hay's Far Eastern policy, so there is no need to conjure up an alleged bargain to account for Britain's retreat in the Caribbean. That retreat is readily explicable on other grounds, as shall appear.

It must be admitted that in this diplomacy of late 1899, as in the Samoan crisis a few months earlier, the popular reaction differed from the truth known to the two governments. The cautious, hard-headed leaders of the British empire did not embrace Hay's *démarche* with the unrestrained joy that the contemporary press, and some later historians, ascribed to them. Although eager for America to participate in Chinese affairs and although welcoming the assurance given by the notes that it was prepared to do so, they had habitually envisaged an Anglo-American partnership directed against other powers. Such a partnership was the apparent objective of the telegram of March, 1898, that had speeded Pauncefote to the White House. But now the United States had ranged itself alone on one side, with Japan, the continental powers, and Great Britain herself lumped together in an undifferentiated mass on the other. Rockhill told the Russian ambassador at Washington that no American government " would adopt an English policy . . . . the administration had solely in view the interests of the country. If they happened to be on lines similar to those declared by Lord Salisbury and others to be in accord with the formal policy of Great Britain, it was a fortunate coincidence." [42] However great their pleasure

of Political and Social Science, Annals, vol. 168 (1933), p. 82, writes: " Our Far Eastern policy was in fact a part of our Caribbean policy." B. A. Reuter, *Anglo-American Relations during the Spanish-American War* (New York, 1924), p. 187, refers to the " unwritten agreement of American protection of British trade in the West in return for American concessions in the Far East."

[42] Rockhill papers, Rockhill to Hay, December 1, 1899. Rockhill wrote

at the emergence of another active champion of the open door policy, such proponents of Anglo-American collaboration as Chamberlain and Balfour must have been disappointed by the manner of the American step. Somewhat disgruntledly the Prime Minister admonished Ambassador Choate not to expect other countries than Britain to accept the commitments asked of them.[43]

Nor were the open door notes framed to fit Britain's special circumstances. Hardly a stone's throw across the bay from her colony of Hongkong lay the leased territory of Kowloon, administered as an integral part of the colony. It would be awkward to apply the self-denying ordinances of Hay's formula to Kowloon, administered so intimately with Hongkong. The Foreign Office at first meditated demanding omission of all reference to leased territories;[44] but as Choate pointed out, since most foreign holdings in China took the form of leases such omission would render the notes largely meaningless.[45] In Britain's view the notes, however imperfect, were better than no American action at all; besides, her astute statesmen doubtless appreciated the risk of disillusioning Americans, who were enthusiastically hailing Hay's intervention as a noble act for which Great Britain should be extremely thankful. Accordingly they decided upon a compromise under which Britain committed herself only with respect to Wei-hai Wei, her other leased territory. (In conformity with this decision, when the Foreign Office was preparing in 1900 a Blue Book on Chinese affairs it arranged with Ambassador Choate to amend their open door correspondence for purposes of publication on the ground that " it would probably be undesirable to show the world that the Hongkong extension was specially excluded. . . .")[46]

Whatever the reaction of government officials, to the ordinary American and Englishman, vaguely aware that the open door

Hay another time that the American policy was " not a British one—for England is as great an offender in China as Russia itself " (Dennis, *Adventures*, p. 186, August 28, 1899).

[43] Choate papers, Choate to Hay, November 1, 1899.
[44] See the draft replies in F. O. 5, 2408.
[45] Choate papers, Choate to Hay, November 1, 1899.
[46] F. O. 5, 2443, Brodrick to Choate, February 27, 1900.

policy was something all good English-speaking people stood for against Germans, Frenchmen, and Russians, Hay's *démarche* appeared not only as a prodigy of diplomatic wizardry but also as a further confirmation of a British-American working arrangement that did good service whenever, as recently in Samoa and perhaps at The Hague, their common interests were jeopardised. Thus the notes undoubtedly gave further impetus to the developing Anglo-American friendship, and helped relieve the irritation following the collapse of the Canadian and canal negotiations in February, 1899. " I know how largely you have yourself contributed for many years in maintaining the good will between England and the United States," Sir William Harcourt, the Liberal leader, wrote Henry White, " and I feel how much you must rejoice in the happy consummation of a policy which is the common object of both nations." [47] No doubt the exaltation of Spanish War days had worn thin, but nevertheless—so went a general belief in both countries—the United States and Great Britain, colleagues in Hay's " partnership in beneficence," were standing together, shoulder to shoulder, through many exciting experiences in 1899.

[47] A. Nevins, *Henry White, Thirty Years of American Diplomacy* (New York and London, 1930), p. 167, March 28, 1900.

CHAPTER 8

War and Diplomacy

EVER SINCE the Canadian and canal negotiations had come to grief in February, 1899, over the Alaska boundary, negotiations between Great Britain and the United States had been bogged down. Dim indeed had grown the prospects for a comprehensive settlement that had seemed so bright during the Spanish-American War. Despite their vaunted friendship, despite much co-operation in Samoa and a common attitude toward the open door in China, the two countries had been able to accomplish nothing at all toward settling their disputes except a temporary demarcation of a small portion of the Alaska boundary. And it was perfectly plain that at least in Alaska and Central America conditions were such that they could not be safely left to run their course much longer. For all the calming effects of the *modus vivendi*, the situation remained explosive in the distant gold country, and the pigeon-holing of Pauncefote's draft for a new canal treaty was not softening one whit the demand for an all-American isthmian waterway that had surged up so irresistibly during the war months. Something would have to be done soon about the boundary and the canal if an outburst was not to occur in the United States.

What could in fact be done? It was easier to appreciate the need than to grasp the means. No diplomats could have been more anxious to resume negotiations than Hay and Pauncefote; few better understood their business or had more sympathetic superiors; yet success had eluded them. Some drastic intervention from outside was required if Britain and American were to break out from the closed circle in which they were groping.

In 1898 the two countries had been snatched out of their habitual relationship and thrown upon a new course by the impact of the Spanish-American War. A year and a half later, when they had become mired in that new course so hopefully entered upon, they were once again shaken up by another conflict, the Boer War, and once again given a fresh and auspicious start. It is a sad but understandable fact that two wars and the threat of a third (in Venezuela) played a prominent, perhaps an indispensable, part in producing the Anglo-American settlement at the turn of the century.

The outbreak of fighting between Great Britain and the Boer republics of South Africa in October, 1899, gave rise to an explosion of anger throughout the world. An unscrupulous empire, swollen in size and laden with booty, was pouncing upon two unoffending little countries in order to plunder their gold mines —so it was commonly asserted. On the Continent the press erupted with a torrent of abuse that revealed in one harsh steady glare the hatred and envy of Britain that had been building up over the years. Talk of a coalition against her resounded on every side, as it had with respect to America the previous year; and the journey of the Russian Foreign Minister, Count Muraviev, to the western capitals lent substance to the rumors. Serious British military reverses in " Black Week " (December 9-15, 1899) foreshadowed, not the anticipated short war, but a protracted conflict for which Britain was ill prepared. With her armies pinned down far from home and with the Continent on fire to humiliate her, Britain's isolation all at once appeared highly precarious. In these circumstances the attitude of the United States was most important. Fortunately for Great Britain the administration and many prominent members of Congress sympathized with her and succeeded with but slight concessions to their numerous antagonists in carrying along the country in a neutrality favorable to her. ". . . the warmth & friendliness of manner shown towards me by the President & all his cabinet is very marked," Pauncefote told Salisbury with relief, " & evidently intended to show their desire to maintain & promote the entente cordiale & the 'unwritten Treaty' which undoubtedly exists in spite of the outcry about the word 'alliance.'" [1]

As regards foreign policy, it was Secretary Hay's opinion that counted as long as McKinley occupied the White House. Although Hay often had trouble pushing through his policies, and frequently bewailed the Senate's disdainful tampering with his cherished treaties, he seems always to have had enough power to veto major ventures he disliked. Few people could have longed for British victory more strongly than John Hay. Apart from his pro-British leanings, he had too lively a dislike of Germans to appreciate Boers, and was too much of an aristocrat to espouse crude farmers on the veldt. On the eve of the war he said solemnly that as long as he headed the State Department no action would be taken " contrary to my conviction that the one indispensable feature of our foreign policy should be a friendly understanding with England "; [2] and his deep emotional feeling for Britain stands out in his message to Henry White to " say many things for me to our friends at the F. O. and to Mr. Balfour —in fact, many more things than I have any business to say." [3] Obviously the United States was not going to take advantage of Britain's predicament in South Africa as long as Secretary Hay controlled foreign policy.

When Theodore Roosevelt entered the White House after McKinley's assassination in September, 1901, the hard-pressed Boers felt a sudden thrill of hope. Might this not be a providential turn of events that would save them? It was true that the new President with the Boerish name had supported Britain early in the war and as a stalwart champion of northern culture had felt certain that " it would be for the advantage of mankind to have English spoken south of the Zambesi just as in New

---

[1] Salisbury papers, January 19, 1900.

[2] W. R. Thayer, *The Life and Letters of John Hay* (2 vols., Boston and New York, 1915) , vol. 2, p. 221, to White, September 24, 1899.

[3] T. Dennett, *John Hay, from Poetry to Politics* (New York, 1933) , p. 263, September 24, 1899.

York." [4] Yet the Boers could expect more sympathy from this cocksure young man than from the benign McKinley. Sobered by the responsibility of his great office, would he not come to the aid of his kinsmen in their dire peril? Perhaps they knew that as the war progressed Roosevelt came to entertain serious doubts about the world importance of what tongue was spoken south of the Zambesi. But even had his sympathies become set on the Boer side—which they had not—an inexperienced President could hardly have reversed the entrenched policy of his renowned Secretary of State and distinguished members of Congress in the few remaining months of the conflict.

Hay's services to Great Britain began before the fighting started, when he rejected an appeal from the Orange Free State for help in arranging arbitration. Six months later, however, when pro-Boer feeling was rampant in America, the administration felt it politically expedient to respond more favorably to a similar appeal, this one addressed to European powers as well as the United States. Accordingly the Secretary forwarded the appeal to Great Britain with an expression of McKinley's "earnest hope that a way to bring about peace may be found. . . ." [5] But Hay was only too glad to drop the matter when Salisbury politely declined mediation.[6] As a matter of fact he had not intended his perfunctory step to be taken seriously; it was not a move for peace but a maneuver in domestic politics. As the Secretary explained to Henry White: ". . . I saw there was nothing to be done with the . . . message but to send it on to you with an expression of the President's platonic desire for peace. If I had done otherwise there would have been a joint resolution rushed through Congress advising us to do it, couched in language which could not have failed to be offensive and injurious. For the present we seem to have spiked their guns." [7]

[4] S. Gwynn, *The Letters and Friendships of Sir Cecil Spring Rice* (2 vols., Boston and New York, 1929), vol. 1, p. 305, December 2, 1899.

[5] State Department, Great Britain, Despatches, telegram received March 10, 1900.

[6] *Ibid.*, White to Hay, March 14, 1900.

[7] A. Nevins, *Henry White, Thirty Years of American Diplomacy* (New York and London, 1930), pp. 151-152, March 18, 1900.

Although the British government understood Hay's intention perfectly well, the press and some members of Parliament displayed resentment.[8] The mediation offer " does not amount to much . . . though it is more than we ever thought of doing when the United States were just beginning to break down the resistance of Spain," the *Times* noted glumly.[9] Such criticism, though natural, resulted from a basic misunderstanding. As it happened Hay had done far more for the British than they realized. The Boers were furious. They had envisaged America as organizing intervention by the great powers; [10] instead, Hay's quick action—he telegraphed instructions to London the very day he received the Boer request—enabled Great Britain to issue a statement that had the effect of preventing other countries from offering mediation without offense, and it put the Washington administration in a position to repudiate any subsequent accusations of partiality that might be raised by Boers or Democrats.[11]

Boer envoys called at the State Department in May, 1900, to plead their cause. They encountered the Secretary in his stiffest mood. " It was a bit discouraging to see our answer lying on the table as we entered and before we had had opportunity to open our mouths," one of them later complained.[12] Their reception by the bland McKinley, while more friendly, was equally unproductive; all they got was some pleasant conversation and a look at the lovely view from the White House. Two years later some other envoys came. But both the new President and the same unfriendly Secretary of State again made it clear that the United States would do nothing. In any case the war was by then fast drawing to its close.

[8] See State Department, Great Britain, Despatches, White to Hay, March 14, 1900. White said the mediation offer had aroused much curiosity and that he had been " besieged by inquiries all day."

[9] *The Times*, March 16, 1900.

[10] A. L. P. Dennis, *Adventures in American Diplomacy, 1896-1906* (New York, 1928), pp. 132-133.

[11] On this point see J. H. Ferguson, *American Diplomacy and the Boer War* (Philadelphia, 1939), p. 142.

[12] Dennis, *Adventures*, p. 133. Regarding the interview see State Department, Miscellaneous Archives, Boer War, 1900-1902.

In pursuing his pro-British policy the Secretary of State encountered both fervent supporters and venomous critics. Undoubtedly his policy ran counter to deep American instincts. It was only natural for Americans to feel a strong bond of sympathy for two sister republics struggling to be free from the far-flung empire against which their ancestors had once fought two wars. And when the Boers, far from being overwhelmed, began to win victory after victory, it was a rare person who could help being thrilled, if only at the spectacle of the underdog turning against the attacker. G. W. Smalley, the London *Times* correspondent, put this "sporting instinct . . . at the bottom of the feeling for the Boers." [13]

The Boers, of course, had a direct appeal for several American minority groups. For people of Dutch descent news from South Africa came close to home. More influential politically, German-Americans tended to side with their beleaguered kinsmen, all the more so because of the violently pro-Boer feeling in the Fatherland itself. But it was the Irish who were the most wrought up. "The Irish and the Germans," John Hay wrote in deep disgust, "for the first time in my knowledge, seem to have joined their several lunacies in one common attack against England and incidentally against the Administration for being too friendly to England. I do not imagine this coalition can survive many months, but for the moment it lifts all our light-weight politicians off their feet." [14] Many Irishmen had highly exaggerated notions as to what they could gain from Britain's preoccupation, and scenting victory they turned with new vigor to their perennial struggle for the old country's freedom. In the great cities of the United States excited Irish orators berated the bloated monarchy across the ocean. A meeting that attracted much publicity was held at Carnegie Hall in New York for the purpose of

[13] *The Times*, April 14, 1900. Theodore Roosevelt's pro-British proclivities were shaken by this consideration: "the . . . warfare has given many people a strong feeling that the Boers must possess altogether exceptional qualities in view of their ability to make such a showing." See E. E. Morison, ed., *The Letters of Theodore Roosevelt* (8 vols., Cambridge, Mass., 1951-1954), vol. 3, p. 20.

[14] Nevins, *White*, p. 151, to White, March 18, 1900.

welcoming Irish delegates just arrived from Europe. One of them, a member of the British Parliament, John Redmond, aroused enormous enthusiasm by declaring roundly: " If Mr. Chamberlain met his deserts he would end his career by hanging upon the nearest lamppost." [15]

As they did after the Civil War, Irish-Americans tried to strike at their hated foe through the part of the empire they could most easily reach—Canada. Theodore Roosevelt gleefully related how he threatened to " clap . . . in jail " and, with a gubernatorial flourish of the Big Stick, succeeded in putting utterly to rout some " belated Fenians " who called at Albany when he was governor of New York, trusting that he as a person of Dutch descent would help them organize raids into Canada.[16] Although reports of impending raids lifted Irish hearts now and then,[17] and at one moment the British consul in San Francisco was seriously perturbed over a rumored plot to destroy the Esquimault dockyards,[18] nothing of consequence occurred to ruffle the border's tranquillity except the apprehension of three dynamiters attempting to sabotage the Welland canal.[19] The only Irish-Americans who actually came to grips with the British were fifty sharpshooters who, under the auspices of the Ancient Order of Hibernians, eluded guardians of the American neutrality law by embarking for South Africa disguised as a Red Cross corps.[20]

Strong feelings such as these were made the stronger by the usual incidents that soon cropped up between the United States as a leading neutral, and Great Britain as a major sea power.

[15] *New York Times*, November 4, 1901. For comments on his speech see *New York Sun*, November 16; *Baltimore Sun*, November 17 and 18; and *New York Tribune*, November 18, 1901.

[16] Ferguson, *Boer War*, p. 66.

[17] *The Times*, December 30, 1899, has a short article on the subject. See *ibid.*, June 12, 1900, for a rumor that the secret Irish society, the Clan-na-Gael, was threatening to make raids in order to prevent the transfer of Canadian troops to South Africa.

[18] F. O. 115, 1185, Pauncefote to Minto, January 20, 1900.

[19] *The Times*, April 23, 25, 1900. See C. O. 42, 875, for a memorandum dated May 17, 1900, on the incident.

[20] Ferguson, *Boer War*, p. 67.

During the first few months of the war four ships carrying goods from New York to Delagoa Bay, adjacent to the Transvaal, were apprehended by British warships and the cargoes detained in South Africa pending adjudication. " Considerable public feeling " was aroused, Hay admitted; and he instructed Ambassador Choate to take up the matter with the Foreign Office.[21] Anxious not to antagonize the United States, Great Britain agreed to pay the shippers the contracted prices for the non-contraband part of the cargo. Nevertheless when she seized a German ship, the *Bundesrath*, on December 29, 1900, Americans for once lined up with Germany; and when she backed down before angry demands from Berlin, they were delighted at the apparent vindication of a traditional principle of their own. " The whole civilised world," the *Washington Times* asserted, " owes gratitude to the German Foreign Office for the clear, irreproachable and decided way in which it settled the affair." [22]

While matters of neutral rights were still filling headlines, the *New York Times* published an account of an alleged interview with the British consul in New Orleans, Arthur Vansittart, in which he was reported to have accused Congress of being guilty of " bombast " and " political buncombe "; to have called senators " mountebanks, double-faced," fond of " talking for show and for votes "; and to have labelled the American people " mercenary in everything that they do. . . ." [23] It seems incredible that the consul could have made such injudicious remarks, and as a matter of fact he denied having even been interviewed.[24] Be that as it may, the *Times* article gave an opening not to be missed by pro-Boers. Abusive remarks were heard in Congress; and a New York Committee to Aid the United Republics of

[21] State Department, Great Britain, Despatches, Hay to Choate, telegram received December 29, 1899. See *ibid.* for a copy of a letter from T. H. Sanderson of the Foreign Office to Choate, December 30, 1899, in which Sanderson stated that an investigation was under way.

[22] E. T. S. Dugdale, ed., *German Diplomatic Documents, 1871-1914* (4 vols., London, 1928-1931), vol. 3, p. 122, Holleben to German Foreign Office, January 21, 1900.

[23] *New York Times*, January 14, 1900.

[24] F. O. 5, 2426, Vansittart to Pauncefote, January 29, 1900.

South Africa rushed off a resolution directing the Secretary of State to investigate the story and "if it be found to be correct . . . take action to uphold the dignity of the Congress and defend the people of the United States from defamatory abuse, by immediately withdrawing the exequatur of said Vansittart. . . ." [25] But after stirring up a sudden surge of anger this incident, too, like that of the cargoes, soon disappeared from public notice.

Further sentiment against Britain was fomented when a one-time United States consul at Pretoria, Charles Macrum, accused the British of having censored his official mail.[26] The charge was taken up by the press; and the unwise appointment of Hay's son, Adelbert, just out of college and completely without consular experience, to succeed Macrum added fuel to the fire.

These incidents occurred during the first four or five months of the war, a time when American enthusiasm was aroused by the gallant Boer resistance. No further comparable incidents took place until much later, when shipments by a British mission in New Orleans of horses and mules to Africa, led to furious accusations of unneutral activity. The State Department felt obliged to investigate,[27] and with the war as good as won Great Britain made no difficulty about withdrawing the offending missions.[28]

None of these incidents amounted to much, but when one considers them in the light of the very considerable sympathy for the Boers it is surprising that they did not stir up a storm

[25] State Department, Miscellaneous Letters, January 17, 1900. See F. O. 5, 2426, Pauncefote to Salisbury, January 22, 1900, for other repercussions.

[26] Ferguson, *Boer War*, p. 100.

[27] *New York Tribune*, April 6 and June 6, 1902; 57th Congress, 1st session, House documents 568 and 649; F. O. 5, 2485, Pauncefote to Lansdowne, February 8, 1902. Henry Adams accused Hay of allowing "the English to come in here, and violate our neutrality on a scale so enormous that . . . both partners are bankrupt"; see W. C. Ford, ed., *Letters of Henry Adams, 1892-1918* (2 vols., Boston and New York, 1938), vol. 2, p. 383, April 6, 1902. According to Cecil Spring Rice Germany tried to use this episode to foment anti-British feeling in America; see Gwynn, *Spring Rice*, vol. 1, p. 351.

[28] F. O. 115, 1239, India Office to Foreign Office, April 24, 1902; Lansdowne to Pauncefote, May 9, 1902. A good deal of material regarding this matter is in State Department, Miscellaneous Archives, Boer War, 1900-1902.

of excitement. What needs explaining is not the pro-Boer sentiment in the United States but its extraordinary moderation,
and its rapid dwindling after the elections of November, 1900.
Even in the summer of 1900, when indignation against Britain
was close to its peak, Lord Pauncefote noted " a remarkable
manifestation of reverence for the Queen as well as of friendliness
and good will towards Great Britain . . ." on the occasion of
his being awarded honorary degrees by Harvard and Columbia.
" The demonstration," he thought, " is all the more significant
and gratifying at the present juncture when popular excitement
consequent on the Presidential Campaign is at its height. . . ." [29]

How can this moderation be accounted for? How was the
government able to carry the country along a path harmful to
the Boers when natural sentiment, powerful minority groups, and
provocative wartime incidents all pointed to another course?
What, in other words, made John Hay's pro-British conduct of
foreign affairs politically possible? Above all, it was the parallel
with the Spanish War. During that recent time of danger Great
Britain had opposed European intervention, had befriended the
United States, and had represented its interests. Now the situation was reversed. With the continental powers beside themselves with angry abuse of Great Britain, and with the United
States representing British interests (though as a matter of fact
Britain asked Germany first),[30] it would have been most incon-
gruous to join in the hue and cry against Britain. " England
stood by us," the *New York Times* reminded its readers. " Let
us stand by her. We had the great help of her moral support.
Let us give her our sympathy and good wishes. The envious and
watchful knew she was our friend. Let all the world know that
we are hers." [31] And in London Ambassador Choate gave assurances that his countrymen were mindful of Britain's great
services.[32] Except for England's friendly attitude in 1898, Theo-

---

[29] F. O. 5, 2428, to Salisbury, July 10, 1900.
[30] Dugdale, *German Diplomatic Documents*, vol. 3, p. 103, Lascelles to
Derenthall, October 3, 1899.
[31] December 13, 1899.
[32] *The Times*, December 19, 1899.

dore Roosevelt thought, " this country would have been swept by such a gust of sympathy for the Boer republics that trouble would almost inevitably have followed." [33]

For another reason, too, it was awkward to be critical. How could Americans hurl their traditional anathemas at British imperialism at the very moment they themselves were crushing Filipinos? If the Spanish-American War presented one thought-provoking parallel, the war in the Philippines presented another. Asked to sign a petition for proffering American good offices in the Boer War, William Jennings Bryan declined on the reasonable ground that " Our refusal to recognize the rights of the Filipinos to self-government will embarrass us if we express sympathy with those in other lands who are struggling to follow the doctrines set forth in the Declaration of Independence." And in a speech he observed pointedly: " Suppose we send our sympathy to the Boers? In an hour England would send back, ' What about the Filipinos? ' " [34]

Some Americans backed Britain because they believed her victory important to United States security. Nowhere was this consideration more prevalent than among the " Large Policy " enthusiasts, now basking in the warmth of popular approval after their glorious little war. If Britain was defeated, Theodore Roosevelt predicted, " in five years it will mean a war between us and some one of the great continental European nations, unless we are content to abandon the Monroe Doctrine for South America. . . ." [35] Another Large Policy stalwart, Henry Cabot Lodge, often but mistakenly depicted as basically anti-British, noted " a very general and solid sense of the fact that however much we sympathize with the Boers the downfall of the British Empire is something which no rational American could regard as anything but a misfortune to the United States." [36] And the

---

[33] Morison, *Letters of Roosevelt*, vol. 2, p. 1437, to White, November 22, 1900.

[34] Ferguson, *Boer War*, p. 183.

[35] *Ibid.*, p. 209, January 30, 1900.

[36] *Selections from the Correspondence of Theodore Roosevelt and Henry Cabot Lodge, 1884-1918* (2 vols., New York and London, 1925), vol. 1, p. 446, February 2, 1900.

great mentor of the Lodge-Roosevelt school, A. T. Mahan, raised
the old cry for Anglo-American solidarity in that focal point of
diplomacy, the Far East: " To this very great impending Eastern
question—in China—I conceive that a cordial understanding . . .
between Great Britain and ourselves, will be a most important
factor. There will be a strong assault, made by those who would
breed discord between the two nations, to use the Transvaal
business as an opening therefor. . . ." [37] After all, imperialism
was for the time being fashionable in the United States; and not
a few Americans would have agreed that, far from blame, Great
Britain deserved gratitude for her sacrificial efforts to uphold
Anglo-Saxon civilisation.

Perhaps the most awkward period for Hay and the administration came during the months before the presidential election of
1900. Hoping to capitalize on pro-Boer sentiment and spurred
on by prominent Irish politicians, Democrats assailed Republicans
for backing Britain. ". . . every effort," Lord Pauncefote reported,
" is being made by the opponents of the present Administration
to prejudice the minds of the public against England especially
in relation to the war in South Africa." [38] Although Bryan and
the Democrats did not succeed in making much political capital
out of the distant struggle they did what they could to be worthy
of their opportunity. " Your friend Bryan, ass that he is," Hay
wrote sarcastically to Henry Adams, " says that the Boer War is
an issue in our campaign—I suppose because the British are
16 to 1." [39] The alluring vision of election day shone brightly
through the Democratic platform's insinuations of Republican
tenderness for Great Britain:

> Believing in the principles of self-government and rejecting,
> as did our forefathers, the claims of monarchy, we view with
> indignation the purpose of England to overwhelm with force
> the South African Republics. Speaking, as we believe, for the
> entire American Nation, except its Republican office holders,

[37] R. Cortissoz, *The Life of Whitelaw Reid* (2 vols., New York, 1921),
vol. 2, pp. 269-270, Mahan to Reid, October 20, 1899.

[38] F. O. 5, 2428, to Salisbury, July 10, 1900.

[39] Ferguson, *Boer War*, p. 125, June 15, 1900.

and for all free men everywhere, we extend our sympathy to the heroic burghers in their unequal struggle to maintain their liberty and independence.[40]

As for the Republicans, they found themselves in a quandary. How to reconcile the administration's pro-British leanings with the undoubted popular appeal of the " heroic burghers "? Their convention almost got out of hand and declared for the Boers. In the end it settled for a plank simply expressing the " hope that a way may soon be found, honorable alike to both contending parties [in Africa], to terminate the strife between them." [41]

By the time of the elections the war was no longer arousing the same absorbed attention. Dramatic and thrilling victories of " Black Week " had been replaced by desultory guerilla fighting that did not lend itself to headlines. Everyone could see that the British were going to win; and McKinley probably lost but few votes because of his indifference to the little South African republics. After the elections interest in the war slackened still more. Never again did the American people recapture their earlier enthusiasm for the Boers. Once the critical year of 1900 had passed, the Secretary of State did not have to worry lest public pressure upset his prudently slanted neutrality.

Thus throughout the conflict John Hay, supported by his two Presidents and by such key congressional figures as Henry Cabot Lodge and Cushman Davis, chairman of the Senate Committee on Foreign Relations, succeeded in committing the United States to a neutrality which, however correct, certainly did no harm to the empire he so admired. The effect of this benevolent American attitude may have been far-reaching. Bülow, the Kaiser's Foreign Minister, thought the failure of the Boer mission to America had made European intervention against Britain " hopeless." [42] One may legitimately envisage Hay's policy as

---

[40] *Ibid.*, p. 197.

[41] " We had great difficulty to prevent the Convention from declaring in favor of the Boers . . . ," Hay stated, June 23, 1900; see *ibid.*, pp. 195-196.

[42] Dugdale, *German Diplomatic Documents*, vol. 3, p. 125; he made this observation on May 28, 1900. The Russian Foreign Minister, Muraviev, in

a contributory factor in clinching German neutrality, and thereby in ensuring that the ring would be held against European intervention while the British armies ground remorselessly ahead to final victory in May, 1902. It is easy to understand why Arthur Balfour invited the Secretary to visit England after the elections of 1900 and why he promised him a heartfelt welcome.[43]

Like the Spanish-American War the Boer War did much to improve Anglo-American relations. No doubt many Americans, apt to portray the British in overly roseate hues during the former conflict, now substituted a good measure of deepest dye; and in their minds the old conception of John Bull as an overbearing bully regained something of its former clarity. This reaction was not universal, of course; other Americans found their affection for Britain kindled afresh by her defiance of the terrible dangers threatening from the Continent.

Whatever the war's net effect on British stock in America, it boosted American stock in Britain. British leaders, although disappointed in the attitude of the American public—Chamberlain told Hay of his discouragement that Britain's motives had been misunderstood all over the world " and especially in the United States, with which it is the first object of my public life to cultivate a good and even an affectionate understanding " [44]— appreciated deeply the manifest friendship and helpfulness of the United States government. As for the British people, they probably judged more from official American policy than from slanderous articles in the American press and venomous orations by Irishmen. In any case, even at its height, pro-Boer agitation across the Atlantic presented a suggestive contrast to vituperation across the Channel. The *Times*—with pardonable exaggeration but some truth—assured its readers that: " At a time when the Continent rings with denunciations of this country . . . it is very

a memorandum of January 25/February 7, 1900, listed American opposition as one point making a coalition impracticable; see W. L. Langer, *The Diplomacy of Imperialism, 1890-1902* (2 vols., New York and London, 1935), vol. 2, p. 665.

[43] Ferguson, *Boer War*, p. 156.
[44] Dennis, *Adventures*, p. 129, July 5, 1902.

cheering and refreshing for the English people to note the sympathy and the intelligent comprehension manifested in the United States . . . . the bulk of American opinion is ranging itself as heartily upon our side in the present quarrel as was English opinion on the side of America in her crusade against misgovernment in Cuba." [45]

More significant, however, than its effect on public opinion—and in this respect it differed from the Spanish War—was the fact that the Boer War, by exposing the British Isles to an array of foes, weakened Britain's international position and therefore her bargaining power. Just as the war with Spain made the United States somewhat dependent on Great Britain, so the Boer War—especially its first phase—made Great Britain somewhat dependent on the United States. We have already noted how Germany triumphed in the partitioning of Samoa because of her rival's South African distractions. Early in 1900 Russia, Britain's arch-foe, delivered another heavy blow: establishment of direct relations with Afghanistan, the stepping-stone to India.[46] And if France could not strike at her foe so directly, she could at least relieve her feelings over the humiliation at Fashoda in violent newspaper rantings against perfidious Albion. It was not a happy time for Great Britain.

Shortly after " Black Week " brought Britain her severest humiliations in living memory, G. W. Smalley wrote: " whatever disputes the United States have with Canada, and there are only too many, they do not prevent the American admiration of Canadian loyalty from being heartily expressed. More than once the suggestion has been heard that this opportunity should be seized to urge the American claims against Canada or England. . . . [It was] not even considered." [47] Smalley was correct in the sense that no member of the administration, least of all the Secretary of State, planned to take advantage of Britain's distresses in

[45] *The Times*, November 6, 1899.
[46] G. P. Gooch and H. Temperley, eds., *British Documents on the Origins of the War, 1898-1914* (11 vols., London, 1926-1938) , vol. 1, pp. 306-307. This unwelcome news was communicated to the British on February 6, 1900.
[47] *The Times*, December 30, 1899.

order to extract advantages in the stalemated Canadian and canal negotiations. Nevertheless her distresses forced her to yield to the United States just as clearly as they did to Germany. Although the United States had not budged one iota from its adamant refusal to arbitrate the Alaska boundary, and although it had agreed to absolutely nothing except a *modus vivendi* favorable to itself, hostilities had hardly commenced when Great Britain, reversing her previous stand, insisted upon Canada abandoning her opposition to changes in the Clayton-Bulwer treaty. It is not necessary to look further than South Africa to understand why the bankrupt canal negotiations of February, 1899, were resumed in early 1900.

CHAPTER 9

The Pauncefote Treaty

BY THE TIME of the Boer War several months had elapsed since that day in February, 1899, when Lord Salisbury told a subdued Henry White that as long as the United States would not arbitrate the Alaska boundary, Great Britain would not sign a canal convention. Ever since then negotiations for modifying the Clayton-Bulwer treaty had been pretty much at a standstill. The convention drafted by Pauncefote lay in the Foreign Office, unsigned; questions of Samoa, China, international arbitration, and South Africa occupied Britain and America. In the United States the call for an American canal had become even more insistent; it would soon force the government to take action, either in cooperation with Great Britain or unilaterally. The American people were going to have their canal no matter what the British might say; so much was certain.

Meanwhile in London, White was continuing to urge early agreement; but apparently relying upon Ambassador Pauncefote's advice, that at least during the year Congress would not authorize a canal, Salisbury, always a calm person, refused to be hurried.[1] Yet the Prime Minister must have had his moments of doubt; after all, two canal bills—the Morgan bill and the Hepburn bill

---

[1] White papers, White to Hay, February 27, 1899: "their information seems to be, presumably through Pauncefote, that no legislation on the Nicaragua Canal is possible this year in any case in Congress and therefore there is nothing to be gained by their giving themselves away in the matters concerning Canada. . . ."

—were before Congress in February, 1899, and the former had passed the Senate by a large majority. To most observers further congressional action must have seemed inevitable. Pauncefote proved right, however. Party conflict arising over one measure sponsored by a Democrat (Senator Morgan) and another by a Republican (Representative Hepburn) resulted in a stalemate in which Congress temporized by shelving both bills and substituting another providing for a special commission to make a thorough survey of all isthmian routes. This bill became law on March 3, 1899, just before Congress adjourned.[2] Great Britain was thereby assured a respite from the threat of provocative American steps at least until sessions resumed in December and possibly until completion of the commission's report, which might not be for two or three years.

The delay was fortunate, for an ugly situation could have arisen had Congress pushed ahead with canal legislation. Ever fearful of new plots in London, the Canadian government was pleading for firmness: let there be no retreat on the Clayton-Bulwer treaty, it urged, without agreement by Washington to arbitrate the Alaska boundary and to safeguard Canadian commercial interests in Puerto Rico.[3] These unrealistic conditions had the backing of the Colonial Office and its chief, Joseph Chamberlain, who was "strongly of opinion"—and so stated several times in 1899—that the Foreign Office should not resume canal talks before getting a "reasonable arrangement" for determining the boundary and before getting assurances of negotiations on American coasting laws.[4] Although the Foreign Office well understood the fatuousness of any such approach, given the uncompromising American temper, it could not lightly disregard the influential Colonial Secretary, to say nothing of the Dominion.[5]

[2] D. C. Miner, *The Fight for the Panama Route: the Story of the Spooner Act and the Hay-Herrán Treaty* (New York, 1940), pp. 85-90.

[3] F. O. 5, 2416, Minto to Chamberlain, telegram received April 10, 1899.

[4] F. O. 55, 392, Colonial Office to Foreign Office, April 17, 1899; F. O. 5, 2416, Foreign Office to Colonial Office, May 6, 1899, Colonial Office to Foreign Office, May 13, 1899.

[5] F. O. 5, 2416, Foreign Office to Colonial Office, May 6, 1899.

Nor was the state of affairs in Alaska much more satisfactory. Hardly had the *modus vivendi* been concluded in October, 1899, when protests from various dissatisfied elements and renewed efforts to reach a permanent boundary settlement began to occupy the attention of British and American statesmen. Their proposal for arbitration along the lines applied in Venezuela having failed, Hay and Pauncefote began to feel their way with utmost circumspection toward arbitration by an even-numbered tribunal, apparently the only procedure offering any hope at all. Pauncefote wrote Salisbury in January, 1900, that he believed the United States would accept such a tribunal, which he knew John Hay to favor; and Ambassador Choate expressed himself similarly a few days later.[6] Lord Salisbury's concern over the uneasy frontier is evident from the eagerness with which he jumped at Pauncefote's suggestion; he telegraphed him immediately to " do all that is in your power " to secure the tribunal.[7] But the Dominion of Canada remained as adamantly opposed as ever.

Here were the two great issues dividing Britain and the United States. As regards both Central America and Alaska strong pressure was being exerted, and was bound to force a change. It would come by common agreement if the statesmen could keep control of events; otherwise it would come by unilateral American action. If the latter, serious, perhaps irreparable, injury would be done to British-American understanding. Yet the two countries, despite elaborate and sustained negotiations, had been able to accomplish no more than a *modus vivendi*, limited in scope and applying to but one controversy.

It has been suggested above that the Boer War broke the impasse into which negotiations had fallen; as a consequence of Britain's vulnerable position she felt compelled to seek renewed negotiations with America. Granted, however, that negotiations resumed, why did they concern the canal rather than the boundary? It was the latter which had proved decisive before the Joint High Commission after all. The explanation lies in the

---

[6] Salisbury papers, January 19 and March 9, 1900; F. O. 5, 2479, Choate to Salisbury, January 22, 1900.

[7] Salisbury papers, February 3, 1900.

Hepburn bill providing for construction and fortification of an American canal. Introduced in December, 1898,[8] it had been superseded by the bill of March, 1899, providing for an investigatory commission. Long before this commission made its report —after extensive surveys it recommended a canal across Nicaragua in November, 1901—Congressional impatience with Britain's procrastination about signing the Pauncefote convention had mounted to a point where many congressmen were prepared to precipitate action, quite regardless of the Clayton-Bulwer treaty. Representative Hepburn reintroduced his bill on December 7, 1899. It was quickly adopted by the committees of both houses to which it was referred. Senator Morgan, who now threw his weight behind the House measure so as not to split the vote, was "quite sanguine" he could steer it through the Senate.[9] All signs pointed to its speedy adoption. "Nicaraguan Canal Will Pass Congress," headlines proclaimed in the New York *Herald* on January 19; "No Longer Any Reasonable Doubt That Its Construction Will Be Authorized During The Present Session Without Waiting for The Walker Report." The administration was alarmed. "This bill," Hay wrote Ambassador Choate, "is in many respects highly objectionable, especially as it absolutely ignores the Clayton-Bulwer Treaty, and, in fact, in many features, is an absolute violation of it." [10]

The Hepburn bill came before Congress at a critical moment in Britain's long history. The object of execration from all over the Continent, she watched with horror as her armies experienced the humiliations of "Black Week" in South Africa. Should the government "delay or refuse signature" of the canal treaty, a Foreign Office memorandum warned, "they would undoubtedly affront the United States Government, and, moreover, it is understood that such action would tend to shake the position of the President," a good friend of the British.[11] Pauncefote had just

[8] See p. 130.

[9] T. Dennett, *John Hay, from Poetry to Politics* (New York, 1933), p. 252, Hay to Choate, January 15, 1900.

[10] *Ibid.* See also F. O. 55, 392, for a telegram from Pauncefote to the Foreign Office dated January 21, 1900, reflecting Hay's agitation.

[11] F. O. 55, 398, memorandum by Larcom, January 26, 1900.

written of the warm friendship being shown by McKinley and the Cabinet.[12] It would have been folly in the extreme to rebuff so friendly an administration, in a world so hostile. And in any case a rebuff would not have been effective; for the United States was on the point of going ahead with a canal regardless of British desires. If Lord Salisbury hesitated at all in these circumstances he may have been persuaded by a personal letter dated January 19, 1900, from Pauncefote, whose analyses and prognostications of canal moves in Washington had always proved reliable:

> I would venture to observe . . . that the proposed convention would be for the benefit of the world at large; that its conclusion at the present time would strengthen the relations between the two nations; that the canal will certainly be made by the U. S. in the face of our opposition & we may have much more difficulty later on in maintaining the " general principle " of the Clayton Bulwer Treaty, whereas the proposed Convention secures all that the world at large can reasonably demand. That the question being one of world-wide interest it seems hardly worth while to make it depend on the issue of the Canadian negotiations which are of a purely local character, especially now that we have practically settled the minor points & that a modus vivendi has been established as regards the Alaska Boundary. The national feeling here about the canal is almost as intense as that regarding the Monroe Doctrine & the opposition of Britain to its construction would undoubtedly impair very seriously the good relations now existing between the two countries, & probably bring back that state of tension which existed at the time of the Venezuelan boundary trouble. America seems to be our only friend just now & it would be unfortunate to quarrel with her.[13]

The next day Hay sent a similar letter to Choate, instructing him to urge the Foreign Office to sign the canal treaty so as to undermine the Hepburn bill. Hay wrote this letter the 15th but delayed sending it so that it would arrive in London with Pauncefote's letter, thus reinforcing its impact.[14]

[12] Salisbury papers, Pauncefote to Salisbury, January 19, 1900.

[13] *Ibid.* Two days later he telegraphed that Hay, " alarmed " over the Hepburn bill, had sent London " urgent request to conclude at once " the canal treaty (F. O. 55, 398, to Foreign Office, January 21, 1898).

[14] Dennett, *Hay*, p. 252.

But what of Canada? The Alaska boundary remained as unsettled as ever; American coasting laws as inflexible. If the Boer War increased the need for Great Britain to come to terms with the United States, it also made it harder for her to alienate Canada, a faithful comrade-at-arms. Lord Salisbury said as much bluntly to Ambassador Choate. But however hard to sacrifice the Dominion, it was harder still to offend her powerful neighbor. Britain's entanglement in South Africa dictated an approach to the United States, and the Hepburn bill specified its subject matter. Accordingly the Colonial Office despatched an important message to Ottawa. It said:

A telegram has been received from Her Majesty's Ambassador at Washington stating that the Hepburn Bill providing for construction of Nicaragua Canal has been reintroduced this session and that Committees of both Houses of Congress have adopted it. Though Bill ignores Clayton-Bulwer Treaty it is believed to be likely to pass and President could not, in view of approaching elections, veto it. United States Government in these circumstances urge that the draft convention communicated to you . . . 20th February 1899 should be concluded immediately. It is believed that the Convention would pass Senate and save situation by rendering it unnecessary for the President to become party to an action unfriendly to this country and seriously embarrassing Her Majesty's Government in the present juncture.

Her Majesty's Government regarded Draft Convention as reasonable and satisfactory *per se*, but they deferred concluding negotiations in the hope of inducing United States Government to come to terms in regard to Alaska Boundary and other questions under discussion by the Joint High Commission.

Her Majesty's Government are deeply conscious of the valuable support received from Canada in the present crisis and would reluctantly abandon any point which might be effectively pressed in pursuance of the wishes of your Ministers.

There is little hope however of an early agreement in the boundary question and it is recognized by public opinion here that claim of United States for the revision of the Clayton-Bulwer Treaty is legitimate.

If Her Majesty's Government further delay or refuse to proceed with Convention, such refusal would be regarded as an affront to United States Government, and would tend to shake position of President whose friendly attitude is in the present condition of public affairs of great importance.

I need not point out what would be the consequences of such a result to Canadian interests, and I trust that your Ministers will recognize that in the interests of the Dominion as well as in those of the rest of the Empire it is necessary that Her Majesty's Government should agree to sign at once. Telegraph reply as soon as possible, as the matter is very urgent.[15]

This forceful appeal was strengthened by a personal message from Joseph Chamberlain who, now that the British armies found themselves bogged down in South Africa, had changed his mind about the Clayton-Bulwer treaty; he asked the Governor-General to use his best efforts to win the Dominion's consent.[16] Lord Minto did not have to exert himself, for the Canadians really had no choice. They realized that the point had been reached where Great Britain was going to modify the treaty no matter what they might wish. Better give way gracefully than be trampled upon. And so after a hastily summoned conference Canada sent the welcome reply that, " Deferring to the strongly expressed views of the Imperial Government that in the interests of the Empire the Imperial Government should agree to the immediate signature of the Convention . . . , and realizing the gravity of those views," she would yield. But in the same breath she manifested her discontent by making one last despairing cry for consolation in Alaska and in her lost Puerto Rican trade.[17]

It only remained for Hay and Pauncefote to resurrect their moribund convention. They signed it on February 5, 1900. It had four articles. By the first Britain released the United States from the obligation not to build a purely American canal. The second listed seven rules, similar to those governing the Suez Canal, for securing the " general principle " of neutralization specified in the Clayton-Bulwer treaty; the most noteworthy of them provided that the canal should be " free and open, in time of war as in time of peace, to the vessels of commerce and of

[15] F. O. 55, 398, Chamberlain to Minto, January 30, 1900.
[16] *Ibid.*, minute by Anderson on Chamberlain to Minto, January 30, 1900.
[17] C. O. 42, 875, Minto to Chamberlain, February 1, 1900. The telegram is also in F. O. 55, 398.

war of all nations on terms of entire equality . . . ," and that it should not be fortified. The third required the United States and Great Britain to invite other countries to adhere to the new convention. The fourth named a time limit of six months for exchange of ratifications (a period subsequently extended to March 5, 1901).[18] In agreeing to these terms Great Britain, after having refused to sign for nearly a year, made a complete capitulation. True, the "general principle" of neutrality remained; but Hay had not asked for its termination. Without conceding anything, in Alaska, Puerto Rico, or anywhere, he had won everything he had been striving for; and the United States after fifty years of frustration had at length rid itself of the most objectionable features of its most unpopular treaty. The Pauncefote treaty represented a signal triumph for the country.[19]

It was not yet law, however. It had still to be approved by the Senate Foreign Relations Committee and be ratified by two-thirds of the Senate. At the outset ratification seemed assured. ". . . I even hoped it might pass unanimously," Secretary Hay admitted later.[20] He should not have been so optimistic; he should have paused to consider the powerful forces arrayed against any such agreement. These forces quickly made themselves felt as the newly signed treaty moved out of the State Department full into the cross winds of Capitol Hill. As a matter of fact, the Secretary of State himself had bolstered the opposi-

[18] F. O. 55, 399, Pauncefote to Salisbury, May 25, 1900; *The Times*, May 7, 1900.

[19] According to press comments cited by *Public Opinion*, vol. 28 (February 15, 1900), pp. 198-199, the *Washington Post*, the Boston *Post*, the Brooklyn *Eagle*, the Chicago *Post*, and the Detroit *News* opposed the treaty; on the other hand the New York *Press*, the *New York World*, the Philadelphia *Inquirer*, the Philadelphia *Ledger*, the *New York Tribune*, the Chicago *Record*, the Baltimore *Herald*, and the *New York Times* favored it. The Paris *Temps*, February 7, 1900, saw the treaty as a British concession made to foster "the Anglo-Saxon alliance." For other continental opinion see *The Times*, February 10, 1900. Sir Charles Tupper was of course annoyed that Canada had got nothing (*ibid.*, February 8, 1900).

[20] C. C. Tansill, *Canadian-American Relations, 1875-1911* (New Haven, 1943), p. 219; Hay wrote this to Choate, December 21, 1900.

tion's strength. According to the two most prominent Republicans on the Senate Committee, Cushman Davis, its chairman, and Henry Cabot Lodge, he had not been sufficiently solicitous of their views. He "neither showed me a draft of the treaty nor told me any of its provisions," Lodge complained; [21] and in the opinion of Whitelaw Reid, the well informed editor of the *New York Tribune*, the "real cause" of the treaty's most important amendment was the "aggrieved feeling" of Senator Davis.[22]

Moreover the treaty had powerful enemies in two New York newspapers—William Randolph Hearst's *Morning Journal*, and Paul Dana's *Sun*. Hardly had it been signed in early 1900 when these papers broke forth in sustained and intemperate denunciations of what they were pleased to depict as Hay's obsequious capitulation to the wily British.[23] The *Sun* in particular waged an "indefatigable campaign" against the treaty, as Pauncefote noted sorrowfully; a campaign no doubt attributable to Dana's dislike of Hay.[24] The Secretary believed that this onslaught frightened several senators into opposing the treaty.[25]

Personal considerations and interested newspaper criticism help

[21] J. A. Garraty, *Henry Cabot Lodge, a Biography* (New York, 1953), p. 211; the complaint was recorded in his journal, December 21, 1900. Hay may not have accorded the senator due deference but he did write to him two days after the treaty's signature that he would "far rather" have the treaty defeated outright "than so changed as virtually to defeat it by a majority"; see R. B. Mowat, *The Life of Lord Pauncefote, First Ambassador to the United States* (Boston and New York, 1929), p. 282. See also A. Nevins, *Henry White, Thirty Years of American Diplomacy* (New York and London, 1930), p. 153, White to Hay, May 16, 1900.

[22] Nevins, *White*, p. 153, White to Hay, May 16, 1900.

[23] *Ibid.*, p. 152.

[24] W. R. Thayer, *The Life and Letters of John Hay* (2 vols., Boston and New York, 1915), vol. 2, p. 236, Hay to Hanna, August 2, 1900: "The whole thing is, Paul Dana wants to get me out of the Cabinet. It is his fourth attempt." F. O. 55, 398, Pauncefote to Salisbury, March 15, 1900. See *The Times*, June 12, 1900, for an article discussing the *Sun*'s anti-British leanings. Hay wrote White, February 10, 1901, that Lodge "beat the Treaty to curry favor with the *Sun* and a few Irish politicians who flatter him" (White papers).

[25] Nevins, *White*, p. 152.

account for the Senate's handling of the treaty. But we must not overlook the fact that strong, well-reasoned arguments could be and were advanced against it. No one presented them more cogently than Theodore Roosevelt, then governor of New York. In a well known letter to John Hay, dated February 18, 1900, he made two points: the treaty endangered United States security by giving enemy ships free use of the canal once they got within the three-mile limit; and it ran counter to the Monroe Doctrine by inviting other countries to adhere.[26] Such arguments doubtless convinced many people.

Two other factors—transcontinental railways and the New Panama Canal Company, a French concern—may have had the greatest influence of all. It goes without saying that the railways opposed the creation of a rival route. But did they intervene to block the Hay-Pauncefote treaty, and if so did they have any success? All one can say is that some newspapers thought they did,[27] and that according to Lord Pauncefote, always a circumspect reporter, "there can be no doubt that it [the campaign against the treaty] has been largely fomented by the great transcontinental Railway interest. . . ."[28] Probably more directly effective was propaganda of the New Panama Canal Company. Organized in 1894 to acquire the holdings of the original French concern, which went bankrupt in 1889, the company wanted desperately to sell its valuable concession, due to expire in 1904; it wanted to sell also the enormous hole it had dug in Panama and all its costly equipment now rotting in the jungle. The more the United States looked to Nicaragua the more frantic

[26] Thayer, *Life and Letters*, vol. 2, pp. 339-341. According to F. W. Holls, Roosevelt after a consultation with Holls, Assistant Secretary of State Hill, Nicholas Murray Butler, and Albert Shaw "issued his manifesto against the Hay-Pauncefote Treaty, which I hope has killed the latter, and also his declination of the Vice-Presidency" (Holls papers, Holls to "My dear Will," March 5, 1900).

[27] *New York Times*, March 12 and December 12, 1900.

[28] F. O. 55, 399, Pauncefote to Lansdowne, December 18, 1900. F. W. Holls wrote: "There is a powerful lobby of transcontinental railroads interested in defeating the whole canal idea . . ." (Holls papers, to Lange, December 5, 1900).

became stockholders of the New Panama Canal Company. Since most Americans were quite unaware of the choice of routes and felt no interest in Panama, the company faced the need to delay a final decision in Washington until the United States could be persuaded of Panama's superior merits.

To accomplish this most formidable task it relied upon an extraordinary American lawyer, William Nelson Cromwell. Since 1896 Cromwell had been conducting one of the most effective lobbies in the by no means poverty-struck history of American lobbying. Now in 1899 he set himself to defeating a treaty that, given the existing fixation on Nicaragua, could lead only to ruin for his clients. Did this resourceful person find a way to influence the Senate Foreign Relations Committee, or did he help convince the Senate itself of the need of amendments? Some newspapers reported that the center of opposition to the treaty consisted precisely of Cromwell and the French company; [29] and according to Cromwell himself, for whatever his claim may be worth, the main credit for the eventual decision for Panama should go to him.[30] One may well suspect that this persuasive individual had much to do with the fate of the Pauncefote treaty. But, again, conclusive evidence is lacking.

Such were the influences brought to bear upon the Senate Foreign Relations Committee as it studied the treaty. After about a month it reported it favorably but with a most important amendment. The Davis amendment, as it was called, declared the non-fortification provision of the Clayton-Bulwer treaty inapplicable " to measures which the United States may find it necessary to take for securing, by its own forces, the defense of the United States and the maintenance of public order." [31] Many informed people have defended the amendment and there is no reason to doubt that, although considerations of personal pique may

[29] *New York Times*, March 12 and December 20, 1900; *The Standard* (London), December 21, 1900; Holls papers, Holls to Lange, December 5, 1900.

[30] Miner, *Fight for Panama*, pp. 123-126.

[31] The committee report is in 56th Congress, 1st session, Senate document 268; it was issued March 9, 1900.

have been present, the majority of the committee sincerely believed with Theodore Roosevelt that the country should not build a canal it could not fortify.

The amendment was very far-reaching, for it cut squarely across the "general principle" of neutralization basic to the Clayton-Bulwer treaty. "It is too childish on their part to suppose that we should accept an amendment so utterly destructive of the ' general principle '...." [32] This was Pauncefote's indignant reaction, and not a few Americans shared his scorn for such nationalistic treatment of the proposed waterway. Even Henry Adams, a person not given to optimistic delusions about politicians, was shocked; he announced "quite seriously" that he would join any party which stood for abolishing the Senate, "even, if necessary, by force." [33] As for John Hay, his whole world seemed to be toppling in ruins. He could hardly believe that even United States senators, whom he despised profoundly, would be so stupid as to endanger a treaty giving America everything, Britain nothing. In a fit of anger and petulance he submitted his resignation on March 13, 1900. Fortunately, however, McKinley refused to accept it. [34]

The treaty was now before the Senate. An agreement giving the United States everything it had been striving to get for fifty years, plus the safeguard of the Davis amendment, would, it might be thought, have been ratified with utmost despatch. But with every passing day of 1900 politics was more and more filling the air. At such times American politicians by a sure instinct steer clear of major agreements with Great Britain, just as they avoid the tariff. Of what help to a senator up for reelection could this canal treaty be? Of what help to the Republican party? It was especially necessary to be wary because the South African war was still arousing intense feelings. How would German-Americans, already critical of the administration's antipathy for the Boers, react to a further accommodation with the

[32] Salisbury papers, Pauncefote to Salisbury, March 9, 1900.

[33] W. C. Ford, ed., *Letters of Henry Adams (1892-1918)* (Boston and New York, 1938), p. 273, March 5, 1900.

[34] Thayer, *Life and Letters*, vol. 2, pp. 226-228.

unspeakable British? Quick to grasp a manifest opportunity, William Randolph Hearst would soon be acquiring his third newspaper, the Chicago *American*, in good measure so as to swing the German vote in the mid-West to the Democrats.[35] Irish opposition, too, could be expected. " The fear of the Irish vote, and probably of the German vote, too, has once more possessed the souls and paralyzed the senses of the Republican politicians," the *New York Times* reported.[36] Although considered pro-British, the Republican party still hoped to keep the German vote, if not to win the Irish. And so, as often before, domestic politics weighed more heavily than international comity; even the canal project would have to be sacrificed to the implacable machine.

The Senate on May 21, 1900, postponed consideration of the treaty until the next session, in December safely after the elections;[37] and a few days later, on June 7, after defeating a resolution offered in desperation by Senator Morgan declaring the Clayton-Bulwer treaty abrogated then and there, Congress adjourned.[38] The decision to delay the vote was all the easier because President McKinley, characteristically passive in such matters, did nothing to support his Secretary's cherished agreement. Hay did not record his feelings, but he may have read with approval an editorial in the London *Times* decrying the "opportunism of Mr. McKinley":

The President has been unable to resist the evidence that there is a community of interests which cannot be ignored between the people of this country and our kinsmen across the Atlantic. But he has been cold and cautious in his recognition of the fact, and, with the Presidential election in his eye, he has done little practically to promote the creation of new ties between the two nations. If he had pressed the question of the Nica-

[35] J. K. Winkler, *W. R. Hearst, an American Phenomenon* (New York, 1928), pp. 170-172.

[36] March 12, 1900.

[37] The senators' timidity in touching anything British in an election year was demonstrated by their reluctance to ratify an obscure and unobjectionable treaty with Britain concerning land tenure (*The Times*, April 14, 1900).

[38] Miner, *Fight for Panama*, p. 101.

ragua Canal Convention . . . the opposition would probably have collapsed.[39]

A year and a half had already elapsed since Ambassador Pauncefote drafted his canal treaty, which had seemed at first so sure of quick acceptance; an even longer period had still to pass before finally a new treaty was signed.

[39] April 30, 1900.

CHAPTER 10

Political Requirements of 1900

DURING the long recess following adjournment the treaty's fate remained uncertain. Still feeling endangered by the international repercussions of her South African adventure, Great Britain was obliged to wait upon American pleasure as to ratification, just as the previous year the United States had had to wait for Britain and Canada to decide about signing. The treaty's drafting had been quick and easy; its signature had been much more difficult; a long, tortuous, often obscure path still lay ahead before its final conclusion. Meanwhile, as summer and autumn months passed, events of compelling fascination were taking place, events that completely overshadowed the treaty for a while and then, when it finally came before the Senate in December, complicated the problem of securing its ratification. These were the siege of the foreign legations in Peking by the Boxers, and the presidential election of 1900.

Originating in anti-foreign sentiment flourishing throughout China in the last years of the century, the Boxer revolt was carried on mainly by a secret society, the Righteous and Harmonious Band, incorrectly known as Boxers.[1] In the spring of 1900 the Boxers, who already had perpetrated scattered outrages against missionaries and native Christians, increased their attacks. Fearing a general uprising some of the western powers in May, 1900, sent reinforcements to protect their legations in Peking;

[1] G. N. Steiger, *China and the Occident: the Origin and Development of the Boxer Movement* (New Haven, 1927), has a good account of the revolt.

the move touched off a violent onslaught against foreigners in many parts of the old empire. Fighting centered in Peking, where communications of the legation area with the outside world were severed. Most people assumed that all westerners in the capital had been slaughtered, as indeed several hundred were elsewhere in the country.

These incredible events gripped the western world all through the summer of 1900. Nothing else—certainly not the canal project —came close to rivaling the terrible fascination of the Peking drama. Horrifying in itself the revolt was the more frightening because it threw into turmoil an area of crucial importance in international diplomacy. Such events did not occur in China at the turn of the century without shaking foreign policies the world over to their core. The long feared partition of the country seemed close at hand, the Anglo-American open door policy a hollow fraud. Thus the revolt presented a fundamental challenge to America's Far Eastern policy—and consequently to the Anglo-American rapprochement based in good measure upon common interests in China. Should China be partitioned a major prop of concord between America and Britain would be knocked out.[2]

Yet the United States could not contemplate joint action with Great Britain in the political atmosphere prevailing during that eventful summer. Many men in the two governments agreed in seeing a Russian hand behind the revolt; but at a time when "every Senator" was telling John Hay, "For God's sake don't let it appear we have any understanding with England" how could the Secretary afford to furnish campaign material to Democrats, already sharpening their knives for an assault on all his works, by establishing a common front with London against St. Petersburg?[3] That American interests might thereby be

[2] On this point see an editorial in *The Times*, March 3, 1900.

[3] T. Dennett, *John Hay, from Poetry to Politics* (New York, 1933), p. 334, June 23, 1900. For a letter from Lodge to White, June 29, 1900, that doubtless reflected the suspicions of many of his associates about Russia see A. Nevins, *Henry White, Thirty Years of American Diplomacy* (New York and London, 1930), pp. 170-171.

advanced made little difference. ". . . anything we should now do in China to take care of our imperilled interests would be set down to 'subservience to Great Britain'"; so lamented the exasperated Secretary of State.[4]

In these circumstances the United States had no choice but to pursue an independent course. In military matters, to be sure, it cooperated with Britain and other countries. That was inevitable in the nature of the case; and the awful peril hanging over the legations prevented serious criticism of a departure from strict precepts of isolationism. While American naval vessels hovered off the China coast, some 5,000 American soldiers participated in an international relief expedition that fought its way inland and relieved the legations on August 14. As for diplomacy, John Hay's famous circular letter sent to the great powers in July, 1900, reflected the exigencies of an election year. Like the open door notes of September, 1899, the letter was sent without prior consultation with Great Britain or any other power. And further to assure Anglophobes soon to cast their ballots, the Secretary of State took pains to publicize the 100 percent Americanism of his step.[5] The circular expressed Washington's hope for a settlement of the crisis that would preserve not only the open door but also the territorial integrity and administrative entity of the entire Chinese empire. The United States hoped thereby to give pause to Russia, whose grip on Manchuria boded ill for American exporters to that area; it boded ill, too, for British, and American, power in the Far East—a consideration that may well have been paramount in Hay's mind.[6]

If the United States felt compelled to act independently of Great Britain, Britain felt the same way with respect to acting with the United States. Military aid, she realized, could not be expected from that country, all the fine talk of Anglo-American

---

[4] Dennett, *Hay*, p. 333, June 23, 1900.

[5] *Ibid.*, p. 309.

[6] For the connection between the Manchurian market and the July circular see C. S. Campbell, Jr., *Special Business Interests and the Open Door Policy* (New Haven, 1951), chs. III and X.

accord in the Far East notwithstanding. Although Lord Salisbury "most emphatically" concurred in the July circular,[7] he
probably did not feel particularly enthusiastic about it, any more
than about the open door notes the previous September. After
all, Hay's polite circular could hardly be counted upon to restrain
the implacable men in the Tsar's war ministry. Yet some counter
to the Russians was essential; and Britain herself, deeply involved
as she was in South Africa, could hardly deliver one. Writing
off the United States she turned, first, to Japan, and then to
Germany. Her ingenious idea of persuading the powers to nominate Japan—the only country with the men on the spot to check
Russia—as their mandatory, ostensibly against the Boxers, did
not work out. More effective, though hardly satisfactory, was
her agreement with Germany. By the Anglo-German treaty of
October 16, 1900, the two signatories pledged themselves to maintain the open door and the territorial integrity of China, and
to confer together if any other country tried to annex Chinese
territory. At the news John Hay at first was thrilled. The treaty
seemed to "confirm and fortify my work"; it was, he wrote
exultingly to his wife, "the greatest triumph of all."[8] But when
he learned, as he soon did, that on German insistence it excluded
Manchuria from its scope, of all parts of China the main object
of Russian expansion, his disillusionment was complete.[9]

Hay's circular, Great Britain's approach to Japan, the British-
German agreement—these were the main diplomatic steps taken
by Washington and London. Although reflecting parallel attitudes toward the Boxer crisis, far from indicating agreed action
they indicated scepticism as to the possibility of such action. In
relatively normal circumstances the two governments might
parade a joint policy in Asia; but if America found itself in the
midst of a presidential election or if Britain felt her vital interests
imperilled, each quickly turned from the other. Nor did the

---

[7] *Foreign Relations of the United States, 1900*, p. 345.

[8] C. S. Hay, ed., *Letters of John Hay and Extracts from Diary* (3 vols.,
Washington, 1908), vol. 3, pp. 199-200, October 29, 1900.

[9] W. R. Thayer, *The Life and Letters of John Hay* (2 vols., Boston and
New York, 1915), vol. 2, pp. 248-249, Hay to Adams, November 21, 1900.

Boxer crisis create among the public in either country an impression of Anglo-American solidarity against other powers, as had the Samoan troubles and the open door notes and in some degree the Hague conference. On the contrary if it led to any comparable impression it was rather one of American-*Russian* harmony. The Secretary of State sorrowfully confessed that " some of the press in England think we have changed our point of view in China, and have taken up one more friendly to Russia than to England." [10] This point must not be overstated, however; certainly no general belief existed that the United States stood on the verge of turning from Britain to Russia.

The Boxer revolt revealed that in a major international crisis Anglo-American understanding was not yet close enough to produce a common front; the election of 1900 revealed that it was at least close enough to furnish a great deal of campaign excitement. With the major parties nominating the same candidates as four years earlier, McKinley and Bryan, another bitter contest, as tense and nerve-wracking as that of 1896, loomed ahead. Although as in most American elections the main issues related to domestic matters, an unusual concern over foreign policy prevailed as a consequence of the Spanish-American War and overseas expansion. Anglo-American relations constituted a prominent subject of debate and one arousing strong emotions. The editor of the London *Times* could hardly have been more mistaken in perceiving " no reason to suppose that Democrats, any more than Republicans " would try to disturb friendly feelings toward Great Britain.[11] On the contrary, far from such forbearance Democrats did their utmost to revive the British bogey; and the campaign had not long been under way before Bryan and his fellow orators were hurling invectives at the administration for being so un-American as to befriend descendants of King George the third.[12]

---

[10] Nevins, *White*, p. 172; E. T. S. Dugdale, ed., *German Diplomatic Documents, 1871-1914* (4 vols., London, 1928-1931) , vol. 3, pp. 131-132. See Nevins, *White*, pp. 177-178, for Henry Cabot Lodge's biting criticisms of Britain's policy in China.

[11] *The Times*, September 11, 1900.

[12] As early as August, 1899, Hay found the Democratic press " ready to

As a matter of fact Democrats had a fertile field to exploit in the Anglophobia still solidly entrenched—according to some it had increased recently [13]—despite the British-American rapprochement. The Russian ambassador at Washington, Cassini, reported " a definite and unmistakable hatred of England, which is fanned by 15 million Irish "; he foresaw in fact an early " violent break " between the two English-speaking countries—a pleasing prospect for Russia with her expansionist ambitions in the Far East.[14] The extent of anti-British feeling may be gauged by the fact that only with considerable difficulty did Republican leaders prevent their convention from adopting a plank demanding annexation of Canada,[15] just as they had trouble in suppressing the plank condemning Britain for the Boer War.

Mention has been made of the electoral clamor about the war.[16] It was only to be expected that the canal question as well would whet the appetite of vote-hungry Democrats. Lord Pauncefote noted that their cry for an " American canal " was making rapid headway.[17] It was no surprise, therefore, when the Democratic convention condemned the canal treaty " as a surrender of American rights and interests, not to be tolerated by the American people," and called—in complete disregard of the Clayton-Bulwer treaty—for immediate construction, ownership, and control of a Nicaragua canal by the United States. Even Republicans, despite their Secretary of State's current negotia-

attack any treaty with England, no matter how advantageous to us, as a hostile act towards Ireland and Germany "; see C. C. Tansill, *Canadian-American Relations, 1875-1911* (New Haven, 1943) , p. 202. See also Dennett, *Hay*, p. 222, Hay to White, September 9, 1899: " Whatever we do, the Bryan party will attack us as slaves of England. All their state conventions put an anti-English plank in their platforms to curry favor with the Irish (whom they want to keep) , and the Germans whom they want to seduce. It is too disgusting to have to deal with such sordid liars."

[13] The British *Review of Reviews*, vol. 21 (1900) , p. 205, cited " the recrudescence of the strong anti-British feeling on the part of the American people."

[14] Dugdale, *German Diplomatic Documents*, vol. 3, p. 131, von Radolin to Chancellor, August 2, 1900. See also Dennett, *Hay*, p. 333.

[15] Dennett, *Hay*, p. 333.

[16] See pp. 181-182.

[17] F. O. 55, 399, to Lansdowne, December 18, 1900.

tions with Britain, went so far as to "favor the construction, ownership, control, and protection of an isthmian canal by the Government of the United States. . . ." It would appear that popular emotionalism barred any quixotic respect for international law.

The *modus vivendi* on the Alaska boundary, too, an arrangement altogether favorable to the United States, came in for criticism, so much so that shortly before the election Hay thought it well to defend himself publicly for having made a good bargain.[18] As a matter of fact, the *modus* had been under fire for some months. The marking of the temporary line, beginning in June, 1900, had touched off protests. From the contested gold fields along Porcupine creek had arrived a petition from 135 miners; denouncing "most emphatically . . . unjust and unwarrantable seizure of vast areas of the public domain . . . which the British, by means of the drag net, the Modus Vivendi, are seizing . . . ," it concluded with a stirring appeal to President McKinley:

> Will you not, Mr. President, act with the people and see to it that these posts are moved back, so our posterity shall have the benefit of the purchase of this land, made under the administration of the G. O. P. which you to-day so worthily represent; and shall not our boys, in years to come, say "Lincoln [sic] purchased these gold fields and hung Old Glory over them, and McKinley kept the Lion at bay and drove him from our forests, and Old Glory hangs there still." [19]

Here was matter to fire the blood of all true patriots! Not only did the Alaska Chamber of Commerce "most heartily endorse" the petition and "most emphatically condemn" the *modus*, but, what was more significant in terms of votes in the approaching election, the Seattle Chamber of Commerce backed up the aggrieved miners with a resolution of its own to the government;[20] and after prompting by the Portland Chamber of Com-

---

[18] Dennett, *Hay*, p. 234; see also Hay's letter to Choate cited in *ibid.*, p. 233.
[19] State Department, Miscellaneous Letters, Emmons to McKinley, July 11, 1900.
[20] *Ibid.*, Alaska Chamber of Commerce to McKinley, September 14, 1900, and Seattle Chamber of Commerce to McKinley, July 23, 1900.

merce, the United States senators from Oregon did likewise.[21] Senator Foster of the state of Washington also forwarded denunciations of the *modus vivendi*, although in this case they arose independently of the Porcupine appeal.[22] Such stirrings among the electorate attested " the state of irritation, generally suppressed, sometimes explosive, in the North-Western States . . ." that G. W. Smalley reported anxiously.[23] No politician could afford to ignore it.

More than against open agreements, however, Democrats declaimed against what they alleged to be a secret British-American alliance. It is indicative both of the dislike of Great Britain, a feeling still to be reckoned with, and of the stupidities of which a presidential election is capable that their platform condemned the " ill-concealed Republican alliance with England. . . ."[24] The allegation was made despite the manifest impossibility of its truth and despite two categorical denials by the Secretary of State. As early as September, 1899, Hay had written an open letter, hundreds of thousands of copies of which were subsequently printed for campaign purposes, denying the existence of such an alliance.[25] Nevertheless, a resolution of the House of Representatives, with an obvious eye on the approaching elections, directed the Secretary of State to disclose " what truth

[21] *Ibid.*, Simon and McBride to Hay, August 1, 1900.

[22] *Ibid.*, Foster to Hay, February 18, 1901; the senator merely enclosed protests from two of his constituents. See also *ibid.*, Department of Interior to State Department, enclosing a letter from J. B. Philip, manager of the Big Salmon Mining and Milling Company, Haines mission, Alaska, May 7, 1900. For protests against various other conditions in Alaska, not specifically relating to the *modus*, see F. O. 5, 2519, Mills to Governor-General, March 5, 1901; F. O. 5, 2482, Hay to Pauncefote, November 27, 1900; F. O. 5, 2482, Pauncefote to Lansdowne, February 13, 1901; F. O. 5, 2482, Pauncefote to Lansdowne, April 9, 1901; State Department, Miscellaneous Letters, Treasury Department to State Department, November 19, 1900.

[23] *The Times*, June 12, 1900. Echoing Smalley's concern was a resolution of the Congress of Chambers of Commerce of the British Empire: " it is of vital importance . . . to press forward a settlement of the Alaska boundary question . . ." (F. O. 5, 2479, to Salisbury, July 31, 1900).

[24] *Outlook*, vol. 65 (1900), p. 637; *The Times*, July 6, 1900.

[25] Dennett, *Hay*, p. 221.

there is in the charge that a secret alliance exists between the Republic of the United States and the Empire of Great Britain." [26] Democratic leaders continued to inveigh against the supposed secret agreement in terms, the British embassy reported, "clearly causing embarrassment to the Administration "; [27] and consequently two days before they adopted their platform the Secretary felt compelled to deny the fantastic allegation again.[28] Obviously improvement of relations with Great Britain was not an unmixed blessing for an incumbent political party in 1900.

The resounding triumph of William McKinley in November— he had a larger popular plurality than any preceding presidential candidate [29]—doubtless encouraged his Secretary of State, who could now continue to push forward his pro-British policy with renewed confidence in its feasibility from the standpoint of party politics. The British, too, were pleased. With Theodore Roosevelt they had no doubt observed that: "No republican of any prominence made any allusion to England . . . save in an entirely friendly spirit. Bryan sought to arouse and trade on Irish, German and Dutch hostility to England, but I do not think he accomplished very much." [30] When the final returns reached London, Ambassador Choate could truthfully say, "the result of the election creates as much interest and gives as much pleasure here as at home." [31]

Comparing the years 1899 and 1900 we find that in the former the United States and Great Britain were thrown together in a number of episodes in which they appeared to present a common front. To be sure, appearance did not altogether square with

[26] State Department, Miscellaneous Letters, February 19, 1900.

[27] F. O. 5, 2392, Tower to Salisbury, October 18, 1899.

[28] Thayer, *Life and Letters*, vol. 2, pp. 233-234, Hay to McMillan, July 3, 1900.

[29] T. A. Bailey, "Was the Election of 1900 a Mandate on Imperialism?" *Mississippi Valley Historical Review*, vol. 24 (1937), p. 43.

[30] E. E. Morison, ed., *The Letters of Theodore Roosevelt* (8 vols., Cambridge, Mass., 1951-1954), vol. 2, p. 1425, Roosevelt to Strachey, November 19, 1900.

[31] E. S. Martin, *The Life of Joseph Hodges Choate as Gathered Chiefly from His Letters* (2 vols., London, 1920), vol. 2, p. 174.

reality. But in 1900 these two countries not only in fact but also in appearance kept well apart from each other. In consequence, whereas at the end of 1899 they had been popularly associated together, at the end of 1900 the presidential elections and the Boxer uprising had had a contrary effect: they had served to disassociate them in popular thinking. The Boer War, too, had stirred up anti-British sentiment in the United States. Undoing much of the good work of 1898 and even of 1899, the year 1900 therefore proved unfortunate for British-American harmony.

The deterioration did not augur well for the Pauncefote canal treaty. As has appeared, the Senate had postponed discussion of it in June for political reasons. Already in early 1900 ratification of the treaty as drafted had seemed unlikely enough; now that elections, Boers, and Boxers had reanimated old prejudices it seemed yet more unlikely. When the second session of the 56th Congress convened on December 3, 1900, Representative Hepburn's canal bill stood high on the Senate's order of business. It had already passed the House the previous May 2 by the decisive vote of 224 to 36, and had been reported favorably two weeks later by Senator Morgan's Committee on Interoceanic Canals. Consideration by the Senate had been promised for December 10. Nicaragua and Costa Rica, through which the projected canal would run, had agreed in principle to the necessary arrangements, and the Walker commission had indicated a favorable route. Pressure for action had mounted to a point where something had to be done.

Worried lest Congress give way and abrogate the Clayton-Bulwer treaty, Republican leaders quickly put Pauncefote's convention before the Senate. They soon discovered, however, that it had no chance without the Davis amendment. To the already large number of advocates of fortification had now been added the transcontinental railroads and the New Panama Canal Company, which seem to have backed the amendment because they thought it would wreck the treaty by rendering it unacceptable to the British.[32] With practically everyone outside the State

[32] *New York Times*, December 20, 1900; *The Times*, December 21 and 24, 1900; *The Standard* (London), December 21, 1900.

Department—the canal's enemies as well as its friends—favoring the amendment its adoption was a foregone conclusion. Fears that Britain might object were quieted by a report, spread mainly by Henry Cabot Lodge, to the effect that a high British official had predicted his government's acquiescence in the amendment; [33] as a matter of fact belief in Britain's readiness to accept, or rather in her inability to resist, practically any change the Senate might make seems to have been general.[34] In view of Pauncefote's earlier scorn it is curious to find him now favoring the amendment's acceptance:

> If I may venture to express my humble opinion it is that it would be wiser to secure the Treaty with amendment, objectionable as it is in principle, than to have no Treaty at all.
> Mr. Hay who strongly opposes the amendment thinks likewise in view of popular clamour for an American Canal free from any conditions and of improbability of the amendment ever having any practical effect.
> President is said to have already accepted the amendment to save the Treaty and I fear that if Treaty were lost he would not have the courage to veto a Canal Bill passed in defiance of the Clayton-Bulwer Treaty, such as the Hepburn Bill which has passed the House and is now pending before the Senate.[35]

The Senate adopted the Davis amendment on December 14, 1900, by the convincing majority of 65 to 17.[36] But before the vote on the treaty as a whole a Republican caucus decided to recommend two further changes: abrogation of the Clayton-

[33] F. O. 55, 399, Pauncefote to Lansdowne, December 9, 1900. Lansdowne instructed Pauncefote to deny the report (Hay papers, Pauncefote to Hay, December 12, 1900). Probably the senator had in mind a report from White quoting Arthur Balfour in that vein (Nevins, *White*, p. 153; the report was made in early April). According to Nevins's account Balfour was agreeable to " amendments "; this would seem to be a mistake for only one amendment (the Davis amendment) had been reported favorably by the Senate Committee by April.

[34] *The Times*, December 10 and 12, 1900.

[35] F. O. 55, 399, Pauncefote to Foreign Office, December 9, 1900. Mowat, *Life of Pauncefote*, p. 285, cites the first paragraph of this telegram, but with quite different wording.

[36] J. A. Garraty, *Henry Cabot Lodge, a Biography* (New York, 1953), p. 215.

Bulwer treaty (the so-called Foraker amendment), and deletion of the article inviting other powers to adhere. As long as the old treaty was being amended almost out of existence anyway, many senators thought it only sensible to scrap it outright; still more senators believed the adherence of other countries would impinge upon the Monroe Doctrine. These critics would have to be placated. A special delegation—Senators Lodge, Foraker, and Aldrich—carried news of the additional changes to the President. McKinley did not reject the Davis amendment, but according to Hay he was " much annoyed " about the two new amendments and warned the senators that Britain would not accept them.[37] Hay himself was of course incensed, all the more so for having just received a report of Boer delight at the prospect of a British-American rift.[38] Unmoved, the Senate ratified the treaty on December 20, 1900, with the three amendments.

Ratification took the ground from under the feet of proponents of the Hepburn bill; since obviously they had no case for unilateral action while the possibility existed of a friendly agreement with Great Britain. By general consent the Senate once again shelved the much postponed bill.

It was now McKinley's problem to deal with a treaty of which he disapproved. He could communicate it to the British as amended, or he could resubmit it to the Senate. Characteristically refusing the role of a strong executive he forwarded it to London.[39]

Would the British accept the amendments? [40] The day before

[37] *Ibid.* F. O. 55, 399, Pauncefote to Lansdowne, December 15, 1900, reporting a conversation with Hay. An editorial in *The Times*, December 15, 1900, said much the same thing. Lodge, however, wrote that the President agreed to " press the amendments upon England to the utmost " (Lodge journal, December 21, 1900, cited by Garraty, *Lodge*, p. 215).

[38] J. H. Ferguson, *American Diplomacy and the Boer War* (Philadelphia, 1939), p. 203.

[39] *The Times*, December 24, 1900, criticized the President for devolving " upon us the responsibility of dealing from an international point of view with a proposal he might have kept within the domain of domestic affairs by the exercise of a little firmness."

[40] The great majority of British newspapers condemned the Senate for the

the Senate approved the treaty, a challenging editorial appeared in the London *Times*:

> The Senators, we are told, in their present mood will ratify no treaty with England but a treaty of surrender. If that is the case the Hay-Pauncefote arrangement is doomed and we are relegated to our rights under the Clayton-Bulwer Treaty. We shall stand upon those rights. It is not the custom of this country to conclude treaties of surrender with any nation— even those whose friendship we value most—and that is a custom from which we have no mind to depart.[41]

The senators were indeed pushing the British government hard. Having already given the United States everything, without compensation, could Great Britain now swallow meekly what looked like a deliberate, unprovoked rebuke?

amendments. The British would have subscribed to a German comment quoted in *The Standard* (London), December 22, 1900: "The fate of the Hay-Pauncefote Treaty in the American Senate shows clearly that the Americans are beginning to apply their too inconsiderate ways, as regards social life, to politics. . . . Since England cannot possibly agree to the most important provisions of the Treaty being set aside, the whole Treaty becomes void. Behind the Hay-Pauncefote Treaty is the Clayton-Bulwer Treaty. This, however, was also annulled by the Senate. America, therefore, takes everything, and England gets nothing. The Americans, on their own authority, annul all their Treaties with England as regards the Nicaragua Canal. This is a public challenge and a mockery of England. Will England take it quietly?"

[41] December 19, 1900.

CHAPTER 11

The Hay-Pauncefote Treaty

GREAT BRITAIN had made a considerable concession to the United States in the first place by modifying the Clayton-Bulwer treaty, all the more so as she herself had got no *quid pro quo* whatever. The United States was now demanding still further concessions. Several months before the Senate's amendments were adopted Valentine Chirol, foreign editor of the London *Times*, wrote what was to prove an illuminating comment:

> A great deal . . . will depend upon the tone in which the opposition in the Senate is conducted. Any attempt to represent the rejection of the obnoxious clauses as a snub to England . . . would certainly tend to harden our hearts over here. . . . Our position in South Africa renders it all the more difficult for us to make, under duress . . . a graceful concession, which under other circumstances we could well afford to make without any loss of dignity. . . . it is, I think, clearly the duty of American Statesmen in the first place to build for our retreat a bridge of unalloyed gold, that is, of friendly suasion and not of menace.[1]

The building of such a bridge was precisely what the United States Senate did not do. Lord Lansdowne, who had just succeeded the aging Salisbury as Foreign Secretary, seems to have felt strongly, more so than the American attitude warranted indeed, that British honor and dignity if nothing else demanded

---

[1] Holls papers, Chirol to Holls, February 20, 1900; Holls forwarded the above excerpt to Cushman Davis, Chairman of the Senate Foreign Relations Committee, on March 7, 1900 (*ibid.*).

a rebuke of what he considered trans-Atlantic boorishness.[2] He complained to Ambassador Choate of the neglect to make " any sort of apology or explanation " in presenting the amended treaty to London,[3] and of " the manner in which . . . the . . . amendments had, so to speak, been thrown at our heads. . . ." [4] Such irregularity rubbed this rather sensitive official the wrong way.

A not inconsiderable part of the sort of annoyance expressed by the Foreign Secretary must be attributed to ignorance of America and of American governmental processes. Few people in Britain understood the constitutional role of the Senate; [5] and Henry Cabot Lodge's well known remark that the Senate, in altering the treaty, was continuing in all friendship the negotiations initiated by Hay and Pauncefote had a measure of truth which Americans but not many Britons could appreciate.[6] Many an Englishman must of course have suspected his ignorance of the vast land across the ocean. But when he turned for enlightenment to the unimpeachable *Times* he found in the frequently expressed opinions of its correspondent in the United States, an American with a formidable reputation, George Washburn Smalley, only the confirmation of his own prejudices. A confirmed Anglophile, Smalley made little effort at objective reporting. His numerous articles, more editorials than factual accounts, grossly misrepresented the American temper at times. This bias could be dangerous, for through his post on the *Times* and his many official connections Smalley had tremendous influence on Anglo-American relations. It was this strategically placed man

[2] Henry Adams, with customary exaggeration but some slight justification, called Lansdowne's frame of mind " sulky, stupid and indiscreet, the worst sort of old-fashioned English short-sightedness." See W. C. Ford, ed., *Letters of Henry Adams (1892-1918)* (Boston and New York, 1938), p. 322, March 18, 1901.

[3] F. O. 55, 405, Lansdowne to Pauncefote, January 14, 1901.

[4] F. O. 55, 406, Lansdowne to Lowther, July 16, 1901.

[5] For an explanation by Pauncefote see *ibid.*, Pauncefote to Lansdowne, January 10, 1901. C. G. Washburn, " Memoir of Henry Cabot Lodge," *Proceedings of the Massachusetts Historical Society*, vol. 58 (1925), p. 336.

[6] *New York Sun*, December 22, 1900; cited by T. Dennett, *John Hay, from Poetry to Politics* (New York, 1933), pp. 257-258.

who in early 1901 was assuring the *Times*'s readers that acceptance of the amendments

> would be an act certain to disturb and likely to embitter the
> relations between the two countries. . . . To accept the dicta-
> tion of the Senate would be to inflame public opinion of both
> sides. On your side would be the sting of surrender, from no
> matter what highest or friendliest impulses, to demands you
> know to be unjust. On our side would be the exultation of
> England's worst enemies and shouts of triumph over her abase-
> ment, followed by immediate preparation for some new experi-
> ment on her endurance.[7]

Who in Britain having repeatedly perused such categorical statements could have helped being swayed to favor rejection of the
treaty, if only for the sake of improving relations with the United
States? The government itself might have found Smalley's assurances embarrassing had it decided to ratify, and F. W. Holls
may have been quite correct in asserting that " If it had not been
for the mischievous mendacity of the London Times correspondent in New York, an agreement [on the Clayton-Bulwer treaty]
would have been arrived at much sooner." [8] Of course, few people
realized that Smalley, a good friend of John Hay's, probably
hoped for the treaty's defeat as a means of saving the Secretary's
face.[9]

Besides injured pride and misunderstanding of the Senate's
action, Great Britain had certain specific complaints about each
of the three amendments. As a matter of fact she had decided,
on Lansdowne's recommendation [10] and with the Prime Minister's
full agreement, to reject the treaty on the basis of the Davis

---

[7] *The Times*, January 16, 1901.

[8] Holls papers, to Charlemagne Tower, October 22, 1901; Holls frequently
criticized Smalley's " mischievous mendacity." To Theodore Roosevelt, Smalley
was a " copper-riveted idiot . . ."; see E. E. Morison, ed., *The Letters of
Theodore Roosevelt* (8 vols., Cambridge, Mass., 1951-1954) , vol. 3, p. 97.

[9] Holls made this point to Chirol, January 25, 1901 (Holls papers) .

[10] F. O. 55, 399, Lansdowne to Salisbury and Salisbury to Lansdowne,
December 10, 1900; memorandum by Lansdowne for the Cabinet, December
13, 1900.

amendment alone.[11] It has sometimes been suggested that her fundamental objection to the Davis amendment, and indeed to the whole treaty, stemmed from dislike of the canal's prospective fortifications.[12] Yet it is not certain that the amendment authorized fortifications at all. It provided that certain regulations, specified in clauses 1 through 5 of article II and designed to ensure the canal's neutrality, should not apply to measures taken by the United States in its own defense. But it was clause 7 that banned fortifications. This clause remained intact in the revised treaty and John Hay, for one, insisted upon its continuing effectiveness.[13] It should be added, however, that Lansdowne was not so sure; he thought it possible to contend that since in the same article one clause permitted " defence " and another forbade " fortifications " " the ' defence ' clause can be so interpreted as to make the ' fortification ' clause of no avail." [14]

More to the point is the decisive fact that the British government did not particularly care whether the canal was fortified or

[11] *Ibid.*, Foreign Office to Pauncefote, December 14, 1900. The decision was taken by the Cabinet on December 13, 1900, contrary to Pauncefote's advice. See *ibid.*, Lansdowne to Salisbury and Salisbury to Lansdowne, December 10, 1900; R. B. Mowat, *The Life of Lord Pauncefote, First Ambassador to the United States* (Boston and New York, 1929), p. 285. The decision was taken before Lodge's warning to White, December 24, 1900, that if Britain rejected the treaty American construction of a canal would only be speeded; see A. Nevins, *Henry White, Thirty Years of American Diplomacy* (New York and London, 1930), p. 155. Too late to influence the decision was a report of a special commission of the Boston Chamber of Commerce appointed at the request of the Isthmian Canal Commission to investigate business interest in a canal; the report took almost exactly Britain's position on the treaty (*The Times*, January 17 and 18, 1901).

[12] R. B. Mowat, *The Diplomatic Relations of Great Britain and the United States* (London, 1925), p. 286; Mowat, *Pauncefote*, p. 284. On the other hand, Dennett, *Hay*, pp. 261-262, and M. P. DuVal, Jr., *Cadiz to Cathay: the Story of the Long Diplomatic Struggle for the Panama Canal* (Stanford, 1940), p. 118, attribute too much significance to the abrogation of the Clayton-Bulwer treaty.

[13] State Department, Great Britain, Instructions, Hay to Choate, December 31, 1900.

[14] F. O. 55, 405, memorandum by Lansdowne, January 15, 1901; see Appendix 5. F. O. 115, 1198, Lansdowne to Pauncefote, January 14, 1901.

not. A significant memorandum drawn up by the Admiralty at the request of the Foreign Office, after examining the probable consequence of an isthmian canal upon British sea power, stated:

> With the exception of the elimination of Article III [inviting other powers to adhere], the amendments inserted by the United States' Senate appear to be comparatively immaterial. . . .
>
> If the canal were fortified, the only change involved would be that the British military forces employed to seize it would have to be larger, and probably more time would be required to complete the work of the expedition.[15]

Lansdowne fully accepted the implication that fortifications would be " comparatively immaterial"; he advised the Cabinet that "while the Davis amendment would strengthen the hold of the United States upon the canal, it would probably not do so very materially " and that " The rule against fortifications was, I believe, of no practical value to us. . . ."[16] The government as a whole doubtless agreed.

Why, then, did Great Britain oppose the Davis amendment? First of all, it seemed good tactics to do so. ". . . I do not see," the Prime Minister told his new Foreign Secretary, "what we shall gain by the Treaty amended by Davis. It is not to be supposed that we shall ever fight on the subject; but we shall have a grievance which is of some value. If we accept the Davis amendment we shall have torn the grievance up with our own hands."[17] Much more important was another point, one which brings up Britain's basic objection to the amended treaty. Her objection was caused not by the amendment as such but by the fact that it stood side by side with the neutrality regulations of

[15] F. O. 55, 405, Admiralty to Foreign Office, January 5, 1901. For the memorandum see Appendix 4.

[16] *Ibid.*, memorandum by Lansdowne, January 15, 1901; see Appendix 5. F. O. 55, 406, memorandum by Lansdowne, July 6, 1901; see Appendix 6.

[17] F. O. 55, 399, Salisbury to Lansdowne, December 10, 1900; note that Salisbury advocated rejecting the treaty on the basis of the Davis amendment alone. When it came to finding compensation Lansdowne confessed his inability to think of anything acceptable to both countries; see *ibid.* for his memorandum, December 13, 1900, printed for the use of the Cabinet.

clauses 1 through 5, regulations which as part of the original treaty she had subscribed to readily. These regulations ordinarily bound Great Britain and the United States alike; however, the United States—*but not Britain*—could obtain release from them by invoking the Davis amendment. In other words, the amendment by itself was supportable; the neutrality regulations by themselves were desirable; the amendment and regulations *combined* weré unendurable. Together they put Britain at a disadvantage she could avoid simply by holding fast to the Clayton-Bulwer treaty.[18]

Even worse than the combination of the neutrality rules with the Davis amendment was their combination with another amendment—excision of article III inviting other powers to adhere. For whereas the Davis amendment placed Great Britain in a worse position than the United States, excision of article III placed her in a worse position than any other country in the world. In time of war Britain alone would be obligated to observe the neutrality rules. We may assume that this discrimination was not intended by the framers of the amendment; apparently Lord Lansdowne was the first to notice it; [19] he surprised Choate when he pointed out to him the unexpected effect of the Senate's step:

> while the United States would have a Treaty right to interfere with the canal in time of war, or apprehended war, and while similar rights would be enjoyed by other Powers, this country alone, in spite of her enormous possessions on the American Continent, in spite of the extent of her Australasian Colonies, and her interests in the East, would be absolutely precluded from resorting to any such action.[20]

[18] F. O. 55, 405, memorandum by Lansdowne, January 15, 1901. See Appendix 5.

[19] See his minute written about January 7, 1901, on Pauncefote's communication to him, December 27, 1900 (F. O. 55, 399).

[20] F. O. 155, 1198, Lansdowne to Pauncefote, January 14, 1901. The Admiralty, too, seems to have grasped the point at an early date, as is suggested by its memorandum cited in the text, p. 217: "With the exception of the elimination of Article III, the amendments inserted by the United States' Senate appear to be comparatively immaterial. . . ." Much the same wording as in Lansdowne's despatch quoted above appeared in his

No country would deliberately consign itself to such inferior status.

The last amendment, though of less substance, stirred up resentment among some officials and perhaps more resentment among the public. This was the unilateral abrogation, and by mere parenthetical clause, of the solemnly contracted Clayton-Bulwer treaty. Even a year later the fancied slight still rankled. " The Senate had declared the Clayton-Bulwer Convention abrogated of its own mere motion, and before any attempt had been made to ascertain our wishes on the point. That, of course, was a proceeding to which no nation could submit." So affirmed the *Times* stiffly.[21] Yet apart from injured dignity the British did not object to terminating the old treaty. The only significant resulting change would be removal of the ban on colonization in Central America. And Lansdowne at least, although admitting that freedom to colonize might be of " substantial importance " to the United States—but not to Britain—would have accepted the amendment had it stood alone.[22] " So far as this amendment was concerned," he admitted, " our complaint had reference rather to form than to substance." [23]

note of February 22, 1901, rejecting the amended treaty; see 63rd Congress, 2nd session, Senate document 474, p. 17; British White Paper, *United States. No. 1 (1901)*. *Correspondence Respecting the Convention signed at Washington, February 5, 1900, Relative to the Establishment of a Communication by Ship Canal between the Atlantic and Pacific Oceans.* Cd. 438. P. 7.

[21] *The Times*, January 16, 1902. " I think," Henry White explained, " the feeling is that they gave us everything we asked without a quibble . . . and that, while there would probably be no real objection to the suspension of the Treaty if asked politely and by regular negotiations to do so, they have not been courteously treated "; see J. A. Garraty, *Henry Cabot Lodge, a Biography* (New York, 1953), p. 216, White to Lodge, January 25, 1901. For a similar reaction on another occasion see H. Nicolson, *Curzon: The Last Phase 1919-1925, a Study in Post-War Diplomacy* (Boston and New York, 1934), p. 141: " for a parliament to refuse ratification of a treaty properly concluded would have been condemned almost as a breach of faith and as highly damaging to the diplomatic credit of the country concerned."

[22] F. O. 55, 405, memorandum by Lansdowne, January 15, 1901; see Appendix 5.

[23] F. O. 55, 406, memorandum by Lansdowne, July 6, 1901; see Appendix 6.

In early 1901 the Foreign Office completed a long despatch, later dated February 22, defining the British position on the amended treaty.[24] At Pauncefote's suggestion delivery to Washington was delayed until Congress adjourned, and until the ratification period expired on March 4, 1901.[25] Congress adjourned for the summer recess on March 9. Two days later Lord Pauncefote called on his friend, John Hay, with whom he had labored so long on the canal dispute, and told him the despatch's melancholy but not unexpected contents. ". . . His Majesty's Government," the ambassador read firmly, " feel unable to accept the Convention in the shape presented to them . . . and prefer, as matters stand at present, to retain unmodified the provisions of the Clayton-Bulwer Treaty." [26]

Another crisis seemed at hand. It threatened to destroy the harmony that had arisen between the two great English-speaking countries. Already for several months the Washington administration had been able to forestall abrogation of the Clayton-Bulwer treaty only with difficulty; now that Britain's hostility to the Senate's amendments stood forth undisguised, an irresistible demand for action could be expected. " If we cannot make a treaty with England which will pass the Senate next December," Lodge wrote, " nothing in the world, in my opinion, will be able to stop the passage of the [Hepburn] canal bill." [27] This controversial measure, it will be recalled, had been shelved the previous December in favor of amending the Pauncefote treaty. As weeks passed with no sign of assent in London some members of Congress, notably the formidable Senator Morgan, had been growing increasingly restive. An old man getting desperate as an isthmian waterway remained tantalizingly just

[24] F. O. 55, 405, Lansdowne to Pauncefote, February 6, 1901.

[25] State Department, Great Britain, Despatches, Choate to Hay, February 19, 1901; F. O. 55, 405, Pauncefote to Lansdowne, February 8 and 20, 1901.

[26] 63rd Congress, 2nd session, Senate document 474, p. 17; *United States. No. 1 (1901)*, p. 7; Lansdowne to Pauncefote, February 22, 1901.

[27] *Selections from the Correspondence of Theodore Roosevelt and Henry Cabot Lodge, 1884-1918* (2 vols., New York, 1925), vol. 1, p. 486, to Roosevelt, March 30, 1901. For a similar statement by Hay see Nevins, *White*, p. 158, June 18, 1901.

out of reach, he began to press hard for the Hepburn bill. Such headway did he make that Smalley sounded the alarm: the bill's passage, he warned his British readers, "would mean very strained, if not critical, relations between England and the United States." [28] After several impassioned appeals to the Senate, Morgan brought his campaign to a climax with an uncompromising demand for immediate abrogation of the Clayton-Bulwer treaty, just five days before Britain gave notice of rejection of the Pauncefote canal treaty. "If Great Britain wants a share of Alaska," he threatened,

> or an entrance into Alaska through the present modus vivendi as a condition precedent of releasing us from the Clayton-Bulwer treaty, she will not get it . . . or if she has a determination that she will pick a quarrel with us . . . she will find that the United States can muster at least . . . 7,000,000 people.
> She will find when that war terminates that the steel band that binds the throne in London with Australia and India and passes through Canada will be rent in twain, and with it down will go the Empire. Tear up that railroad which Great Britain built through Canada and all the powers of the world can not preserve the British Empire in its integrity.[29]

At first glance little hope now existed of a negotiated modification of the treaty. How could common ground possibly be found between Britain's categorical rejection of the Senate's amendments, and the Senate's equally firm insistence on an all-American canal? In actual fact, however, the prospect was not so bleak as it appeared. Despite their recent disagreement Washington and London were basically in accord in a determination to

---

[28] *The Times*, February 25, 1901.

[29] *Congressional Record*, vol. 35, p. 18, March 6, 1901; *ibid.*, vol. 34, pp. 2884-2887, 3517-3519; *The Times*, March 7, 1901; D. C. Miner, *The Fight for the Panama Route: the Story of the Spooner Act and the Hay-Herrán Treaty* (New York, 1940), p. 107. The Foreign Office doubtless felt happier about such threats as Morgan's because of a report from Pauncefote to the effect that McKinley viewed the Hepburn bill as "permissive and not mandatory," and that therefore, though he would not veto it, neither would he use the power it bestowed to initiate construction; in short the Clayton-Bulwer treaty would not be abrogated even if the Hepburn bill passed (F. O. 55, 399, Pauncefote to Salisbury, December 14, 1900).

prevent a major breach. In his note rejecting the amended treaty Lansdowne had carefully held out a hope of further discussions: Great Britain, he had declared, " would sincerely regret a failure to come to an amicable understanding. . . ." [30] John Hay and Lord Pauncefote, who would bear the brunt of renewed negotiations, were dedicated men, it is perhaps not too much to say; as long as they remained in office no one could despair of British-American friendship. In each country, moreover, conditions in the spring of 1901 were in several respects more favorable to agreement than during the preceding winter. In the United States the political position of President McKinley, a good friend of Britain's, had strengthened. Not only were national elections no longer imminent, but the President's decisive victory in November had increased his personal prestige as well as the Republican majority in the Senate. Facilitating McKinley's control of the party was the colonial patronage now assuming sizable proportions with the new empire's consolidation. The *Times* noted the resulting " wide field for ' conciliatory ' operations among Senators who are only technically hostile "; [31] and Senator Lodge sagely cautioned the President to keep " *all* questions of patronage . . . in abeyance . . . until the English treaty . . . is out of the way." [32]

Although hard to assess the state of public opinion, it seems probable that Americans were better disposed to Great Britain than they had been in the latter part of 1900, all the irritation over the canal treaty notwithstanding. The death of the aged and greatly respected Queen Victoria on January 22, 1901, may have had much to do with this. For one thing it had the immediate effect of postponing hasty action on the Hepburn bill as pleaded for by Senator Morgan.[33] More important was the genuine and widespread sorrow—" more in the nature of personal grief than of international political concern," the *Literary Digest*

---

[30] 63rd Congress, 2nd session, Senate document 474, p. 17; *United States. No. 1 (1901)*, p. 7; Lansdowne to Pauncefote, February 22, 1901.

[31] *The Times*, April 13, 1901.

[32] *Selections from Roosevelt and Lodge*, vol. 1, p. 507, October 17, 1901.

[33] *Congressional Record*, vol. 35, p. 16, March 6, 1901.

thought—and the solemn mood attendant upon the end of an era, that were awakened in America.[34] Resolutions expressing sympathy were adopted by the legislatures of Washington, North Carolina, Wyoming, Utah, and Maine.[35] The Philadelphia *Record* could declare that ". . . Queen Victoria was the peer of our Washington " without arousing the horrified cries that would have resounded in an earlier decade.[36] As for the new monarch, Edward VII, the emotionalism over the well loved Queen extended to her son, too, and even to the somewhat tarnished cause of British-American friendship; thus the influential *New York Tribune* doubtless reflected a prevalent belief in stating that " he may be relied upon . . . to continue the course pursued by his mother from the very outset of her reign, namely, the development of sentiments of friendship and unity between the two great English-speaking nations, who are bound together by ties of kinship, by community of speech, of jurisprudence, and of character—that is to say, by ties far more lasting than mere treaties, made to be broken." [37]

As for Great Britain, although her fortunes in South Africa had improved, new dangers loomed in another quarter. Once again war clouds were gathering in the Far East. A showdown with Russia apparently imminent, Japan began pressing frantically for British assurances of help. During March, 1901, the very month in which London turned down the amended canal treaty, the British Cabinet was meeting time after time to consider these pleas.[38] The flare-up in the Far East did not prevent

[34] *Literary Digest*, vol. 22 (January 26, 1901), p. 91. F. W. Holls noted the effect of the Queen's death in inducing Americans to think more kindly of Great Britain (Holls papers, to Chirol, January 25, 1901). For official expressions of sorrow see State Department, Great Britain, Instructions, Hay to Choate, January 22, 1901.

[35] State Department, Miscellaneous Letters, January 22, 25, February 7, 27, 28, 1901, respectively. The Senate and the House adopted similar resolutions (*ibid.*, Great Britain, Instructions, Hay to Choate, January 22, 1901).

[36] *Literary Digest*, vol. 22 (February 2, 1901), p. 122.

[37] *Ibid.*, p. 119. For other press comment see *Public Opinion*, vol. 30 (January 31, 1901), pp. 138-141.

[38] W. L. Langer, *The Diplomacy of Imperialism, 1890-1902* (2 vols., New York, 1935), vol. 2, p. 720 ff.

Britain from rejecting the treaty as planned several months earlier, but it would be surprising if it did not make her more amenable to renewed negotiations with America. Were fighting soon to commence it would be folly to prolong the break with the powerful trans-Atlantic republic over the Clayton-Bulwer treaty.[39]

At no point in his career as Secretary of State does John Hay show to better advantage than when, refusing to yield to his profound discouragement over the apparent wreck of his labors of the last few years, he set himself grimly to starting all over again. The Senate's transformation of his treaty had been a terrible blow. On January 18, 1901, the young Charles Gates Dawes, a future ambassador to Great Britain, noted: " John Hay is sick of grippe . . . . he is making the mistake of considering the Senate attacks on the Hay-Pauncefote treaty . . . as in some way reflecting upon him personally, and . . . he grows excited and agitated when discussing the matter . . . . this feeling on his part is wearing him out physically for it adds worry to the hard work which he has had to perform." [40] Mastering his depression Hay, a few days after his disheartening interview with Lord Pauncefote, conferred with several senators about the desirability of making an entirely new treaty.[41] By March 25, 1901, just two weeks after receiving Lansdowne's note, he felt sure enough of his ground to propose further negotiations to Pauncefote.[42] Receiving a favorable reply he instructed Alvey Adee, his invaluable chief assistant at the State Department, to prepare a draft.[43]

[39] A curious indication that people in Britain still thought well of Americans is given by a telegram from the Lord Mayor of Liverpool, January 1, 1901: " The citizens of Liverpool send hearty greetings on opening of twentieth century to the people of the United States " (State Department, Miscellaneous Letters) .

[40] C. G. Dawes, *A Journal of the McKinley Years* (Chicago, 1950) , pp. 260-261.

[41] F. O. 55, 405, Pauncefote to Lansdowne, March 23, 1901; W. R. Thayer, *The Life and Letters of John Hay* (2 vols., Boston and New York, 1915) , vol. 2, pp. 259-260, March 28, 1901; Garraty, *Lodge*, p. 216.

[42] 63rd Congress, 2nd session, Senate document 474, p. 19; F. O. 55, 405, Pauncefote to Lansdowne, March 26, 1901.

[43] Hay papers, Adee to Hay, April 8, 1901. The " first sketch " was ready

Taking unusual pains not to ruffle senatorial sensibilities, Hay reviewed it with Senators Foraker, Lodge, Cullom, Frye, Fair-banks, Spooner, and others.[44] (Senator Davis had recently died.) Within a month he had another canal treaty ready for British consideration.

The Secretary had done more than that. He had ready not only a new canal draft, he had also voluminous papers (soon shaped into two draft treaties) developing a settlement of most of the Canadian questions that had been before the Joint High Commission two years earlier.[45] With an admirable vigor and breadth of imagination he had reacted to the total collapse of negotiations, not with caution but with boldness: with a proposal to go, in effect, much of the way back to that hopeful month of August, 1898, when with the Joint High Commission convening in Quebec and F. W. Holls raising the canal question in London, Great Britain and the United States in high confidence were embarking upon a quest for an overall settlement. When that ambitious, perhaps overly ambitious, plan had come to grief six months later, Hay, as has appeared, abandoned it in favor of a more deliberate piecemeal approach. Now after two years of frustration with nothing to show except the *modus vivendi*, he was turning again to an attack on all fronts, with the significant difference that negotiations this time were to be conducted through normal channels instead of by another high commission. The resourcefulness and suppleness of his diplomacy were again manifest.

Before describing the new canal treaty something should be said about the two new Canadian treaties, given to Pauncefote on May 10, 1901.[46] One of them dealt with the disputed boundary of Alaska; the other with most of the other Canadian questions.

April 8; Adee wrote: " In wrestling with Article IV, I have endeavored 1st, to give it the sense of Senator Lodge's explanation, made in his state-ment given to the press December 21, 1900. . . . 2nd, to reserve silently the right to fortify, to the end of preserving the canal from attack. . . ."

[44] Choate papers, Hay to Choate, August 5, 1901.

[45] F. O. 55, 406, Pauncefote to Lansdowne, April 25, 1901; 63rd Congress, 2nd session, Senate document 474, pp. 19-21.

[46] F. O. 5, 2482, Pauncefote to Lansdowne, May 10, 1901.

As for the latter proposed treaty, it received little attention in the face of concentration on the much more dangerous canal and boundary questions, and no further mention need be made of it. But an account must be given of the proposals relating to Alaska, for they marked a significant step toward the eventual boundary agreement of 1903 and they affected the negotiations, which we must consider shortly, that followed from Hay's new canal draft and resulted in the Hay-Pauncefote treaty of 1901.[47]

The boundary proposals grew out of discussions that had been proceeding on and off since the conclusion of the *modus* of October, 1899. Lord Salisbury's eager injunction to Pauncefote in early 1900, to " do all that is in your power " to establish an even-numbered tribunal, will be recalled.[48] Thus encouraged, Pauncefote had settled with Hay upon a plan for reviving the Joint High Commission; after reconvening, its sole function would be to sign an agreement for arbitration on the model of the unratified Olney-Pauncefote arbitration treaty of 1897, that is, by three Americans and three Britons, an agreement that Pauncefote would meanwhile try to reach with the American commissioners of Quebec and Washington.[49] Accordingly, about the time the Boxers were raising havoc in China, the ambassador was having a series of informal talks with Fairbanks, Foster,[50] and Kasson, and also with Hay; supplemented by correspondence between Fairbanks and Sir Wilfred Laurier, these talks proved so fruitful that in September, 1900, Pauncefote prophesied early success.[51] His optimism proved misplaced. The presidential

[47] The text of the Alaska treaty is on pp. 22-25 of the British White Paper, *United States. No. 1 (1904)*. *Correspondence Respecting the Alaska Boundary*. Cd. 1877. F. O. 5, 2482, Pauncefote to Lansdowne, May 10, 1901.

[48] See p. 188.

[49] Salisbury papers, Pauncefote to Salisbury, March 9, 1900.

[50] It is easy to see the connection between the talks and the appearance in *The Independent*, vol. 52 (1900), pp. 1420-1422, " A Permanent Method of Arbitration with Great Britain," of an appeal by John Foster for another Olney-Pauncefote treaty, an appeal which was published just when the establishment of an even-numbered tribunal (as specified in that treaty) seemed not unlikely.

[51] Salisbury papers, to Salisbury, September 14, 1900; the American commissioners, however, demurred to the proviso of the treaty of 1897 for

election and recriminations attendant upon the Senate's rejection of the canal treaty provided an unfavorable atmosphere; and the apparent failure of canal negotiations enhanced Canadian bargaining power and consequently her resolution to oppose an even-numbered tribunal.[52] Nevertheless from these discussions of 1900 had emerged ideas that Secretary Hay incorporated in his Alaska draft of May, 1901; indeed it must be said that that draft reflected Pauncefote's labors as much as those of his friend in the Department of State.

A comparison between the draft of 1901 and the final treaty of 1903 shows their close overall resemblance, in fact their word for word identity in most parts. Like the treaty the draft provided for a tribunal of "six impartial jurists of repute," three from each country; they would answer two questions concerning the Anglo-Russian treaty of 1825: the first as to the boundary in and near Portland channel, the second as to whether Russia possessed an unbroken coastal strip. These questions as worded in 1901 [53] compared closely with the equivalent part of the final

Supreme Court justices to constitute the American side of the tribunal. See also F. O. 5, 2482, Chamberlain to Minto, January 18, 1901.

[52] There seems also to have been some Colonial Office opposition to such a tribunal; see C. O. 42, 885, minute by "G. D.," June 4, 1901.

[53] The exact wording, almost identical with part of article IV of the final treaty, was as follows:

" 1. Referring to Article III of said Treaty of 1825 between Great Britain and Russia, was it intended thereby that the line of demarcation should be traced from the southernmost point of the island, now known as the Prince of Wales Island, along the parallel of 54° 40′ north latitude to the passage now commonly known and marked on the maps as the " Portland Channel," and thence along the middle of said channel northward until said northward line shall reach on the mainland of the continent the 56th degree of north latitude?

" If not, how should said line be traced to conform to the provisions of said Treaty?

" 2. In extending the line of demarcation northward from said point on the parallel of the 56th degree of north latitude, following the crest of the mountains situated parallel to the coast until its intersection with the 141st degree of longitude west of Greenwich, subject to the condition that when such line should exceed the distance of 10 marine leagues from the ocean, then the boundary between the British and the Russian territory

treaty. Hay's draft pointed to the ultimate solution in another way: for the first time an American proposal did not designate Dyea and Skagway as being reserved to the United States.[54]

We may now turn to an analysis of Hay's new canal treaty, which he handed to Pauncefote on April 25, 1901.[55] It differed in three respects from the treaty as amended by the Senate and rejected by Great Britain. Britain's objection to the amended treaty, it will be recalled, lay not so much in the amendments as such as in the combination of two of them with the specified neutrality rules. People at the time did not generally grasp this point. Assuming that Britain's hostility was based on the amendments in themselves, few saw any possibility of compromise between her and the Senate. It was to John Hay's great credit that he penetrated to the root of the difficulty and perceived its simple solution. His new treaty provided that the neutrality rules should be binding, not upon the two countries alike, but upon the United States *alone*. By this change he transformed the whole aspect of the negotiations. For now Britain no longer had to contemplate circumstances in which she would be at a

should be formed by a line parallel to the sinuosities of the coast, and distant therefrom not more than 10 marine leagues, was it the intention and meaning of said Convention of 1825 that there should remain in the exclusive possession of Russia a continuous fringe or strip of coast on the mainland, 10 marine leagues in width, separating the British possessions from the bays, ports, inlets, havens, and waters of the ocean, and extending from the said point on the 56th degree of latitude north to a point where such line of demarcation should intersect the 141st degree of longitude west of the meridian of Greenwich?

If not, how should said line of demarcation be traced to conform to the provisions of said Treaty? "

It should be noted that two other questions were added in 1903 that specifically mentioned the possibility of the boundary cutting across heads of inlets.

[54] F. O. 5, 2482, Minto to Chamberlain, August 23, 1901; State Department, Miscellaneous Archives, Alaskan Boundary, 1899-1903, British embassy to State Department, February 28, 1902. Sir Wilfrid Laurier insisted that as a practical matter the draft did safeguard American possession of Dyea and Skagway.

[55] F. O. 55, 406, Pauncefote to Lansdowne, April 25, 1901; 63rd Congress, 2nd session, Senate document 474, pp. 19-21.

disadvantage as compared with every other country. Her principal objection both to the Davis amendment and to deletion of
the article inviting the adherence of other powers therefore disappeared. All at once optimism returned to Washington and
London.

A difficulty remained, however. Although now rendered innocuous, the Davis amendment had been subjected to so much
press abuse that its reenactment would be awkward for Britain.
On the other hand the Senate would never ratify an instrument
denying the United States a free hand in wartime. Again Hay
found a simple but decisive solution. The amended treaty had
stipulated that " The canal shall be free and open, in time of
war as in time of peace. . . ." The new draft struck out not only
the Davis amendment but also, as an offset, the words " in time
of war as in time of peace. . . ." The Secretary's reasoning was
shrewd. If the treaty itself did not provide for its continuing
effectiveness in wartime, then it could be contended that by
virtue of the usual effect of war in terminating treaties the United
States, if at war with Britain, would be relieved of treaty encum-
brances and hence legally free to act as it wished in the canal
area.[56]

The new draft contained two other changes. With the Davis
amendment scrapped, the Senate would certainly not accept the
ban on fortifications (in article II, clause 7). It was therefore
deleted. Second, the parenthetical clause abrogating the Clayton-
Bulwer treaty now attained the dignity of a separate article, a
purely formal change calculated to ease British sensibilities.

A comparison of Hay's draft with each of the contrasting
positions taken by the Senate and Great Britain makes apparent
its ingenuity. The Senate had stipulated that the United States
be free to take measures of defense, had refused to permit other
countries to adhere, and had provided for supersession of the
Clayton-Bulwer treaty. The new draft met each of these demands
fully. As a matter of fact, it went further than the Senate with
respect to the right to fortify; for whereas the earlier treaty as

[56] For the offsetting nature of the phrase " in time of war " see 63rd
Congress, 2nd session, Senate document 474, pp. 23 and 64.

amended contained a section prohibiting fortifications the new draft said nothing at all on the subject. As for the British objections, the draft met them also with one possible qualification.[57] No longer would Britain find herself tied to neutrality obligations from which the United States could escape at any time and which Britain's great rivals on the Continent would never even assume. And no longer could she complain of casual abrogation of the Clayton-Bulwer treaty. The one point still bothering the Foreign Office concerned the continued exclusion of countries other than the two signatories. "It will . . . be impossible for us to agree to give way altogether upon this point . . . ," Lansdowne advised the Cabinet; but in the same breath he indicated a compromise formula that, as shall appear, was to be reached without difficulty.[58] The risk taken by the Foreign Secretary in turning down the Senate's amendments had paid off; he now had a far more satisfactory convention, and the Hepburn bill still was not law.

Thus by changing a few words here and there the apparently irreconcilable had been reconciled. Further negotiations had still to be undertaken, seven months more were to pass before ratification, but in essence and even in wording with but few exceptions the Hay-Pauncefote treaty of November, 1901, was as good as concluded with John Hay's draft of April.[59]

The back of the difficulty having been broken, Hay wanted the final touches put upon the treaty in Great Britain. He had produced a set of articles that the Senate, he this time had good reason to believe, would accept. It was now a matter of satisfying the British. The Secretary therefore suggested that Lord Pauncefote, who more than any other Englishman was familiar with details of the treaty and who moreover could be counted

[57] For Pauncefote's comments on the draft see F. O. 55, 406, Pauncefote to Lansdowne, April 25, 1901.

[58] *Ibid.*, memorandum by Lansdowne, July 6, 1901. See p. 233 for the formula, and Appendix 6 for the memorandum.

[59] Lodge's remark that "although the draft was written by Mr. Hay, the treaty was really made and perfected in London" is highly misleading. The treaty was "perfected" in London but it was "really made" in Washington. For the remark see Washburn, "Memoir of Lodge," p. 337.

upon to fight for it, as well as for the two Canadian treaties, should spend the summer in England.[60] The suggestion proving acceptable, negotiations were held in abeyance pending the ambassador's arrival in London in early June.

In the meantime the curious figure of F. W. Holls, who three years before had initiated the first phase of negotiations, again entered the picture. At dinner in April, 1901, at Arthur Balfour's residence he discussed the developing canal question with his host and with Lord Lansdowne. According to Holls's subsequent account the three of them traced the outlines of an agreement remarkably similar to the one finally concluded.[61] In July he reappeared in London; much to Choate's annoyance—" He has been here for the last week in most offensive form . . . ," the ambassador complained to Hay[62]—Holls attempted, unsuccessfully, to intrude himself upon the negotiators. Was he merely a self-appointed busybody? It is clear that on this occasion he had no connection with the State Department. A good guess is that he was speaking for Henry Cabot Lodge and Theodore Roosevelt. Holls was closely associated with Roosevelt, and fully shared his dislike of the original canal treaty.[63] What more likely than that the new Vice-President, deeply interested in the canal question as he was, should have asked his friend to explain in London his and Lodge's reasons for supporting the amendments?

With Pauncefote's arrival in London, consideration of the three draft treaties resumed in earnest, mainly in frequent conferences between him and Ambassador Choate.[64] At a Cabinet meeting on July 8, 1901, Lord Lansdowne submitted Hay's canal proposals, together with a long explanatory memorandum of his own.[65] This memorandum seems to have been decisive. In it the

[60] F. O. 55, 406, Pauncefote to Lansdowne, May 7, 1901.

[61] Holls papers, Holls to Balfour, December 17, 1901; Choate wrote Hay, July 31, 1901, that Holls saw only Balfour and Chamberlain (Hay papers).

[62] Hay papers, July 26, 1901.

[63] See Holls's letter supporting the Senate's amendments in *The Times*, January 1, 1901.

[64] 63rd Congress, 2nd session, Senate document 474, pp. 22-24.

[65] F. O. 55, 406, dated July 6, 1901, printed for the use of the Cabinet. See Appendix 6.

Foreign Secretary took up one by one the three Senate amendments, and demonstrated that the sting had largely been removed from them by Hay's modifications. From that time on, London raised no substantial objection to the new draft.

It still remained to hear from Ottawa, particularly in regard to the two Canadian treaties. The British wanted a comprehensive settlement. They recognized that in offering parallel negotiations on the canal and boundary controversies the United States had given Canada gratuitously a bargaining weapon which she might never get again and which she would be foolish not to use to the utmost.[66] They did their best to persuade her to take advantage of Hay's offer.[67] Far from heeding the plea Sir Wilfrid Laurier unhesitatingly spurned not only the Alaska treaty but Hay's other Canadian treaty as well. Holding fast to the Dominion's consistent position, he sternly denounced a tribunal of six on the ground that it would not ensure finality. He was equally adamant about the second draft treaty. He saw nothing good in it. The British commissioners on the Joint High Commission had refused to settle any other issue until the Alaska boundary was determined. Why abandon this excellent position? "The fact is," Laurier asserted flatly, "that on basing a Treaty upon the negotiations of the Joint High Commission . . . a gross injustice would be perpetrated towards Canada." [68]

Sir Wilfrid's short-sighted intransigence annoyed the British government. His attitude was "very unsatisfactory," a Foreign Office memorandum declared.[69] Besides, it revealed a danger of Canadian misunderstanding that could prove awkward. Ottawa seemed to be thinking in terms of matching one treaty against another, so that if the United States did not make concessions to Canada, Great Britain would not give way over the canal. Should this belief take root and should Laurier continue to reject

[66] Similarly, Senator W. P. Frye of Maine urged Hay to make a canal agreement but to " please avoid Canadian matters, and especially the Alaskan boundary question " (State Department, Miscellaneous Letters, May 2, 1901).

[67] F. O. 5, 2479, Chamberlain to Minto, July 27, 1901.

[68] F. O. 5, 2482, Laurier to Minto, August 14, 1901; Minto to Chamberlain, August 24, 1901.

[69] *Ibid.*, memorandum by Villiers, September 14, 1901.

American overtures, Britain would be in a dilemma: conclusion of a canal treaty would outrage Canada; refusal to do so would outrage the United States. ". . . we ought . . . ," Lansdowne warned, " to say nothing either to the Canadians or the U. S. govt. suggestive of the idea that there is to be a transaction, and that the three treaties are interdependent." [70] He again urged the Canadians to negotiate before it was too late; meanwhile they could discuss the draft treaties with Sir John Anderson, the Colonial Office official, soon to arrive in Ottawa.[71]

Sir Wilfrid may have been obdurate, but nothing could now stop rapid progress toward a Hay-Pauncefote treaty. In short order Lansdowne and Pauncefote prepared a counter-draft.[72] It differed but little from Hay's draft. What was perhaps the main change reflected the Foreign Minister's discomfiture over the failure to provide for adherence of other powers. To remedy this defect the counter-draft simply stipulated that only those countries observing the neutrality rules could use the projected waterway. Another change—one that was to have a bearing upon the Panama Canal tolls controversy between Britain and America in 1912—specified that traffic charges should be " just and equitable." Finally a new article guarded against possible adverse consequences of changes in sovereignty in the canal area.

It is unnecessary to follow details of the bargaining during that summer of 1901.[73] From the moment Hay submitted his proposals to Pauncefote in April the two countries had been in substantial accord. Lansdowne's modifications caused little difficulty. Nor did a point which he and Pauncefote several times told Choate was absolutely indispensable:

they must have something to satisfy Parliament and the British public that in giving up the Clayton-Bulwer Treaty, they had retained and reasserted the " general principle " of it, that the canal should be technically neutral and should be free to

[70] *Ibid.*, memorandum by Lansdowne, September 14, 1901.

[71] *Ibid.*, Colonial Office to Foreign Office, September 14, 1901.

[72] 63rd Congress, 2nd session, Senate document 474, pp. 25-31, Lansdowne to Lowther, August 3, 1901.

[73] They can be found in 63rd Congress, 2nd session, Senate document 474.

all nations on terms of equality, and especially that in the contingency supposed of the territory on both sides the canal becoming ours, the canal, its neutrality, its being free and open to all nations on equal terms, should not be thereby affected. . . .[74]

At one point Pauncefote, who carried on the detailed discussions with Choate, became agitated over the consideration that the treaty, commonly known as the Nicaragua treaty, might be construed by the United States as not applying to Panama should construction unexpectedly take place there.[75] His fears were readily allayed by an express stipulation that—as Washington had assumed anyway—the treaty applied to " whatever route may be considered expedient. . . ." Otherwise, apart from a few stylistic revisions, the Hay draft carried through word for word to the final Hay-Pauncefote treaty.

One development did trouble the negotiators. Just when they were on the verge of putting the treaty into final shape came the terrible news of the shooting of President McKinley on September 6, 1901. Eight days later he died, and the ebullient Theodore Roosevelt became President. Unlike his predecessor, recognized as a moderate and conciliatory man, Theodore Roosevelt was pretty much an unknown quantity as far as his attitude to Britain was concerned. The one thing people did know about him was his much publicized denunciation of the original canal treaty.[76] Rumors were spreading that he intended to replace John Hay; if true, a major turning-point in Anglo-American relations would be at hand. No wonder the diplomats in London were worried. Their fears proved unfounded. When the Secretary of State met the new President at the Washington railway station Roosevelt hastened to assure him both as to his treaty and as to his office. At the news the anxious negotiators heaved a heartfelt sigh of relief. Choate " was very much rejoiced," he

[74] State Department, Great Britain, Despatches, Choate to Hay, September 29, 1901.

[75] 63rd Congress, 2nd session, Senate document 474, pp. 44-45, Choate to Hay, September 27, 1901.

[76] See p. 195.

wrote the President, " to hear from the Secretary of State that you are in perfect accord with him in regard to the Isthmian Canal Treaty. . . ." [77]

As a matter of fact the death of the well loved McKinley gave rise to such universal expressions of sympathy in Britain as to unite the two countries in a mood of shared grief. Ambassador Choate described the British sorrow: As McKinley lay wounded " voices of affection and sympathy . . . came to us from the great English speaking communities in the most distant regions of the earth, . . . manifesting a unity of spirit, and fraternal sympathy among all the scattered nations who speak the English tongue. . . ." And when he seemed on the road to recovery, " An intense feeling and expression of relief pervaded the city and the whole country, which could hardly have been more emphatic and universal if the King himself . . . had been rescued from a similar peril." Then came word of the President's death. Upon the embassy poured " a deluge of messages . . . in every form; letters, telegrams, resolutions, minutes of municipal and corporate bodies, and from every description of association. . . . The letters from private persons were in vast numbers. . . ." The Court went into mourning. A memorial service was held at Westminster Abbey, and another at St. Paul's under the auspices of the Lord Mayor and conducted by the Archbishop of Canterbury.[78] " Enough to say . . . that nothing like it [the " overwhelming demonstration of grief and sympathy throughout Great Britain "] was ever seen before . . . in any country." [79] The ambassador could well conclude that " the general disposition here towards us just now is better than ever . . ." and that consummation of

[77] Choate papers, Choate to Roosevelt, September 28, 1901.

[78] State Department, Great Britain, Despatches, Choate to Hay, October 9, 1901; E. S. Martin, *The Life of Joseph Hodges Choate as Gathered Chiefly from His Letters* (2 vols., London, 1920) , vol. 2, p. 199; Hay papers, Choate to Hay, September 14, 1901.

[79] State Department, Great Britain, Despatches, Choate to Hay, September 21, 1901. Even the illness of Mrs. McKinley the preceding June had occasioned so many enquiries in London that Choate asked for daily bulletins (*ibid.*, Choate to Hay, May 17, 1901) .

the canal treaty was assured.[80] Like Queen Victoria, President
McKinley did good service to the cause of British-American
friendship by his death, as well as during his life.

Theodore Roosevelt's advent to power had one immediate consequence upon the canal negotiations. It brought his intimate
friend, Henry Cabot Lodge, into great prominence. Earlier in
the summer Lodge had been in London, where in several conversations with Arthur Balfour, soon to be Prime Minister, and
Lord Lansdowne he had explained and defended the Senate's
stand on the earlier, Pauncefote treaty, doubtless elaborating
along the lines laid down by F. W. Holls to the same men three
months earlier.[81] At Choate's wise suggestion the senator, returning to London from the Continent, was now taken into full
confidence.[82] Lodge contributed in a minor way to the treaty's
wording and, what was far more important, became an enthusiastic convert who promised wholehearted support in the Senate.[83]

With agreement at hand the British government made one last
effort to win over Canada. Suggesting there might still be time
to get "indirect advantage" from the canal talks, Joseph
Chamberlain telegraphed Laurier an urgent plea to negotiate
on the basis of Hay's two draft treaties at the "earliest possible
date." [84] In Ottawa Sir John Anderson added his own appeal.[85]
All was in vain. The Canadians refused to budge.[86] Their stubbornness was to cost them dear. By the time the Alaska boundary
question came to the fore again, a year later, they no longer had
any bargaining weapons. Of course it may have been too late

[80] 63rd Congress, 2nd session, Senate document 474, p. 43, Choate to Hay,
September 25, 1901.

[81] *Ibid.*, p. 24; F. O. 55, 406, Lansdowne to Lowther, July 16, 1901; Washburn, "Memoir of Lodge," pp. 336-337.

[82] State Department, Great Britain, Despatches, Choate to Hay, September
25, 1901; 63rd Congress, 2nd session, Senate document 474, p. 43.

[83] Lodge was responsible for the interposition of the words "country or"
in article IV (63rd Congress, 2nd session, Senate document 474, pp. 45-48).

[84] F. O. 5, 2479, Chamberlain to Minto, October 8, 1901.

[85] F. O. 5, 2482, memorandum by Villiers, October 21, 1901.

[86] F. O. 5, 2479, Minto to Chamberlain, October 15, 1901.

even in 1901 to seek advantage from the canal negotiations, but Canada made it impossible for Britain to find out.

The treaty's signature was held up for Lord Pauncefote's return to Washington. He sailed from England on October 26. On November 18, 1901, he and the Secretary of State signed a canal treaty for the second time. Congress convened on December 2. Presented with a document meeting all their requirements the senators wasted no more time over the Hepburn bill. Strongly supported by Lodge, who had returned three weeks before Pauncefote, and by his powerful friend in the White House, the treaty was easily ratified on December 16 by 72 votes to 6.[87]

Three years of hard work, and many grievous disappointments, had been experienced since John Hay had written Senator Morgan not to expect protracted negotiations.[88] Since then the Secretary in despair had offered his resignation. On a number of occasions an unbridgeable rift between America and Britain had appeared almost inevitable. But as John Hay and Lord Pauncefote surveyed the new treaty named after them, but bearing also the imprint of McKinley, Choate, Roosevelt, Lodge, and of Salisbury, Balfour, Chamberlain, and Lansdowne, they could have felt proud of their part in surmounting an obstacle that for over fifty years had been bedeviling relations between their countries.

Some resentful voices there were, to be sure, in Canada; and on the Continent disgruntled commentators, deprived of an Anglo-American break, depicted the treaty as an utter humiliation for Great Britain.[89] In the United States the treaty was viewed as a major diplomatic victory. Americans would have agreed with Henry Adams's ironical remark:

[87] The six were Bacon, Blackburn, Culberson, Mallory, Teller, and Tillman; paired with Depew, Hanna, and Sewell (for the treaty) were Bailey, Elkins, and Rawlins. The text of the treaty is in 63rd Congress, 2nd session, Senate document 474, pp. 292-294.

[88] Dennett, *Hay*, p. 249; the letter was dated December 27, 1898.

[89] Such Canadian and Continental comments may be found in *The Times*, November 20, 1901, and January 16, 1902.

With infinite effort he [Hay] had achieved the astonishing diplomatic feat of inducing the Senate, with only six negative votes, to permit Great Britain to renounce, without equivalent, treaty rights which she had for fifty years defended tooth and nail. This unprecedented triumph in his negotiations with the Senate enabled him to carry one step further his measures for general peace.[90]

Most Americans would have agreed also with the more balanced and accurate judgment of Lord Pauncefote:

As for ourselves we have surrendered no right worth keeping & have saved for the world at large the great principle of the Clayton-Bulwer Treaty, which Congress would undoubtedly have scattered to the winds, had we not come to terms. There is a general feeling also that our attitude has been generous & friendly & that the Treaty will do much to keep up our good relations.[91]

Great Britain may have surrendered no major right but she had taken a long step toward surrendering power in Central America and the Caribbean.[92] The important Admiralty memorandum mentioned above [93] pointed to the obvious fact that a canal would strengthen America as against Britain; it concluded: " To sum up the situation from a purely naval and strategical point of view . . . the preponderance of advantage from the canal would be greatly on the side of the United States, and . . . the navy of the United States would derive such benefits from the existence of the canal, that it is not really in the interests of Great Britain that it should be constructed." Of course it was not the Hay-Pauncefote treaty that caused the shifting balance of power in the New World. Britain had no choice but to meet

[90] H. Adams, *The Education of Henry Adams, an Autobiography* (New York, 1928) , p. 423.

[91] F. O. 5, 2458, Pauncefote to Lansdowne, November 22, 1901. See also *The Times*, December 18, 1901: " In Washington everybody considers the action of the Senate on the Canal Treaty as a new pledge of amity with England."

[92] This is emphasized by J. A. S. Grenville, " Great Britain and the Isthmian Canal, 1898-1901," *American Historical Review*, vol. 61 (1955) , pp. 48-69.

[93] See p. 217, and Appendix 4.

American wishes. Gone was the time when she could hold the Caribbean along with all the other vital seas of her empire. Hard pressed as she was in 1901 by Boers in South Africa, and by Germans, Russians, and Frenchmen elsewhere, she wisely granted in generous spirit what she could not have prevented by force.[94]

[94] See Choate's tribute to "the friendly spirit and desire to agree" of Lansdowne and his colleagues (State Department, Great Britain, Despatches, to Hay, October 5, 1901).

CHAPTER 12

Adjustment and Change

THE Hay-Pauncefote treaty not only ended the dangerous canal controversy; it also paved the way toward adjustment of all remaining controversies. It had much the same effect as removal of part of a log-jam. We have seen that Ottawa had tried to tie together the two principal Anglo-American disputes in the belief Great Britain could get more in Alaska as long as she could brandish the Clayton-Bulwer treaty over the United States. But the Dominion had overestimated that treaty's bargaining power, and had underestimated the likelihood of accord in Central America. Disregarding repeated warnings from the mother country that negotiations were progressing smoothly, she woke one day to find a new canal treaty concluded and the main basis of her diplomacy with the United States undermined. She lay exposed, far more vulnerable to American pressure than before.

Of the remaining issues it was the complex problem of defining the Alaska boundary that clamored for attention. Fisheries, fur seals, reciprocity—these were matters of undoubted significance; but demarcation of the boundary was a *sine qua non* of stable Anglo-American relations. If it could be defined, other disputes could be taken lightly on the sure assumption of their being resolved in due course; if not, British-American friendship might not long outlast the Spanish War that had brought it to light.

In recent months disturbing reports had been coming from the north country. During the preceding summer of 1901, about

240

the time Pauncefote went to London to carry the canal discussions to a successful conclusion, rumors were rife that Great Britain was on the verge of seizing Skagway and presenting America with a *fait accompli*; the signal for the *coup* would be the hoisting of the Union Jack over the offices of the White Pass and Yukon Railway, the town's highest point.[1] However unfounded, these reports alarmed Americans in the area; and on June 24, 1901, an excitable lawyer named Miller, perhaps hoping to nip a nefarious British plot in the bud, cut down the Canadian flag on the customs house.[2] Americans applauded the stalwart deed; Canadians angrily denounced it, insisting they had as much right to display the flag as Americans did to fly the Stars and Stripes over their customs houses in Canada; and as the governor of Alaska said, " The whole incident is regrettable because it is calculated to inflame and engender hostile feelings as hardly anything else could do." [3] The time had come to deal with Skagway firmly, a special American Treasury agent reported on completing a tour of investigation.[4] Fortunately Miller's foolish act did not provoke any Canadian to retaliate; and the incident was closed when the United States apologized and when it and Britain agreed to discontinue flying flags over their customs houses located within the other's jurisdiction.[5]

Nevertheless Alaska continued to cause concern. Just two days after signature of the Hay-Pauncefote treaty an alarming telegram was received in London from Governor-General Lord Minto:

[1] F. O. 5, 2457, Adee to Lowther, September 7, 1901.

[2] *The Daily Alaskan* (Skagway), June 25, 1901, has an account of the incident.

[3] State Department, Miscellaneous Letters, Secretary of the Interior to Hay, July 13, 1901, enclosing a letter from J. G. Brady, governor of Alaska, to the Secretary of the Interior, June 29, 1901.

[4] *Ibid.,* Treasury Department to State Department, November 27, 1901, enclosing a letter from J. F. Evans dated October 27, 1901.

[5] *Ibid.,* F. O. 5, 2485, report of the committee of the Privy Council, December 23, 1901; F. O. 115, 1261, Hay to Pauncefote, January 7, 1902; F. O. 5, 2484, Villiers to Pauncefote, February 18, 1902; F. O. 115, 1238, Lansdowne to Pauncefote, February 18, 1902.

Rumours of contemplated rising of American miners in Yukon intended to overthrow local government are not without foundation. United States miners largely outnumber British. Police garrison at Dawson being strengthened. I inform you at once so that possible complications with United States may be avoided.[6]

The Skagway police had uncovered evidence of a conspiracy to seize Canadian territory in the Yukon.[7] The news sent a thrill of excitement through Washington, London, and Ottawa. Was the long-feared insurrection at hand? Sir Wilfrid Laurier was seriously perturbed; and Great Britain appealed to Washington "to exercise a moderating influence on the American miners."[8] It looked very much as though Americans, having just levelled charges of British plotting at Skagway, were about to take action themselves;[9] part of British North America might shortly be going the way of Florida, Oregon, Texas, and California—other frontier areas that had been so injudicious as to admit large numbers of Americans. Alerted to the danger, Ottawa ordered mounted police to stand guard on routes to the Yukon; it despatched secret agents to Skagway and Seattle, believed to be the conspiracy's headquarters.[10] The United States warned the commanding general in Alaska to prevent Alaska being used as a base against Canada, and instructed officials in Eagle City and Juneau to enforce the neutrality laws in the event of trouble.[11]

Possibly because of these precautions nothing of consequence happened. As a matter of fact, the conspiracy probably never did assume serious proportions. No one of standing except the mayor

[6] F. O. 5, 2479, to Chamberlain, November 20, 1901.

[7] F. O. 5, 2505, memorandum by comptroller of Northwest Mounted Police, December 19, 1900.

[8] F. O. 5, 2479, Lansdowne to Pauncefote, November 22, 1901; Minto to Chamberlain, November 23, 1901.

[9] See F. O. 5, 2510, Minto to Chamberlain, February 1, 1902, for a report that the Yukon conspiracy might be connected with the Skagway flag incident.

[10] F. O. 5, 2505, Minto to Chamberlain, December 20, 1901.

[11] F. O. 5, 2479, Pauncefote to Lansdowne, November 23, 1901; State Department, Miscellaneous Letters, Interior Department to Hay, November 27, 1901, and War Department to Hay, November 29, 1901.

of Skagway was connected with it; and it was apparently conceived and organized largely by owners of amusement halls and gambling houses, partly to make money, partly in the hope of putting the Alaska question so vividly before the American people as to force Britain either to yield or to fight.[12] Nevertheless the situation on the frontier remained menacing. The governor of Alaska advised keeping " a gunboat constantly in these waters ";[13] the mounted police thought trouble after the break-up of ice in the spring " quite possible ";[14] Laurier feared an emergency in April or May.[15] The Canadian collector of customs at Skagway, a respected man of sound judgment, told Lord Minto that the coastal population, much of it Irish-American, was " intensely dissatisfied "; that Seattle was full of irresponsible " scum "; and that danger lurked along Porcupine creek because of its precious minerals.[16] Almost as he spoke, miners of the Porcupine, who already had petitioned McKinley,[17] were preparing another resolution to put before his successor, Theodore Roosevelt:

we firmly believe that the young man that tackled the Lions in their den among the N. Y. Police commissioners, who throttled vice & immorality also corruption in high places while Governor of the Empire State, & faced clouds of lead & steel in a Southern Clime, will be equal to this task, & we leave our interests with you Mr. President believing our inter-

---

[12] F. O. 5, 2505, memorandum of White, December 19, 1901, and F. O. 5, 2510, Minto to Chamberlain, February 1, 1902. For further information about the revolt see F. O. 5, 2479, Pauncefote to Lansdowne, December 9, 1901, and Hay to Pauncefote, December 16, 1901; F. O. 5, 2505, Minto to Chamberlain, December 20, 1901; State Department, Miscellaneous Letters, Interior Department to Hay, January 3, 1902; F. O. 115, 1261, Hay to Pauncefote, January 7 and 10, 1902; P. C. Jessup, *Elihu Root* (2 vols., New York, 1938), vol. 1, pp. 391-392.

[13] State Department, Miscellaneous Letters, Interior Department to Hay, January 3, 1902; the governor deprecated prophecies of trouble, however.

[14] F. O. 5, 2505, memorandum of White, December 19, 1901.

[15] *Ibid.*, Minto to Chamberlain, December 20, 1901.

[16] F. O. 5, 2510, Minto to Chamberlain, February 1, 1902.

[17] See p. 206.

ests are the Nations [sic] interests and you by Gods [sic] help will guard them sacredly.[18]

It was doubtless because of his awareness of the ominous state of affairs in the gold country rather than because of this heady exhortation, however, that the young tackler of lions wisely ordered additional troops to proceed to southern Alaska; [19] they might be an indispensable element of stability in the spring, when ice began to melt in the north and men everywhere became restless. After all, April and May were favorite months for American rebellions.

Thus nothing could have been plainer than the need for Britain and the United States, now that they had at length resolved their protracted dispute in Central America, to come to grips with the one great danger still outstanding. Despite the obvious need, however, despite the stronger diplomatic position of the United States after the canal treaty, a long rough road had to be traversed before finally the Alaska boundary was drawn in late 1903.

We have seen the extent to which the new British-American friendship depended on an American conviction of British sympathy during the struggle with Spain. It was therefore with some consternation that Great Britain in early 1902 heard official German accusations that she, through the venerable Pauncefote, had in fact taken the lead in 1898 in agitating for European intervention against the United States. Here was a most unwelcome shaft aimed close to the heart of the carefully nurtured friendship between the two English-speaking nations. It was rendered the more deadly by news that no less a personage than the Kaiser's brother, Prince Henry, was soon to visit America. Just as a large part of America's liking for Britain dated from the Spanish War, so a large part of its dislike of Germany sprang

[18] State Department, Miscellaneous Letters, January 19, 1902, the miners of Porcupine, by H. F. Emmons, to Roosevelt; see *ibid.*, March 26, 1902, for a petition from the Chilkat Indians to " the Great White Father " raising the alarm about " the King George Men."

[19] Jessup, *Root*, vol. 1, pp. 391-392; Roosevelt ordered the troop movement on March 27, 1902.

from a legend about the same conflict, the legend of the deliberately hostile conduct of a German naval officer, Vice-Admiral von Diederichs, toward the American squadron at Manila Bay in 1898.[20] Prince Henry, also a naval officer, had commanded the German squadron at Hongkong when Commodore Dewey arrived there in the spring of that year. The appearance of this exalted being in the United States, therefore, might convey to Americans a suggestion, however unavowed, of German penance for her sins of 1898. Once absolved, Germany could hope to find for herself a warm spot in American affections, perhaps even to replace the British there, the more so if her allegations of British perfidy in 1898 should strike a responsive note across the Atlantic.

The German attack had its origin in a controversy raised by G. W. Smalley in December, 1901, when he took it into his head to revive in the august columns of the London *Times* the story of the good British and the wicked Continentals during the Spanish War. There is some reason to think he had got wind of a projected campaign to disseminate aspersions upon Britain's role at that time and hoped to forestall it by striking first.[21] It was easy for a man of his talents to suggest a parallel between these former attitudes and the existing continental hatred of Britain—and the existing American support of Britain—during the Boer War. Smalley's historical analogies attracted a certain amount of attention in the United States,[22] some commentators being so unkind, however, as to cast aspersions upon the genuineness of Britain's friendship in 1898.[23]

But interest in the Smalley controversy was slight compared with that arising when at this juncture a member of the Liberal

[20] See p. 53. T. A. Bailey, "Dewey and the Germans at Manila Bay," *American Historical Review*, vol. 45 (1939), pp. 59-81, demolished any remnants of the myth that had lived on.

[21] A somewhat similar line of thought occurs in an article entitled "Our Friends in 1898," *New York Tribune*, January 1, 1902.

[22] *The Times*, December 26, 1901.

[23] Pauncefote reported "efforts made in certain quarters [before January 20, 1902] to misrepresent the facts to the detriment of His Majesty's Government" (F. O. 5, 2517, Pauncefote to Lansdowne, January 31, 1902).

opposition, Henry Norman, arose in the House of Commons to ask the government for information about the moves for intervention in April, 1898. Why Norman put the question can only be conjectured. As a former American correspondent of the Liberal journal, the *Daily Chronicle*, and as a graduate of Harvard University, he had many connections with the United States. Perhaps he had no other motive than curiosity; perhaps he wanted to help Smalley strike a shrewd blow for Anglo-American unity, a cause dear to his heart.[24] There is no reason to suspect him of trying to stir up the storm that followed.[25] Answering the question on January 20, 1902, Lord Salisbury's son, Lord Cranborne, Under-Secretary for Foreign Affairs, denied that Britain had participated in any mediation proposal unfriendly to the United States.[26] Although couched in moderate terms his answer seemed to imply that Britain alone had prevented intervention; and British and American newspapers were shortly stressing this theme frequently and unreservedly.[27]

Cranborne's statement and subsequent press comment in Great Britain and the United States created an extraordinary sensation. The statement, Pauncefote reported joyfully, had a "most important and decisive effect" on American opinion and "entirely baffled" current attempts to disparage Britain's friendship.[28]

[24] A. Vagts, *Deutschland und die Vereinigten Staaten in der Weltpolitik* (2 vols., New York, 1935), vol. 2, p. 1400.

[25] In a letter to the editor Norman denied prearrangement between himself and the government (*The Times*, February 14, 1902); since he belonged to the opposition, his assertion would seem to be correct—a point that Great Britain made to Germany (F. O. 5, 2517, Lascelles to Lansdowne, February 14, 1902). See also Vagts, *Deutschland*, vol. 2, pp. 1402-1403.

[26] *Parliamentary Debates*, vol. 101, p. 311.

[27] See Vagts, *Deutschland*, vol. 2, p. 1401, for an Associated Press statement, claiming the "highest authority" in Great Britain, that Germany, France, and Russia, the three powers intervening in the Far East at the time of the Sino-Japanese War, were behind the mediation move of 1898. The Foreign Office later asserted that it would not have selected the Associated Press for an official communication (*ibid.*, p. 1408).

[28] F. O. 5, 2517, Pauncefote to Lansdowne, January 31, 1902. See also *New York Evening Post*, January 21, 1902; *Evening Star* (Washington), January 21, 1902; and *New York Tribune*, January 22, 1902.

But the American reaction was as nothing compared to the European. Reviewing press articles around the world the *Literary Digest* found the powers falling over themselves, each trying to prove that it alone had been America's true friend in 1898.[29]

Of all countries it was Germany that was most indignant about Cranborne's explanation.[30] The Kaiser had long been jealous of the special niche in American esteem reserved for his rivals across the North Sea; and he now seems to have suspected the British government of instigating Norman's question with malice aforethought so as to spoil his brother's forthcoming trip. Early in the morning of February 12, 1902, an indignant Kaiser William descended upon the British embassy in Berlin. Informed that the ambassador, Sir Frank Lascelles, was still asleep, the Kaiser stamped upstairs to his bedroom, seized hold of the recumbent Englishman's little finger, and squeezed it until he awoke. It was "rather too strong," he told the startled diplomat, for Great Britain to be claiming the exclusive merit of having staved off intervention four years earlier when in point of fact Germany herself could rightly claim much of the credit, and the Berlin government had therefore just published a reply in the *North German Gazette* to Cranborne's charges.[31]

The government also released two official documents regarding the matter. One of these was Holleben's version of the identic telegram drawn up at the famous meeting of the foreign representatives in Washington on April 14, 1898.[32] The other read as follows:

Telegram. Berlin, 15 April, 1898. The Imperial Secretary of State to His Majesty the Emperor and King. Decypher.

---

[29] *Literary Digest*, vol. 24 (February 1, 1902), p. 137.

[30] In Washington the German ambassador, Holleben, sent Hay a memorandum complaining that "England wishes to impair the friendly relations between Germany and the U.S. which relations arouse the jealousy of England"; see A. L. P. Dennis, *Adventures in American Diplomacy, 1896-1906* (New York, 1928), p. 74. For the reaction in Germany see Vagts, *Deutschland*, vol. 2, pp. 1400-1410.

[31] F. O. 5, 2517, Lascelles to Lansdowne, February 14, 1902.

[32] See p. 33. This document was apparently an independent version prepared by the German ambassador; see Appendix 1.

Your Majesty's Ambassador in Washington telegraphs: "The English Ambassador today very decidedly took the initiative in suggesting a new collective action on the part of the representatives of the Great Powers here. We conjecture that the Queen Regent [of Spain] has made representations in this sense to the Queen of England. The six representatives are telegraphing to their Governments in the following sense at the wish of the English Ambassador: [The identic telegram followed.]

"My personal feelings with regard to such a proceeding are those of coldness. Holleben."

(signed) Bülow.

Marginal note by His Majesty to the Ambassador's last sentence.

"I consider it completely mistaken, useless and therefore hurtful. . . . I am against taking this step." [33]

Germany's disclosure launched a furious debate. All over Europe and America Britain's many enemies took up the attack with whoops of delight. German newspapers gloated at the apparent exposure of British hypocrisy; "the Parisian press is making as much as possible of the question . . . ," the British ambassador to France reported; [34] St. Petersburg published a communiqué putting the blame for the mediation proposal squarely on Pauncefote.[35] Some publicists went all the way back to the Civil War in their search for proof of British malevolence toward America.[36]

---

[33] *Official Gazette*, February 12, 1902. Referring to the German documents in his *Anglo-American Memories, Second Series* (New York and London, 1912) , p. 182, G. W. Smalley quotes a "high personage in Washington" as saying (though he gave no evidence) : "I do not believe the Imperial ink on the margin of Holleben's four-year-old dispatch was dry when the press telegram was sent from Berlin." According to Holleben, Pauncefote told the French ambassador when leaving the meeting of April 14, 1898, that the Americans were "brigands"; see *Die Grosse Politik der Europäischen Kabinette, 1871-1914* (40 vols., Berlin, 1924-1927) , vol. 15, p. 30. R. B. Mowat, *The Life of Lord Pauncefote, First Ambassador to the United States* (Boston and New York, 1929) , pp. 217-218, ridicules the story.

[34] F. O. 5, 2517, Monson to Lansdowne, February 17, 1902; F. O. 115, 1238, Villiers to Pauncefote, February 24, 1902.

[35] *Journal de Saint-Pétersbourg*, February 23, 1902.

[36] *Literary Digest*, vol. 24 (March 29, 1902) , p. 417. Goldwin Smith thought

Thus assailed on all sides, Great Britain moved to defend herself. On releasing her own documents Germany had challenged Britain to do as much.[37] But Britain declined. " Ld. L. [Lansdowne] thinks," Cranborne explained to Chamberlain,

> that, at the present moment, our declarations have given us the best of the position and that it is not likely to be bettered by any publication. The fact is that our ordinary practice of doctoring papers for publication is not open to us in the present instance, where we should be under an honourable obligation not to publish anything which is not rigidly genuine, and there are several expressions which would not look very well in public. (What private communications are there of which that cannot be said?) [38]

Despite some pressure in Parliament, the government refused to alter its stand. This was, a spokesman asserted firmly, " not a case in which papers of a confidential character can be published, and this decision must be adhered to." [39] Nor would Lord Pauncefote defend himself publicly, thinking it beneath his dignity to embark upon an angry altercation in Washington.[40] So again the government had recourse to a public statement by Cranborne in the Commons:

> Whatever opinions were expressed by Lord Pauncefote during the discussion which was of an informal character were personal to himself and not in persuance of any instructions from Her Majesty's Government. The discussion resulted in an agreement by the Ambassadors to forward an identical telegram to their respective Governments suggesting a further communi-

it well to counter such charges by writing an article defending Great Britain; see "England and the War of Secession," *The Atlantic Monthly*, vol. 89 (1902) , pp. 303-311.

[37] F. O. 115, 1239, Lascelles to Lansdowne, February 24, 1902.

[38] J. Amery, *The Life of Joseph Chamberlain* (London, 1951) , vol. 4, pp. 187-188; the letter is dated February 15, 1902, the day after the German documents were published.

[39] *The Times*, March 1, 1902; cited by Vagts, *Deutschland*, vol. 2, p. 1408.

[40] F. O. 5, 2517, Pauncefote to Lansdowne, February 13, 1902. Wayne McVeagh, a former Attorney General and ambassador to Italy, and John Foster defended Pauncefote in the *Washington Post* (Mowat, *Pauncefote*, pp. 221-222) .

cation to the Government of the United States. On the receipt of this message Her Majesty's Government at once replied objecting to the terms of the proposed communication as injudicious. Two days later Lord Pauncefote was informed that Her Majesty's Government had resolved to take no action. We had at the time no information of the attitude of the German Government.[41]

We have already seen that although Lord Pauncefote had, in his own words, " strongly advocated at the meeting an identic telegram . . . counseling action . . . ," [42] he did not convince his superiors. Neither the Cabinet nor Queen Victoria—a Foreign Office memorandum stated explicitly that Holleben's surmise regarding the Queen " had no foundation in fact " [43]—had instructed him to arrange mediation, and Balfour rejected the identic telegram suggested by Pauncefote. But the American people did not know this.

Hard upon release of the German documents came the visit of Prince Henry. He arrived at New York on the *Kronprinz Wilhelm* on February 23, 1902. After nearly three weeks of incessant receptions, parades, speeches and other public activities, culminating in the launching of a yacht for his imperial brother by the President's daughter, the vivacious Alice, he set sail on the *Deutschland*, his expiatory mission successfully performed. He had, the Philadelphia *Press* believed, revealed " the Kaiser . . . as a long-headed statesman who may easily give his British friends cause to wonder and ponder." [44] Cause to wonder he no doubt did give; yet it seems clear that the consequence of neither the visit nor the publication of the documents was profound. Certainly the President and the Secretary of State were not swayed to Germany.[45] As for less prominent Americans, once their

[41] *Parliamentary Debates*, vol. 103, p. 40, February 14, 1902.

[42] F. O. 5, 2517, Pauncefote to Lansdowne, February 13, 1902. See p. 37.

[43] F. O. 115, 1239, Lansdowne to Pauncefote, April 9, 1902, enclosing memorandum dated March 8, 1902, marked " printed for the use of the Cabinet." See Appendix 1. Since the memorandum was prepared for Foreign Office use, not for publication, it must be accepted as true.

[44] *Literary Digest*, vol. 24 (July 24, 1902) , p. 103. See also *Public Opinion*, vol. 32 (January 23, 1902) , p. 101; *ibid.* (March 6, 1902) , pp. 296-297.

[45] According to Smalley, whose writings must however be taken with

initial surprise had worn off they had time to reflect that Pauncefote had acted as dean and that in any case his government had opposed mediation. Some wavering of belief in British good faith doubtless there was; some weakening even; but certainly Americans on the whole did not view this undignified contest for their friendship seriously enough to cause any lasting change of outlook. Many newspapers, indeed, regarded the whole affair— " the shrieks of angry housemaids pulling caps over the policeman," John Hay called it [46]—as rather ludicrous.[47]

Nevertheless the German documents did make a fairly deep impression for two or three weeks. Britain " had lost much ground," Holleben rejoiced; [48] and most Americans probably would have agreed with the Philadelphia *Ledger* that Germany had had the best of the argument.[49] Joseph Chamberlain, who had unusual facilities for gauging trans-Atlantic opinion through official channels and through frequent letters from his wife's American relatives,[50] found that opinion " rather critical," " wavering or even inclining to Germany in this controversy "; deeply perturbed, he urged the government to do something " to set ourselves right with the American people. . . ." [51] It is in its short-run effect, notably in its effect on the complicated problem of defining the Alaska boundary, that the episode's main significance is to be found. For a while it complicated that problem yet more. To the extent that American Anglophobes

caution, the President told him, " Not only do I not believe this Berlin story, but I know it is false " (Smalley, *Memories, Second Series,* p. 185) . See also Smalley's article, " That German Experiment," *Collier's Weekly,* vol. 31 (August 29, 1903) , pp. 18-19. See Holls papers, Holls to Lange, February 14, 1902, and Holls to Halle, April 16, 1902.

[46] Dennis, *Adventures,* p. 74, Hay to Roosevelt, February 15, 1902.

[47] See *Literary Digest,* vol. 24 (February 22, 1902) , p. 246.

[48] Vagts, *Deutschland,* vol. 2, p. 1409.

[49] *Public Opinion,* vol. 32 (February 20, 1902) , p. 229; *Literary Digest,* vol. 24 (February 22, 1902) , p. 246.

[50] ". . . letters usually passed every week between the households on opposite sides of the Atlantic "; see J. L. Garvin, *The Life of Joseph Chamberlain* (3 vols., London, 1932-1934) , vol. 3, p. 296.

[51] Amery, *Chamberlain,* p. 188, to Lansdowne, February 25, 1902; and p. 189, to Lansdowne, March 7, 1902.

found aid and comfort in the German allegations and in Prince Henry's mission, Secretary Hay's freedom to negotiate was curtailed. And Lord Pauncefote was so shaken by the attack on his veracity—Henry Adams found him "almost broken up"[52]— that he could not give full attention to other matters during the last months of his life. Indeed, according to his friend Smalley the attack hastened his death some three months after the German charges were made.[53] If true, that would be significance enough of the whole absurd squabble.

Even had the squabble not occurred it would have been difficult to follow up the Hay-Pauncefote treaty with an early Alaska agreement. For the moment conditions simply were not suitable for negotiations. A long chapter was drawing to its close, and diplomacy would have to await its conclusion. Pauncefote died on May 24, 1902; his successor did not reach Washington until October; in the meantime diplomacy perforce marked time. Lord Salisbury's health was failing, too. No longer could the old statesman, who had contributed so notably to the new understanding between his country and the United States, meet all the responsibilities of his office. His wife's death had been a terrible blow; it had contributed to the lethargy, absent-mindedness, growing slowness of mind described by his biographer.[54] Everyone knew that he was only waiting for victory in the Boer War— that interminable conflict he had disliked from the beginning— in order to retire. The aged Prime Minister had no inner urge to sponsor new enterprises; younger men after him could do that; he only wanted to tidy up what had already been started, and then get out.

The monarchy, too, was in a somewhat uncertain state. Queen Victoria had long been dead; but the new ruler, Edward VII, had not yet been crowned. And even after all preparations for the

---

[52] W. C. Ford, ed., *Letters of Henry Adams (1892-1918)* (Boston and New York, 1938), p. 372, February 16, 1902.

[53] *The Times*, May 26, 1902; *Literary Digest*, vol. 26 (February 14, 1903), p. 237.

[54] A. L. Kennedy, *Salisbury, 1830-1903, Portrait of a Statesman* (London, 1953), p. 307.

coronation had been completed and the guests assembled, the King's sudden illness required a postponement of the ceremony, thereby intensifying the atmosphere of uncertainty. The great Victorian age had perhaps ended; was the Edwardian really to begin?

Across the Atlantic the new Roosevelt administration had not long been in office. It would take time for it and for the country at large to get over the shock of McKinley's assassination; it would take time for the President to become accustomed to his new responsibilities and to formulate his own program. It was one thing for him to allow finishing touches to be put on the Hay-Pauncefote treaty, already substantially concluded when he unexpectedly became President; it was quite another to think through from the beginning the intricate Alaska question and authorize a fresh start. Throughout his first year in office Roosevelt could say little more about that question than that he disliked Hay's draft boundary treaty of May, 1901, and that if he had been President then he would not have sanctioned it. A "quite despondent" John Hay told Lord Pauncefote at the end of March, not long before the ambassador's death, that "the President considers the claim of the United States is so manifestly clear and unanswerable that he is not disposed to run the risk of sacrificing American territory under a compromise which is the almost certain result of an Arbitration." ". . . clear and unanswerable"—one wonders whether these words stirred up along the corridors of the Foreign Office disquieting memories of the memorable phrase, "clear and unquestionable," that had been applied to another British-American boundary dispute, that of the Oregon boundary, more than half a century earlier, when President Polk, too, rejected arbitration. The most that President Roosevelt would agree to, Hay told the ambassador, was a tribunal recording, not a verdict, but merely its members' "reasoned opinions." Pauncefote believed that Roosevelt must be under heavy pressure from western states and from pro-Boer and Irish groups.[55] Such pressure could not be taken lightly in

[55] F. O. 5, 2510, Pauncefote to Lansdowne, March 28, 1902.

the face of an approaching election by a young man only accidentally and precariously in power. Trudging across the countryside with the British military attaché, the President declared roundly that he would not touch the Alaska boundary question until the Boer War was over.[56] A week earlier an overwhelming majority of American newspapers had been " jubilant " over the unexpected rout of a British general, Lord Methuen, in South Africa. " Let sleeping dogs lie! " Roosevelt admonished Ambassador Choate.[57]

As a matter of fact, when the President turned to miners, it was not gold miners of the far north but coal miners right at home who occupied his thoughts. The great coal strike which broke out in May, 1902, was one of the most formidable labor upheavals in American history. The very least of its threats pointed squarely at the new administration in the mid-term elections. Miners of Alaska might be restive but they did not vote; until the strike was settled they would have to take second place to those of Pennsylvania. Meanwhile they could be restrained by the additional troops sent north in March.

Thus for several months of 1902 the prevailing atmosphere in both the United States and Great Britain was unpropitious for vigorous diplomacy. Both governments stood their ground, waiting for more favorable circumstances to crystallize.

One apparent exception existed, an enormous one it must be confessed, to this diplomatic inactivity. The Anglo-Japanese alliance, signed January 30, 1902, represented a far-reaching step, indeed a departure from Britain's policy of isolation, hard to reconcile with a somnolent Prime Minister and an end-of-the-age atmosphere. But the decisive phase in negotiations came in 1901; and in any case Britain was pretty much forced into the agree-

---

[56] Ford, *Letters of Adams,* p. 382, March 30, 1902; the President had said much the same thing to Smalley on February 18, 1902; see C. C. Tansill, *Canadian-American Relations, 1875-1911* (New Haven, 1943) , p. 223; see also Choate papers, Hay to Choate, January 7, 1902.

[57] Choate papers, Choate to Hay, July 19, 1902; Hay to Choate, January 7, 1902: " The President seems to think that sufficient to the day is the evil thereof. . . ."

ment by Japan's flirtation with Russia.[58] A few words should be said about the impact of this famous alliance upon Anglo-American relations. On the whole Americans judged the British step favorably; they would have agreed with Ambassador Choate who, reporting the new treaty to Washington, said, " It seems to me greatly to fortify the policy of the ' open door '. . . ." [59] In other words the alliance was interpreted as another confirmation, comparable to but more conclusive than the Anglo-German treaty of 1900,[60] of Britain's whole-hearted acceptance of John Hay's open door principles. As for the British, implicit in their favorable reception of this change from past policy lay an assumption that America was in some sense a third party to the treaty. A writer pointed out that in a debate in Parliament " Mr. Norman remarked that ' the interests of the United States in this matter were identical with our own.' Viscount Cranborne had no doubt that ' in this agreement we shall command the general approval of the Government of the United States.' Sir Henry Campbell-Bannerman had a word on the ' similarity of peaceable commercial interests and other material interests,' between England, Japan and the United States in the Far East; and Mr. Balfour said that the Treaty would do much to place upon a solid and permanent foundation the interests common to the whole of the commercial world and ' not least of our American brothers.' " [61]

The end of these months of adjustment and marking time came during the summer of 1902. To be sure, in the United States the coal strike continued to bedevil the administration; the mid-term November elections drew nearer; the President remained

[58] W. L. Langer, *The Diplomacy of Imperialism, 1890-1902* (2 vols., New York and London, 1935) , vol. 2, pp. 782-783.

[59] State Department, Great Britain, Despatches, Choate to Hay, February 12, 1902.

[60] See p. 203.

[61] Sydney Brooks, " America and the Alliance," *The Fortnightly Review* (1902) , p. 555. See *Literary Digest*, vol. 24 (March 15, 1902) , p. 365, for the view of the *Hamburger Nachrichten* that the alliance was nothing but a British trick to entangle the United States with herself, and for the interpretations of other newspapers; see also *ibid.* (May 24, 1902) , p. 704.

firm against compromise in Alaska. But to Great Britain the treaty of Vereeniging, signed May 31, at long last brought peace in South Africa. And in August, Edward VII was at length crowned King and Emperor. Then, the interregnum terminated, the Edwardian age formally began. In the meantime Lord Salisbury, unable to wait for the deferred coronation, resigned on July 10. His nephew, Arthur Balfour, succeeded him as Prime Minister. The younger, stronger man's "sympathies with us will be more *active* than Lord Salisbury's were," Choate predicted.[62] The new British ambassador, Sir Michael Herbert, took up residence in Washington in October, eager to mark his promotion by ending the boundary impasse.[63] In short, the war was over, the King was crowned, new faces were in Downing Street and the British embassy; suddenly circumstances had changed in a manner favorable to active diplomacy.

It was on the Canadian side, however, that the really decisive change occurred. In that summer of 1902, as the Boer War drew to its close and the King stood ready to be crowned, statesmen from all over the British empire assembled in London for a conference of colonial Prime Ministers. Sir Wilfrid Laurier headed the Canadian delegation. Lord Minto was also there. According to a subsequent account, Clifford Sifton, Canadian Minister of the Interior, and several other members of the Cabinet, fearful lest Laurier be seduced by British wiles, warned him before leaving Ottawa not to agree to submit the Alaska boundary dispute to an even-numbered tribunal; Laurier, Sifton asserted, promised to uphold Canada's position "without flinching." [64] If the Prime Minister did in fact give this assurance he changed his attitude soon after arriving in Great Britain.

Calling at the Foreign Office on June 25, 1902, Ambassador Choate was surprised to hear Lansdowne suggest his taking advantage of the presence in London of the Canadian officials to resume negotiations on the dormant boundary question. Choate

[62] Hay papers, to Hay, July 19, 1902.

[63] C. S. Hay, ed., *Letters of John Hay and Extracts from Diary* (3 vols., Washington, 1908), vol. 3, p. 264.

[64] J. W. Dafoe, *Clifford Sifton in Relation to His Times* (Toronto, 1931), p. 217. Dafoe claims to have got this story straight from Sifton.

demurred somewhat, mainly on the ground of the inadvisability of reviving a sore and delicate subject in an election year; but after some further reflection he cabled to Washington for instructions.[65] The prompt reply authorized negotiations but warned that " the President . . . thinks the Canadian claim has not a leg to stand on and that compromise is impossible." [66] Thus fortified, the ambassador called on Lansdowne again, on July 2. The Foreign Minister renewed his suggestion; he went further: he offered two concessions of utmost significance to the eventual settlement. First, he said that no matter what an arbitral board might decide, the United States must have Dyea and Skagway—Canada did not want them; second, he said that if the question to be arbitrated could be properly framed, he would not oppose "your way of constituting the Court. . . ." [67] Since Canada had stubbornly rejected an even-numbered tribunal from the beginning of the controversy (unless two of the members were neutrals) , most recently when she had refused Hay's draft treaty of May, 1901, and the United States equally stubbornly had rejected an odd-numbered tribunal, these unexpected concessions struck at the root of the deadlock.

Choate suspected that Lansdowne's change of front originated not in London but with Sir Wilfrid Laurier; and in several subsequent conversations he and Henry White had with the Canadian he found this suspicion confirmed.[68] Indeed there can be little doubt that Lansdowne was speaking for Sir Wilfrid. It is true that Laurier's biographer has denied that the Prime Minister did in fact make any such concessions.[69] Against that we have Choate's statement to Hay and a similar statement by the ambassador to Lansdowne.[70] Clifford Sifton likewise accused

---

[65] F. O. 5, 2510, Lansdowne to Raikes, June 25, 1902; State Department, Great Britain, Despatches, Choate to Hay, June 29, 1902.

[66] Hay papers, Choate to Hay, July 5, 1902; Choate received the reply July 1, 1902.

[67] *Ibid.*

[68] Hay papers, Choate to Hay, July 5 and 19, 1902.

[69] O. D. Skelton, " Dafoe's Sifton," *Queen's Quarterly*, vol. 39 (1932) , p. 6.

[70] Hay papers, Choate to Hay, July 5 and 19, 1902; F. O. 5, 2510, Lansdowne to Raikes, July 16, 1902.

his chief of giving way in London.[71] We have, also, testimony of Sir John Anderson that seems conclusive. In a minute addressed to Joseph Chamberlain, Sir John said plainly: " It seems to me that Sir W. Laurier after making all the trouble of the last three or four years has made an abject surrender of all the U. S. ask for." And Chamberlain confirmed this judgment in a minute of his own: " I gathered that Sir W. Laurier was in a conceding mood." [72]

Laurier did not return to Canada until October, when he told his dismayed Cabinet what had transpired. Although some members contemplated trying to force him to retract, they could not have done so without precipitating a row which in the political situation then existing would have endangered the Liberal government. As it was, the Cabinet was at odds over a private campaign by the Minister of Public Works, J. I. Tarte, for tariff revision; and Sir Wilfrid, hardly off the boat, had created a sensation by dismissing him.[73] Furthermore the Prime Minister himself was in such poor health that despite his long absence he soon had to depart for warmer climates in the United States. Obviously the moment was not propitious for disgruntled ministers to stir up more trouble.

It was the astonishing about-face by Sir Wilfrid Laurier that cleared the way to the boundary agreement of 1903. Theodore Roosevelt would still hesitate to jeopardise territory he believed incontestably American, but in the end he would yield without too much difficulty. And Great Britain, as has appeared, had for long been ready to pay almost any price for a settlement. So decisive were the Prime Minister's concessions, especially his acceptance of an even-numbered tribunal, that every effort must be made to explain them. Nothing more need be said as to the

[71] Dafoe, *Sifton*, pp. 217-218.

[72] C. O. 42, 890, minute by Anderson, September 1, 1902. See also F. O. 5, 2510, Anderson to Villiers, July 18, 1902, for Sir John's marginal explanations of why he toned down a draft Foreign Office despatch for transmission to Washington that had been submitted to him for comment: " too strong if we contemplate giving way "; " In the present mood of the Dominion Govt. the dft appears to be too emphatic on some points."

[73] Dafoe, *Sifton*, p. 217; *Literary Digest*, vol. 25 (November 8, 1902) , p. 608.

profound effect of the Hay-Pauncefote treaty in weakening Canada's bargaining strength *vis-à-vis* the United States; Laurier doubtless understood the new situation and was influenced by it. But this was not the only influence upon him. Judging by the statements of some of the participants, he gave way simply from concern over the dangerous state of affairs in the gold country. Lansdowne gave this explanation to Choate. Why risk stirring up a hornet's nest when all was proceeding so well under the *modus vivendi* of 1899, the puzzled ambassador asked him. ". . . there was a risk," the Foreign Minister answered, "of serious trouble arising should there be discoveries of gold . . . within the disputed area." [74] And Sir Wilfrid himself said the same thing to both the ambassador and Henry White. [75] Nevertheless this consideration alone seems inadequate, and Choate himself put little stock in it. No particular reason existed in the summer of 1902 to anticipate early gold strikes along the desolate border. Besides, cold weather, that season Lord Salisbury thinking of Alaska used to hail with relief as " our mutual friend the winter," [76] was drawing near. The real explanation, Choate believed, lay somewhere in Canadian politics or in Laurier's personal position. [77] And indeed, though Sir Wilfrid's motives cannot be demonstrated with certainty, the ambassador does appear to have been close to the mark.

We must now turn to an area far removed from the gold fields of Alaska—to Newfoundland and her great fisheries. For not only do developments there need consideration on their own merits; they need consideration also because they point to a likely reason for the Canadian Prime Minister's strange reversal in London.

Life was not easy at the turn of the century for the hardy

[74] F. O. 5, 2510, Lansdowne to Raikes, June 25, 1902; State Department, Great Britain, Despatches, Choate to Hay, June 29, 1902.

[75] F. O. 5, 2510, Lansdowne to Raikes, July 16, 1902; Hay papers, Choate to Hay, July 19, 1902; A. Nevins, *Henry White, Thirty Years of American Diplomacy* (New York and London, 1930), pp. 192-193, White to Hay, June 28, 1902.

[76] F. O. 5, 2510, Lansdowne to Raikes, July 16, 1902.

[77] Hay papers, Choate to Hay, July 19, 1902.

inhabitants of Britain's oldest colony. Harassed by French fishing fleets based on the "French shore," [78] her sales restricted on the Continent by lavish French bounties and in the American market by the tariff, Newfoundland was seeking to raise her meagre standard of living.[79] A decade or so earlier, in 1890, the Blaine-Bond convention, by lowering duties on her major exports to the United States, had afforded a tantalizing glimpse of riches behind the American tariff wall; but before the convention became effective Great Britain, under pressure from Canada which objected that it would prejudice her own reciprocity negotiations with the United States,[80] insisted on postponement. Ever since then Britain's apparent partiality had been a sore subject in Newfoundland.

Ten years passed. Near the end of 1900 Sir Robert Bond, Premier of Newfoundland, revived the reciprocity question, asking for permission to ratify the Blaine-Bond convention, or if Washington considered it defunct to negotiate a new treaty.[81] Great Britain could not with propriety turn down her colony again. She had allowed Canada ample time for making arrangements with the republic; it was not Newfoundland's fault that Canada had failed.[82] Consequently the Colonial Secretary, Joseph Chamberlain, informed Lord Minto in early 1901 of Newfoundland's desire, adding hopefully that he supposed Canada would no longer object.[83]

The news created consternation in Ottawa. Laurier quickly replied that Canada most certainly would object, that any such

[78] P. T. McGrath, "The Anglo-French-American Shore," *North American Review*, vol. 174 (1902), pp. 113-123.

[79] F. O. 5, 2482, McCallum to Chamberlain, November 23, 1900; F. O. 115, 1239, Villiers to Raikes, June 4, 1902, enclosing minutes of the Newfoundland Executive Council, December 14, 1901.

[80] F. O. 5, 2482, note signed "A. L." (A. Law) on the back of a Colonial Office communication to the Foreign Office dated December 17, 1900; Strathcona to Chamberlain, March 1, 1901; Bond to Chamberlain, April 18, 1901.

[81] *Ibid.*, McCallum to Chamberlain, November 23, 1900; Bond to Chamberlain, April 18, 1901.

[82] *Ibid.*, Bond to Chamberlain, April 18, 1901.

[83] *Ibid.*, January 11, 1901.

treaty would in fact be "highly prejudicial" to her. Aware as he of course was of Pauncefote's current talks with Fairbanks, Foster, and Kasson, looking to recall of the Joint High Commission, he maintained that Newfoundland could gain more by making common cause with Canada when sittings resumed.[84] Already fearful lest Canadian bargaining power be curtailed as a result of the canal treaty then under negotiation, Laurier feared still further curtailment if the United States reached agreement with Newfoundland. ". . . I ask in what position would Canada be," he indignantly wrote Lord Minto, " to conduct successful negotiations, either with respect to fisheries alone, or a general arrangement . . . if the United States once understood that they could, by means of a separate agreement with Newfoundland, obtain, to a large measure, and without an equivalent to Canada, those privileges, which, in negotiations with the United States, have hitherto constituted our most valuable asset? " [85]

Such a prospect was grim enough, but another consideration probably alarmed the Prime Minister far more. The vision of confederation with Newfoundland lay close to his heart. He felt reluctant, however, to acquire an area where France enjoyed extraordinary treaty rights; for he could then anticipate entanglements with that country and hence with his own French-Canadian constituents.[86] But by the end of 1901, according to Minto, Laurier, "hitherto . . . strongly . . . averse to any negotiations [with Newfoundland] till after the settlement of the

[84] *Ibid.*, Minto to Chamberlain, January 12, 1901. See p. 226.

[85] *Ibid.*, February 16, 1901.

[86] On the French shore complication see *ibid.*, Minto to Chamberlain, January 16, 1901: " Prime Minister looks forward to Newfoundland joining Confederation at no distant date, present conditions in the island encouraging this view. He is, therefore, averse to separate negotiation between Newfoundland and United States of America, which assembly of Commission would at any rate render unnecessary; but he cannot suggest confederation to Newfoundland while French shore difficulty exists." See also *ibid.*, Laurier to Minto, February 16, 1901; Chamberlain to Minto, March 27, 1901; Minto to Chamberlain, September 4, 1901; Colonial Office to Foreign Office, October 10, 1901.

French Shore question," had become so eager for early confederation that he had " laid aside his apprehensions of friction with France, and consequently with French Canada. . . ." The Governor-General added: " I have no doubt that my Government will oppose any attempt at a separate Treaty negotiation between Newfoundland and the United States . . . and that the entrance of Newfoundland into Canadian confederation might tend to obviate future friction." [87]

Such were the meditations of Sir Wilfrid Laurier when to his horror he learned about Great Britain's change of mind and encouragement of her colony's reciprocity aspirations. At once he grasped the possible consequences. If Newfoundland should make a treaty with the United States, he predicted, " the idea of political union with Canada would become less and less an object to the people of Newfoundland, and . . . instead of being drawn towards the Canadian Confederation, they would be more and more drawn in another direction"—toward the great republic.[88] Did Sir Wilfrid Laurier look still further? Did he see that the consequences of reciprocity might not stop with precluding the confederation he so ardently desired? It would be strange if he did not perceive the possibility of Canada finding herself blocked on the east by an Americanized Newfoundland lying squarely athwart her sea lanes to Europe and, should the Alaska boundary dispute be decided adversely, hemmed in on the west by an American coastal strip. Manifest indeed, he may have feared, would then be the course of destiny: let Newfoundland once drift into the American orbit, and the Stars and Stripes would soon be floating over the Dominion herself. Perhaps he recalled that it was only fifty years after France lost Newfoundland in 1713 that she lost all her Canadian holdings as well, and that Blaine in 1890 had been influenced by the hope of acquiring Canada when he made his abortive treaty with Sir Robert Bond. Whether Sir Wilfrid's vision did extend that far or not, it is

[87] *Ibid.*, Minto to Chamberlain, September 4, 1901; Colonial Office to Foreign Office, October 10, 1901.

[88] *Ibid.*, memorandum of Laurier, February 16, 1901; Strathcona to Chamberlain, March 1, 1901.

easy to understand why he fought hard to stem the tide toward reciprocity in 1901 and 1902.

Unfortunately his proffered bait of a resumption of the Joint High Commission did not prove tempting. The spring of 1901 came, but no commission; instead, Sir Robert Bond arrived in Ottawa from London, strong in British approval, and pressed Sir Wilfrid most embarrassingly to withdraw his opposition. Thus cornered, the Prime Minister could do no more to calm his unwelcome visitor than allude hopefully to prospective new sittings " at an early date "; if they did not materialize, he promised, he would " then be prepared to have the whole subject reconsidered." [89] That was not much, but it sufficed to hold off serious pressure for nearly a year, until the spring of 1902.

By then, Joseph Chamberlain had become impatient. Believing that Newfoundland could " no longer be reasonably opposed," he took steps to bring the reciprocity question to a head.[90] But the colonial conference was imminent, and Canada made the reasonable request for further delay until Laurier could present her case in London.[91] Great Britain, although she did " not see any Imperial reasons sufficient to justify further delay . . . ," agreed to wait if Newfoundland would; and after further discussion Newfoundland gave her consent.[92]

Such was the situation confronting Sir Wilfrid when he arrived in London in June, 1902, for the colonial conference. Unless he could muster extraordinary powers of persuasion Newfoundland would be permitted to go ahead and negotiate; if successful in concluding a treaty she would, he gravely feared, drift further from the Dominion toward the United States. Laurier's unexpected concessions at the conference have been mentioned. In the absence of documentary evidence one can only conjecture as to why he made them. But it is impossible not to believe that

[89] F. O. 115, 1239, Lansdowne to Bond, May 21, 1901; F. O. 5, 2482, Chamberlain to Minto, April 26, 1901.

[90] F. O. 115, 1239, Colonial Office to Foreign Office, April 12, 1902; the Foreign Office approved on April 17.

[91] *Ibid.*, Minto to Chamberlain, May 6, 1902, enclosed in Villiers to Raikes, June 4, 1902.

[92] *Ibid.*, Chamberlain to Minto, May 9, 1902; Villiers to Raikes, June 4, 1902.

he was influenced by a hope of staving off the dreaded rapprochement between Newfoundland and the United States. Hitherto
he had been holding out the prospect of the Joint High Commission reconvening. But that prospect had worn dreadfully
thin. Over a year before, Joseph Chamberlain had told Lord
Minto bluntly that in the absence of " any scheme for adjusting
the Alaska boundary question . . . it would appear to be useless
to reassemble the Commission." [93] His statement went to the
root of Laurier's dilemma. The Joint High Commission had
come to grief once precisely because no such scheme acceptable
to Canada could be devised. Eager to fend off the catastrophe
of United States-Newfoundland reciprocity, Laurier must have
realized the futility of trying to beguile people any longer with a
defunct Joint High Commission unless he changed position radi-
cally on Alaska matters. Realizing, too, Great Britain's anxiety
for a boundary settlement, he could hope to swing her from Newfoundland by a striking demonstration of Canadian cooperation
in reaching one. And so it was, we may well suspect, that Sir
Wilfrid convinced himself that he had no recourse but to renounce the Dominion's claim to Dyea and Skagway—which he
knew she could never get anyhow—and accept an even-numbered
tribunal. Only through creating a distinct prospect of accord
in Alaska could he prepare the way for the commission's revival;
and even if it should prove too late to prevent Newfoundland
from entering into negotiations with the United States, he could
still expect Great Britain to be reluctant to approve an actual
treaty while the possibility existed of attaining through the commission a comprehensive settlement not only for Newfoundland
but for Canada as well.[94]

[93] F. O. 5, 2482, Chamberlain to Minto, January 18, 1901.
[94] I have found no direct confirmation of this conjecture in the Laurier
papers, but there is evidence of the Premier's continuing apprehension about
an agreement between the United States and Newfoundland, which he feared
would prevent union between Canada and Newfoundland. See William Smith,
writing for Sir Robert Bond, to Laurier, June 9, 1902 (Laurier papers, Series
A; C-794) ; C. Edwin Kaulbacke, M. P. from Nova Scotia, to Laurier, September 11, 1902 (*ibid.*, Series A; C-795) ; and especially a letter from W. S.
Fielding, Canadian Minister of Finance, written by express authority of

As matters worked out, it did prove too late to stop reciprocity negotiations. Reconvening the Joint High Commission would take time, even assuming it could be managed at all; and Britain doubtless felt unwilling to ask Newfoundland to wait again. Besides, she may have considered that in any case reciprocity negotiations could be transferred to the commission should it be revived. Accordingly Great Britain gave Newfoundland the permission she so keenly desired. The ensuing negotiations need some attention on their own account, and also because of their probable connection with the boundary accord the next year.

Sir Robert Bond appeared in Washington in August, 1902, and with the support of the British embassy opened discussions with the State Department.[95] In the absence of John Hay on his summer vacation negotiations proceeded slowly, but by the middle of October a convention similar to the Blaine-Bond convention was ready for signature.[96] About that time Bond, doubtless aware that Henry Cabot Lodge's son-in-law, Robert Gardner, was running for the House of Representatives in the mid-term elections the next month in the congressional district where the fishing town of Gloucester, Massachusetts, was located, sent the Senator a copy of the draft treaty, together with a long analysis defending it. Lodge forwarded the draft to W. H. Jordan, collector of the port of Gloucester; and on receiving an adverse report some days later, told John Hay that he could not accept the treaty for fear of throwing the district to the Democrats;

Laurier, to Bond, September 15, 1902 (*ibid.*) : " May I venture to suggest that you hold yourself free in your negotiations [in Washington] respecting commercial and fishery interests, and that at an early day, at some point on the other [North American] side of the water which may be mutually convenient, a meeting (either formal or informal) of representatives of Newfoundland and Canada be held for the purpose of making a further effort to agree upon terms of union, which you would feel able to recommend to your people."

[95] F. O. 5, 2484, Lansdowne to Raikes, August 18, 1902. For an account of some of the considerations before the negotiators see P. T. McGrath, " The Atlantic Fisheries Question," *The Atlantic Monthly*, vol. 90 (1902), pp. 741-748.

[96] F. O. 5, 2489, Herbert to Lansdowne, October 12, 1902; F. O. 5, 2487, Raikes to Villiers, September 15, 1902.

he asked the Secretary to reshape the treaty to fit Gloucester's desires and not to sign it until after the elections.[97] Hay did postpone signature but he did not consult the fishermen; to have complied with their demands would obviously have rendered the treaty meaningless to Newfoundland. However, according to Sir Michael Herbert, who had recently arrived in Washington to assume his duties as ambassador, Lodge indicated to Hay that if the treaty were amended so as to remove the Newfoundland duty on American boots and shoes, he would support it after all in the belief that the accruing benefit to the leather industry of Lynn (in the same congressional district as Gloucester) would offset any injury to the fishermen.[98] Unable at first to persuade Sir Robert to accept such an amendment, Secretary Hay nevertheless signed the treaty on November 8, 1902.[99] It was submitted to the Senate for ratification when the new Congress met in December after the election.[100]

The Hay-Bond treaty was well received by much of the American press. "A reciprocity treaty with Newfoundland, once in operation," predicted the Minneapolis *Tribune*, echoing Sir Wilfrid Laurier's line of thought, "will draw England's oldest colony and the United States very close together. The step to practical free trade between them will not be long or difficult. Newfoundland's interests will be ours, and she will stay out of the Dominion." [101] Nonetheless a storm of criticism broke forth among fishing interests of Massachusetts and Maine. Despite the fact that his son-in-law had been safely elected, despite the further

[97] Lodge's telegram to Hay, October 16, 1902, is in Hay papers; F. O. 5, 2489, Herbert to Lansdowne, October 19, 1902.

[98] F. O. 115, 1244, Herbert to Lansdowne, November 7, 1902.

[99] F. O. 5, 2489, Herbert to Lansdowne, October 25, 1902; F. O. 115, 1267, Herbert to Hay, November 5, 1902. For the text of the treaty and for Roosevelt's message transmitting it to the Senate see 57th Congress, 2nd session, Senate document 49.

[100] Probably because of Lodge's attitude Roosevelt hesitated to submit the treaty to the Senate; he agreed only when Hay threatened to resign; see J. A. Garraty, *Henry Cabot Lodge, a Biography* (New York, 1953), pp. 236-238.

[101] For this and other citations on the subject see *Public Opinion*, vol. 33 December 18, 1902), p. 774.

fact that Newfoundland, alarmed by the tide of opposition, now agreed to include boots and shoes on the free list,[102] Lodge set himself adamantly against ratification.[103] At hearings before the Senate Committee on Foreign Relations he gave prominence to hostile resolutions adopted by the Central Labor Union of Gloucester and by the Gloucester Master Mariners' Association,[104] and to criticism advanced by delegations from Massachusetts and Maine.

Within a week or so Secretary Hay saw the game was up; ratification could not be obtained in the near future, if ever. " I regret to say," Herbert telegraphed the Foreign Office on December 18,

> that Secretary of State informed me this morning that Treaty has now no chance of passing the Senate owing to the strong opposition of the four New England senators. I asked him whether any further concession on the part of Newfoundland would mend matters and he replied in the negative. Deputation from Maine and Massachusetts was very hostile yesterday and informed Senate that owing to cold storage facilities bait privileges were no longer so valuable to American fishermen. Fear it is no use Premier coming here.[105]

Thus largely to conciliate one small town and one son-in-law, national interests of tremendous possible consequence were sacrificed. Such was Henry Cabot Lodge's influence that he prevented the treaty from even reaching the floor of the Senate until 1905, when it was amended beyond possibility of acceptance

[102] F. O. 115, 1244, Herbert to Lansdowne, December 5, 1902.

[103] Reporting the arrival at the capital of Lodge and Gardner, the Washington *Evening Star*, November 20, 1902, predicted that the senator would oppose the treaty because it was inimical to the interests of Gloucester fishermen, " who form so considerable a portion of the constituency of Representative Gardner."

[104] 57th Congress, 2nd session, Senate document 50. See also *ibid.*, Senate document 14, for twenty-seven pages of papers and statistics regarding Gloucester and New England fisheries presented by Lodge; *ibid.*, Senate document 78, for other papers presented by him; and *ibid.*, Senate document 94, for the protest of a New York fisheries company against ratification.

[105] F. O. 5, 2489.

by Newfoundland. John Hay never forgave him for what he believed to be an unscrupulous betrayal.[106]

Nevertheless, Sir Wilfrid Laurier's concessions in London remained accomplished facts. And of course the treaty itself, for all its shelving, was not yet dead in 1902 and 1903; it was still before the Foreign Relations Committee and the Committee had the power, however unlikely its use, to present it to the Senate for ratification. Conceivably it might do so should Ottawa become too recalcitrant about a boundary settlement. It may be, though there is no documentary proof, that that unpleasant possibility hanging over his head helped keep Sir Wilfrid in line when Alaska developments shortly took a most unwelcome turn.

One can be more certain about the adverse effect of another matter upon the Dominion's fortunes: the sudden and unexpected emergence of a new international crisis in the Caribbean Sea. The crisis this time concerned not Cuba but the Republic of Venezuela.

---

[106] For Hay's reaction see Dennett, *Hay*, ch. 35; Garraty, *Lodge*, pp. 236-238.

CHAPTER 13

Venezuelan Interlude

THE LATEST in a long series of military adventurers, Cipriano Castro, seized control of Venezuela in 1899. His position was weak, and for several years disorders continued to plague the country as various other chieftains sought to oust their rival from his lucrative post. Vain, arrogant, and grasping, Castro in his fierce struggle to keep himself in power showed little regard for others. Foreign residents suffered from the incessant fighting; foreign debts were not paid. Because of the proximity of the British island, Trinidad, British persons and property more than those of any other great power suffered from the unscrupulous Venezuelan's high-handed proceedings. Castro's numerous enemies used the island as a convenient base. Searching out his foes and incensed by what he denounced as criminal laxity on the part of the British authorities, Castro did not hesitate to transgress upon British rights in Trinidad as well as in his own country.[1] Next to Britain, Germany probably had greatest cause for complaint, though her grievances were mainly of a financial nature. Several other countries in Europe, and the United States[2] and Mexico in the New World, likewise suffered from the dictator's exactions.

All attempts to persuade Castro into more righteous ways having failed, Germany and Great Britain began to consider

[1] A. Maurice Low, " Venezuela and the Powers," *Review of Reviews*, vol. 27 (1903), pp. 39-43.

[2] For American claims see 60th Congress, 1st session, Senate document 413.

using force. Squarely in their way stood the great dogma of American foreign policy, the Monroe Doctrine. Utmost caution would be advisable, in view of the rise in American sea power since the war with Spain, if force was to be applied within the scope of that sacrosanct doctrine. Great Britain had already experienced United States sensitiveness in regard to that very South American country. Memories of President Cleveland's intemperate censure at the time of the Venezuelan boundary dispute in 1895 still lingered unpleasantly in London; and however agreeable to squelch the obnoxious Venezuelan, that could not be done at the expense of Anglo-American understanding. Nor would Germany wish to jeopardize her recent efforts to cultivate American good will by a violent incursion into the delicate Caribbean area; she, too, would have to observe the limits imposed by Monroe.

The accession to the presidency of Theodore Roosevelt in September, 1901, threatened to complicate still further the problem of coercing Castro. For would not this intense, impetuous young man, who had rejoiced at Cleveland's stand in 1895 and who had denounced the Pauncefote canal treaty as not coming up to his standards for the Monroe Doctrine, view European intervention in the New World much less tolerantly than the lamented McKinley? Perhaps he would have, except for one aspect of his complex nature not yet as evident as it would soon become. This was his contempt for Latin American countries, a contempt giving rise to the conviction that they could be kept in line only through close supervision. When still Vice President he had told his German friend, Speck von Sternburg, "If any South American country misbehaves toward any European country, let the European country spank it." [3] And now in his first annual message to Congress, on December 3, 1901, he made a most welcome statement to the two European countries anxious to do some spanking: "We do not guarantee," he assured the world, "any state [within the scope of the Monroe Doctrine] against punishment if it misconducts itself, provided that punish-

[3] H. F. Pringle, *Theodore Roosevelt, a Biography* (New York, 1931), p. 283; Roosevelt so stated July 12, 1901.

ment does not take the form of the acquisition of territory by any non-American power." With these comforting words before them, Great Britain and Germany could begin to think very seriously about chastising the arrogant Castro.

Which country first sounded out the other as to joint intervention is not clear. According to Baron von Eckardstein, the German chargé d'affaires at London, Francis Villiers, Assistant Under-Secretary of State at the British Foreign Office, told him on January 2, 1902, that the Cabinet was going to discuss Venezuela and that when circumstances in that country became clearer it might approach Germany about common action.[4] But this statement, as the Kaiser noted, was " Too vague! ";[5] and in the absence of corroboratory material in the British archives it does not seem justifiable to interpret it as evidence of a considered British overture.[6] If the Cabinet did discuss Venezuela it apparently decided that circumstances were not clear enough; for it took no step to concert plans with Germany until six months later, and then only after German initiative.

As a matter of fact we do know that, whatever may have been the case with the British, the Germans were giving careful thought to a display of force. Just eight days after the President's encouraging message to Congress the German ambassador at Washington, Holleben, left a memorandum with John Hay asserting that negotiations with Venezuela were " hopeless " and that " measures of coercion " might be required. In interviews with Hay and Roosevelt the next day Holleben emphasized his country's determination to respect the Monroe Doctrine.[7] Doubtless appreciating this courteous advance notice about a matter

[4] A. Vagts, *Deutschland und die Vereinigten Staaten in der Weltpolitik* (2 vols., New York, 1935) , vol. 2, pp. 1542-1543; a short digest of Eckardstein's telegram to the German foreign office is given in *Die Grosse Politik der Europäischen Kabinette, 1871-1914* (40 vols., Berlin, 1924-1927) , vol. 17, p. 242.

[5] *Grosse Politik*, vol. 17, p. 243, note 1.

[6] H. C. Hill, *Roosevelt and the Caribbean* (Chicago, 1927) , Vagts, *Deutschland*, and D. Perkins, *The Monroe Doctrine, 1867-1907* (Baltimore, 1937) , cite Eckardstein's statement to show that Great Britain approached Germany.

[7] 57th Congress, 1st session, House executive document 1, vol. 1, pp. 192-194.

which in strict law did not concern the United States, neither the Secretary of State nor the President raised any objection.[8]

The administration's calmness notwithstanding, a few American and British newspapers, apparently getting wind of Holleben's message, saw fit, quite inexcusably, to conjure up visions of a German plot against the Monroe Doctrine.[9] Had London and Berlin paid due heed to this foolish agitation, as indicating the ease with which excitement could mount, they might have spared themselves much embarrassment a year later.

Perhaps intervention in Venezuela would have occurred at the beginning instead of at the end of 1902 except for the Kaiser. When Bülow, the German Chancellor, having prepared the ground in Washington, asked his imperial master for permission to approach London, the Kaiser, vexed by the developing quarrel over intervention in 1898 just before the Spanish War, vetoed another intervention until after Prince Henry's visit to the United States.[10] Consequently not until July 23, 1902, the prince's mission successfully accomplished, did Count Metternich, the new German ambassador at London, discuss with Lord Lansdowne possible measures against Venezuela.[11] Lansdowne was quite ready to confer, and over the next four or five months the two men looked into methods of joint action. By November they were pretty well in accord. On the 8th of that month the Kaiser landed in Great Britain for a twelve-day visit. He was greeted with a storm of abuse.[12] The hostile attitude of the

---

[8] *Ibid.*, p. 195.

[9] *Public Opinion*, vol. 32 (January 9, 1902), p. 36. See S. W. Livermore, "The Venezuelan Crisis of 1902-1903," *American Historical Review*, vol. 51 (1946), p. 458, for a letter from Rear Admiral Taylor to Admiral Dewey showing that some naval officers were contemplating war with Germany.

[10] *Grosse Politik*, vol. 17, p. 243, marginal note dated January 21, 1902.

[11] G. P. Gooch and H. Temperley, eds., *British Documents on the Origins of the War, 1898-1914* (11 vols., London, 1926-1938), vol. 2, pp. 153-154, Lansdowne to Buchanan, July 23, 1902.

[12] "The Emperor's official reception had been brilliant; the attitude of the public extremely hostile. . . . Even before he landed a chorus of protest had been raised in the Press." Such was the uproar that Balfour thought it necessary to protest the "fantastic inventions" in a speech at the Guild-

public and press should have convinced the British government of the perils of association with a country whose people had been so bitterly critical during the Boer War. But Lansdowne went ahead with his plans. He assured Metternich that it seemed "only reasonable that if we agreed to act together in applying coercion, we should also agree that each should support the other's demands, and should not desist from doing so except by agreement." [13] This informal understanding was the famous "ironclad bargain," as the British press came disgustedly to call it, that bound Britain to Germany.

Only then, on November 13, 1902, did Sir Michael Herbert, Pauncefote's successor at Washington, advise Secretary Hay of his country's plans, a step that Germany had taken nearly a year earlier.[14] In view of Britain's assiduous cultivation of American good will, in view of her recent altercation with Germany over respective roles in April, 1898, in view too of her rough handling by the United States during the Venezuelan boundary dispute seven years earlier, it seems extraordinary that she concluded the "ironclad bargain" with so little apparent concern for American susceptibilities.[15] How is this behavior to be explained? Does

hall; see É. Halévy, *A History of the English People in the Nineteenth Century* (6 vols., New York, 1949-1952), vol. 5, pp. 132-133.

[13] British Blue Book, *Venezuela. No. 1 (1903). Correspondence Respecting the Affairs of Venezuela.* Cd. 1399. P. 146; this assurance was given November 11, 1902. For his part Metternich responded on November 21 that Germany was "willing to intervene jointly in support of the collective German and English claims, without discriminating between the various classes of claims, it being understood that joint action will be maintained unless terminated by mutual agreement" (*ibid.*, p. 155).

[14] *Venezuela. No. 1 (1903)*, p. 145, Lansdowne to Herbert, November 11, 1902; and p. 147, Herbert to Lansdowne, November 13, 1902. Herbert spoke to Hay on November 13.

[15] One would expect Great Britain to have been particularly careful about a Caribbean venture just then, because she had only recently finished defending herself against a charge relating to another alleged activity on her part in the Caribbean. The United States minister to Cuba had complained to Washington that his British colleague was trying to dissuade Cuba from ratifying a reciprocity treaty with the United States. Choate and Hay seem to have fully accepted a sweeping British denial. See State Department, Great Britain, Despatches, Choate to Hay, October 28, 1902; F. O. 5,

it suggest that Britain attached less importance to American friendship than has been suggested in the above pages; that although willing enough to curry American favor if entirely convenient to herself, she would not scruple to push that country aside whenever even slight interests of her own were at stake, or whenever negotiations with a great European power were afoot?

It is conceivable that the British leaders, forced to cope with a rapid sequence of distracting occurrences during that summer— Pauncefote's death, the end of the Boer War, Salisbury's retirement, the King's sudden illness, the postponed coronation—overlooked the significance of Lansdowne's talks with Metternich. Arthur Balfour replaced his uncle as Prime Minister in July, the very month Germany suggested joint intervention. By the time the new government got around to reviewing Venezuelan affairs, it may have found that plans had progressed to a point from which it felt unable to withdraw. Such an explanation must be regarded with great caution, however. Balfour, a firm believer in the American connection—" through all my political life my most fondly cherished hope," he wrote in early 1903 [16]— was not the man to be forgetful of the powerful republic. And Joseph Chamberlain, another staunch champion of the United States, still had tremendous authority in the government.[17]

More probably Britain's apparent carelessness about America was attributable to errors of judgment. One cannot help but think that had Pauncefote still been at his post British policy would have evolved differently. Deprived of mature counsel from America during the interregnum after the great ambassador's death, just when intervention was being planned, the government seems simply to have underestimated the dangers.

2484, Lansdowne to Herbert, October 17 and 30, and November 19, 1902; Hay papers, Choate to Hay, October 27, November 19, 1902.

[16] B. J. Hendrick, *The Life of Andrew Carnegie* (2 vols., New York, 1932), vol. 2, p. 183, to Carnegie, January 30, 1903.

[17] Chamberlain left England to visit South Africa on November 26, 1902; he did not return until March 14, 1903; thus he was absent throughout the intervention. But he must have known about the plans, which had been substantially completed before he left.

Mindful of Roosevelt's reassuring message to Congress and expecting Castro to collapse quickly before a naval demonstration, it did not anticipate friction with Washington. ". . . if the occupation were prolonged, troublesome international questions might arise between the Powers concerned and the United States Government," Lansdowne predicted, with the obvious implication that a brief occupation would lead to no trouble.[18] However, he did propose to Metternich that the United States be invited to participate; but refrained from pressing the point when the ambassador showed no interest.[19] The timing of the intervention, too—it began shortly after the mid-term congressional election— suggests that the British were trying to be careful about America; certainly they did not wish to create any pre-election embarrassment for a friendly administration.

Consideration must also be given to another matter. However highly Great Britain regarded the American tie, she could not overlook all others; clearly she could not overlook relations with the formidable power across the North Sea. When Lord Lansdowne became Foreign Minister in 1901 he wrote that although he had few preconceptions he did have one: that Britain should bend "every effort" to improve relations with Germany.[20] Anglo-German negotiations looking to an alliance do not fall within the scope of this work. By 1902 they had nearly failed, in part owing to the reluctance of Lord Salisbury to foresake splendid isolation.[21] But in July the old Prime Minister retired,

[18] Gooch and Temperley, *British Documents*, vol. 2, p. 160, memorandum dated December 2, 1902; Perkins, *Monroe Doctrine*, p. 332. Villiers said to Eckardstein about January 2, 1902: "We are perfectly satisfied here that the *present* Government of the United States will not interfere with any European Power which may think it opportune to take energetic measures for pressing for the fulfilment of private claims against any of the South American Republics as long as no permanent seizure of a sea-port or territory is intended" (Vagts, *Deutschland*, vol. 2, p. 1543).

[19] Perkins, *Monroe Doctrine*, p. 332.

[20] Lord Newton, *Lord Lansdowne, a Biography* (London, 1929), pp. 196-197.

[21] For his famous memorandum of May 29, 1901, arguing against an alliance see Gooch and Temperley, *British Documents*, vol. 2, pp. 68-69. Lansdowne recognized that the American tie presented an obstacle to closer

and in July Count Metternich suggested partnership against the obnoxious Castro. May it not be that Lord Lansdowne, envisaging joint action as an opening wedge to friendship with Germany, judged that the gains from such action would outweigh the slight risks? [22] If so, he displayed a serious lack of imagination, for the intervention aroused such an outcry against Germany as virtually to end hopes of an alliance.

Like the President's message, Hay's response to Sir Michael's warning of November 13 was reassuring. Although the United States would regret the use of force, he said, it did not object to steps to obtain redress provided no territory was taken. [23] Herbert, although at his new post only a few weeks, had already become uneasy; he made a penetrating observation: " I wish we were going to punish Venezuela without the aid of Germany, for I am not sure that joint action will be very palatable here." [24] He saw that people in America, as in Britain, viewed the Kaiser's rising empire with considerable distaste.

Once Great Britain and Germany had concerted plans, events developed rapidly. On December 7, 1902, they delivered ultimatums to Venezuela, and the next day broke off diplomatic relations. On the 9th they captured four Venezuelan gunboats, two of which were destroyed by the Germans. [25] On the 10th British troops landed for a short while at La Guayra. On the

understanding with Germany; in a memorandum of November 11, 1901, he listed five difficulties to such an understanding; the fourth was: " The risk of entangling ourselves in a policy which might be hostile to America. With our knowledge of the German Emperor's views in regard to the United States, this is to my mind a formidable obstacle " (*ibid.*, p. 78) .

[22] For the cordial relations between the British and German governments in July, 1902, in contrast to the tension between the two peoples see Halévy, *History of the English People*, vol. 5, p. 131.

[23] *Venezuela. No. 1 (1903)* , p. 147, Herbert to Lansdowne, November 13, 1902.

[24] Newton, *Lansdowne*, p. 256, to Lansdowne, November, 1902.

[25] Most writers state that Germany sank three boats. According to a memorandum of the German embassy at Washington, dated December 18, 1902, Germany captured three boats, of which one was manned by Germans and sailed to Trinidad and two, proving unseaworthy, were destroyed; see *Foreign Relations of the United States, 1903*, pp. 422-423.

11th they imposed a " pacific " blockade of the principal Venezuelan ports, and two days later bombarded the forts at Puerto
Cabello. Meanwhile Italy, which also had claims against Venezuela, had joined the two allies; the part she played, however,
was of little consequence and may be ignored in this account.
On December 20 the three countries proclaimed a formal blockade, to become effective the 25th. It was not lifted until February
14, 1903.

That these exciting developments in an area of great strategic
consequence attracted American notice, it goes without saying.
Although not on the whole particularly agitated at first, press
comment tended to criticize the intervention as unnecessarily
harsh: the act of bullies picking on a defenseless victim. Inevitably some concern for the Monroe Doctrine was voiced, and
destruction of the gunboats aroused real anger. Editorials
denounced this unwise deed as " an act of hostility without giving
due notice of war . . ." and " comparable to acts of wanton
devastation in warfare, which have long been discountenanced
by civilized nations "; about the mildest comment was that it
should be noted " with surprise and with regret." [26]

As for the administration, it gave no sign of perturbation.
Although we can be sure that neither Theodore Roosevelt nor
John Hay welcomed the appearance of German warships so close
to the future canal, both doubtless relished the spectacle of
retribution catching up with the unsavory Castro. And Hay at
least must have felt reassured by the presence of British ships,
and Roosevelt by the knowledge that in October his Caribbean
squadron had been supplemented by three additional squadrons,
all under the command of the redoubtable Admiral Dewey.

Having in effect given advance consent, the United States
made no protest. Its only sign of disapproval was a *pro-forma*
warning that it did not admit the legality of a so-called pacific
blockade; if a blockade had to be imposed let it be a war one.[27]

[26] *Public Opinion*, vol. 33 (December 18, 1902), p. 778. The quotations
are from, respectively, the New York *Evening Post*, the *New York Times*,
and the *New York Tribune*.

[27] *Foreign Relations, 1903*, p. 452, Hay to White, December 12, 1902; and

The United States readily consented to assume charge of British interests in Venezuela, as it had just done in South Africa and as Britain had done for American interests during the Spanish War.[28] Accordingly when Castro, infuriated at being brought to bay, threw into prison all Britons and Germans he could seize, the American minister at Caracas, Herbert W. Bowen, went straight to the dictator himself and succeeded in obtaining their release; moreover he offered asylum in the American legation, and got police protection for the British and German legations.[29]

Venezuela soon realized that her adversaries were in dead earnest. Knowing full well that she, no more than the Boers, could expect sympathy from a State Department headed by John Hay, she deliberately made her appeal to the American people, a much more promising source of comfort, and consistently tried to associate the United States with her own cause.[30] The impossibility of armed resistance being evident, she appealed through Washington for arbitration. But Hay contented himself with forwarding the appeal to London without comment, a routine act not calculated to awaken apprehension in Whitehall.[31]

One person in London, however, perceived the latent perils. In charge of the American embassy in the absence of Ambassador Choate on leave, Henry White was an invaluable man to have on the spot. Long resident in Britain, he had a wide circle of influential friends whose confidence and affection he had earned; through informal dealings with them he had often demonstrated his ability to supplement most happily the formal diplomacy of the State Department. With Hay, Pauncefote, Choate, and Herbert, he was one of that remarkable group of diplomats to whom part of the credit for the Anglo-American settlement must

pp. 454-455, White to Lansdowne, December 13, 1902. J. W. Foster, *Diplomatic Memoirs* (2 vols., Boston and New York, 1909), vol. 2, p. 293, takes credit for the American stand against a pacific blockade.

[28] *Venezuela. No. 1 (1903)*, p. 154, Lansdowne to Herbert, November 25, 1902.

[29] F. O. 80, 447, Herbert to Lansdowne, December 10, 1902; F. O. 80, 448, Herbert to Lansdowne, December 11, 1902.

[30] F. O. 80, 447, Herbert to Lansdowne, December 5, 1902.

[31] F. O. 80, 448, White to Lansdowne, December 13, 1902.

be attributed. During the Venezuelan crisis White again displayed his talent for personal diplomacy. Remaining in the capital throughout the emergency, he took it upon himself to warn repeatedly his good friend Arthur Balfour, Lord Lansdowne, and several of his other prominent acquaintances of his " grave fears . . . lest Great Britain . . . antagonize American public feeling." [32] He called often upon the Prime Minister, and nearly every day and sometimes several times a day upon the Foreign Minister.[33] The bombardment at Puerto Cabello on the 13th, the same day he delivered Castro's request for arbitration to the Foreign Office, was just the sort of incident he dreaded. Unfortunately that important day found Lord Lansdowne at his country seat, Bowood, and other members of the government likewise away from London; not until the 16th could the Cabinet be convened.[34] As soon as the Foreign Minister returned on the 15th, White hastened to see him. It was probably at this interview that Lansdowne told him in strict confidence the welcome news that Great Britain would not land troops in Venezuela.[35]

Before the Cabinet could meet, a debate was held in Parliament; and the anxiety with which many members viewed relations with the United States against the dark Venezuelan background, speedily manifested itself. Speaking for the government, Lord Cranborne was quick to remind them, and perhaps the President too, of Roosevelt's now all-important assurance the previous December: " As the House is aware, in a celebrated passage in his Message to Congress, the President announced that

[32] State Department, Great Britain, Despatches, White to Hay, Decmber 15, 1902.

[33] *Ibid.*, White to Hay, February 14, 1903. Another American who foresaw the dangers was Andrew Carnegie; he sent a strong message to his friend, John Morley, who forwarded it to the Prime Minister (Hendrick, *Carnegie*, vol. 2, p. 179). In this connection it is instructive to note that White found Britain's cooperation with Germany particularly unpopular in commercial circles and in the City of London (State Department, Great Britain, Despatches, White to Hay, December 17, 1902).

[34] State Department, Great Britain, Despatches, White to Hay, December 13 and 15, 1902.

[35] *Ibid.*, White to Hay, December 15, 1902.

in insisting on a South American Republic meeting its international obligations no European Power was infringing the Monroe doctrine." Cranborne doubtless had in mind auditors on the far side of the Atlantic as well as at home when he cast Great Britain in the role of traditional champion of that doctrine.[36] But all the noble lord's eloquence did not soothe the members. Lord Charles Beresford, whose exertions in behalf of the open door in China have been noted, warned against anything " of any kind, sort, or description that would be in the least way provocative of irritation or animosity on the part of the United States "; Henry Norman, the unwitting instigator of the altercation with Germany over Pauncefote's role in April, 1898, showed insight into American ways when he warned that however well disposed the United States government might be, it was " peculiarly susceptible to public opinion, and public opinion may from one week to another take a much keener interest in this matter, which may make the position more serious for this country "; and Arthur Lee, a friend of Roosevelt's, made another valid point in reporting the harm done Britain's cause in America by her fraternization with the distrusted Germans.[37] White, who had followed the debate closely, noted an " earnest desire " that the country do nothing which Americans might interpret as violating the Monroe Doctrine.[38]

Thus when the Cabinet met on December 16 it had disconcerting evidence of uneasiness in Parliament. It had also disconcerting news from across the Atlantic. The day before, White had visited the Prime Minister in his private room at the House of Commons; there he had " unburdened very frankly " his concern over mounting American resentment. The chargé believed he had made a deep impression upon his friend.[39] The

[36] *Parliamentary Debates*, vol. 116, p. 1263; the debate was held on December 15. In the House of Lords Lansdowne was careful to thank the United States for Bowen's help at Caracas (*ibid.*, p. 1108).

[37] *Ibid.*, pp. 1278, 1279, 1286.

[38] State Department, Great Britain, Despatches, to Hay, December 17, 1902.

[39] White papers, White to Hay, December 17, 1902. A. Nevins, in *Henry White, Thirty Years of American Diplomacy* (New York and London, 1930),

extent of the Cabinet's misgiving is evident from the decisions it at once took. First, at the instigation of the Prime Minister himself,[40] it decided to announce publicly that very day that British troops would not land in Venezuela.[41] Assurance against a landing could be expected to stiffen Castro's resistance; and Britain's willingness to take this chance was a measure of her eagerness to conciliate America. Second, the Cabinet agreed to accept in principle Venezuela's offer of arbitration as forwarded by the State Department; this decision, however, it kept secret pending German compliance. Third, it decided to impose a general blockade; but, again in deference to American wishes, and opposed to those of Germany, it decided against a " pacific " blockade in favor of one admittedly involving a state of war.[42]

Welcome as was Britain's promise of no land fighting it did not remove the anger beginning to rise in the United States at the spectacle of European navies attacking a weak New World republic, and over the fact that European warships were barring American ships no less than those of other countries. On December 16 Sir Michael Herbert reported a " growing feeling of irritation in Congress " and a conviction that Great Britain was being used by her ally; [43] three days later this irritation had

p. 210, refers to this interview but dates it incorrectly as on or before December 13.

[40] State Department, Great Britain, Despatches, White to Hay, December 16, 1902 (second telegram of that date).

[41] *Parliamentary Debates*, vol. 116, pp. 1290, 1489. Britain's decision may have been hastened by a report that the chairman of the powerful Senate Committee on Foreign Relations, Shelby Cullom, had said that the United States should take prompt action if troops marched inland (*New York Times*, December 15, 1902, cited by Perkins, *Monroe Doctrine*, p. 342).

[42] *Foreign Relations, 1903*, pp. 454-455, White to Lansdowne, December 13, 1902; F. O. 5, 2489, Herbert to Lansdowne, December 16, 1902; *Parliamentary Debates*, vol. 116, p. 1490. According to Perkins, *Monroe Doctrine*, p. 330, Great Britain and Germany had already reached an understanding on December 6 that the blockade should be a war one. It would appear, however, from the accounts of United States Ambassador Tower at Berlin and Henry White at London that Germany agreed to a " pacific " blockade on December 14 or 15; see *Foreign Relations, 1903*, p. 421, Tower to Hay, December 17, 1902, and p. 454, White to Hay, December 17, 1902.

[43] Gooch and Temperley, *British Documents*, vol. 2, p. 162, to Lansdowne,

become an "explosion of feeling" against Germany.[44] Annoyance with Britain, though not as intense, was increasing too. Restless and suspicious, the House of Representatives adopted a resolution asking the Secretary of State for all the Venezuelan correspondence; [45] and John Hay told Herbert and von Quadt, the German chargé d'affaires, that he feared other, more bellicose resolutions.[46] Clearly the intervening powers would have to proceed with utmost caution, if congressional and public sentiment in America was not to become so agitated as to force the administration's hand.

Accordingly Hay, having received no reply to Castro's request for arbitration which he had forwarded to London, and not knowing that the British had already decided upon arbitration in principle, abandoned his hitherto passive stand; he telegraphed White on December 16 to make urgent representations regarding the "great desirability" of arbitration. This White did at an interview with Lord Lansdowne on the 17th.[47] Since German consent to arbitrate had by then been given to London—it reached the Foreign Office shortly before White called with Hay's communication [48]—the Cabinet quickly agreed to arbitrate (except for certain reserved claims), and also to request Theodore Roosevelt to be the arbitrator.[49] Obviously intent to remain on good terms with Washington, Lansdowne asked White to

December 16, 1902; the telegram did not arrive until the 17th, too late to influence the important decisions taken by the Cabinet on the 16th.

[44] Newton, *Lansdowne*, p. 256, Herbert to Lansdowne, December 19, 1902.

[45] *Congressional Record*, vol. 36 (December 18, 1902), pp. 423-424.

[46] *Grosse Politik*, vol. 17, p. 269, von Quadt to German foreign office, December 18, 1902; see also Livermore, "The Venezuelan Crisis," p. 464.

[47] *Foreign Relations, 1903*, pp. 453-454; White must have couched his urgent representations in strong language, for he wrote Hay that Lansdowne would appreciate the communication's suppression when the correspondence was published (State Department, Great Britain, Despatches, White to Hay, December 18, 1902).

[48] State Department, Great Britain, Despatches, White to Hay, December 18, 1902.

[49] *Foreign Relations, 1903*, p. 455, White to Hay, December 18, 1902 (second telegram of that date); *Venezuela. No. 1 (1903)*, p. 177, Lansdowne to Herbert, December 18, 1902.

make a special point of informing Hay and Roosevelt that Britain's decision had been arrived at independently of American pressure and " that His Majesty's Government are the better pleased to find that they had of their own accord adopted a course which would find favor with the Government of the United States." [50] Roosevelt's nomination met with approval in Britain, and in America also; and for several days enthusiastic editorials appeared on the subject in many British newspapers.[51]

It would be folly to picture London as acting only out of consideration for the United States. It had plenty of evidence that people in Britain, too, abhorred the Venezuelan adventure, that they felt a revulsion from an enterprise that involved partnership with Germans and that alienated Americans. " People here *loathe* the German alliance, and what's more, they have had their bellyful of all military operations for a good long while "; so John Morley, the well known Liberal, told Andrew Carnegie.[52] The sinking of Venezuelan gunboats evoked as much

[50] State Department, Great Britain, Despatches, White to Hay, December 18, 1902 (second telegram of that date). The present work is not a suitable place for another analysis of Roosevelt's claim to have compelled Germany to arbitrate through a virtual ultimatum to her ambassador; see W. R. Thayer, *The Life and Letters of John Hay* (2 vols., Boston and New York, 1915), vol. 2, ch. 28. There can be no doubt, however, from the evidence presented above, that no ultimatum was delivered before Germany consented to arbitrate on December 17. The possibility remains that the President spoke strongly to Holleben or Sternburg later on, sometime in early 1903. Whatever the truth, it is certain that both Roosevelt's and Thayer's accounts need considerable correction. For this controversy see Hill, *Roosevelt and the Caribbean*, ch. 5; J. F. Rippy, *Latin America in World Politics, an Outline Survey* (New York, 1931), ch. 11; Vagts, *Deutschland*, vol. 2, ch. 15; Perkins, *Monroe Doctrine*, ch. 5.

[51] *Foreign Relations, 1903*, pp. 459-460, White to Hay, December 22, 1902; State Department, Great Britain, Despatches, White to Hay, December 24, 1902.

[52] Hendrick, *Carnegie*, vol. 2, p. 182, letter dated December 27, 1902. Feeling had also been aroused against Germany because of her hostility in connection with the proposed evacuation of Shanghai. To the British, Germany seemed intent on turning a deaf ear to Russian encroachments in Manchuria while encouraging China to push Great Britain out of Shanghai and the Yangtze valley. See Balfour's indignant memorandum dated Novem-

indignation in Britain as in America.[53] Resolutions adopted by various churches and peace organisations denouncing intervention and all its works began to arrive at the Foreign Office at an early date; cumulatively they represented a significant body of opinion.[54] Soon Rudyard Kipling's famous if unedifying poem was printed in the London *Times*; mincing no words it referred to Germans as "the Goth and the shameless Hun" and excoriated the "secret vow Ye have made with an open foe!"[55] Although the *Times*, like Lord Lansdowne who characterized the poem an "outrage,"[56] demurred at the phrase "open foe" it had to confess that Kipling had expressed a sentiment that "unquestionably prevails far and wide throughout the nation."[57] The truth is that there occurred such an upsurge of protest as to astonish government officials.[58] Lord Lansdowne considered the violence of feeling "extraordinary."[59] Count Metternich believed that it, together with pressure from the United States, would prove irresistible; as early as December 16, when opposition was just beginning to manifest itself, the ambassador regret-

ber 4, 1902, to the King in B. E. C. Dugdale, *Arthur James Balfour, First Earl of Balfour, K. G., O. M., F. R. S., Etc.* (2 vols., New York, 1937), vol. 1, p. 279.

[53] See State Department, Great Britain, Despatches, White to Hay, December 15, 1902, for White's appraisal of British opinion.

[54] The more important resolutions were the following: Committee of International Arbitration and Peace Association, December 16, 1902 (F. O. 80, 448), and December 24, 1902 (F. O. 80, 449); Bristol branch of the committee, December 16, 1902 (F. O. 80, 448); Tyneside branch of the committee, December 17, 1902 (F. O. 80, 449); Committee of the Northamptonshire Federation of Free Churches, December 17, 1902 (F. O. 80, 448); League of Liberals (*The Times*, December 19, 1902); Incorporated King's Lynn Forward Association (representing 1,000 working men), December 21, 1902 (F. O. 80, 449); Fulham Congregational Church (by unanimous decision of over 1,200 members), December 22, 1902 (*ibid.*); Peace Society and International Arbitration Association, Manchester auxiliary, December 23, 1902 (*ibid.*).

[55] December 22, 1902.

[56] Newton, *Lansdowne*, p. 258, to Herbert, January 2, 1903.

[57] *The Times*, December 22, 1902.

[58] Nevins, *White*, pp. 211-212, White to Hay, December 31, 1902; A. Fitzroy, *Memoirs* (2 vols., London, 1925), vol. 1, p. 117.

[59] Newton, *Lansdowne*, p. 258, to Herbert, January 2, 1903.

fully advised his government that Germany should withdraw from the venture as soon as she honorably could.[60]

Once Venezuela and the intervening powers had committed themselves in principle to arbitration, the sense of urgency evaporated. Yet the critical period was still to come. From the beginning, as we have seen, Venezuela pinned her hopes on enlisting the sympathies of the American people, whose reverence for the Monroe Doctrine she well appreciated. Her offer to arbitrate, relayed to London through the State Department, was nicely calculated to appeal to uninformed American idealism.[61] Venezuela now made another clever move: she conferred full powers on the American minister at Caracas, Herbert W. Bowen, to negotiate on her behalf.[62] This shrewd stroke must have been most unwelcome at the Foreign Office. For no matter how Britain reacted she risked turning American sympathies more strongly to Venezuela: if she spurned a respected United States diplomat, she would offend his compatriots; if, on the other hand, she agreed to negotiate with Bowen, Americans would tend to side with him—and therefore with Venezuela. The British minister at Caracas had already warned against Bowen, describing him as a " mischievous man " whose participation in negotiations would be " suicidal." [63] Not surprisingly, Lansdowne told White that Britain preferred Roosevelt as arbitrator to Bowen as negotiator; and he repeated his request for the President's services.[64]

From Roosevelt's letters it is obvious that the role of defender of the revered doctrine and arbiter among the great powers

[60] *Grosse Politik*, vol. 17, p. 266, to German foreign office, December 16, 1902.

[61] The suggestion of the Venezuelan consul in London that the New York brokers, I. and W. Seligman and Company, undertake the settlement of Venezuela's debt, may have represented another attempt to enlist American sympathies; see State Department, Great Britain, Despatches, White to Hay, December 19, 1902; E. E. Morison, ed., *The Letters of Theodore Roosevelt* (8 vols., Cambridge, Mass., 1951-1954), vol. 3, p. 386.

[62] *Foreign Relations, 1903*, p. 456, Hay to White, December 18, 1902.

[63] F. O. 80, 448, Haggard to Lansdowne, December 18, 1902.

[64] *Foreign Relations, 1903*, p. 456, White to Hay, December 19, 1902; *Venezuela. No. 1 (1903)*, p. 182, Lansdowne to Herbert, December 22, 1902.

appealed to his vanity and romantic nature.[65] He would have relished playing the part; and as a matter of fact he was prepared to do so had that been necessary to get arbitration.[66] But since the United States itself had claims against Venezuela and also since any verdict would have been bitterly resented somewhere, it would have been both improper and injudicious for him to have served as arbitrator. It was apparently John Hay who restrained his chief's eager impulses. Having done so, the Secretary adopted the wise plan of persuading the countries concerned to have recourse to the new Hague tribunal instead of to the White House.[67] With that, the President formally declined to serve. Disliking the prospect of being out of the picture altogether, however, he offered to help arrange preliminaries of arbitration and suggested that the powers meet in Washington to that end.[68]

Great Britain now had to determine what to do about the awkward Bowen. She regretted Roosevelt's decision of course.[69] Indeed it was evident that she could contemplate with no great enthusiasm the prospect of negotiating in the American capital, under the watchful eye of the American President, and with the American minister to Venezuela, the very country with which she was embroiled. On the other hand, it would not do to affront Theodore Roosevelt. While she was considering this dilemma, an opportune telegram arrived from Herbert:

> I have received a private note from Secretary of State, informing me that the selection of Mr. Bowen as the representative of Venezuela has not been due to any suggestion put

[65] See his three letters of December 26, 1902: to Albert Shaw (Morison, *Letters of Roosevelt*, vol. 3, pp. 396-397), to Carl Schurz (*ibid.*, p. 397), and to Grover Cleveland (*ibid.*, p. 398).

[66] *Foreign Relations, 1903*, p. 464, White to Lansdowne, December 27, 1902.

[67] British consent was given December 22; see *Venezuela. No. 1 (1903)*, p. 182, Lansdowne to Herbert, December 22, 1902. White predicted such consent as early as the 19th (State Department, Great Britain, Despatches, White to Hay, December 19, 1902).

[68] *Foreign Relations, 1903*, p. 464, White to Lansdowne, December 27, 1902.

[69] Newton, *Lansdowne*, p. 258, Lansdowne to Herbert, January 2, 1903.

forward by the United States Government. If objections are raised by the Powers concerned to the choice of Mr. Bowen the President would be disposed to refuse him permission to act, but at the same time the President desires to lend all possible friendly offices in order to secure a satisfactory agreement between the parties interested.

Mr. Hay has further informed me in conversation that, in the event of Mr. Bowen's acting, he would receive no instructions from the Department of State here, and would be absolutely independent as far as the United States Government are concerned.[70]

With his usual solicitude Secretary Hay had taken care to relieve Britain's fears that by negotiating with the American she would find herself dealing in effect with Washington instead of Caracas. Such assurance made it easier to accept Bowen. Furthermore, time would be lost if Britain turned him down, time for other incidents to occur, time for a further hardening of American tempers. Before doing anything herself Great Britain had to consult Germany; and the Wilhelmstrasse felt most disgruntled about the rapid Americanization of her venture. But under British urging she gave in. Accordingly Britain consented on January 9, 1903, to negotiate with Bowen, in Washington as Roosevelt wished; she would make a direct settlement, or would refer the controversy to The Hague if Venezuela so preferred. Her only condition was that Castro accept certain stipulations regarding the exclusion of reserved claims.[71] (She intimated, however, that if Washington disliked these stipulations she would consider modifying them.) [72]

---

[70] F. O. 5, 2489, to Lansdowne, December 31, 1902. In the same vein White assured Lansdowne that Bowen's designation was not due to prompting by the United States, and that a suggestion by Castro, that a New World country be chosen to arbitrate, was not supported by the United States; see *Venezuela. No. 1 (1903)*, p. 186, Lansdowne to Herbert, January 1, 1903.

[71] For the final steps to this agreement see *Venezuela. No. 1 (1903)*, p. 186, White to Lansdowne, January 1, 1903; pp. 191-192, Lansdowne to White, January 5, 1903; p. 194, White to Lansdowne, January 9, 1903. See also *Foreign Relations, 1903*, pp. 465-469. For the German and British conditions see *ibid.*, pp. 427-428 and 461-462.

[72] *Foreign Relations, 1903*, p. 461, White to Hay, December 24, 1902.

Nothing could have been more obvious in these developments than Britain's solicitude for the United States. She appeared resolved to make amends for her initial mistake of plunging ahead without adequate consideration of American sensibilities. She had hastened to comply with the slightest and most gently expressed American wish; she had overcome German distaste for arbitration, for a belligerent blockade, and for negotiating with Bowen; she had committed herself publicly not to fight on Venezuelan soil.[73] These were extraordinary acts of deference by the world's greatest sea power.

As the year drew to its close, a retrospective mood seized upon statesmen in Washington and London. Theodore Roosevelt, who considered the controversy practically settled as early as December 26,[74] exuded complacency. He wrote characteristically to Grover Cleveland:

> It is just six years since you took action in the Venezuela case. I have always been proud of the fact that I heartily backed up what you then did. . . . It seems to me that you have special cause for satisfaction in what we have succeeded in accomplishing this time in connection with getting England and Germany explicitly to recognize the Monroe Doctrine in reference to their controversy with Venezuela and in getting all of the parties in interest to accept arbitration by the Hague court. I congratulate you heartily on the rounding out of your policy.[75]

As for Anglo-American relations, Sir Michael in Washington and White in London, both of whom agreed with Roosevelt in thinking intervention about concluded, believed no real damage had been done. " The Administration," Herbert reported, " has been most friendly throughout, and, if the dispute be referred without delay to arbitration, which at the moment of writing seems probable, it will be almost safe to affirm that the friendly relations between Great Britain and the United States, instead

---

[73] See Nevins, *White*, pp. 211-212, White to Hay, December 31, 1902, for White's praise of Lansdowne's " perfect " courtesy.

[74] See his letter of that date to Taft (Morison, *Letters of Roosevelt*, vol. 3, p. 399).

[75] *Ibid.*, p. 398, December 26, 1902.

of being impaired, have, if anything, been strengthened by the Venezuelan incident." [76] Even so perspicacious an observer as Henry White, who had kept harping on the hidden dangers, believed the incident had done more good than harm.[77]

A less complacent note was sounded by the American press. Although editorials often portrayed acceptance of arbitration as a triumph for the Monroe Doctrine (and occasionally as a triumph for the Hague tribunal),[78] yet according to *Public Opinion* if the affair taught any one lesson it was that the nation must rearm. Thus the Boston *Journal* believed that " the country has just been given a vivid reminder that the Monroe doctrine is not self-enforcing. . . . A heavier battle-line is sure to follow from these startling events on the southern edge of the Caribbean." " The Monroe doctrine cannot be maintained with words alone. . . . Build a mighty navy! " the New York *American and Journal* exhorted its many readers.[79] Strongly critical as it was

[76] Gooch and Temperley, *British Documents*, vol. 2, p. 164, to Lansdowne, December 29, 1902. There exist one or two indications that Herbert may have misunderstood. Edward Farrer, a well known Canadian newspaper man visiting Washington, wrote: " Much bitterness has been created in Washington against England by the Anglo-German expedition against Venezuela. I am told on high authority that the President has indulged in some very plain speaking to Sir Michael Herbert . . ."; see O. D. Skelton, *Life and Letters of Sir Wilfrid Laurier* (2 vols., New York, 1922) , vol. 2, p. 142. But probably this letter was written toward the end of January, when American exasperation against Britain had mounted. Thus Henry Cabot Lodge wrote to Henry White on February 3, 1903: " the English *Government* appears to be no more friendly than that of Germany. Why the Government should run contrary to the feelings in their own country and take the very great risk of arousing bitter feelings here is something hard to understand"; see C. C. Tansill, *Canadian-American Relations, 1875-1911* (New Haven, 1943) , p. 236.

[77] Nevins, *White*, p. 216, to Hay, December 31, 1902.

[78] *Public Opinion*, vol. 34 (January 1, 1903) , p. 3. Few Americans, certainly, agreed with a widely noticed editorial by the unconventional journalist, Henry Watterson, that the lesson of the Venezuelan affair was that the Monroe Doctrine should be scrapped; this unfashionable suggestion met with overwhelming repudiation in some 300 replies in the American press; see *ibid.* (January 8, 1903) , p. 38; only the St. Paul *Dispatch* and the Knoxville *Journal* are cited as agreeing with Watterson.

[79] *Ibid.*, vol. 33 (December 25, 1902) , p. 805.

of both Great Britain and Germany, the press nevertheless tended to make a distinction: Germany was the evil genius in the episode; she had duped the British leaders (but not the British people) .[80] American dislike and distrust of Germany, which had been so marked ever since Vice-Admiral von Diederichs made the mistake of annoying Dewey at Manila Bay, and still more since Germany stood against Britain and America in Samoa, had risen by the end of 1902, because of the intervention, to a pitch that Michael Herbert thought " truly remarkable." [81]

The one statesman furthest from a sense of satisfaction at the turn of the year was the German ambassador, Holleben. Held responsible by his government for the abysmal depths to which German prestige had sunk in the United States, as well as, it may be, for the failure to convince Americans of Britain's guilt in 1898, the ambassador was summarily recalled to Berlin.[82] Although calculated to improve relations with America, the dismissal in actual fact stirred up indignation. The poor ambassador was being made the scapegoat for Berlin's stupidities, Americans conjectured; and if the report was true that he was to be succeeded by Roosevelt's friend, Baron Speck von Sternburg, the Kaiser was insulting American intelligence by attempting to win the country through so transparent a device.[83] Great Britain could not escape some attribution of guilt by virtue of her association with the Kaiser; but she gained something, too, in the sense that not a few Americans hailed the British squadron as a most welcome restraining hand upon German truculence.[84]

---

[80] *Ibid.*, p. 808.

[81] Gooch and Temperley, *British Documents*, vol. 2, p. 164, to Lansdowne, December 29, 1902.

[82] Rumor had it that he had further incensed the Kaiser because William had almost been snubbed when he offered a statue of Frederick the Great to be erected in Washington in commemoration of Prince Henry's visit; see *Public Opinion*, vol. 34 (January 22, 1903), p. 100, *Literary Digest*, vol. 24 (June 7, 1902), p. 760. For other comments on the ambassador's recall see *ibid.*, vol. 26 (February 14, 1903), p. 236; *The Times*, January 9, 1903.

[83] *Public Opinion*, vol. 34 (January 22, 1903), pp. 99-100.

[84] Gooch and Temperley, *British Documents*, vol. 2, pp. 163-164, Herbert to Lansdowne, December 29, 1902; for a similar British interpretation see

The distinction drawn by the press between the blockading powers was no doubt attributable mainly to memories of their roles, or fancied roles, during the Spanish-American War. It was attributable also to occasional offerings of homage by British public figures—but not by Germans—to the doctrine of President Monroe, and even more to the marked contrast between British and German press comment. Whereas the principal German newspapers and publicists supported the intervention and blamed the United States for interfering, the British press with few exceptions inveighed against the government for cooperating with Germany and for slighting America.[85] There was much truth in the London *Daily Mail*'s contention, after the blockade had been lifted, that Britain got out of the scrape as well as she did because of the British press, not the British government.[86]

The decision to negotiate in Washington having been taken, diplomacy lapsed while the foreign representatives waited for the U. S. S. *Dolphin* to carry Bowen across the Caribbean. Landing at Charleston, he hurried to the capital where he presented himself at the British embassy on January 21, 1903. He immediately repeated a request he had made prior to leaving Venezuela, that the blockade be raised before negotiations commenced. But Great Britain, like Germany, would not agree to ease pressure upon Castro until either a direct settlement had been reached or the dispute referred to The Hague.[87] After all, Venezuela had not yet signed an acceptance of the British conditions regarding reserved claims.

The very day discussions commenced in Washington a serious incident erupted on the Venezuelan coast. While Bowen's ship was steaming toward America one of the blockading German warships, the *Panther*, was fired upon by the fort of San Carlos

Sir Almeric Fitzroy's notation of January 13, 1903, in his *Memoirs*, vol. 1, p. 117.

[85] *Public Opinion*, vol. 34 (January 1, 1903), p. 10, citing the London *Daily Mail*, the London *Post*, the *Manchester Guardian*, the Liverpool *Post*, and the *Westminster Gazette*.

[86] *Ibid.* (February 19, 1903), p. 233.

[87] *Venezuela. No. 1 (1903)*, pp. 208-209, Lansdowne to Herbert, January 12, 1903.

at Maracaibo. Four days later, on January 21, several German ships bombarded and destroyed this decrepit citadel.[88] The harsh and foolish deed jolted American attention back to the Caribbean. It was bad luck for Germany that the *Panther* was the same ship that several months before had sunk a Haitian ship (an incident that at the time had aroused no excitement in the United States),[89] and more recently had destroyed the two Venezuelan gunboats. "Are people in Berlin crazy?" asked Theodore Roosevelt angrily. "Don't they know that they are inflaming public opinion more and more here? Don't they know that they will be left alone without England?"[90] A veritable storm of criticism of Germany now swept the country.[91] She was likened to "an eighteenth century pirate such as Blackbeard and Morgan"; the bombardment was called "one of the most wantonly reckless acts on record," and "a piece of treacherous misconduct hardly paralleled in all modern history."[92] The Philadelphia *Press* may well have been correct in asserting that the *Panther* had undone in a day much of Prince Henry's good work.[93] For once, Sir Michael Herbert did not gloat over abuse of Britain's ally. ". . . after the bombardment," he wrote, "I was very nervous as to what was going to happen, for complications with Germany mean trouble for us."[94]

[88] *Grosse Politik*, vol. 17, p. 274. It was the *Panther* that, dropping anchor at Agadir on July 1, 1911, precipitated the second Moroccan crisis. The date of the bombardment is usually but incorrectly given as January 17.

[89] *Public Opinion*, vol. 33 (September 18, 1902), p. 360.

[90] Vagts, *Deutschland*, vol. 2, p. 1595.

[91] *Public Opinion*, vol. 34 (January 8, 1903), p. 35, and *ibid.* (January 29, 1903), p. 131.

[92] *Ibid.* (January 29, 1903), p. 138; *Literary Digest*, vol. 26 (January 31, 1903), p. 141; *Review of Reviews*, vol. 27 (1903), pp. 135-136.

[93] *Literary Digest*, vol. 26 (January 31, 1903), p. 141. See *Public Opinion*, vol. 34 (January 22, 1903), p. 99, for an account of a series of apparently concerted allegations against Germany that suddenly broke out in the American press. Among other things Germany was charged with trying to steal a canal concession and with being responsible for America's failure to purchase the Danish West Indies.

[94] Newton, *Lansdowne*, p. 259, to Lansdowne, January 30, 1903. A few days earlier he had written: "there is a feeling of intense irritation in the

The trouble for his own country that Sir Michael foresaw would doubtless have been greater had not British opinion condemned the bombardment almost as vehemently as American. The naval commander-in-chief in the West Indies sharply criticized his German colleague in a telegram to the Admiralty; Arthur Balfour, "much annoyed and perturbed," told Henry White that "his anxiety is equal to mine for settlement"; members of Parliament lamented that their constituencies were up in arms against the "ironclad bargain." [95] Such was the outcry that government officials, as well as the general public, attacked the tie with Germany. White reported members of the Cabinet as demanding an immediate end of the blockade even at the price of a break with Germany.[96] Although the American people could not read these diplomatic papers, they could read the London *Times*'s dry remark that "Such proceedings as the bombardment of San Carlos do not tend to inspire with confidence . . ."; [97] and they could read cables of the London correspondents of American newspapers who unanimously depicted Great Britain as most critical of Germany.[98] Ruefully, Ambassador Metternich

United States against Germany, and in default of an early settlement there may be an outburst of feeling which may produce a strained situation and place the President in a position of serious embarrassment . . . (Gooch and Temperley, *British Documents*, vol. 2, p. 166, to Lansdowne, January 26, 1903).

[95] Gooch and Temperley, *British Documents*, vol. 2, p. 165, telegram of January 23, 1903; State Department, Great Britain, Despatches, White to Hay, January 24, 1903.

[96] State Department, Great Britain, Despatches, to Hay, January 28, 1903. White stated on the 26th that the British government did not consider itself bound to Germany "beyond point at which in its own opinion satisfactory settlement has been made and will decline further cooperation should Germany not be expressly satisfied with settlement and wish to continue blockade" (*ibid.*, to Hay).

[97] January 26, 1903.

[98] *Public Opinion*, vol. 34 (January 29, 1903), p. 138. The one sour note was Beresford's charge that the Monroe Doctrine was under attack, a charge that was doing considerable mischief in America according to Smalley (*The Times*, January 16 and 17, 1903); *Public Opinion*, vol. 34 (January 22, 1903), p. 99. Beresford claimed to have been misquoted.

confessed that the British were blindly accepting, not the assurances of their own ally, but the slanderous statements of Castro.[99]

The hue and cry about the *Panther* did not provide a happy
atmosphere for negotiations. Prospects for early settlement were
further dimmed by a demand put forward by Bowen shortly
after discussions commenced in Washington, namely, that all
countries having claims against Venezuela be paid on an equal
basis, whether they had participated in the blockade or not.[100]
To the blockading powers it seemed grotesquely unfair that
countries that had borne the brunt of forcing Castro to disgorge
should be treated equally with countries that had done nothing.[101]
They insisted upon preferential treatment. Bowen, likewise,
stood firm. Negotiations appeared to be collapsing.

This exasperating deadlock, coming on top of the San Carlos
bombardment, gave rise to a wave of pessimism in the United
States, a wave the more exaggerated because the setback was so
unexpected. Instead of subsiding, the dispute suddenly appeared
to be just getting started. And where it would end, who could
say? Apprehension and impatience mounted ominously across
the country. Having just stood with Venezuela over the bombardment, the American press, mindful perhaps that Americans
too had claims, again aligned itself with Venezuela in character-
izing the British and German position " unreasonable and unjust
to other claimants." ". . . it is impossible," the *New York Times*
declared firmly, " not to view the claim they have set up [for
preference] as an obstruction to the progress of peace negotiations. . . . We are weary, and something more than weary, with
German explanations and protestations and with British apolo-
gies for the German alliance, coupled with ministerial assurances

[99] E. T. S. Dugdale, ed., *German Diplomatic Documents, 1871-1914* (4
vols., London, 1928-1931), vol. 3, pp. 164-165, to Bülow, February 4, 1903.

[100] 58th Congress, 2nd session, Senate document 316, p. 1039, to Herbert,
January 27, 1903; State Department, Great Britain, Despatches, White to
Hay, January 28, 1903. Another hitch arose from Germany's demand for
immediate cash payment of a large sum; however, she soon lowered her price
(*Foreign Relations, 1903*, p. 472, White to Hay, January 30, 1903).

[101] *Venezuela. No. 1 (1903)*, p. 219, Lansdowne to Herbert, January 26,
1903.

of undying friendship for ourselves." [102] Ever a close observer
of the American mood, Henry White kept exhorting his British
friends to end the blockade quickly—or face an explosion in the
United States.[103] And the President himself warned von Sternburg, the Kaiser's new representative at Washington, that " public
opinion . . . was growing more and more irritated." [104]

Any trans-Atlantic flare-up was of course unwelcome in London. But a flare-up at the end of January, 1903, was doubly
unwelcome. For not only did it threaten good understanding
with America; it threatened the very life of the government. The
new session of Parliament would convene on February 17. Given
the existing British unrest the Balfour ministry believed an early
end of the blockade " absolutely necessary." [105] Thus endangered,
it took special pains to reassure the British and American people.
Twice within a week during the critical period of early February
when Bowen was rejecting preferential treatment, Cabinet ministers publicly stressed Britain's true devotion for the republic.
In Birmingham a rising young politician, Postmaster-General
Austen Chamberlain, speaking for his famous father, proclaimed
that there was " no nation in the world with whom we were so
closely knit as with our cousins across the Atlantic," and " no
nation in the world that had so heartily and loyally accepted
the Monroe Doctrine " as Great Britain.[106] The Secretary of
State for India, Lord George Hamilton, laid " it down as a
cardinal and primary axiom of our foreign policy that, consistently with the maintenance of our interests and honour, we should
do nothing to alienate a people who are nearer to us in language,
in kinship, and in sentiment than any other nation in the

[102] *Public Opinion*, vol. 34 (February 5, 1903) , p. 169.

[103] State Department, Great Britain, Despatches, White to Hay, January 28,
1903.

[104] Gooch and Temperley, *British Documents*, vol. 2, p. 168, Herbert to
Lansdowne, January 31, 1903.

[105] *Ibid.*, p. 171, Lansdowne to Herbert, February 7, 1903. See also *Foreign
Relations, 1903*, p. 475, White to Hay, February 10, 1903; Dugdale, *German
Diplomatic Documents*, vol. 3, p. 165, Metternich to Bülow, February 4, 1903.

[106] *The Times*, February 2, 1903.

world." [107] And a prominent opposition spokesman, Sir Edward Grey, castigated the Conservatives for cultivating good relations with Germany at the expense of those with the United States.[108] Certainly the air teemed with fine phrases from high sources during early February.

Yet all the fine phrases did not terminate the blockade, nor did they settle the deadlock over preferential treatment. The British government now made a determined effort to come to terms with Bowen. First of all—so Lansdowne instructed Herbert —let Theodore Roosevelt be approached again; true, he had refused to arbitrate the whole controversy; but would he not arbitrate the one question of preference that was holding up everything? [109] If not, let this point be referred to the Hague tribunal. In either eventuality, the other, less disputed points, on which as a matter of fact Sir Michael and Bowen stood on the verge of agreement, could be included in a protocol for early signature in Washington. Or if Bowen should make trouble about a protocol—he had just angered the British by publishing a private letter from Sir Michael and by inspiring a press report of disagreement among the Washington representatives of the blockading powers [110]—the other points, too, could go to The Hague.[111] Thus in one way or another agreement could be reached in short order and the blockade raised before Parliament met.

[107] *Ibid.*, February 9, 1903. About this time, on January 30, 1903, the Prime Minister wrote to Andrew Carnegie, though this was not known publicly, that "the one thing on which they [the British people] are agreed" was a desire for the closest possible relations with the United States (Hendrick, *Carnegie*, vol. 2, p. 183) ; and King Edward was "really very outspoken" to Henry White about his American sympathies (Nevins, *White*, p. 212).

[108] Halévy, *History of the English People*, vol. 5, p. 135; speech of February 6, 1903.

[109] *Venezuela. No. 1 (1903)*, pp. 222-223, to Herbert, January 30, 1903.

[110] Gooch and Temperley, *British Documents*, vol. 2, p. 169, Herbert to Lansdowne, February 4, 1903; State Department, Great Britain, Despatches, White to Hay, February 7, 1903; White wrote that the British feared a settlement could not be reached through negotiations with Bowen.

[111] Gooch and Temperley, *British Documents*, vol. 2, pp. 171-172, Lansdowne to Herbert, February 7, 1903.

In accordance with these instructions Sir Michael, after making a final and fruitless attempt to reach agreement directly with Bowen, formally asked Theodore Roosevelt to adjudicate the question of preference. Again the President declined; indeed there was little likelihood that having once refused to arbitrate he would now change his mind.[112] The next step was to submit the protocol to Bowen; it embraced all the points at issue except that of preference. One last difficulty remained. Bowen, although prepared to accept the British protocol (which, he assured Herbert, was " very creditable to you and to the British Government ") ,[113] would not accept the German one; and Great Britain, bound by the " ironclad bargain," felt unable to sign until Germany did likewise.

It was an exasperating state of affairs. At any moment another inflammatory incident might occur on the Venezuelan coast. Who could foresee how Americans would react? Already dangerously impatient, they might drive the administration to extreme measures. Something like that had happened in April, 1898; and the Spanish War had resulted. ". . . Germany takes an impossible stand," Theodore Roosevelt complained angrily.[114] And a solemn and courageous warning from Sir Michael Herbert showed that the sands were fast running out in the United States:

> I feel myself bound [he telegraphed Lansdowne] to warn your Lordship that a great change has taken place in the feeling of this country towards us since . . . December 27th last, and that our good relations with this country will be seriously impaired if this Alliance with Germany continues much longer. The time has almost come, in American opinion, for us to

[112] *Foreign Relations, 1903*, pp. 473-475, Herbert to Hay, and Hay to Herbert, February 6, 1903; British Blue Book, *Venezuela. No. 1 (1903)*. *Correspondence Respecting the Affairs of Venezuela*. Cd. 1399. P. 227, Herbert to Lansdowne, February 6, 1903.

[113] 58th Congress, 2nd session, Senate document 316, p. 1041, Bowen to Herbert, February 10, 1903; Gooch and Temperley, *British Documents*, vol. 2, p. 172, Herbert to Lansdowne, February 7, 1903; *Foreign Relations, 1903*, p. 475, White to Hay, February 10, 1903.

[114] Morison, *Letters of Roosevelt*, vol. 3, p. 423, to Theodore Roosevelt, Jr., February 9, 1903.

make the choice between the friendship of the United States and that of Germany.[115]

The sands were fast running out in Great Britain, too. Only a few days remained before Parliament was to assemble. Lord Lansdowne summoned Count Metternich to the Foreign Office. Speaking " with the utmost frankness," he impressed upon him how " almost intolerable " Britain's position would be if she were forced to break off negotiations because Bowen, although agreeable to the British terms, would not accept " extreme German demands." Lansdowne dismissed the ambassador with what Metternich probably understood as a notification that if Germany did not back down, Britain would abandon the alliance: " I said [he wrote Herbert] that we had no intention of deserting Germany, but that it was absolutely necessary that we should endeavour to find some way out of the difficulty." [116]

Possibly Germany would have moderated her demands even without this stern admonition. Metternich had made perfectly clear to his superiors the perils for the Balfour government if no accord were reached before Parliament convened; certainly Berlin preferred Balfour, Lansdowne, and Chamberlain to Lord Rosebery and the Liberals. Whatever the explanation, the fact is that Germany quickly brought her protocol into line. On February 13, 1903, each of the blockading powers signed protocols with Bowen setting forth the agreed points and providing for reference to the Hague tribunal of the one undetermined question of preferential treatment. Certain claims were to be settled by early cash payments, the great bulk of which would go to Germany; remaining claims were to be referred to mixed commissions. It was here that Theodore Roosevelt at last found a suitable place for himself. Although dissuaded from serving as arbitrator, the President now agreed to nominate umpires in the likely event the mixed commissions divided equally.

[115] Gooch and Temperley, *British Documents*, vol. 2, p. 172, Herbert to Lansdowne, February 7, 1903.

[116] *Ibid.*, pp. 172-173, February 9, 1903; on January 28, 1903, King Edward told Metternich of his strong desire to see intervention concluded immediately (*Grosse Politik*, vol. 17, pp. 281-282).

Venezuela having thus signed acceptable terms, the powers raised the blockade on February 14, 1903. In the nick of time, just three days before Parliament opened, the unexpectedly protracted and hazardous intervention was at length concluded.

The British ministers must have heaved a sigh of relief at their narrow escape. As though to dispel once and for all the politically dangerous charges of unfriendliness toward the United States, Prime Minister Balfour, in a speech at Liverpool, made a remarkable obeisance to the Monroe Doctrine:

> the Monroe doctrine has no enemies in this country that I know of (Cheers.) We welcome any increase of the great influence of the United States of America upon the great Western Hemisphere. . . . I go further, and I say that, so far as I am concerned, I believe it would be a great gain to civilization if the United States of America were more actively to interest themselves in making arrangements by which these constantly recurring difficulties between European Powers and certain States in South America could be avoided.[117]

A hundred years earlier, British power in the Caribbean stood virtually unchallenged. Fifty or sixty years earlier, Great Britain and the United States confronted each other on somewhat more equal terms there, and were not far from blows over which was to be supreme. Ever since then Britain had beaten a slow retreat before the rising young republic. A year or so earlier, by the Hay-Pauncefote treaty, she had handed over her canal rights in Central America to the United States. She was now, if the Prime Minister was to be believed, handing over most of the western hemisphere.

[117] *The Times*, February 14, 1903. A former Prime Minister, Lord Rosebery, viewed the intervention much less happily. During a debate in the House of Lords on March 3, 1903, he said: " I frankly say that, for my part, I wish to dismiss this ignominious and pitiable transaction as quickly as possible from my memory just as I wish to and have dismissed the former episode of Venezuela from my memory also. The only reason for which it interests me . . . is in regard to the effect which it may have on our relations with Germany and with the United States. I cannot believe, whatever may be thought by the noble marquis [Lansdowne] as to the effect of his policy on the United States, that it can be a happy one " (*ibid.*, March 3, 1903) .

Throughout the whole intervention the British people, more than their government it must be said, had made no bones about their detestation of a course of action that appeared to place Germany above the United States in British esteem. On the eve of the new session of Parliament a great meeting was held in London. Its object was to demand the basing of another naval squadron in the North Sea, which would stand guard against the enemy across those waters. The British public had made its choice between Germany and the United States. Soon, and in no small measure because of the unpopular Venezuelan involvement, the government, too, would have to abandon hope of an understanding with Berlin.

Despite the steady friendship of the British public and press, despite the "great regard" (to quote Henry White) of the British government, too,[118] despite even the Prime Minister's prostration before the Monroe Doctrine, an ugly cloud had been drawn over the Anglo-American understanding. As far as Theodore Roosevelt was concerned, "The English behaved badly in Venezuela. . . ."[119] "Is it . . . nothing," G. W. Smalley inquired worriedly, "to the British Foreign Secretary that by his entanglement with Germany he for some weeks put a great strain on American good will to England, checked for a time what had been the steady growth of that good will, gave new life to the distrust always fostered by the enemies of England in the United States, and made it difficult for this Government to persevere in its friendly purpose?"[120] The friction arose just at the climax of negotiations over the Alaska boundary. We must now turn to those crucial negotiations.

[118] *Foreign Relations, 1903*, p. 476, White to Hay, February 14, 1903.

[119] *Selections from the Correspondence of Theodore Roosevelt and Henry Cabot Lodge, 1884-1918* (2 vols., New York and London, 1925), vol. 2, p. 37, to Lodge, June 29, 1903.

[120] *The Times*, March 4, 1903.

CHAPTER 14

The Hay-Herbert Treaty

WHEN Sir Michael Herbert arrived in Washington in October, 1902, to fill the post left vacant following Lord Pauncefote's death the previous May, a complicated situation confronted him. Sir Robert Bond was already there, pushing hard for a reciprocity treaty; Sir Wilfred Laurier had recently withdrawn his opposition to an even-numbered tribunal for the Alaska boundary arbitration; and soon Great Britain and Germany would be intervening in Venezuela, and thereby provoking dangerous misgivings in the United States. Soon, too, the American mid-term elections would be imposing their stultifying effect upon diplomacy.

For the moment the new ambassador's main preoccupation was with Alaska, where prospects for settlement had so unexpectedly brightened. Peaceful conclusion of that crucial and long-standing controversy would mark his promotion most happily. But when Sir Michael called at the State Department on October 17 he found the Secretary of State in a gloomy mood.[1] Three months before, Hay had informed Theodore Roosevelt of Laurier's concessions at London, but sure in his own righteousness the President had been anything but conciliatory. "In my judgment it is not possible to compromise . . . ," he had asserted stoutly. "I think the Canadian contention is an outrage pure and simple."[2] He would agree only to a commission of six,

[1] F. O. 5, 2510, Herbert to Lansdowne, October 17, 1902.
[2] E. E. Morison, ed., *The Letters of Theodore Roosevelt* (8 vols., Cambridge, Mass., 1951-1954), vol. 3, p. 287, to Hay, July 10, 1902. See also C. C. Tansill,

"but I think I shall instruct our three commissioners when appointed that they are in no case to yield any of our claim." [3] Obviously Roosevelt had not changed his mind since that day in March, 1902, when a disconsolate John Hay told Pauncefote that his new chief would not arbitrate, and that he could propose therefore nothing but a tribunal giving a reasoned opinion. The Secretary could propose no more to the new ambassador in October.[4] Thus in contrast to the recent softening in Canadian intransigence, American intransigence had hardened; for the President was insisting upon not only an even-numbered tribunal but one not authorized to render a decision.

The Dominion made no difficulty about agreeing to the President's terms provided the tribunal's terms of reference gave her own contentions equal prominence with American.[5] But when Sir Michael called at the State Department with this answer on December 8, he discovered American policy now veering along on a new tack. The United States was willing, Hay said, for the tribunal to return not a reasoned opinion but a final decision.[6] Just why Roosevelt changed his mind from October is not entirely clear; but it is reasonable to find part of the explanation in his stronger political position, and hence greater willingness to take risks, following the party's decisive victory in the November elections.[7] Presumably, too, the developing blockade of Venezuela made itself felt. Within a few days the President was to put pressure on the British to submit that dispute to arbitration. He must have perceived that what was sauce for the goose was sauce for the gander; that he would weaken his own effectiveness in Venezuela if too obdurate over American interests in Alaska.[8]

Canadian-American Relations, 1875-1911 (New Haven, 1943), p. 225, Hay to Roosevelt, July 14, 1902, and p. 226, Roosevelt to Strachey, July 18, 1902.

[3] Morrison, *Letters of Roosevelt*, vol. 3, p. 294, to Hay, July 16, 1902.

[4] F. O. 5, 2510, Herbert to Lansdowne, October 17, 1902.

[5] *Ibid.*, Chamberlain to Minto, October 31, 1902; Foreign Office to Herbert, December 6, 1902; Herbert to Lansdowne, December 8, 1902.

[6] *Ibid.*, Herbert to Lansdowne, December 8, 1902.

[7] See *Public Opinion*, vol. 33 (November 13, 1902), p. 611.

[8] Lord Newton, *Lord Lansdowne, a Biography* (London, 1929), p. 261,

Since Sir Michael welcomed the new American suggestion, Hay drew up a draft treaty; it was ready on December 18. Modelled closely on his draft of May, 1901, it nonetheless met British and Canadian objections so fully, Herbert thought, that he could report the Secretary as yielding on almost all points.[9] Like the canal treaty, it demonstrated Hay's genius at devising compromises. The draft, which unaltered became the final treaty, provided for a tribunal of " six impartial jurists of repute who shall consider judicially the questions submitted to them "; three appointed by each side; a majority of four to decide. Each jurist would " subscribe on oath that he will impartially consider the arguments and evidence presented to the tribunal and will decide thereupon according to his true judgement."

It remained to secure Canadian approval. This might not be easy. Britain had already sounded out Ottawa's reaction to the proposition of a tribunal empowered to make an award. The Canadians had hedged. They could express no opinion, they replied, until they knew both the treaty's text and the tribunal's composition.[10] Their evasiveness irritated Great Britain.[11] Enmeshed in the critical developments in the Caribbean, her friendship with the United States shaken, she could ill afford further complications in Alaska. She wanted a settlement more than ever. The treaty's text was now available for Ottawa's consideration, and Hay was pressing for action so as to allow time for ratification

wrote: " as President Roosevelt had forced arbitration upon the Powers concerned in the Venezuela question, it was hardly possible to refuse it in the case of Alaska. . . ." In asking Roosevelt to serve as arbitrator in the dispute with Venezuela, Britain may have hoped to influence him in favor of arbitration over Alaska.

[9] F. O. 5, 2510, December 19, 1902. Herbert mildly protested that section 5, article 4, gave prominence only to the American contention, but he soon dropped the point (State Department, Miscellaneous Archives, Alaskan Boundary, 1899-1903, Herbert to Hay, December 18, 1902). For the draft of May, 1901, see pp. 227-228.

[10] F. O. 5, 2510, Colonial Office to Minto, December 11, 1902; F. O. 115, 1244, Herbert to Lansdowne, December 12, 1902. Canada's reply was received at the Colonial Office on December 15.

[11] F. O. 5, 2510, Foreign Office to Herbert, December 24, 1902.

before Congress adjourned in March.[12] Holding out the hope
of a tribunal composed of three Supreme Court justices, the
Lord Chief Justice of England, and two high Canadian judges,
Great Britain on January 12, 1903, urgently summoned Canada
to make up her mind.[13] As with the Boer War on an earlier
occasion, the threat of war with Venezuela had moved her to
speak bluntly to her colony.

Sir Wilfrid Laurier had just returned to Ottawa from Virginia,
where he had been recuperating from a serious illness. Harassed
by various considerations pointing to opposite conclusions, he
had a hard choice to make. Laurier had known for about a
month that Sir Robert Bond's reciprocity treaty, the forestalling
of which had been one reason for his concessions at the colonial
conference, was not likely soon to emerge from the Senate Foreign
Relations Committee. No longer, therefore, did he face the
same pressing need to moderate his stand on the boundary question in order to sustain the prospect of confederation with Newfoundland. Moreover among his colleagues, already in some
disarray over his dealings in London, he found a hearty distaste
for the Hay-Herbert draft. Their opinions could not be treated
lightly. On the other hand, the Prime Minister's own honor was
involved, for he had largely committed himself during the summer. Besides, should he change his position the possibility existed
of the Senate's reviving Bond's Newfoundland treaty.

More important from a national and imperial point of view
was the dangerous involvement with Venezuela. On January 12,
1903, the day Great Britain adjured Canada to approve the draft,

---

[12] *Ibid.*, Herbert to Lansdowne, December 25, 1902.

[13] J. S. Ewart, *The Kingdom of Canada, Imperial Preference, the Colonial
Conferences, the Alaska Boundary, and Other Essays* (Toronto, 1908), p. 303.
Herbert had led the Foreign Office to expect nominations of Supreme Court
justices in a telegram of December 8, 1902 (F. O. 5, 2510); but see *ibid.*
for his despatch of the same date citing Hay as stating that it would be
difficult to secure the nomination of these justices owing to pressure of
business. In his telegram Herbert reported Hay's hope of not more than one
Canadian appointment; Herbert himself recommended that no Canadian
be appointed, but the Colonial Office disapproved (*ibid.*, Lansdowne to
Herbert, December 10).

the situation in the Caribbean was still fraught with peril. A prominent Canadian journalist wrote Sir Wilfrid about a disturbing talk with Senator Shelby Cullom, chairman of the Foreign Relations Committee, who had " frankly said that while he should like to accommodate you [Laurier, with regard to Alaska], he was afraid that the Venezuela affair had for the moment pretty well undermined the good understanding between the United States and England." [14] News had just arrived of Bowen's appointment to negotiate with the blockading powers. It was not the moment to jeopardize Venezuelan negotiations and further to embroil America and Britain by standing stubbornly against the Hay-Herbert treaty.

Another consideration may have weighed heavily with Ottawa. In November, 1902, the Canadian Privy Council had before it information that an American army officer, Lieutenant G. T. Emmons, who had been sent to Alaska to look for boundary markers, had discovered a Russian stone house, presumably a boundary monument, near the summit of the Dalton Trail. The monument was much more than ten marine leagues from tidewater in an area where Canadian sovereignty had hitherto been unquestioned.[15] " The evidence if reliable is very detrimental to our case," a Foreign Office official in London admitted; [16] and Theodore Roosevelt was so "very much impressed " that he contemplated demanding even more territory.[17] If the Canadians put any stock in the monument they may have concluded they would risk little or nothing by arbitrating.

But they yielded only grudgingly, possibly because Laurier

[14] O. D. Skelton, *Life and Letters of Sir Wilfrid Laurier* (2 vols., New York, 1922) , vol. 2, pp. 142-143; the journalist was Edward Farrer.

[15] Concerning the Privy Council report see C. O. 42, 889, report dated November 12, 1902, and F. O. 5, 2510, Minto to Chamberlain, November 15, 1902. For Emmons's discovery see *New York Times*, August 31, 1902; Washington *Evening Star*, October 29, 1902; *New York Tribune*, October 30, 1902.

[16] Note initialed " A. L." (A. Law) on the back of Herbert's despatch to Lansdowne, October 31, 1902 (F. O. 5, 2510) .

[17] Morison, *Letters of Roosevelt*, vol. 3, p. 405, Roosevelt to Hay, January 14, 1903.

wanted to make a show of resolution for the benefit of his colleagues. They asked Great Britain to try yet again to persuade the United States to accept either a tribunal composed partly of independent jurists, or else the Hague court.[18] This reversion to an old and threadbare theme was greeted with sweeping condemnation in London and Washington. " In my opinion," Lord Minto, obviously nettled, asserted, " the action of my Ministers is most unsatisfactory. . . . Sir Wilfrid has for long recognized that he could not get the arbitration he wanted, and much open to criticism as the present proposed Tribunal may be, he had no doubt fully made up his mind to accept it at once, till some other influence was brought to bear on him." [19] And both John Hay and Theodore Roosevelt categorically refused to countenance any such proposition.[20] It was just at that time that the Germans destroyed the fort at San Carlos, and that American resentment against the blockading powers was soaring to a dangerous pitch. Great Britain could wait upon her dilatory colony little longer. " Telegraph reply as soon as possible," the Colonial Secretary wired Lord Minto on January 19.[21]

[18] 58th Congress, 2nd session, Senate document 162. Alaskan Boundary Tribunal. *Proceedings of the Alaskan Boundary Tribunal, Convened at London, under the Treaty between the United States of America and Great Britain, Concluded at Washington January 24, 1903, for the Settlement of Questions between the Two Countries with respect to the Boundary Line between the Territory of Alaska and the British Possessions in North America* (7 vols., Washington, 1903), vol. 5, part 4, p. 17. British White Paper, *United States. No. 1 (1904)*. *Correspondence Respecting the Alaska Boundary.* Cd. 1877. P. 38; Minto to Colonial Office, January 13, 1903.

[19] Further Correspondence Respecting the Boundary between the British Possessions in North America and the Territory of Alaska, Printed for the use of the Foreign Office. November, 1904. Confidential (8296). Minto to Colonial Office, January 13, 1903.

[20] *Ibid.; United States. No. 1 (1904)*, pp. 38-39; Herbert to Lansdowne, January 18 and 19, 1903; their refusals were made when Britain approached the United States along the lines requested by Canada.

[21] *United States. No. 1 (1904)*, p. 39. Laurier had already written to Minto: " In asking that another effort should be made to have the Tribunal modified as we suggest, it is not because we have any serious hope of having that request granted, but we want to protest to the end again what we regard as an unsatisfactory Tribunal for the final settlement of this long-pending

What could Canada do? Once again, as during the Boer War when Britain had demanded her consent to modify the Clayton-Bulwer treaty, she found herself in an impossible position. To dig in her heels and refuse to budge would be to risk being shoved aside and losing everything. She had no real choice except to yield. " My Ministers," Minto telegraphed, " whilst still regretting that proposed Tribunal will not be constituted so as to insure certainty of a final decision being reached on the reference, being satisfied with the terms of that reference, will agree to accept Treaty as contained in the draft submitted to them." [22]

At five o'clock on the afternoon of January 24, 1903, in John Hay's library, the Secretary and Sir Michael signed the Hay-Herbert treaty; Hay sealed it with Lord Byron's ring, " having nothing else in the house." [23] The treaty represented a signal triumph for Hay, who had persevered with patience and adroitness throughout four and a half years. He was justified in calling it " substantially the same treaty " he had sponsored several years earlier.[24] Pauncefote, too, could have claimed much of the credit; for, as has been noted, its substance and to a large extent its very wording followed the draft of May, 1901, for which he and the Secretary of State had been responsible.

With the treaty's signature another long step had been taken toward the conclusion later in the year of the protracted controversy that had blocked Canadian-American agreements since 1898 and had threatened to disrupt British-American understanding. Two further complications, however, had still to be surmounted before the " impartial jurists of repute " could assemble to make

controversy. If Herbert cannot succeed then let him sign the Treaty as it is " (Further Correspondence, Minto to Onslow, January 13, 1903) .

[22] *United States. No. 1 (1904)*, p. 40, Lansdowne to Herbert, January 23, 1903; the date of Minto's reply is not given. Ewart apparently overlooked the White Paper in asserting, *Kingdom of Canada*, p. 304, that Canada's reply had not been published.

[23] C. S. Hay, ed., *Letters of John Hay and Extracts from Diary* (3 vols., Washington, 1908) , vol. 3, p. 264; W. R. Thayer, *The Life and Letters of John Hay* (2 vols., Boston and New York, 1915) , vol. 2, p. 318.

[24] Hay, *Letters and Diary*, vol. 3, p. 264.

their award: the United States had to ratify; Canada's resentment on learning the tribunal's composition had to be appeased to a point where she would cooperate. Each of these matters will be considered in turn.

Although Hay, rendered wise by sad experience, had prepared the treaty in close consultation with Henry Cabot Lodge and other members of the Senate Committee on Foreign Relations and had shown it to over thirty senators before handing it to Herbert, and although the American press had appraised it favorably enough, the Secretary's usual tribulations with " that unspeakable Senate " soon commenced.[25] Just as the hostility of a small group in the northeast had prevented ratification of his treaty with Bond, so another minority, this one in the northwest, threatened to wreck the Hay-Herbert treaty. It was particularly the shipping and trading interests of the state of Washington that denounced it as endangering American control of the Lynn Canal.[26] Near the end of January, 1903, Representative Jones of that state introduced a hostile resolution in the House; a week later G. W. Smalley predicted that northwestern opposition would prevent ratification.[27] And after a " long and very serious " talk with the President, F. W. Holls wrote the day before the Senate voted that the treaty had " no chance whatever of being ratified." [28]

But fortunately for the United States, Henry Cabot Lodge

[25] F. O. 5, 2510, Herbert to Lansdowne, December 19, 1902; C. G. Washburn, " Memoir of Henry Cabot Lodge," Massachusetts Historical Society, Proceedings, vol. 58 (1925), pp. 339-340; Literary Digest, vol. 26 (February 7, 1903), p. 177. The reference to the Senate is in a letter, October 29, 1900, from Hay to his wife in Hay, Letters and Diary, vol. 3, p. 199.

[26] See the harsh but not unfair comment of J. W. Dafoe, Clifford Sifton in Relation to His Times (Toronto, 1931), p. 240: " Actually, the power and prestige of the United States were being exploited, to the embitterment of relations with a friendly country, in the hope that it might divert to the port of Seattle some of the trade of the Klondike, which would flow in Canadian channels if there was an all-Canadian approach to that region."

[27] Congressional Record, vol. 36 (January 27, 1903), p. 1347; Further Correspondence, Herbert to Lansdowne, January 29, 1903; The Times, February 6, 1903.

[28] Holls papers, to Strachey, February 10, 1903.

had no politically minded son-in-law on the west coast; moreover he had collaborated closely in the drafting, more closely than in the case of the Bond draft; and he had assurances from the President regarding the tribunal's composition that convinced him that America at worst would not lose.[29] He gave the treaty his powerful support. Nonetheless, clever strategy was required to obtain ratification, for many senators disliked the treaty. The first step was for its sponsors to create an impression that consideration would be deferred, because of mounting antagonism, until an extra session some months later.[30] Then Lodge took command. Being warned by several of his colleagues that they would not vote to ratify without assurances as to the American commissioners, he got the President's permission to tell the Senate in confidence who was to be named.[31] For the afternoon of February 11, 1903, the Senate's time was allotted to Senator Morgan of Alabama. Anticipating a long and boring occasion numerous senators, including many opposed to the treaty, prudently absented themselves. Morgan's speech lived up to the dismal expectations, and no listener seems to have minded when Lodge interrupted to propose consideration of executive business prior to adjournment. On the motion being adopted, the Senate went into executive session for forty minutes; there Lodge presented the Hay-Herbert treaty.[32] Following a few perfunctory remarks a vote was taken, and the treaty declared ratified without a roll-call or the listing of yeas and nays. A test vote the next day for reconsideration, although defeated, indicated that the treaty lacked the necessary two-thirds. " I do not believe," Holls

[29] Washburn, " Memoir of Lodge," p. 340.

[30] This is stated in an unsigned editorial doubtless written by Albert Shaw in *Review of Reviews*, vol. 27 (1903) , p. 276; since Shaw opposed the treaty his statement may have been unduly prejudiced.

[31] Washburn, " Memoir of Lodge," p. 340. A long letter to the *Washington Post*, February 2, 1903, from former Secretary of State John Foster, strongly supporting the treaty, may have won over some senators. According to Herbert it would " carry much weight with the Senate " (Further Correspondence, to Lansdowne, February 3, 1903) . Foster's letter was printed as Senate document 136 (57th Congress, 2nd session) .

[32] *Congressional Record*, vol. 36, p. 2036.

wrote indignantly, "that ever before a trick of this character has been resorted to in voting upon a measure of really serious importance." [33]

Be that as it may, the treaty was now law for Americans. It still had to be ratified by Great Britain, a procedure that would have been a formality but for the outspoken resentment in Canada. When its terms became known, much of the Canadian press blew up. Editorials condemned the "obstinacy of the Americans," "their utterly preposterous claims," "United States bad faith," "a member [of Congress] . . . who must have been drunk in speaking of the Alaska matter." *The Evening Telegraph* of Toronto deplored American diplomacy as exemplifying "the arts, graces, and appetites which are exhibited by the highway robber in private life. . . ." [34] A connection between Britain's acceptance of the treaty and her current entanglement in Venezuela was widely suspected. Is the treaty, the Toronto *World* inquired disgustedly, "a friendly overture to the United States in order to atone for the folly of Great Britain's co-operation with Germany in the blockade of Venezuela? If so, are the blunders of British diplomats to be paid for at the expense of the interests and dignity of Canada?" [35] And *The Telegram* of Winnipeg affirmed: "The United States had proposed a form of arbitration between Great Britain and Venezuela which Great Britain had accepted. What was fair in that case should have been fair in the Alaskan boundary case." [36]

On February 14, 1903, Secretary Hay told Sir Michael the

[33] This account is based mainly on a letter from Holls to Strachey, February 13, 1903 (Holls papers); like Shaw, Holls opposed the treaty, and his account may be prejudiced. Substantially the same account occurs in *Review of Reviews*, vol. 27 (1903), p. 276. See also W. C. Ford, ed., *Letters of Henry Adams, 1892-1918* (2 vols., Boston and New York, 1938), vol. 2, p. 397: "Hay astounded himself and me by getting his Alaska Treaty through the Senate without a vote"; and *Congressional Record*, vol. 36, p. 2068.

[34] *Literary Digest*, vol. 26 (February 14, 1903), p. 235.

[35] *The Times*, January 27, 1903. See *ibid.*, for the assertion of J. I. Tarte, the dismissed Canadian minister, that the treaty represented an American effort to clear the way for a trade treaty with Canada.

[36] *Literary Digest*, vol. 26 (February 14, 1903), p. 235.

identity of the three American "impartial jurists of repute":
Elihu Root, Senator George Turner, and Henry Cabot Lodge.
Root was Secretary of War in the government charged with
upholding the United States case; Turner not only was publicly
committed [37] (though not in such extreme terms as Lodge),
but he represented the state of Washington, of all states the one
that stood to lose most from a verdict for Canada; and Lodge
had made public speeches calling the British claim " monstrous "
and as "manufactured and baseless" as any claim ever put
forward.[38]

These appointments were such gross travesties of the spirit
of the treaty and the preceding negotiations as to make one
wonder how even the bumptious Theodore Roosevelt could have
made them. On being informed of the American nominations
Sir Michael Herbert expressed "great disappointment" to Hay,
who "said that he agreed with me, but that the fault was not
that of the President. . . ." [39] In appraising Roosevelt's part in
the boundary settlement, one must bear in mind his sincere
belief that Canada not only had no case but knew it. In his
view, therefore, the tribunal was not a means of finding the
truth—that was known already—but a device to help a friendly
country, which had blundered through deference to an obstreper-
ous colony, climb down from an untenable position.[40] Rather
than petty carping about appointees, two of whom were his
intimate friends anyhow, he deserved gratitude for his chivalrous
forbearance in agreeing to negotiate at all. It must also be
remembered that Roosevelt expected to place at least one
Supreme Court judge, and perhaps two, on the tribunal; however, all the judges refused to serve on the ground of impro-

[37] Further Correspondence, Hodgins to Lansdowne, February 16, 1903.

[38] *Boston Herald*, October 17 and December 28, 1902; in the December
speech he had termed the claim one "that no self-respecting nation could
possibly admit."

[39] Further Correspondence, Herbert to Lansdowne, February 14, 1903;
see also his letter to Lansdowne, February 21, 1903, in Newton, *Lansdowne*,
p. 262.

[40] See his statement to Holls (Holls papers, Holls to Strachey, February 10,
1903).

priety.[41] And of course it may have been politically unavoidable to name such stalwarts. In all probability, however, the President could have reassured the Senate by appointing men equally but less flagrantly committed; he would thereby have spared Canadian feelings, and enhanced his own reputation with posterity.

Herbert's telegram giving the disagreeable news of the nominations put the British government in a predicament. Although the Canadians had grudgingly consented to Britain's signing the treaty, they had refused to approve it themselves without knowing the identity of the American commissioners.[42] The British leaders must have realized perfectly well that Canada's reaction to the naming of Lodge, Root, and Turner would be violent, and that she would expect to be consulted before negotiations proceeded further. But there was another consideration. News of the American appointments reached London on February 14, simultaneously with the lifting of the Venezuelan blockade. It was only a week earlier that Herbert had sent his dramatic message to Lord Lansdowne: " I feel myself bound to warn your Lordship that a great change has taken place in the feeling of this country towards us. . . ." [43] All indications pointed to an ominous temper across the Atlantic. In these circumstances it would have been madness for the Balfour government to offer the flagrant provocation of rebuffing such key figures as Lodge and Root, not to mention Turner. The government did not need Ambassador Herbert's advice to appreciate that " the con-

[41] Hay told Herbert that " all the Justices had declined to sit " (Further Correspondence, Herbert to Lansdowne, February 14, 1903). However, Roosevelt may have approached two judges only. According to T. A. Bailey, " Theodore Roosevelt and the Alaska Boundary Settlement," *Canadian Historical Review*, vol. 18 (1937), p. 125, he asked Holmes and White; Roosevelt himself wrote: " I asked two judges . . . to serve " (*ibid.*, p. 127); and J. W. Foster, *Diplomatic Memoirs* (2 vols., Boston and New York, 1909), vol. 2, p. 199, says Roosevelt offered the appointments to two judges. Hay wrote Choate, April 3, 1903, of his " great disappointment " at Justice White's refusal to serve (Choate papers).

[42] F. O. 5, 2510; *United States. No. 1 (1904)*, p. 35; Minto to Onslow, December 15, 1902. The British could have argued that this statement had been invalidated by Canada's subsequent consent to the signing.

[43] See p. 297.

sequences would be too grave to contemplate." [44] Political consequences at home, too, might be grave. A break with the United States would lend weight to the repeated charges of frivolous disregard of American susceptibilities. But should a boundary accord be reached before the new session of Parliament convened on February 17, such charges might be nipped in the bud.

Documentary evidence is lacking, but it would be surprising if the thought did not occur to the British ministers that sound policy called for presenting Canada with the *fait accompli* of ratification before she could make trouble about the American nominations. At any rate the government did not tell Ottawa about Herbert's unwelcome telegram from Washington for some days, not until the King had ratified the treaty on February 17 and had so announced publicly in his speech on the convening of Parliament. Only on the 18th did it inform Canada of the distressing news. [45]

If Canada reacted with such violence to the treaty's signature, her reaction on learning the names of the American commissioners can easily be imagined. Even the American press criticized the "impartial jurists," especially Lodge. "President Roosevelt ought not to have appointed him to the place," the Springfield *Republican* said flatly; another Republican journal, the Hartford *Courant*, declared, "he does not bring the judicial mind." "It is not likely that England will get anything she is not entitled to from that trio," the Louisville *Courier-Journal* safely predicted. [46] The Dominion's uneasy suspicion that she was again slated for victimization on the altar of Anglo-American friendship seemed confirmed. [47] Root was not too bad and Turner supportable; but Canadians felt about Lodge much as Henry Adams described: ". . . Cabot is the real pill. Whenever Canada raises a bristle, Theodore roars like a Texas steer, and ramps round the ring screaming for instant war, and ordering a million men

[44] Newton, *Lansdowne*, p. 262, Herbert to Lansdowne, February 21, 1903.

[45] *United States. No. 1 (1904)*, p. 45, Onslow to Minto, February 18, 1903.

[46] *Literary Digest*, vol. 26 (February 28, 1903), p. 293.

[47] She had felt this even before hearing about the appointments; see Further Correspondence, Minto to Onslow, February 9, 1903.

instantly to arms." [48] So incensed were the Prime Minister and his Cabinet that they were inclined to break off negotiations. ". . . my Ministers call attention to the fact," Lord Minto telegraphed,

> that they agreed to a Court of six members on the stipulation expressed in the Treaty that the members of the Court would be impartial jurists, and on the further confidential assurance . . . that Judges of the highest Courts of the United States would be appointed. . . .
> My Ministers most strongly represent that these conditions, having been material in causing their assent to the Treaty, should be made good; otherwise the ground upon which was based their assent would be changed, and it is feared that the whole situation would require reconsideration. [49]

The Colonial Office agreed; "it should be seriously considered" whether Britain should proceed further with the treaty, it maintained. [50] But the Foreign Office did not agree, and it carried the Cabinet. Accordingly a long, carefully worded explanation was despatched to the agitated Canadians on February 26:

> His Majesty's Government were as much surprised as the Dominion Government at the selection of Mr. Elihu Root, and of Senators Lodge and Turner, to be the American members of the Tribunal, and cannot but feel, with the Canadian Government, that their appointment fails to fulfil in their complete sense the conditions laid down in Article I of the Convention.
> The situation is full of difficulty, and His Majesty's Government earnestly desire to have the concurrence of the Canadian Government in dealing with it. It should, in their opinion, be borne in mind that the three gentlemen selected, all of them occupy conspicuous positions in the public life of the United States. A refusal to accept them as members of the Tribunal would unquestionably be greatly resented by the United States' Government, and by the American people generally.

[48] Ford, *Letters of Adams*, vol. 2, p. 399.

[49] Further Correspondence, Minto to Onslow, February 23, 1903; *United States. No. 1 (1904)*, p. 45, dates a somewhat different version of the telegram February 21.

[50] Further Correspondence, to Foreign Office, February 20 and 23, 1903.

It is true that the attitude of Senator Lodge has on various occasions been pronouncedly hostile to the Canadian contentions; but it is noteworthy that quite recently he took the leading part in disarming the hostility of the Senate towards the Treaty, and in bringing about its acceptance by that body.

Be this, however, as it may. His Majesty's Government are convinced that it would be of no avail to press the United States to withdraw the three names which they have put forward.

It would be easy to raise a discussion upon the fitness of the three American Representatives, but success in an argument of this nature would not only be barren of practical results, but would not improbably have the effect of sowing the seeds of lasting ill-will between the two countries.

His Majesty's Government are, therefore, virtually in the position of having to choose between, on the one hand, breaking off the negotiations altogether, or, on the other hand, accepting the American nominations, and appointing as their colleagues British Representatives appropriate to the altered circumstances of the case.

His Majesty's Government would regard the first alternative as a grave misfortune in the interests of both countries and of the Dominion of Canada. They would, in view of the restrictions under which the Tribunal is to carry out its work, prefer that the inquiry should proceed, in the confident expectation that it would not prejudice Canadian or British interests, while, even in case of failure, the result of its labours would probably be to collect much important information as to controverted points, and thereby to facilitate a reasonable settlement at some future time.

It would seem desirable that Lord Minto should urge his Ministers to weigh these considerations carefully. In the event of their sharing the opinion above expressed, His Majesty's Government hope that they will favour them with an expression of their views as to the manner in which the British side of the Tribunal might most advantageously be composed.[51]

The Laurier government was in no mood for counsels of moderation, however. While considering what retort to make to this clever statement, it received the staggering news of another

---

[51] *Ibid.*, Villiers to Colonial Office, February 25, 1903; Onslow sent the message to Minto on February 26 with one or two insignificant changes. A much abbreviated version of the message appears in *United States. No. 1 (1904)*, pp. 45-46.

fait accompli: Great Britain and the United States had exchanged ratifications on March 3; the treaty was now as secure as law could make it. Without even waiting for Canada's answer, Britain had put her in a predicament from which she could hardly escape.

To the Canadians this precipitate step seemed to confirm their worst fears as to the mother country's basic contempt for them. ". . . Sir W. Laurier called upon me yesterday," the Governor-General reported anxiously,

> extremely annoyed at the exchange of the ratifications of the Treaty, before my Government had sent an official reply to your telegram of the 26th February. He considers it a " slap in the face for Canada." Hitherto, while regretting the President's action, he has in conversation with me taken a calm view, and had personally quite decided to accept the President's nominations, but the announcement of the final ratification of the Treaty has had the most unfortunate effect. He considers that the interests of Canada have been treated with discourtesy.[52]

Again the Colonial Office sided with the Dominion. ". . . the Canadian Government had . . . reason," it admonished the Foreign Office stiffly, "to presume that until their reply was received no step would be taken which would irrevocably commit His Majesty's Government and them to taking part in the proceedings of a Tribunal which they could not regard as being constituted, so far as the American members were concerned, in the manner stipulated in the Convention creating it." [53]

[52] Further Correspondence, to Onslow, telegram received March 9, 1903; see also Minto to Onslow, March 7, 1903: " My Ministers are much dissatisfied at the exchange of ratifications . . . prior to the official reply to your telegram of the 26th February."

[53] *Ibid.*, March 27, 1903. Joseph Chamberlain landed at Southampton returning from his trip to South Africa on March 14; he was therefore back in the Colonial Office at the time this statement was made; earlier Colonial Office statements of 1903 did not of course necessarily express his opinions. Against this attack the Foreign Office defended itself as follows: " The exchange of ratifications . . . was a mere formality, which in no way affected the terms of the Convention, and it seems to Lord Lansdowne that after the announcement in His Majesty's speech this formal exchange could not have been avoided, and that no advantage would have resulted from

However angry, and however understandable its anger, Ottawa again had no alternative but to fall in line. Events had proceeded much too far for any other course to be conceivable. Nevertheless the government's pique is manifest in the message of surrender that Minto sent London on March 6:

> If the whole matter were now open to be dealt with entirely from the point of view of Canadian interests my Ministers would hesitate to advise any further participation in the proceedings in which there has been so serious a departure from good faith.
>
> My Ministers have observed from the press, and have also been officially informed, that, while the matter is still under their consideration, the Treaty has been confirmed by His Majesty's Government and an exchange of ratifications has already taken place at Washington. It is presumed that this fact precludes further discussion, and my Ministers will therefore proceed to do whatever is necessary on their part to make good the engagements of His Majesty's Government, but they must reserve the right to submit to the Dominion Parliament the whole correspondence or such a statement of the case as will clearly explain the whole matter, and especially the manner in which the consent of Canada was obtained.[54]

Poor Canada! Step by step she had been beaten down. Laurier's acceptance at London of an even-numbered tribunal had alarmed his colleagues, but in the circumstances they had felt obliged to acquiesce; the Ottawa government had disliked the Hay-Herbert draft and had given very lukewarm approval of its signature, but Great Britain had signed notwithstanding; she had ratified the treaty before informing Canada of the objectionable appointments; and when Canada, learning of them, asked for reconsideration, Great Britain had clinched matters by exchanging ratifications. ". . . the British Government deliberately decided about a year ago," Clifford Sifton concluded,

---

its postponement" (*ibid.*, Villiers to Colonial Office, March 28, 1903). One cannot help wondering, however, if this point was well taken in view of the Foreign Office's remark on February 25, quoted above, p. 315, that Britain had the alternative of "breaking off the negotiations altogether. . . ."

[54] *Ibid.*, to Onslow, telegram received March 7, 1903.

to sacrifice our interests at any cost, for the sake of pleasing the United States. All their proceedings since that time were for the sake of inveigling us into a position from which we could not retire. I am bound to say that we have been pretty easy prey. . . .

It is, however, the most cold-blooded case of absolutely giving away our interests . . . which I know of, and I do not see any reason why the Canadian press should not make itself extremely plain upon the subject.[55]

Such no doubt was the prevailing belief of the Laurier government and throughout the country generally. No wonder that a disgruntled Dominion contemplated the tribunal's forthcoming sessions with apprehension.

[55] Dafoe, *Sifton*, pp. 221-222.

CHAPTER 15

Settlement in Alaska

THE SELECTION by the United States of such known partisans
as Lodge, Root, and Turner raised the question among British
and Canadian statesmen whether they were not now compelled
to make similar appointments to the boundary tribunal themselves. Attempting to soften the Dominion's wrath over the
American nominations, the British government made the ill-
considered suggestion of naming commissioners " appropriate to
the altered circumstances of the case." [1] But Lord Minto, the
Governor-General, although he thought the United States had
behaved " quite disgracefully," had the good sense to disagree;
he saw that if Britain likewise appointed publicly committed
men she would miss an opportunity of showing up the United
States before the world, and the tribunal itself would be stripped
of any remaining dignity and weight.[2] It was partly because
of his stand that Ottawa rejected London's suggestion and asked
for selection of " Judges of the higher Courts, who in the best
sense of the words would be impartial jurists of repute . . .";
it recommended the Lord Chief Justice of England and two
Canadian jurists.[3]

[1] Further Correspondence Respecting the Boundary between the British
Possessions in North America and the Territory of Alaska, Printed for the
use of the Foreign Office. November, 1904. Confidential (8296). Onslow to
Minto, February 26, 1903.

[2] John Buchan, *Lord Minto, a Memoir* (London and New York, 1924),
p. 171; see p. 168 for Minto's unflattering view of American politicians.

[3] British White Paper, *United States. No. 1 (1904). Correspondence*

Having spurned Canada's wishes as to the American members, Great Britain now took her advice. She appointed Lord Alverstone, the Chief Justice; and the Dominion appointed Sir Louis A. Jetté, Lieutenant-Governor of Quebec province and formerly a member of the Supreme Court of Quebec, and (following the death of the original nominee, Justice Armour) A. B. Aylesworth, a prominent lawyer who had refused appointment to the Canadian Supreme Court.[4] Alverstone was a senior permanent member of the judiciary, although as a former Attorney General he was not innocent of political considerations; and Aylesworth and Jetté, even if unshakeable proponents of their country's case, stood at the top of the Canadian legal profession. The three men fitted much more closely than did Lodge, Root, and Turner the description of " impartial jurists of repute "; and no doubt these scrupulous nominations, with the implied rebuke to the United States, gave Canada a pleasant feeling of moral superiority.

Besides letting her colony name two commissioners Great Britain entrusted to it the preparation of the British case.[5] This difficult task was assigned to Clifford Sifton, Minister of the Interior. Its difficulty came mainly from the intrinsic weakness of the principal Canadian contentions; but it came also from the fact that Sifton's American counterpart was that long-standing bane of Canadian negotiators, John Foster. This disputatious individual could be relied upon to have at his finger tips the most exhaustive and meticulous knowledge of every possible argument for the United States.

Under the Hay-Herbert treaty each party could have two months from the exchange of ratifications (from March 3, 1903, that is) for preparing its case; each could have a further two

Respecting the Alaska Boundary. Cd. 1877. P. 47, Minto to Onslow, March 6 and 7, 1903.

[4] United States. No. 1 (1904), p. 48, Foreign Office to Colonial Office, March 11, 1903; Minto to Chamberlain, March 17, 1903; p. 49, Minto to Chamberlain, July 23, 1903. Armour died July 11; he had been Puisne Judge of the Supreme Court of Canada. Alverstone (then Sir Richard Webster) had argued against the United States in the Venezuelan boundary arbitration.

[5] Ibid., p. 48, Foreign Office to Colonial Office, March 11, 1903.

months for preparing its counter-case, a period the tribunal could extend, however, if " necessary by reason of special difficulties which may arise in the procuring of . . . additional papers and evidence "; and each could have two more months for preparing its written argument. Thus six months, barring special difficulties, were allotted to preliminaries before the tribunal convened. Soon discovering she needed more time, Canada through Great Britain asked the United States for another few weeks.[6] The request led to an angry altercation which added one more grievance to the Dominion's already well stocked supply.

Henry Cabot Lodge and Elihu Root wanted to be back in Washington by November, 1903—Lodge to attend a special session of Congress, Root to prepare his War Department's annual report. If the tribunal should convene later than September 3 (six months from the exchange of ratifications) they might not be able to render a decision in time for their deadlines. Consequently they vehemently opposed extension, especially Lodge. To accommodate them Canada dropped her request for more time and delivered the British case on the specified day. However, on receiving the American case and realizing the complexities of preparing a counter-case, she pressed most urgently for an extension:

> With regard to the request for an extension of time, it will be impossible fully to present the reply to the United States' Case unless it is acceded to, and the [Hay-Herbert] Convention expressly contemplates such an application. A refusal of the latter would entail the presentation of the British Counter-Case in an incomplete form, which would be as unsatisfactory to the Tribunal as to His Majesty's Government, and His Majesty's Government cannot think that the United States Government

[6] 58th Congress, 2nd session, Senate document 162. Alaskan Boundary Tribunal. *Proceedings of the Alaskan Boundary Tribunal, Convened at London, under the Treaty between the United States of America and Great Britain, Concluded at Washington January 24, 1903, for the Settlement of Questions between the Two Countries with respect to the Boundary Line between the Territory of Alaska and the British Possessions in North America* (7 vols., Washington, 1903), vol. 5, part 3, pp. 5-7, Herbert to Loomis, March 13, 1903; Herbert to Hay, March 23, 1903.

would be prevented by any question of personal convenience from giving favourable consideration to the request.[7]

Lodge was indignant. Believing that the Canadians, whose dislike for him he well knew, were stalling in order to get rid of him, he asked Theodore Roosevelt to " take a stiff tone " against delay. Roosevelt did not want the controversy dragging on into the presidential elections the next year; he was only too willing to oblige his good friend. Assuring Lodge that Britain had " behaved badly in Venezuela " and would not be permitted to " do any shuffling now," he instructed Secretary Hay to oppose an extension. ". . . if the English decline to come to an agreement this fall, under any pretense, I shall feel that it is simply due to bad faith . . . ," he declared stoutly.[8]

John Hay shared neither his chief's impatience nor his doubts as to Britain's good intentions,[9] but under the lash of Lodge and Roosevelt he had no choice except to stand on the strict letter of the treaty and deny the relevance of the special difficulties cited by Canada; besides, he wanted to present Congress with a decision before it convened.[10] A series of increasingly acrimonious notes passed back and forth between Washington and London,[11] the argument coming to a head when Britain served notice that

[7] Further Correspondence, Lansdowne to Herbert, June 16, 1903.

[8] Selections from the Correspondence of Theodore Roosevelt and Henry Cabot Lodge, 1884-1918 (2 vols., New York and London, 1925), vol. 2, p. 32, Lodge to Roosevelt, June 23, 1903; p. 37, Roosevelt to Lodge, June 29, 1903; E. E. Morison, ed., The Letters of Theodore Roosevelt (8 vols., Cambridge, Mass., 1951-1954), vol. 3, p. 507, Roosevelt to Hay, June 29, 1903; J. A. Garraty, " Henry Cabot Lodge and the Alaskan Boundary Tribunal," New England Quarterly, vol. 24 (1951), p. 471, Lodge to his daughter, July 28, 1903.

[9] T. Dennett, John Hay, from Poetry to Politics (New York, 1933), pp. 359-360, Hay to Roosevelt, July 2, 1903. Hay disliked Roosevelt's aggressiveness; he offered to resign on July 23, 1903, but Roosevelt refused the offer (ibid., p. 360).

[10] Choate papers, Hay to Choate, May 5, 1903.

[11] For the notes see Alaskan Boundary Tribunal, vol. 5, part 3, p. 12, Sifton to Foster, May 15, 1903; p. 14, Foster to Sifton, May 25, 1903; pp. 25-27, Herbert to Hay, June 12, 1903; pp. 27-30, Hay to Herbert, June 16, 1903; pp. 41-42, Raikes to Hay, June 23, 1903. See also Further Correspondence, Lansdowne to Herbert, June 16, 1903.

if the United States did not change its stand she "would be fully justified in refusing to proceed further in the matter. . . ." [12]

Here was indeed ground for grave concern. Was it really possible that agreement would not be reached after all? A failure could have serious consequences. Dangers still lurked in the gold country. If at that late hour with a settlement actually in sight negotiations should collapse, exasperation and impatience would be sure to rise ominously along the disputed frontier. A shot in the night could cause an explosion. In the spring of 1903 Roosevelt's friend, F. W. Holls, was expressing concern lest the thousands of American emigrants to the northwest create an Outlander problem as acute as the one in Johannesburg that had helped bring on the Boer War. [13]

As a matter of fact, however, Britain had no intention of calling off the tribunal. Although she felt obliged to make a show of determination for Canadian benefit, she would not risk a break with the United States. Washington understood this; the danger as seen from there was not that the tribunal would fail to meet but that it would meet later than the President wished. Britain's resolute stand, therefore, called for a resolute rejoinder; and resolution was one quality that never failed Roosevelt and Lodge. They drew up a vigorous warning against delay, in the form of a letter signed by Roosevelt and addressed to the senator. [14] If the tribunal did not reach a verdict by November, the President wrote, ". . . I should ask Congress at its next meeting [in November] to make an appropriation to enable me to run the line on our own theory. . . . When Congress assembles I must be able to report the success or failure of the negotiation so that action can be taken accordingly." [15] Lodge then departed for London with the letter.

[12] *Alaskan Boundary Tribunal*, vol. 5, part 3, pp. 50-52, Raikes to Hay, July 1, 1903; pp. 55-56, Loomis to Raikes, July 6, 1903.

[13] Holls papers, Holls to Stead, March 6, 1903; Holls to de Bildt, April 15, 1903.

[14] Garraty, "Alaskan Boundary Tribunal," p. 471, Lodge to his daughter, July 28, 1903.

[15] *Selections from Roosevelt and Lodge*, vol. 2, p. 39, Roosevelt to Lodge, July 16, 1903.

Arriving there on July 26, he showed this near ultimatum to Ambassador Choate and Henry White—it "alarmed" White—in the expectation that through them the stern message "would percolate through to the British Government. . . ." [16] He called also on Lord Alverstone, Joseph Chamberlain, and Prime Minister Balfour, impressing upon each the President's determination to have a decision by November. All were most cooperative, and Chamberlain promised to put pressure on Ottawa.[17] Roosevelt's letter had probably percolated through by then, adding its weight to Lodge's own urgings. And at this very moment another presidential communication arrived in London, addressed to Supreme Court Justice Oliver Wendell Holmes, then vacationing in Europe:

> I wish to make one last effort to bring about an agreement through the commission, which will enable the people of both countries to say that the result represents the feeling of the representatives of both countries. But if there is a disagreement I wish it distinctly understood, not only that there will be no arbitration of the matter, but that in my message to Congress I shall take a position which will prevent any possibility of arbitration hereafter; a position, I am inclined to believe, which will render it necessary for Congress to give me the authority to run the line as we claim it, by our own people, without any further regard to the attitude of England and Canada.

". . . if you happen to meet Chamberlain again," the President wrote encouragingly, "you are entirely at liberty to tell him what I say . . ."; and it did not need as clever a man as Holmes to take the hint and warn the Colonial Secretary.[18]

[16] J. White, "Henry Cabot Lodge and the Alaska Boundary Award," *Canadian Historical Review*, vol. 6 (1925), p. 340; J. White's statement that Lodge wrote to Roosevelt on July 25 about having shown the letter to Henry White is not correct, for Lodge only landed at Liverpool on the 26th. Garraty, "Alaskan Boundary Tribunal," p. 471, Lodge to his daughter, July 28, 1903.

[17] Garraty, "Alaskan Boundary Tribunal," pp. 474-476, Lodge to his daughter, July 29, 30, 31, 1903.

[18] Morison, *Letters of Roosevelt*, vol. 3, pp. 529-530, July 25, 1903; P. C. Jessup, *Elihu Root* (2 vols., New York, 1938), vol. 1, p. 400. When the

Under the combined influence of these two threatening statements from the White House and the disquieting presence in London of the powerful senator from Massachusetts it was no wonder that the British government ceased talking about postponement. Clifford Sifton had just proposed mid-October as a suitable date for convening; [19] but Britain sided against her colony and agreed that the tribunal would meet on September 3, the earliest date the United States could demand under the treaty.[20] Canada had no recourse but to follow suit; and Henry Cabot Lodge, his mission accomplished, departed happily for sight-seeing on the Continent.

Britain's characteristic deference to the United States stemmed no doubt, in this instance as in others, from the basic requirements of her overall foreign policy that have been noted. Those requirements did not change during 1903. In so far as international developments of that year affected Anglo-American relations, they served to bring the two countries closer together. Since the Venezuelan intervention the German menace had been looming larger, both in London and in Washington. In 1903,

award was rendered Roosevelt wrote exultantly to Holmes: "If you will turn back to the letter I wrote you in July last, and which you showed to Chamberlain, you will notice how exactly the Alaska boundary decision went along the lines I there indicated. I cannot help having a certain feeling that your showing that letter to Chamberlain and others was not without its indirect effect on the decision" (Roosevelt papers, October 20, 1903); see also Roosevelt's letter to Justice White, October 19, 1903 (*ibid.*). See M. A. De W. Howe, *James Ford Rhodes, American Historian* (New York and London, 1929), p. 121, for an account of a meeting at the White House in 1905 at which Roosevelt indicated that as a result of his letter to Holmes the British government "tipped the wink to the Chief Justice." Writers have tended to take the President at his word, but there is little doubt that he was mistaken. The letter to Holmes probably influenced the decision not to postpone the hearings, but almost certainly it had much less influence on the award than did a letter from Hay dated September 20, 1903 (see pp. 332-333).

[19] *Alaskan Boundary Tribunal*, vol. 5, part 3, p. 63, Sifton to Foster, July 29, 1903; pp. 63-65, Foster to Sifton, August 4, 1903; pp. 65-66, Loomis to Choate, August 4, 1903.

[20] *Ibid.*, p. 66, Choate to Hay, August 7, 1903; see also Choate papers, Choate to Hay, August 14, 1903.

moreover, Russian pressure in the Persian Gulf, in Central Asia, in Tibet, in Manchuria was continuing to worry Britain. It was worrying Theodore Roosevelt, too, particularly the pressure against Manchuria. Shortly before the boundary tribunal convened he told Hay that he felt "thoroughly aroused and irritated" at Russian conduct in Manchuria; that he did not intend to back down; and that he was "year by year growing more confident that this country would back me in going to an extreme in the matter." [21] If British-Russian animosity helped to keep the United States and Great Britain together, so did the growing British-French friendship. Since going to the Foreign Office Lord Lansdowne had made it a prime objective to put an end to the years of friction with France; and in 1903 his policy showed definite signs of being successful. In the spring of that year King Edward made his famous trip to Paris, and in July President Loubet visited London. Before many months the Entente Cordiale would be concluded. Americans welcomed the impending rapprochement between their new friend and their comrade of the Revolution. A tendency could be observed, the German chargé d'affaires at London reported unhappily to Chancellor von Bülow, toward a "Dreibund" consisting of the United States, Great Britain, and France.[22]

Roosevelt had now got his way as regards the date of convening; but right up to the award on October 20, 1903, he continued to breathe forth threats about the dire consequences sure to follow a deadlocked decision. These threats were not simply the irrepressible outbursts of a highly-strung, self-righteous man sure of everything but his hold upon the presidency; they were an essential ingredient in his overall strategy. The President's master plan had two parts. He had completed the first when by naming Lodge, Root, and Turner he had made certain the United States at least would not lose; he was now engaged with the second, intended to ensure it would win.[23] To that end he

---

[21] Morison, *Letters of Roosevelt*, vol. 3, p. 520, July 18, 1903.

[22] *Die Grosse Politik der Europäischen Kabinette, 1871-1914* (40 vols., Berlin, 1924-1927), vol. 17, p. 576, May 17, 1903.

[23] See his candid explanation to his son, October 20, 1903 (Roosevelt papers).

wrote a succession of strongly worded letters, addressed to various American officials but intended for the edification of Lord Alverstone, the tribunal's key member. Roosevelt confidently expected the British government to become aware of their uncompromising tone, and he hoped it would then see the advisability of making clear to the Chief Justice its requirement of a decision. His letter of July 16 to Lodge and his letter to Holmes have been noted. These were but two of many such messages.

If the British made difficulties, he wrote another time, he would " declare the negotiations off, recite our case in the message to Congress, and ask for an appropriation to run the boundary as we deem it should be run " (to Lodge, June 29, 1903) ; [24] ". . . I shall probably, if they fail to come to an agreement, bring the matter to the attention of Congress and ask for an appropriation so that we may run the line ourselves " (to Hay, June 29) ; [25] ". . . I do hope she [Britain] will understand that if we can't come to an agreement now nothing will be left the United States but to act in a way which will necessarily wound British pride " (to Hay, July 29) ; [26] " if on the main issue the British hold out and refuse to agree with us I shall at once establish posts on the islands and sufficiently far up the main streams to reduce at all the essential points of our claim to actual occupancy, and shall then ask Congress to appropriate money for at least a partial survey of the territory between the posts. This will not be pleasant to do and it will be still less pleasant for the English . . ." (to Root, August 8) ; [27] in the event of " captious objections on the part of the English, I am going to send a brigade of American regulars up to Skagway and take possession of the disputed territory and hold it by all the power and force of the United States " (to Turner, about August 8) ; [28] " I hope the British will see reason. If they do not, it will be unpleasant for us, but it will be far more unpleasant for Great Britain and Canada " (to Root,

[24] *Selections from Roosevelt and Lodge*, vol. 2, p. 37.
[25] Morison, *Letters of Roosevelt*, vol. 3, p. 507.
[26] *Ibid.*, pp. 532-533.
[27] *Ibid.*, p. 546.
[28] Jessup, *Root*, vol. 1, p. 396.

August 20) ; [29] " I wonder if the jacks realize that while it may be unpleasant to us, it will be far more unpleasant to them, if they force the alternative upon us; if we simply announce that the country is ours and will remain so, and that so far as it has not been reduced to possession it will be reduced to possession, and that no further negotiations in the matter will be entertained " (to Hay, September 21) ; [30] " a deadlock . . . would leave me with no alternative but to declare as courteously, but as strongly as possible, that the effort to reach an agreement having failed, I should be obliged to treat the territory as ours, as being for the most part in our possession, and the remainder to be reduced to possession as soon as in our judgment it was advisable—and to declare furthermore that no additional negotiations of any kind would be entered into " (to White, September 26) ; [31] " I do wish they could understand that this is the last chance, and that though it will be unpleasant for us, if they force me to do what I must do in case they fail to take advantage of this chance, it will be a thousandfold more unpleasant for them " (to Root, October 3) ; [32] " The plain fact is that the British have no case whatever, and when this is so Alverstone ought to be satisfied, and indeed must be satisfied with the very minimum—simply enough to save his face and bring an adjustment " (to Lodge, October 5) .[33]

One can readily understand, in the light of this barrage, why the President was not willing to entrust to his Secretary of State the stern business of drawing boundary lines; John Hay, he felt certain, was much too gentle a person; his own Big Stick was required.[34]

Under the Hay-Herbert treaty the six jurists were required to take an oath to " consider judicially " the questions before them. According to Lord Lansdowne the British government made it

[29] *Ibid.*, p. 397.

[30] Morison, *Letters of Roosevelt*, vol. 3, p. 603.

[31] A. Nevins, *Henry White, Thirty Years of American Diplomacy* (New York and London, 1930) , p. 199.

[32] Morison, *Letters of Roosevelt*, vol. 3, p. 613.

[33] *Ibid.*, p. 616.

[34] White papers, Sullivan to White, October 6, 1925.

a rule when once a case had been committed to a tribunal not to try to influence the verdict.[35] We shall see that it did not altogether follow this rule as regards the Alaska tribunal.[36] As for the American government, far from making a point of not interfering, it seems to have made a point of doing just the opposite. Several of Roosevelt's letters quoted above were addressed to one or another of the American commissioners, two of them during the hearings after they had taken an oath to be impartial; all of them were intended to influence the award. Moreover, after appointing Lodge, Root, and Turner, the President sent them an outline of his views as to the proper verdict.[37] Clearly these were improper communications. Elihu Root, who did not want to serve in the first place, did make some effort to act judicially. His reply to the President's suggestion about the verdict came close to being a rebuke; and in London he tried to create an impression of impartiality by residing in a different hotel from that occupied by the American counsels and John Foster.[38] But solicitude for appearances did not prevent him, and it certainly did not prevent Turner, and Lodge least of all, from consulting on several occasions with Henry White and Joseph Choate (who as ambassador stood in the shoes of Theodore Roosevelt) as to a suitable verdict; and nothing could be more obvious than the fact that the American commissioners developed their findings, not by reference to the true meaning of the treaty of 1825, but by reference to what they thought American public opinion would support. The decision, in short, was not judicial but diplomatic.[39]

[35] Choate papers, Choate to Hay, October 20, 1903.

[36] See the evidence in several pages of this chapter showing that Balfour and perhaps Lansdowne got in touch with Alverstone; see also similar evidence regarding Anderson and Laurier (pp. 335, 336, 338).

[37] Morison, *Letters of Roosevelt*, vol. 3, pp. 448-449, March 17, 1903. Jessup dates this letter March 25 and Root's reply refers to it as being dated then (Jessup, *Root*, vol. 1, p. 395).

[38] Jessup, *Root*, vol. 1, p. 392, Root to Taft, August 11, 1903; p. 395, Root to Roosevelt, March 28, 1903; pp. 396-397, Root to Turner, July 22, 1903.

[39] According to the London *Daily Express*, October 21, 1903, quoted by J. W. Dafoe, *Clifford Sifton in Relation to His Times* (Toronto, 1931),

The tribunal opened as scheduled on September 3, 1903. After taking an oath to be impartial, electing Alverstone president, and agreeing to finish oral arguments by October 9 (Lodge wanted to sail October 21), they adjourned for a few days so preparations could be completed.[40] Four points, known as questions 2, 3, 5, and 7 from their listing in article IV of the Hay-Herbert treaty, occupied most of their attention when they reconvened on September 15. The other three questions were less controversial, and may be disregarded. Questions 2, 3, 5, and 7 were:

" What channel is the Portland Channel? " (Question 2.)

" What course should the line take from the point of commencement to the entrance to Portland Channel? " (Question 3.)

Between the parallel of the 56th degree of north latitude and the 141st degree of west longitude was it the intention and meaning of the treaty of 1825 " that there should remain . . . a continuous fringe, or strip, of coast on the mainland, not exceeding 10 marine leagues in width, separating the British possessions from the . . . ocean . . . ? " (Question 5.)

" What, if any exist, are the mountains referred to as situated parallel to the coast, which mountains, when within 10 marine leagues from the coast, are declared to form the eastern boundary? " (Question 7.)

p. 227, Roosevelt said: " This is the greatest diplomatic victory of our time." Very possibly he did make some such statement, but this newspaper report cannot be accepted as conclusive evidence. See also J. W. Foster, *Diplomatic Memoirs* (2 vols., Boston and New York, 1909), vol. 2, p. 209.

[40] For the hearings see the seven volumes of *Alaskan Boundary Tribunal.* Jacob M. Dickinson, David T. Watson, Hannis Taylor, and Chandler P. Anderson served as counsels for the United States. Hay had asked Choate to serve as counsel; Choate wisely refused, stating that the role would be incompatible with his position as ambassador; see E. S. Martin, *The Life of Joseph Hodges Choate as Gathered Chiefly from His Letters* (2 vols., London, 1920), vol. 2, pp. 220-228. Robert Lansing was solicitor of the American agency; O. H. Tittman, W. C. Hodgkins, O. T. Cartwright, T. J. Newton, and F. R. Hanna were on the American agent's staff. Attorney General Sir Robert Finlay, Solicitor General Sir Edward Carson, Christopher Robinson, F. C. Wade, L. P. Duff, A. Geoffrion, S. A. T. Rowlatt, and J. A. Simon served as counsels for Great Britain; W. F. King and A. P. Collier were on the British agent's staff.

Of these, question 5 was much the most important, for on its answer depended whether or not one or more Canadian waterways would bisect the American coastal strip.

In the case of five of the commissioners the answers did not depend on the extensive arguments that day after day, in tedious speech after tedious speech, were advanced before the tribunal.[41] Aylesworth and Jetté seem to have been as fully (though not as publicly) committed as Lodge, Root, and Turner before ever they reached London. The whole burden of decision thus rested squarely on the shoulders of Alverstone, who was in effect the arbitrator: if he agreed with the Americans the Alaska boundary dispute would at last be resolved; otherwise the tribunal would break up in deadlock, and presumably Theodore Roosevelt would carry out his threats. Beset on the one hand by Canadians prophesying a dismal future for the empire unless he stood with them, as Lord Herschell had done, and on the other hand by Americans warning of ruin for the still fragile trans-Atlantic friendship unless he did just the opposite, the Lord Chief Justice occupied an unenviable position.

As the hearings proceeded, Alverstone's hope to compromise became evident: he would decide for the United States on the main point—whether the coastal strip was broken or not (question 5)—and compensate Canada by awarding her all four disputed islands in the Portland Canal (question 2) and by narrowing the coastal strip to the maximum extent feasible (question 7). Question 5 was never in doubt; the Chief Justice steadily supported the American contention that the coastal strip was unbroken, and the Canadian commissioners appeared ready to accept defeat. Questions 2 and 3 also appeared settled, since Alverstone took "very decisively" the Canadian view and the American commissioners seemed disinclined to make trouble.[42] The disposition of the four little islands was "not a very serious point" for the United States, as Lodge admitted; but for Canada

[41] The decision, Lodge wrote Roosevelt, "does not depend on the arguments" (*Selections from Roosevelt and Lodge*, vol. 2, p. 61, September 29, 1903).

[42] *Ibid.*, p. 58, Lodge to Roosevelt, September 24, 1903.

it was another matter: the islands were believed to have tremendous strategic importance as commanding Port Simpson,
expected to be the western terminus of the Dominion's transcontinental railroad.[43] Question 7, on the other hand, caused
violent controversy until almost the last day. In the opinion of
Lodge, Root, and Turner, Lord Alverstone in resolving to narrow
the coastal strip was attempting the impossible: he was attempting to conjure from the vast welter of Alaskan mountains an
imaginary range by arbitrarily selecting and stringing together
a number of disconnected peaks. They set themselves deter-
minedly against any such procedure. Their opposition did not
stem from conviction as to the meaning of the treaty of 1825,
but from a belief that Alverstone's range was too manifestly
ridiculous to be defended against critics in America. ". . . we
must," Lodge explained to Roosevelt, "as Turner well pointed
out, rest whatever line we are conceding, upon a *tenable* theory
on which we can stand at home." [44]

But how to drive the Lord Chief Justice, a determined man
himself, to a tenable theory? About two weeks after the hearings
commenced, Henry White received an opportune letter from
John Hay; it gave rise to a train of developments that in all
likelihood had a decisive effect in swinging the Englishman to
the American side. In all probability this letter had considerably
more direct effect upon the eventual verdict than did the much
better known letter from Roosevelt to Justice Holmes cited
above.[45] For some time the Secretary of State, as has appeared,
had been subjected to the impatient prodding of Theodore
Roosevelt, ever fearful of a slip-up fatal to his nomination in
less than a year. Just as Hay had felt obliged to refuse post-

[43] Garraty, "Alaskan Boundary Tribunal," p. 485, Lodge to his daughter,
September 25, 1903; White wrote Hay, September 19, 1903: "There seems
to be unanimity in thinking the Canadians have a good case upon the
Portland Canal . . ." (Nevins, *White*, p. 197) ; Further Correspondence,
Minto to Onslow, February 9, 1903.

[44] *Selections from Roosevelt and Lodge*, vol. 2, p. 59, September 24, 1903;
Garraty, "Alaskan Boundary Tribunal," p. 485, Lodge to his daughter,
September 25, 1903.

[45] See p. 324.

ponement of the hearings, so now he felt obliged to intervene again. ". . . this is the last time we shall admit this question to any form of judicature . . . ," he wrote White in words echoing his forceful chief.

> The President, at my earnest persuasion, consented to this Tribunal, because I felt sure we could convince any great English lawyer, that our contention was just. He was not so sanguine, but agreed to try the experiment, to enable the British Government to get out of an absolutely untenable position, with dignity and honor. If the Tribunal should disagree he will feel he has done his utmost, and will make no further effort to settle the controversy. He will hold the territory, as we have held it since 1867, and will emphasize the assertion of our sovereignty, in a way which cannot but be disagreeable to Canadian amour propre. And all the labor of the last few years, to bring about a closer friendship between the two governments will have gone for nothing.
>
> And this, after I have heard from Laurier, and Pauncefote, directly, *that they know they have no case.*
>
> I will not believe it till the verdict is in.[46]

This forthright statement reached White as he was about to leave for a weekend at Balfour's home in Whittingehame, East Lothian. Knowing Hay well, he must have understood that the Secretary could not have brought himself to write so provocatively without grave reason. Presented with such an unequivocal reconfirmation of the President's intransigence, White thought it advisable to ask Root how Alverstone's views were turning. If unsatisfactorily, would Root advise showing the letter to the Prime Minister? As it happened, Root and his two colleagues were seriously concerned over the effect upon Alverstone of a powerful speech just delivered before the tribunal by Sir Edward Carson, one of the British counsels. The arrival of Hay's letter, coinciding with White's trip to Scotland, furnished an opportunity not to be missed. Root advised White to speak frankly to Balfour; "the highest considerations of friend-

---

[46] White papers, September 20, 1903. Hay had written White, April 10, 1903, that a private messenger sent by Laurier to Washington said: "Sir Wilfrid knows, and all of us know, that we have no case"; see C. C. Tansill, *Canadian-American Relations, 1875-1911* (New Haven, 1943), p. 239.

ship between the two countries," he said, "require that the Foreign Office should know how serious the consequences of disagreement must necessarily be. . . ." And Henry Cabot Lodge, in true Rooseveltian style, urged him to suggest that Alverstone be confronted with the practical situation, namely, that if there were no award " The United States will remain in possession of all the disputed territory, and will take possession of any points not occupied." [47]

Accordingly White on the afternoon of Sunday, October 4, had a long talk with his friend the Prime Minister in which he described the grave situation likely to follow a stalemate. Explaining Alverstone's strategic position on the tribunal, he intimated that it was desirable for the Chief Justice to be informed of the Cabinet's anxiety for a decision.[48] His measured warning impressed Balfour deeply. Failure to render an award, the Prime Minister said, would be disastrous; he said, too, that he attached more importance to a settlement than to any other issue before him—a strong statement, particularly when one considers that he was then engrossed with a Cabinet crisis resulting from Joseph Chamberlain's recent resignation and from the Duke of Devonshire's resignation the very day White arrived at Whittingehame. And back in London a few days later, the Prime Minister said much the same thing to Henry Cabot Lodge.[49]

A day or two after this Sunday conversation Balfour's confidential secretary, J. S. Sanders, had two interviews with Lord

[47] Jessup, *Root*, vol. 1, pp. 399-400, White to Root, October 1, 1903; Tansill, *Canadian-American Relations*, pp. 254-255, Root to White and Lodge to White, October 2, 1903.

[48] A. L. P. Dennis, *Adventures in American Diplomacy, 1896-1906* (New York, 1928), p. 155, Hay to Roosevelt, October 29, 1903.

[49] Garraty, " Alaskan Boundary Tribunal," p. 489, Lodge to his daughter, October 9, 1903; C. G. Washburn, " Memoir of Henry Cabot Lodge," Massachusetts Historical Society, *Proceedings*, vol. 58 (1925), p. 341; Nevins, *White*, p. 200, White to Hay, October 20, 1903. Not long before, Balfour had told Carnegie that: ". . . I have no wish, public or private, nearer my heart than that of securing and preserving genuinely good relations with the U.S.A., whom I do not in any sense regard as a foreign community "; see B. J. Hendrick, *The Life of Andrew Carnegie* (2 vols., New York, 1932), vol. 2, p. 194, July 28, 1903.

Alverstone. Although there is no record of what he said and although the Chief Justice did not immediately come to terms with his American colleagues, it seems clear enough that the Prime Minister through his secretary had brought home to Alverstone the dangers of a deadlock.[50] From that time at least, the Chief Justice understood all too clearly the imperatives of an award—which meant his deciding with Lodge, Root, and Turner.

Oral arguments terminated on October 8, 1903, and the jurists had then to frame their decisions. Ten days were required. They met for the first of a series of conferences among themselves at the Foreign Office on October 9. Despite the message from Balfour, the Chief Justice continued to hold firm on narrowing the coastal strip (question 7); he stayed with Lodge, Root, and Turner on the all-important point of the unbroken coastal strip (question 5), and with Aylesworth and Jetté on the Portland Canal line (questions 2 and 3). But he was, or so it seemed to the perturbed Canadians, preparing to shift toward the American position. " I think," Sifton cabled Sir Wilfrid Laurier, " that Chief Justice intends to join Americans deciding in such a way as to defeat us on every point. We all think that Chief Justice's intentions are unjustifiable, and due to predetermination to avoid trouble with United States. Jetté and Aylesworth are much exasperated, and considering withdrawing from Commission."

[50] Nevins, *White*, p. 200, White to Hay, October 20, 1903; White's letter does not make it clear whether it was Sanders or Balfour himself who spoke to Alverstone, but probably it was the former. Nevins, *White*, dates the letter incorrectly on p. 201; and in his quotation of the letter the name Sanders is misspelled. White's account is supported by a letter from Lodge to his daughter dated October 5, 1903 (Garraty, " Alaskan Boundary Tribunal," p. 488) : " Balfour is deeply anxious for a decision, a fact I may say to you in the deepest confidence made known to Lord Alverstone today." Four days later, however, the senator wrote less positively: ". . . I think that fact [Balfour's anxiety for a decision] has reached Lord Alverstone . . ." (*ibid.*, p. 489, October 9, 1903). In addition to Sanders, Sir John Anderson of the Colonial Office is known to have spoken to Alverstone, though he argued not for a decision but for the justice of Canada's case regarding the Portland Canal (Further Correspondence, memorandum of Minto, November 11, 1903).

But Laurier, a moderate and level-headed person, instructed the Canadians to stay on the job and put up a "bitter fight" for the Portland Canal islands, where the validity of the Dominion's case was "beyond doubt. . . . Shame Chief Justice and carry that point," he urged. "If we are thrown over by Chief Justice, he will give the last blow to British diplomacy in Canada. He should be plainly told this by our Commissioners." [51]

After three days of animated discussion the commissioners seemed close to an agreement on questions 2, 3, and 5. On October 12 Lord Alverstone read an opinion favorable to America on question 5, but conceding Canada all four disputed islands in the Portland Canal. Agreement as to the width of the coastal strip, however, appeared as remote as ever, with the Englishman holding fast to his theory of selected peaks, and Lodge, Root, and Turner rejecting it as "fundamentally untenable." Lodge drew the Chief Justice aside and told him "the situation practically, that this was the only chance of a settlement, that if Canada broke off here she would get nothing & that now she might get the Portland Channel but that we could not take his mountains." Nevertheless Alverstone did not budge; if he was going to decide for the United States on the main issue he was going to get as much as possible for the Dominion on the subsidiary points. For two days more the weary commissioners wrangled over question 7; then, discouraged, they decided on the morning of the 14th to adjourn for the afternoon and the next day. "I do not think we shall agree . . . ," Lodge predicted despondently. [52]

A crisis was at hand, so ominous a one that the Americans despatched a telegram sounding out Washington on an eighteen months' adjournment. [53] But first they conferred with White and

[51] Dafoe, *Sifton*, pp. 228-229, Sifton to Laurier, October 7, 1903; the date of Laurier's reply is not given. His instruction to Sifton shows that the Canadian government, too, was not above interfering with the tribunal.

[52] Garraty, "Alaskan Boundary Tribunal," pp. 490-491, Lodge to his daughter, October 12 and 14, 1903; see also his letter to Roosevelt, October 12, 1903 (*Selections from Roosevelt and Lodge*, vol. 2, p. 69).

[53] State Department, Great Britain, Despatches, Choate to Hay, October 15, 1903; although signed by Choate, the telegram was drafted by the three commissioners. It might seem from Alverstone's stubbornness that Balfour's

Choate. A second letter from Hay to White had just arrived, reiterating Roosevelt's familiar refrain that in the event of deadlock the President would "regard our case as proved—and act accordingly"; [54] and the Americans decided that another application of the Big Stick was called for. Ten days had elapsed since Henry White had administered the last one for the benefit of Balfour; it was now Ambassador Choate's turn. Only a few hours after the tribunal adjourned on the 14th the ambassador was closeted with Lord Lansdowne at the Foreign Office.[55]

> I told him [he wrote Hay] that there was a supreme necessity for this boundary question to be settled by this Commission, and that there never would be another opportunity, that the President in signing this Treaty had gone as far as he could possibly go; that he would never in the event of this Commission failing, consent to an arbitration for the settlement of this boundary, and that if he were inclined to do so, as he certainly was not and never would be, the Senate could by no possibility be induced to consent to any such thing . . . . that after having given this opportunity to the Canadians to establish their claim and they having failed to do so, he would have to send to Congress the fact of failure . . . and at the same time he could not hesitate to assume the full responsibility of government over the disputed territory, and must continue to treat it all, as it always had been treated, as United States property, and this he must do openly and emphatically; that now was the last chance to settle the question, that only by the decision of this tribunal, which would be final without

message to him through Sanders had been fruitless. But White's retrospective judgment doubtless had the correct explanation, and the crisis was not as acute as Lodge, Root, and Turner thought: ". . . I only attributed it [the apparent deadlock] to Lord Alverstone's very natural and proper desire to do the best and make all the fight possible for the Canadians on the question of the width of the *lisière*, and I never for a moment doubted that the undercurrent of diplomacy, the force and quiet working of which you and I appreciate . . . , would bring about a decision in the end" (Nevins, *White*, p. 201, White to Hay, October 20, 1903). See also Choate papers, Choate to Hay, October 21, 1903.

[54] Tansill, *Canadian-American Relations*, p. 252; letter dated September 30, 1903.

[55] On that very day Great Britain and France had concluded their general treaty of arbitration, pointing the way to the Entente Cordiale.

any action of the Senate, could Canada get anything whatever of what she claimed.

To this rolling Rooseveltian thunder Choate appended, now in the lighter vein of Henry White, a description of Lord Alverstone's discomfiture, hard beset as he was by his Canadian colleagues; the Chief Justice, he asserted, "was entitled to the support of his own government. . . ." The ambassador left the Foreign Office, satisfied that Lansdowne and Balfour would, " if they had not already done so, tell Lord Alverstone what they thought as to the necessity of agreeing upon that line, and that the present chance of settling the controversy ought not to be lost." [56]

Documentary evidence is lacking that Lansdowne and Balfour did in fact convey the hint; but the sequence of events makes it seem almost certain that if they did not, it was only because they knew the Chief Justice had already been sufficiently indoctrinated. On October 14 Alverstone was still insisting upon his mountain range " with great force & some heat " but the very next day, after Choate's plain words to the Foreign Minister, he went out of his way at a dinner of The Pilgrims in order to assure Elihu Root that he would do his utmost to secure an award. And when all six commissioners reconvened on the 16th following their recess, the Chief Justice displayed the same urgent mood. Hardly had Lodge arrived at the Foreign Office when

[56] Hay papers, Choate to Hay, October 20, 1903. Doubtless Choate did speak to Lansdowne along the lines he described to Hay; but one wonders whether the ambassador, writing after the award had been rendered, did not see the wisdom of overstating the force of his warning to Lansdowne, partly for the sake of the record, partly to clear himself with Roosevelt, whose uncompromising tone he seems to have been copying; Choate may have thought it advisable to demonstrate that he, as well as his subordinate, Henry White, could get results. It should be noted that the ambassador had second thoughts about his report of the interview with Lansdowne in his letter of the 20th; he asked Hay to destroy the letter (Choate papers, October 21, 1903), and then cabled Hay that the report was " possibly misleading. These were only my conclusions not from anything said by him [Lansdowne] but from the necessity of the situation as it then appeared" (Hay papers, October 23, 1903).

Alverstone "looking very anxious . . . bore me off to his own room & told me matters were reaching a crisis & something must be done "; in full conference a few minutes later, he insisted on a decision being reached and despite the sullen ire of Aylesworth and Jetté, who perceived the drift of events, showed himself at long last ready to abandon his cherished peaks.[57]

The verdict was now near. When Lodge and Root appeared at the Foreign Office early on the 17th, Lord Alverstone again hustled them off to his private room; without further demur he consented to a compromise line for the coastal strip they had devised since the previous meeting. But a curious and unexpected development now occurred. On their way to the meeting, the two Americans had stopped at the embassy to get Washington's reply to their suggestion of an adjournment. The President was agreeable, the reply stated, provided announcement could be made that the United States was getting an unbroken coastal strip; in that case he was even willing to give Canada all four Portland Canal islands.[58] The matter is not altogether clear, but it appears that, despite Roosevelt's readiness to yield as regards ownership of the islands, Turner blandly announced at this decisive meeting on the 17th that the Portland Canal line, presumably accepted by all the commissioners five days earlier, and certainly accepted by Alverstone then, must now be redrawn so as to hand over two of the islands to the United States; otherwise the Americans would not sign, and the agreement, at last virtually concluded, would collapse.[59]

[57] Garraty, "Alaskan Boundary Tribunal," pp. 492-493, Lodge to his daughter, October 19, 1903.

[58] Choate papers, Hay to Choate, October 16, 1903.

[59] At least this is what Sifton told Minto three weeks later (Further Correspondence, memorandum of Minto, November 11, 1903) : " He (Sifton) said that the truth of the matter was that he had reason to believe that an attempt would be made by the United States' Commissioners practically to 'jockey' Lord Alverstone, though he did not use that word, and to induce him to believe that if he could come to a favourable decision on certain points connected with the mainland, they would raise no objection to the Portland Channel frontier. He was afraid of this, and mentioned the matter to Sir John Anderson, who saw Lord Alverstone on the matter. Exactly what Sifton expected occurred, Lord Alverstone was induced to take

Up to that late moment the four islands had been considered as a group: either Canada or the United States would get all four. Quite understandably, therefore, the Canadians were outraged when Alverstone, mindful perhaps of the admonition as to Britain's need for an award, reversed his decision of the 12th and voted with Lodge, Root, and Turner to give two of the islands, Kannaghunut and Sitklan, to the United States—a verdict that Sifton called "wholly indefensible" and Laurier "one of those concessions which have made British diplomacy odious to Canadian people. . . ." [60] However that may be, the Lord Chief Justice had ended the boundary dispute.

The resulting award, formally announced on October 20, 1903, was almost wholly favorable to the United States. By a vote of four to two it got an unbroken coastal strip, although not as wide a one as the American commissioners would have liked,

a favourable view of the United States' contentions on the mainland, but when they were required to be correspondingly reasonable on the Portland Channel they got out of it, and when the matter was about to be finally decided, they put up Turner to stand out absolutely for Tongass Passage [running between the islands], on the understanding that if that was not agreed to, they would refuse entirely to come to the Canadian terms. Sifton was also given to understand that Lord Alverstone was under the impression that the Canadian Government hoped for an award, and for a final settlement above everything else. He considered this so important that he saw Lord Alverstone himself on the subject, and explained to him the entire incorrectness of any such view, and that in the event of no award there was very good reason to hope for final settlement by diplomatic action. He strongly impressed upon him that there was no idea of accepting an award irrespective of the rights of the case. . . . Sifton said that . . . they were prepared in recognition of prior occupation by the United States on the Lynn Canal to give the whole of that inlet to the United States, he believed that their argument as to the possession of other inlets would have held good . . . with a firm front shown by us. . . ." I have found no evidence to support Sifton's contention that Turner's demand had been contemplated from an early stage of the proceedings. Regarding this episode see also Dafoe, *Sifton*, pp. 231-232; Garraty, "Alaskan Boundary Tribunal," p. 493, Lodge to his daughter, October 19, 1903; White, "Alaska Boundary Award," pp. 345-346.

[60] Dafoe, *Sifton*, p. 233. For a detailed, hostile analysis of Alverstone's decision see J. S. Ewart, *The Kingdom of Canada, Imperial Preference, the Colonial Conferences, the Alaska Boundary, and Other Essays* (Toronto, 1908), pp. 310-347.

and Kannaghunut and Sitklan islands at the entrance of Portland Canal. To her intense disappointment Canada got nothing but Pearse and Wales islands.

"So it ends," Lodge wrote his daughter gleefully just before he and Turner sailed on the 21st.[61] "It has been a great transaction, more momentous perhaps than the world thinks. The decision is a great victory for us, but better than that is the final removal of the one dangerous question from the relations of two great nations. More I will tell you when we meet, & especially of the courage and fairness of Lord Alverstone, who has had a hard part to play." [62]

It was a bitter defeat for the Dominion of Canada, made the worse by having lost on the Portland Canal where her claim had seemed incontestable and victory assured. Aylesworth and Jetté refused to sign the award, denouncing it roundly as prearranged. "This is not the first time that British diplomacy has proved costly to Canada," declared the Toronto *World*, indignantly accusing the tribunal of being "loaded." [63] "The decision," the *Montreal Gazette* charged, ". . . is due to the imperial desire to enhance American goodwill, to which many Canadian issues have previously been sacrificed." [64] Other Canadian newspapers, too, broke forth in angry and sarcastic comments: "The finding will arouse strong and lasting indignation"; "it was to be expected that Great Britain would consider her own interests rather than ours, and it is undoubtedly to her interest to be friendly toward the United States . . ."; "The genius of British diplomacy and the naval and military strength of Britain will never be employed to thwart the greed of the United States"; "Had we better not make sure of our title to the Hudson Bay coast and the fringe of territory that skirts the Arctic Ocean? Some enterprising American may settle there"; "Canada is that

[61] Despite the consideration of his annual message to Congress (advanced by Lodge in arguing against postponement of the hearings) Root did not sail until October 30; see Martin, *Choate*, vol. 2, p. 236.

[62] Garraty, "Alaskan Boundary Tribunal," p. 494, Lodge to his daughter, October 19, 1903.

[63] October 19, 1903.

[64] Richard Jebb, *Studies in Colonial Nationalism* (London, 1905), p. 49.

portion of North America which the United States doesn't want." [65] Seriously concerned, Governor-General Minto telegraphed the Colonial Office that: " Public and newspapers here assume that decision of Alaska Commission is based on compromise with the United States of America Commissioners, and not on judicial finding. Feeling here very bitter in consequence. Publication of official statement that Case was decided on its merits urgently necessary." [66]

Particularly violent was the feeling toward the Lord Chief Justice. Canadians commonly regarded him as little if any better than a deliberate traitor; and Aylesworth and Jetté made public charges against their former colleague so intemperate that Minto advised the British government that the accusations " require to be stiffly resented." [67] Even the London *Times* called it " regrettable that Lord Alverstone, after coming to a fresh conclusion about the two little islands, did not make the nature of his decision clear to his Canadian colleagues. . . ." [68] Yet the Chief Justice always insisted on the strictly judicial character of his decision. To a letter from Sir Wilfrid Laurier denying that he had acted judicially Alverstone replied: " I desire to state most explicitly that the decisions . . . were judicial . . ."; and several

[65] *Literary Digest*, vol. 27 (October 31, 1903), p. 587. The quotations are from, respectively, *The Globe* (Toronto); *The Daily Witness* (Montreal); *The Evening Telegraph* (Toronto); *The Free Press* (Ottawa); *Montreal Herald*.

[66] Further Correspondence, Minto to Lyttelton, October 26, 1903.

[67] *Ibid.*, Minto to Lyttelton, November 18, 1903; both the Colonial Office and the Foreign Office rejected Minto's advice (*ibid.*, Foreign Office to Colonial Office, December 21, 1903). In a report to the press on October 21, 1903, Aylesworth and Jetté asserted that the two American islands commanded the entrance to Portland Canal and to Port Simpson and therefore destroyed the strategic value of Pearse and Wales islands. Such an outcry was raised in Canada about Alverstone's " treachery " in changing his mind about the islands that the Foreign Office thought it necessary to get a definitive report on the strategic importance of Kannaghunut and Sitklan islands. Both the Division of Military Intelligence and the Division of Naval Intelligence agreed that the two American islands had no strategic value whatsoever. See *ibid.*, October 21, 22, and 23, 1903, for letters of the Military Intelligence Division, War Office, and of the Naval Intelligence Division, Admiralty.

[68] October 27, 1903.

years later he wrote in his memoirs: " The papers [in the boundary case] were very voluminous, and after studying them carefully and hearing all the arguments, I came to the conclusion that I could not support the main contention of Canada as regarded the boundary, and acting purely in a judicial capacity, I was under the painful necessity of differing from my two Canadian colleagues." [69]

Perhaps the key to explaining Alverstone's verdict lies in his comment on Laurier's reproachful remark that " The consideration that the two islands of Sitklan and Kannaghanut have no value whatever either strategic or otherwise is not a judicial consideration and has simply to be set aside." The Englishman rejoined: " I wholly dissent from this view. I am clearly of opinion that in determining judicially the questions submitted to the Tribunal . . . it was our duty to take into consideration the value and importance to the parties negotiating of all parts of the territory to which the Treaty applied." Although many people would deny that the jurists had this duty—and would even insist that their duty was *not* to consider these matters— Lord Alverstone was justified, if such was in fact his conception of the Tribunal's true function, in saying that Laurier had no right to accuse him of deciding on non-judicial grounds.[70]

As one would expect, the United States reacted to the award almost as enthusiastically as Canada reacted unfavorably; and Great Britain likewise rejoiced that the protracted and dangerous controversy, of which she was heartily sick, was finished with.

[69] Viscount Alverstone, *Recollections of Bar and Bench* (New York and London, 1914), pp. 240-241. It may be significant that this statement refers only to " the main contention," whereas the criticism directed against him referred chiefly to his decision on a subsidiary point—the Portland Canal islands. For Alverstone's well known statement in his Guildhall speech, November 9, 1903, see Jebb, *Colonial Nationalism*, p. 46.

[70] O. D. Skelton, *Life and Letters of Sir Wilfrid Laurier* (2 vols., New York, 1922), p. 157. Theodore Roosevelt wrote a defense of Alverstone which is revealing as to the President's frank conception of the non-judicial nature of the award: " If the decision had been rendered purely judicially, *the Canadians would not have received the two islands which they did receive at the mouth of the Portland Canal* . . ." (Morison, *Letters of Roosevelt*, vol. 3, pp. 665-666, to Lee, December 7, 1903) .

Canadian-American relations deteriorated for a while,[71] but that did not worry most Americans in the least. As far as they were concerned, the Dominion was at length getting just desert for a preposterous and dishonest claim.[72] And from the standpoint of Anglo-American relations the award could only be welcomed. It "removes from the field of controversy the one point of serious difference that might possibly disturb the harmony of the two great Anglo-Saxon nations," the *New York Tribune* declared. And whereas north of the border Alverstone was a deep-dyed villain, to Americans he was a shining hero. "What man in the history of either of the two English-speaking peoples will have done a finer or more important thing?" asked the *New York Sun*; and according to the Philadelphia *Press* "Lord Alverstone has done one of those great services to righteousness and humanity which advances the moral standards of a man's time." [73]

Although John Hay was to remain in the State Department almost two years more, until his death in 1905, the boundary award proved the culminating point of his career. It was, he wrote his daughter, "one of the greatest transactions of my

---

[71] Sifton wrote John Foster that he did not anticipate much Canadian bitterness toward the United States (Dafoe, *Sifton*, p. 236); but more trust can be put in Sir Richard Cartwright's confidential remark to Lord Minto that he feared "dangerous demonstrations of feeling in Canada against the United States" (Further Correspondence, memorandum of Minto, November 13, 1903). See also P. E. Corbett, *The Settlement of Canadian-American Disputes, a Critical Study of Methods and Results* (New Haven and Toronto, 1937), p. 22.

[72] Americans would have sympathized with Carnegie's reference to Canada in a letter to Balfour, July 23, 1903: "How would you like Scotland to be flaunting the Stars and Stripes along the border, boasting its allegiance to the Republic; raising objections to your making treaties, as Canada did with the Nova Scotia [Newfoundland ?] and United States treaty; raising what you consider trumped-up claims to territory, as she does on the Pacific Coast, and which she does only because she knows Britain is in reserve behind her? They would never have been heard of otherwise" (Hendrick, *Carnegie*, vol. 2, p. 190).

[73] *Literary Digest*, vol. 27 (October 24, 1903), p. 535.

life." [74] On becoming Secretary of State five years earlier he had set himself to wiping the slate clean of Anglo-American differences and to consolidating the new Anglo-American friendship. Few statesmen have realized their ambitions so completely. With the settlement of the Alaska boundary dispute, after conclusion of the Hay-Pauncefote treaty two years earlier, Secretary Hay could feel confident that he had played a major part in putting relations between the two English-speaking countries on a firm basis not likely to be seriously endangered in the future.

[74] C. S. Hay, ed., *Letters of John Hay and Extracts from Diary* (3 vols., Washington, 1908), vol. 3, p. 282, October 19, 1903.

CHAPTER 16

Conclusion

IT WAS at a decisive moment in British-American history that President McKinley appointed John Hay Secretary of State. The month before, in August, 1898, the armistice in the Spanish-American War had been concluded, the Joint High Commission had assembled at Quebec, and the United States had approached Great Britain informally about building a purely American canal. The recent Klondike gold rush and America's impatient determination to have its own isthmian canal, had created a delicate situation that could easily have become explosive if not handled with the utmost care by British and American—and Canadian—statesmen.

Fortunately, however, the Spanish War had produced for the time being an extraordinary change of attitude toward Great Britain in the United States, so that many Americans who habitually had viewed Britain as the arch-enemy now saw her as a staunch friend, a friend who had rallied to their aid in a time of peril. Fortunately, too, Great Britain herself, beginning to feel dangerously isolated in an increasingly hostile world, appreciated the importance of American friendship. Both countries, furthermore, found themselves sharing the same general approach toward the great current issue of international diplomacy —how to deal with the disintegrating Chinese Empire. Thus realization of the need of an agreement and the possibility of fruitful negotiations coincided. After long discussion, many

346

difficulties, and grievous disappointments, the Anglo-American settlement of 1898-1903 resulted.

Looking back several years after the Alaska boundary award, Theodore Roosevelt told his old mentor, A. T. Mahan, " The settlement of the Alaskan boundary settled the last serious trouble between the British Empire and ourselves as everything else could be arbitrated. . . ." [1] Reciprocity, North Atlantic fisheries, and Bering Sea fur seals—these were in 1903 the only remaining issues of any significance; and they, unlike the emotional canal and boundary controversies, were no longer of a nature to endanger Anglo-American understanding and even Anglo-American peace. Indeed when Roosevelt wrote Mahan in 1911, the fisheries dispute, that oldest of Anglo-American disputes, had already been settled through arbitration, and in that very year an international arrangement was inaugurated for protecting the seals. Although in that year, too, a Canadian-American reciprocity treaty failed, partly because of the Dominion's bitter memories of the boundary settlement, commercial relations between those countries came in time to be regulated under a new American reciprocity.

Other controversies would, of course, occur in future years— concerning, notably, Panama Canal tolls, neutral rights during the first World War, war debts, Far Eastern and Near Eastern policy; but never again, once the clash over canal policy in Central America and once the perils lurking along the Alaska boundary were removed, has an issue arisen that appeared possibly incapable of peaceful settlement. Despite the many disagreements, the Anglo-American understanding that was reached between 1898 and 1903 has proved enduring.

---

[1] J. F. Rhodes, *The McKinley and Roosevelt Administrations, 1897-1909* (New York, 1922), p. 260, letter dated June 8, 1911. Roosevelt was of course delighted with the award; " Congratulate you and thank you heartily on behalf of American people," he telegraphed Lodge, Root, and Turner when it was announced (Roosevelt papers, October 20, 1903) ; see also his letter to Justice White, October 19, 1903 (*ibid.*) .

Appendices

Excerpt from Confidential Foreign Office Memorandum [1]

The text of the identic telegram drawn up by the French Ambassador, and adopted by the meeting [in Washington, April 14, 1898], was received at the Foreign Office on the 15th April. In the course of the day the Austro-Hungarian Ambassador communicated, confidentially, a telegram from M. Hengelmüller, the Austro-Hungarian Representative at Washington, written apparently before the meeting, and strongly urging on his own behalf a collective representation to the same effect as that advocated by the subsequent telegram of the Ambassadors. Count Deym was instructed to ask for our opinion on this suggestion, and whether we should be disposed to join in such a representation if all the other Powers could do so.

Shortly afterwards, the French Minister in London inquired what view Her Majesty's Government took of the identic telegram received from the Ambassadors.

The replies returned to Lord Pauncefote that evening, and to Count Deym and M. Geoffray on the following day, were all to the same effect, viz., that Her Majesty's Government were ready to join in any representation agreed upon by the other Powers in favour of peace, and to express their earnest hope that the declaration of an armistice by Spain might appear to the President, as it appeared to them, to afford an opportunity for a peaceful settlement. But that it seemed to them very doubtful whether it would be wise to express any judgment on the attitude of the United States, or whether such a step would be conducive to the interests of peace.

On the 17th April, after further consideration of the situation at Washington, but without knowledge of the decision taken by other

[1] F. O. 115, 1239. Printed for the use of the Foreign Office, March 8, 1902; see also Lansdowne to Pauncefote, April 9, 1902.

Governments, Her Majesty's Government informed Lord Pauncefote that they considered it better, at all events for the time, to abstain from action of any kind.

Until the recent publication by the German Government, it has never been intimated to His Majesty's Government, either by Lord Pauncefote himself, or by any other Government, that he was supposed to have been primarily instrumental in obtaining the dispatch of the identic telegram. The statement made officially in the " Gazette de Saint-Pétersbourg," that the identic telegram was a translation of Lord Pauncefote's draft is obviously untrue, as will be seen by a comparison of the two texts. It is further to be observed that the message sent by Dr. von Holleben as published in the "Imperial [Official ?] Gazette " corresponds neither with Lord Pauncefote's draft nor with the message drafted by the French Ambassador and adopted by the meeting, but is an independent version compiled apparently by himself, though in substance it conforms to the French draft and not to Lord Pauncefote's. It is important to note that the Austro-Hungarian Government had received an independent suggestion from their Representative at Washington, recommending strongly the course proposed in the identic telegram, without any reference to the opinion of his English colleague, and that neither that Government nor the Government of France suggested that the telegram originated from a British initiative.

His Majesty's Government must, therefore, maintain that Dr. von Holleben misapprehended the share taken by Lord Pauncefote in the discussions of the meeting, and that in any case the responsibility for the identic telegram rested with the meeting generally. It is undeniable that the draft actually adopted varied materially from Lord Pauncefote's original sketch (which he appears, being a ready " rédacteur," to have prepared for the convenience of the meeting), and that Dr. von Holleben's surmise that the suggestion was made by Lord Pauncefote in consequence of an appeal from the Queen of Spain to the late Queen Victoria, had no foundation in fact.

APPENDIX 2

CONFIDENTIAL

Board of Trade to Foreign Office [2]

Board of Trade, *February 2, 1899*

Sir,

I AM directed by the Board of Trade to acknowledge the receipt of your letter of the 25th ultimo, inclosing a copy of a despatch from Her Majesty's Ambassador at Washington, transmitting a draft Convention supplemental to the Clayton-Bulwer Treaty.

With reference to your request to be furnished with the observations of the Board of Trade with regard to the matter, and also to the last paragraph of my letter of the 5th ultimo, I am directed to inclose, for Lord Salisbury's information, copy of a Memorandum and Statistical Tables with regard to the commercial aspects of the Nicaraguan Canal which have been prepared in this Department.

I am further directed to offer the following observations with regard to the terms of the draft Convention inclosed in your letter:—

1. Generally speaking, and subject to the observations made below, the Board of Trade see no objection to the provisions of the draft Convention on commercial grounds. The clause (Article II (1)) guaranteeing equality of treatment appears to be amply sufficient to protect the interests of this country against differential treatment.

With reference, however, to this point, I am to observe that the above Article of the proposed Convention appears to be inconsistent, both with the provisions of section 20 of the Bill introduced into the United States' Senate by Senator Morgan, of which the text was recently forwarded to this Department by the Foreign Office, and also with the terms of the Concessions from Nicaragua and Costa Rica to the Maritime Canal Company on which that Bill is stated to be based. In Appendices I and II of the Board of Trade Memorandum inclosed the text of certain Articles in the Senate Bill and Concessions are set out, from which it will be observed that a reduction of 50 per cent. in transit dues is secured to Nicaraguan and Costa Rican vessels and to other vessels which carry their produce. The Central American Republics are also placed in an exceptional position as regards the closing of the canal to war vessels of their enemies in time of war. These privileges (which formed part of the consideration given by the Company to the Nicaraguan and Costa Rican Governments in return for the Concession) are specially secured by section 20 of the Senate Bill. The Board of Trade recognize that a Bill in progress, with the present form of which they are only imperfectly acquainted, cannot afford guidance in regard to the meaning of a proposed international instrument; but as the ratification of any Convention will rest with the Senate they think it right to point out the inconsistencies alluded to above which might otherwise cause difficulties at a later stage of the negotiations.

I am to add that should it be thought proper to admit the special privileges accorded under the Concessions to the Republics of Nicaragua and Costa Rica as an exception to the general principle of equality of treatment, the Board of Trade see little objection to such a course on commercial grounds, though it might form an inconvenient precedent.

2. In Article I of the proposed Convention the exclusive right of providing for the regulation and management of the canal is left to the United States, subject to the provisions of the present Treaty. This provision would give to the United States the exclusive right to fix the scale of transit dues.

No doubt the interest of the United States in attracting vessels to the canal as well as their large interest in the actual trade and shipping passing through it (which is estimated by the Board of Trade at 46 per cent. in the case of the trade and 25 per cent. in the case of the shipping) may to a large extent be relied on to secure reasonable regulations and dues. On the other hand, as the main proprietors of the canal the United States may desire to keep the dues rather high, and the influence of the American railway interests is likely to be exercised in the same direction.

The Board of Trade have generally held that the Maritime Powers chiefly interested in a canal of this kind should, so far as possible, have some say as regards dues. In the present case their estimates lead them to suppose that of the shipping likely to pass the Nicaraguan Canal at the outset, about 47 per cent. will be engaged in trade to or from ports of the British Empire, and about 60 per cent. will carry the British flag. No further comment is necessary to show the magnitude of the interest of this country in the regulations and charges of the canal.

The Board observe that there is no effective provision in the Concessions for any limitation of transit dues, such as is contained in the Suez Canal Concession, which limits the navigation dues to 10 fr. per ton of shipping and 10 fr. per passenger. It is true that Article 52 of the Nicaraguan Concession provides that the dues shall be reduced if the dividends amount to more than 15 per cent., but this limit is so high that it is unlikely to operate for many years to come.

I am, accordingly, to suggest, for Lord Salisbury's consideration, the desirability of endeavouring to insert in the proposed Convention some stipulations with regard to the limitation of the canal dues.

In case his Lordship concurs in principle in this suggestion, I am to point out that the stipulation might either provide for a maximum limit of dues (which might or might not be the same as that embodied in the Suez Canal Concession), or for a sliding-scale arrangement under which an increase of profits above a certain point should entail a proportionate reduction of dues. If the latter form of arrangement were adopted it would be necessary to provide for the publication of accounts.

On the whole, in view of the difficulty of fixing a reasonable maximum on the information at present available, the Board of Trade are disposed to prefer some sliding-scale arrangement, if practicable, and they would be prepared at a later stage, if desired, to offer more definite suggestions as to the form which the stipulation might take.

3. The above are the only matters specially affecting the Board of Trade to which they desire to draw attention. The Foreign Office have, no doubt, considered the form of Article 1 in so far as its language may appear to affect the rights of Nicaragua and Costa Rica.

As regards the adhesion of other Powers, the Board do not clearly gather from Article III of the Convention whether the proposal is that the signatures of Representatives of other Powers are to be obtained to the present Convention, or that the United States should conclude identical Conventions with other countries. As the position of the canal as regards neutrality in case of a war in which the United States are engaged would probably be different in the two cases, this is a point which appears to deserve attention, but doubtless it has been duly considered by the Foreign Office and the Admiralty.

I am, &c.

Courtenay Boyle

APPENDIX 3

CONFIDENTIAL

Intelligence Division to Foreign Office [3]

The Director of Military Intelligence presents his compliments to the Under-Secretary of State for Foreign Affairs, and, in compliance with the request contained in Mr. Villiers' letter of the 22nd ultimo, begs to forward herewith a short Memorandum in which is briefly set forth, in general terms, the effect on the naval and military position of the Empire by the construction of a ship canal across the Isthmus of Darien, together with some suggestions as to the compensation which, in the Director's opinion, might reasonably be demanded by Great Britain for any concessions made to America in connection with the Clayton-Bulwer Treaty. A few remarks have been added on the financial aspect of the enterprise which may not be without interest.

Sir Thomas Sanderson will not fail to notice that the matter is one which largely affects the navy, and Sir John Ardagh would therefore venture to submit, for the consideration of Lord Salisbury, that it might be advisable to approach the Admiralty with a view to obtaining the opinion of their Lordships on the whole question.

The inclosures contained in Mr. Villiers' letter are returned herewith.

Intelligence Division, 18, Queen Anne's Gate,
London, *January 3, 1899.*

INCLOSURE

Memorandum respecting the Clayton-Bulwer Treaty

The acquisition by the United States, of Cuba, Porto Rico, Hawaii, and the Philippines—their intention to raise their regular army to the number of 100,000—and to make a very large addition to their navy—are alone sufficient to modify very materially the strategical position both naval and military, of Great Britain, in the Atlantic and Pacific, as well as in the Dominion of Canada, in the event of war with the United States.

---

[3] F. O. 55, 392. Printed for the use of the Cabinet, January 10, 1899.

The long land frontier of the Dominion will henceforth be exposed at the outbreak of such a war to an attack from regular forces drawn from a body four times as numerous as that hitherto maintained.

The Imperial fortresses and coaling stations of Halifax, Bermuda, St. Lucia, Jamaica, and Esquimalt; the Atlantic and Pacific ports of the Dominion; the West Indian Islands, the Australasian Colonies, Borneo, Singapore, Hong Kong and Wei-Hai-Wei, will all be subjected to an increased risk proportioned to the development of the naval forces which may be employed to attack them; and this latter risk will be affected in a high degree by the construction of a ship canal at Panamá or Nicaragua, and by the nature of the control exercised over it.

The Clayton-Bulwer Convention of the 19th April, 1850, engages Great Britain and the United States not to occupy, fortify, colonize, or exercise dominion over Nicaragua, Costa Rica, the Mosquito Coast, or any part of Central America; to promote the construction of a canal, and the establishment of a free port at each end, and to protect the canal when completed; to invite other States to enter into similar stipulations; and to extend the same to all interoceanic communications, whether by canal or railway, across the isthmus.

From a commercial point of view, these conditions are excellent; but they have practically acted as an insuperable bar to the construction of a canal, for the following reasons:—

1. It is extremely doubtful that a canal for purely commercial purposes would be a remunerative investment.

2. The American people are fully aware of the great strategical advantage which a ship canal under their exclusive control would confer upon their navy; and have recently had this brought home to them conspicuously by the necessity of their warships having to circumnavigate South America in order to pass from the Pacific to the Atlantic and *vice versá*; and they perceive what an intolerable restriction on their freedom of movement might arise from the control of the canal being shared with this country, or with an international body, or with the Isthmian States.

3. Great Britain considers that the construction of a canal across the isthmus would impair her maritime supremacy, increase the responsibilities of her navy, and conduce to the development of rivals to her mercantile marine.

For many years there has been a growing desire in the United States for the abrogation of the Clayton-Bulwer Convention, but it was felt that the terms were so reasonable and so unequivocal from an international point of view, that if such a claim were submitted to arbitration the verdict would certainly be given for Great Britain. This conviction had, probably, no slight influence in the rejection of the Arbitration Convention, and it may, not unreasonably, be inferred that the Clayton-Bulwer Convention was the rock upon which it foundered.

Both the President and the Senate have revived the canal scheme within the last few days from the stand-point of the United States' control, and in view of the results of the war with Spain it is quite natural that Americans should regard the construction of this link between the Atlantic and the Pacific, as more important and more urgent than before.

Commercial interests, which were formerly the chief factor in the discussion, have now been superseded by the obvious requirements of the new position acquired in the Pacific, and these may be expected to have a preponderating influence in favour of a guarantee by the United States' Government, of the interest on the requisite capital, whether there be a prospect of the enterprise being a paying concern or not.

The maximum liability would probably not exceed 1,000,000*l.* per annum for thirty years, and the advantage to be derived would be cheaply purchased at this price, even on the supposition that the tariff for transit was fixed on so low a scale as to be unremunerative.

In peace a canal with moderate dues would attract a large custom, and confer a great and continuous benefit upon our merchant ships, and it would ordinarily be a material convenience to our ships of war.

But if we were engaged in hostilities with the United States, the advantage would certainly at the outset lie with them, so long as they held the canal.

This is a question for the Admiralty; but even a superficial consideration of it would seem to indicate that the mere existence of such a canal under American control would impose upon us the necessity of maintaining stronger squadrons than we have hitherto regarded as sufficient in these waters.

The practical question now before us is the *quid pro quo* which would be adequate to induce us to consent to the abrogation of the Clayton-Bulwer Convention or its modification in terms which would be acceptable to both parties.

The *sine quâ non* of the United States is exclusive control, to the exclusion of joint or international control. Assuming this concession there still remain many clauses and conditions in the Convention which are susceptible of retention.

Some of the joint declarations might become unipartite, some may admit of modification, and some may be inadmissible.

We, on our part, should expect a sound Arbitration Treaty, adhesion to the open-door policy, a benevolent settlement of outstanding questions in Canada and elsewhere, special consideration for the West India Islands, facilities on the Alaska coast, a readjustment of boundary in the San Juan Straits, and other matters of mutual interest—to receive a treatment calculated to cement the ties and promote the intercourse which should bind us together, and which it is now desirable more than ever to maintain on a secure basis.

Upon some such conditions the commercial advantages which we shall enjoy during a peace of prolonged duration from the use of the canal may more than counterbalance the distant risk to which exclusive American control will undoubtedly expose us in war with the United States.

It is a matter of secondary importance whether the Panamá or the Nicaragua route be selected.

Thirty millions have already been spent on the Panamá Canal, and a like sum is required to complete it. The estimates for the Nicaragua Canal range from twelve to thirty millions. Taking the larger figure, the interest on capital at 3 per cent would amount to 900,000*l.*, administration and maintenance might require 600,000*l.*, making a total annual charge of 1,500,000*l.*

The estimates of tonnage which would pass through vary from 300,000 to 7,000,000 tons annually, while that which actually passes the Suez Canal is 12,000,000 tons, paying a tariff of about 5*s.* per ton.

At that rate, 6,000,000 tons would be required to make an isthmian canal remunerative, or, if the transit tonnage amounted to 1,500,000, a tariff of 1*l.* per ton (which would probably be found prohibitive) would be required to earn the same amount.

It may be surmised that at first the canal would not even pay working expenses, and that there would be no interest earned upon capital for a great many years.

But even if this unfavourable forecast should prove correct, and the capital interest should fall entirely upon a United States' guarantee, it may be contended—and it would probably be accepted by patriotic Americans—that the money would be well spent, and that there would be a prospect of eventually recovering it.

The Suez Canal has cost 24,000,000*l.*, and now pays 20 per cent. on the nominal value of its shares. If the traffic through the American isthmus should ever attain the same magnitude (12,000,000 tons), the receipts at the same rate of tariff would amount to 3,000,000*l.*, which would probably allow of dividends of 8 per cent. upon capital.

National pride and sentiment are strongly engaged in this project, and it may be anticipated that the United States will not be deterred from undertaking it by financial considerations.

J. C. Ardagh, Major-General,
Director of Military Intelligence

December 9, 1898.

APPENDIX 4

CONFIDENTIAL

Admiralty to Foreign Office [4]

Admiralty, *January 5, 1901.*

Sir,

WITH reference to your letter of the 24th ultimo, I am commanded by my Lords Commissioners of the Admiralty to request you will state to the Marquess of Lansdowne, that they have had under consideration the Hay-Pauncefote Convention, which was signed at Washington on the 5th February, 1900, together with the amendments introduced by the Senate of the United States, on which they beg to offer the following observations, which are confined to the naval and strategical issues involved in the event of war with the United States:—

2. The two essential conditions governing the use of the Isthmian Canal at such a time are:—

(i.) The control of the canal would rest with that Power which was able to place a superior naval force in position to command the approaches to either entrance, quite independently of Treaties or Agreements with the United States alone.

(ii.) No belligerent even though in superior naval force, would be able to pass his ships through the canal unless he were assured that the passage could be made with safety.

3. With reference to the first condition it is believed to be the firm intention of the United States to provide herself with a fleet sufficiently powerful to insure to her the command of the Caribbean Sea and of American waters on the Pacific Coast. It is difficult to see how Great Britain can prevent this if the latent resources of the United States are considered.

4. Great Britain unaided can hardly expect to be able to maintain in the West Indies, the Pacific, and in the North America Stations, squadrons sufficiently powerful to dominate those of the United States and at the same time to hold the command of the sea in home waters, the Mediterranean, and the Eastern seas, where it is essential that she should remain predominant. With the accepted relative standard of

[4] F. O. 55, 405. Printed for the use of the Cabinet, January 9, 1901.

naval strength it would be essential in order to place Great Britain in a position to acquire the command of the sea on the coasts of America that the neutrality of the European Powers should be absolutely assured. Whether such neutrality could be absolutely relied upon is a question on which the Admiralty are not in a position to form an opinion.

5. The assurance of a safe passage through the canal which is the second condition, is dependent upon the arrangements made for controlling its working. In the case of the Suez Canal the Board of a French Company, on which Great Britain is represented, manages the traffic; but the Power which commands the sea has assumed control of the weak government of Egypt, and in war time would be able to regulate the traffic if it saw fit. Under the Hay-Pauncefote Convention the exclusive right of managing the Isthmian Canal is vested in the United States' Government; the territory through which the canal passes belongs to a weak Central American State, which, if the necessity arose, would be as much at the mercy of the commanding sea Power as is Egypt at that of Great Britain. If the United States were that Power she would not need to land a man to secure the control, as the management would, under the Convention, be already in her hands. She would be able to pass her own ships through the canal in time of war while denying its use to those of her enemy. Under the amended Convention she would be in a better position in time of war than is Great Britain with regard to the Suez Canal at the present moment.

6. On the other hand, if Great Britain is the commanding sea Power, she would be unable to pass her ships through a canal managed by the Agents of the United States' Government without first removing them and replacing them by her own. This would have to be done either by arrangement with the Government of the Central American State in question, or by dispatching a military expedition, as was done in the case of Egypt.

7. With the exception of the elimination of Article III, the amendments inserted by the United States' Senate appear to be comparatively immaterial, and introduce no new principle into the question. They only strengthen the hold which the United States would have had on the canal under the original Convention, in time of peace, and accentuate the necessity of ousting the United States' Agents in time of war, before British ships can use it.

8. If the canal were fortified, the only change involved would be that the British military forces employed to seize it would have to be larger, and probably more time would be required to complete the work of the expedition.

9. It should be noted that the argument has tended to show that the traffic would be stopped by a superior naval force controlling the sea, but that it could only be kept open by controlling, in addition,

the country through which the canal passed. It may be added, that if the command of the sea were disputed, the traffic could still be carried on, but at considerable risk.

10. Whether it would be worth while for this country, if she had the power, to attempt either to block the Isthmian Canal or to keep it open in time of war with the United States, depends upon the following considerations:—

The strategic effect of an isthmian canal under the Hay-Pauncefote Convention, in the event of war with the United States, would be that the United States might be able to transfer its ships quickly from one ocean to the other.

At the commencement of the war, while leaving sufficient ships to assure the command in British Columbian waters, she might be able to pass the bulk of her force to the Atlantic, where the war would probably be decided, or if her force in the Atlantic were to admit of it, she might be able to quickly reinforce the American squadron on the coasts of China or British Columbia. The United States would derive great advantages from keeping the canal open to her ships.

On the other hand, the advantages which Great Britain would derive from a free passage to her ships of war, if this were possible, would be only secondary, as she has few ships in the Pacific to transfer to the decisive point in the Atlantic, and the reinforcements to China could be more readily sent viâ Suez. The object of Great Britain would be to close the canal to her enemy, which could probably be done efficiently, for all practical purposes, by a blockading squadron, but only completely by military occupation.

11. The Admiralty have not dwelt in this letter on the diplomatic and political issues involved, nor have they referred to the commercial aspects of the case.

12. They, however, take the opportunity of calling Lord Lansdowne's attention to the attached paper written by the President of the United States' Naval War College,[5] which may be considered to represent the official view taken by the American navy on the subject, and shows the great advantages which they hope to gain not only strategically during war, but to American trade during peace, by shortening the distances between the Atlantic ports of the United States and the Pacific ports of North and South America, as well as many of the Asiatic and Australian ports, in a much greater degree than the corresponding distances from England to the same places, which will enable them to compete with the British carrying trade on advantageous terms.

[5] Not printed; the article referred to is C. H. Stockton, " The American Interoceanic Canal. A Study of the Commercial, Naval, and Political Conditions," *Proceedings of the United States Naval Institute*, vol. 25 (1899), pp. 753-797.

13. To sum up the situation from a purely naval and strategical point of view, it appears to my Lords that the preponderance of advantage from the canal would be greatly on the side of the United States, and that, in case of war between Great Britain and the United States, the navy of the United States would derive such benefits from the existence of the canal, that it is not really in the interests of Great Britain that it should be constructed.

I am, &c.

Evan MacGregor

APPENDIX 5

CONFIDENTIAL

Memorandum on the Amendments proposed by the Senate of the United States to the Hay-Pauncefote Convention of February 5, 1900 [6]

My despatch of the 14th instant to Lord Pauncefote contains a full account of Mr. Choate's explanation of the amendments made by the Senate in the Hay-Pauncefote Convention. His argument was, in fact, an appeal to our forbearance, and an attempt to minimize the practical importance of the amendments.

The despatch deals at some length with the second and third amendments.

The effect of the first (that in Article II, which declares the Clayton-Bulwer Treaty to be "hereby superseded") can best be understood by reference to the attached copy of the Treaty, in which I have marked the only provisions which, so far as I have been able to ascertain, are not replaced by new provisions covering the same ground in the Hay-Pauncefote Convention.

Although the Convention has been constantly described as supplementary to the Treaty, and although it contains frequent references to the latter, it is a self-contained instrument, and its provisions do in effect almost entirely supersede those of the Treaty.

I doubt whether these surviving provisions of the Clayton-Bulwer

[6] F. O. 55, 405. Printed for the use of the Cabinet, January 16, 1901.

Treaty, which are only two in number, and which are marked A and B, are of much use to us.

Under A, the surviving provision in Article I the two Powers agreed that neither would occupy, or fortify, or colonize or assume or exercise any dominion over any part of Central America, nor attain any of the foregoing objects by protection afforded to, or alliance with, any State or people of Central America.

There is no similar Agreement in the Hay-Pauncefote Convention. If, therefore, the Treaty be abrogated *en bloc* both Powers will recover their freedom of action in Central America. We should be free to extend the limits of British Honduras, and to resume the Protectorate over the Mosquito Coast.

Whether we should be likely to avail ourselves of this liberty, and whether its restoration is of any value to us, is more than doubtful.

For the United States, on the other hand, the recovery of their rights might have a substantial importance, while as a matter of sentiment it would certainly seem, in the estimation of the American people, an important diplomatic achievement.

Under the other surviving portion of the Treaty (part of Article VI) provision is made for Treaties with the Central American States in furtherance of the object of the two Powers, and for the exercise of good offices should differences arise as to the territory through which the canal will pass.

But as it is expressly stipulated in Article I of the Hay-Pauncefote Convention that the canal is to be constructed " under the auspices " of the United States, and as the whole object of the Convention is to give to that Power an undivided interest in all that concerns its construction, I find it difficult to conceive that we should ever desire, in virtue of this provision of the earlier document, to enter into stipulations with the Central American States, or to assert a Treaty right to use our good offices with them for the purpose of facilitating the execution of " the great design." There is, moreover, nothing in the Convention to prevent us, if we were so minded, from entering into communication, or exercising our good offices, with the Central American States, in case difficulties should hereafter arise between them and the United States.

I therefore regard the retention of provision B as of no value to us, and if the third amendment stood alone I should be in favour of coming to terms with regard to it.

We might perhaps re-enact in the Convention any parts of A and B which seemed to us really worth retaining, and then agree to the abrogation of the Clayton-Bulwer Treaty. That contract has for half a century been cordially detested in America, and the United States' Government would probably sacrifice something in order to be able to say that they had finally got rid of it.

The other two amendments present more formidable difficulties.

I have already circulated the important Memorandum prepared by the Admiralty as to the naval and strategical aspects of the case. The Memorandum shows that, while the Davis amendment would strengthen the hold of the United States upon the canal, it would probably not do so very materially. This important admission should not be lost sight of.

On the other hand, Senator Lodge's argument, quoted with approval by Mr. Choate, appears to me to have considerable force. If the United States' Government were under no international obligations in the matter, we could not blame them for insisting upon their right to take the necessary steps for defending their own canal in the event of their being threatened by another Power. We could not, if they were free agents, expect them to bind themselves by a contract which they intended to respect not to interfere in such a case with the canal or its surroundings.

During the course of our negotiations with the French Government in 1887 we constantly insisted that the Khedive and the Sultan were entitled to the right of taking measures for the defence of Egypt, in spite of anything contained in certain Articles of the Convention. We even urged that they were entitled to call in allies to assist them.

It is true that the Khedive and the Sultan are the territorial Rulers of the country traversed by the Suez Canal, and that the United States' Republic do not own the territory which the Nicaragua Canal will traverse.

On the other hand, Article I of the Hay-Pauncefote Convention gives the United States the right of constructing the canal under " the auspices " of their own Government, as well as " all rights incident to such construction, as well as *the exclusive right of providing for the regulation and management of the canal*." These reservations, and the fact that the canal is to be built with American money, would, I think, justify the United States' Government in contending that what was reasonable in the one case would not be unreasonable in the other, were it not for the fact that by the Clayton-Bulwer Treaty we and the United States have already bound ourselves to respect the neutrality of the canal in all circumstances. It is now suggested that this obligation should remain in force so far as we are concerned, and that the United States should be released from it. The result of such a one-sided arrangement deserves attentive examination. It would, as I pointed out to Mr. Choate, result that, while we should be debarred by Treaty from any warlike action in or around the canal, the United States would be able to resort to such action to whatever extent they might deem necessary in order to secure their own safety. In other words, we should be in a worse position than if we had no Treaty at all.

The attempt to show that Article II (7) of the Convention, which forbids the fortification of the canal, would counteract the Davies [*sic*] clause, seems to me to fail entirely. The two Rules are inconsistent, and I am satisfied that the " defence " clause can be so interpreted as to make the " fortification " clause of no avail.

The invidiousness of the Davies [*sic*] amendment stands out in stronger relief when we come to consider the effect of the third amendment. This strikes out Article III of the Convention, under which the Contracting Parties are bound to invite the adhesion of the other Powers, who will therefore not be subject to the Self-denying Ordinance which we are to accept. It follows that while France and Russia could with a clear conscience disregard any of the restrictions imposed by the Convention, and while the United States would by the express provisions of the new Convention retain the right of deneutralizing it, Great Britain alone, in spite of her vast maritime interests, in spite of her Colonial possessions in Australia and North America, would be precluded from taking steps to secure her interests in this important waterway.

If any modification of the Convention, such as the Davis amendment, is to be taken into consideration by us, we shall certainly have to insist upon qualifying it by the addition of a clause corresponding with Article XI of the Suez Canal Convention.

But for the present I recommend that a despatch be addressed to Lord Pauncefote recapitulating the history of the negotiations and the reasons for which the amendments of the Senate seems [*sic*] to us inadmissible.

If our refusal should retard the construction of the canal, we need not trouble ourselves with regrets. There can be no question that the existence of an Isthmian Canal, whether neutralized or defended, will strategically be disadvantageous to us. The Admiralty Memorandum which I have already quoted is, I think, conclusive on this point; and the official literature of the United States is not less convincing.

Should the Convention fall through, and the United States decide to persevere with the project, we shall, of course, contend that the Clayton-Bulwer Treaty remains in force. It will, I think, be impossible for the United States' Government to dispute this in the face of their repeated admissions. But the Hepburn Bill, or some such measure authorizing the construction of the canal, would no doubt in that event be passed.

My impression, however, is that if Lord Pauncefote uses firm but conciliatory language in the sense which I have suggested, an alternative proposal will be made to us on the part of the United States' Government.

L. [Lansdowne]

Foreign Office,
January 15, 1901.

APPENDIX 6

Memorandum [7]

Our refusal to accept the amendments inserted by the Senate in the Hay-Pauncefote Convention has led, as we anticipated, to a further proposal on the part of the United States' Government. I circulate, with an explanatory Memorandum by Mr. Villiers, a new draft Convention which Mr. Hay has prepared in consultation with a number of prominent Senators, and which Lord Pauncefote has been asked to submit to us privately in the first instance.

Lord Pauncefote's opinion may, I think, be summarized as follows:

He thinks the Senate would probably accept the new draft as it stands. He believes that an attempt to recast it would probably be fatal to its chance, and he inclines to the view that with one or two amendments which he suggests, the new addition might be accepted by His Majesty's Government.

We should, I believe, all of us be glad to find an amicable solution of this troublesome question. The conditions are, moreover, more favourable than they were, for whereas the inconsiderate action of the Senate last year justified us then in insisting on our strict rights and in pressing our objections to the utmost, it is open to us, now that we are approached in a very different spirit by Mr. Hay, to deal somewhat less strictly with him so far as matters of form are concerned. We ought also to take into account the fact that Mr. Hay has laid before us not only this draft of a Convention relative to the construction of the Interoceanic Canal, but also a scheme for determining the Alaska boundary by arbitration, and a draft Treaty dealing with a number of the outstanding Canadian questions which we had hoped to settle in 1899, but which were left open by the Joint High Commission appointed in that year [*sic*].

On the other hand, however much we may desire an amicable settlement, it will be impossible for us to abandon abruptly the strong position which we took up in our despatch of the 22nd February, a despatch which was regarded with approval here, and was admitted in the United States to be a moderate and reasonable statement of the British Case.

---

[7] F. O. 55, 406. Printed for the use of the Cabinet, July 8, 1901.

In form the new draft differs from the old Convention, under which the High Contracting Parties, after agreeing that the canal might be constructed by the United States, agreed to adopt certain rules as the basis upon which the canal was to be neutralized. In the draft now before us the United States intimate to us *their* readiness to adopt somewhat similar rules as the basis of the neutralization of the canal. I do not know, however, that this change of form is one to which we need seriously object.

The three amendments inserted by the Senate, and objected to by us in our despatch of the 22nd February, 1901, are dealt with as follows:—

(A.) *Supersession of the Clayton-Bulwer Treaty.*

As to this amendment we stand where we did, for the Treaty is superseded in the first Article of the new draft.

I pointed out, however, in a Memorandum circulated to the Cabinet on the 15th January, 1901,[8] that the Hay-Pauncefote Convention in its original form contained provisions which did in effect almost entirely supersede those of the Treaty. I showed that there were only two provisions of the Treaty which were not covered by the Convention, and that neither of them were of great importance to us, and I said that if this amendment had stood alone I should have been in favour of coming to terms with regard to it. In our despatch we objected to the amendment, not so much upon the ground that it would be materially injurious to us, as upon the ground that the Treaty was an international contract of unquestionable validity, and that, according to well-established national usage, it ought not to be abrogated or modified, save with the consent of both the parties to the contract. So far as this amendment was concerned, our complaint had reference rather to form than to substance.

Lord Pauncefote's new Article III provides for the case in which the sovereignty of the territory through which the canal is intended to pass might fall into the hands of the United States, or of any other foreign Power. I do not see how the United States could object to this stipulation. They could scarcely contend that a change in the ownership of the territories adjoining the canal would relieve them of their obligation to maintain its neutrality.

(B.) *Reservation by the United States of the Right to Defend the Canal.*

To this amendment we objected very decidedly (see despatch [February 22, 1901], p. 3). The objectionable provision does not appear in the

[8] Appendix 5.

present draft, from which, however, is also omitted Rule 7 of Article II of the original Convention, under which the Contracting Parties were forbidden to fortify the canal. The two Rules were, as I pointed out at the time, antagonistic. I think we may be content to have them both omitted; but attention will, no doubt, be called to the omission of Rule 7, as suggesting that the right to fortify is not renounced.

The Rule against fortification was, I believe, of no practical value to us: the United States would not be likely to spend money on expensive works at the mouth of the canal or throughout its course, nor, if they did, would the control of the canal in time of war depend upon the presence or absence of such works.

(C.)   *The High Contracting Parties not to be obliged to bring the Convention to the notice of other Powers and to invite them to adhere to it.*

The Article excised by this amendment has not been restored, and as to it we stand where we did in the spring. It will, I think, be impossible for us to agree to give way altogether upon this point, but Lord Pauncefote's proposal for dealing with the matter seems to me sufficiently to meet the requirements of the case. If his words are added to Article III, Rule 2 [marginal query: 1 ?], it will no longer be possible for us to contend, as we contended in our despatch, that we should be placed in a position of marked disadvantage compared with other Powers.

Any Power which gives its adherence will incur the obligation to observe the Rules described in Article III, and no non-adhering Power will be able to claim a right to use the canal.

The omission of the words " in time of war as in time of peace," from Article III, Rule I, is the alteration which we shall find most difficult in justifying. The fact that the words occur in the original text renders their disappearance significant. Were it not for this, we might rely upon the fact that there are no limiting words in Article I, which, therefore, might be presumed to apply in time of war as well as in time of peace, that in Article II it is said that the canal shall " *never* be blockaded, &c.," and that in Article VI it is stipulated that the plant, establishment, buildings, &c., of the canal shall " in time of war as in time of peace " enjoy complete immunity from attacks or injury by belligerents, and from acts calculated to impair their usefulness as part of the canal. But it will not be forgotten that throughout the discussions which have taken place in the United States, prominent politicians have constantly insisted that under no circumstances could the United States preclude themselves from the right of adopting, when their country was at war, whatever measures were best calculated to secure its safety, even if such measures involved temporary deneutralization of the canal. The United States could not, it was said, refuse to take such measures, when the time came, without dereliction of duty, and they would be dishonest if they promised not to take them without the intention of keeping their word.

As a matter of practical politics I do not think we need object. Assuming the United States and Great Britain to be at war and assuming a British ship of war to have forced its way through the squadron which might be watching one end of the canal, could we expect the United States to give that ship facilities for passing through the canal from end to end in order that she might, as soon as she re-entered extra-territorial waters, renew her attack upon American shipping? Or, again, should we, if we were at war with the United States, be in the least likely to risk the safety of our ships by endeavouring, even if the canal were ostensibly open, to pass them through it? The Admiralty, in a paper which was circulated to the Cabinet, have advised us that the real control of the canal will probably remain with that Power which is able to place a superior naval force in a position to command the approaches to its entrances, and that no belligerent, even in superior naval force, would attempt to pass his ships through the canal unless he could be sure that the passage could be made with safety. The latter condition is never likely to be present while the United States hold the banks. It seems to me, therefore, that for all practical purposes, we should in substance gain nothing, even if we were to secure on paper the right of passing our ships through the canal in time of war as well as in time of peace.

I quote in support of this view the following passage from a paper entitled " An Isthmian Canal from a Military Point of View," [9] read before the American Academy of Political and Social Science: —

" An isthmian canal, to be of service to the United States, presupposes that passage to it, through it, and from it is assured. But passage to or from it in case of war with a strong naval Power could only be maintained by a strong naval force. If the canal bristled with guns from one end to the other, it would be of no use to the United States while a powerful hostile fleet dominated the Carribean [sic] Sea. The nation that controls the adjoining seas will in time of war control passage through the canal, no matter which one has possession."

The despatch of the 22nd February does not seem to me to tie our hands, should we desire to concede this point now. In that despatch, we showed reasons against a unilateral arrangement, under which the United States would enjoy the right, not enjoyed by the other Con-

[9] P. C. Hains, " An Isthmian Canal from a Military Point of View," *Annals of the American Academy of Political and Social Science*, vol. 17 (1901), pp. 397-408. Punctuation and spelling are slightly different in the above excerpt as compared with the original article.

tracting Party, of taking, even in time of peace, whatever steps they thought necessary for the purpose of defending the canal. Under the present proposal no such right is sought by the United States, although the draft is so worded as to render it possible for them to contend, when war has actually broken out, that they are no longer bound by any of the Rules which govern its neutralization. In such a case, however, we should be entirely emancipated from the restrictions now imposed upon us by the Clayton-Bulwer Treaty, and should find ourselves equally free with the United States to act in whatever way we thought best for our own interest.

L. [Lansdowne]

Foreign Office,
July 6, 1901.

Bibliographical Note

To a very considerable extent the present book is based on archival material of the United States Department of State and the British Public Record Office. These enormous collections are indispensable for any study of Anglo-American diplomatic relations. Of the two I have found the British material more informative. This is partly because it is less well known; unlike the State Department material, it has hardly been used at all by other writers on subjects relating to American history around the turn of the century. The British material thus supplements and sometimes corrects conclusions derived from non-British sources alone. But I have also found the British material more informative simply because it is more voluminous. Besides the usual diplomatic correspondence, it includes a vast amount of correspondence between the Colonial Office and Ottawa, which is most enlightening with respect to Canadian-American controversies. The principal series in the Public Record Office concerning Anglo-American relations around 1900 are F. O. 5 and F. O. 115; other noteworthy series are F. O. 55, F. O. 80, and C. O. 42. This Public Record Office material is not at present available to the student for dates after 1902, but the Foreign Office kindly permitted me to use its unpublished 1903 *Further Correspondence Respecting the Boundary between the British Possessions in North America and the Territory of Alaska* (Confidential, 8296), which has a great deal of information about the Alaska boundary controversy. Some of the British archival material has been published in: G. P. Gooch and H. Temperley, eds., *British Documents on the Origins of the War, 1898-1914* (11 vols., London, 1926-1938); White Paper, *United States. No. 1 (1898)*. *Despatch from Professor D'Arcy Thompson Forwarding a Report on His Mission to Behring Sea in 1897*. Cd. 8702; White Paper, *United States. No. 2 (1898)*. *Joint Statement of Conclusions Signed by the British, Canadian, and United States' Delegates Respecting the Fur-Seal Herd Frequenting the Pribyloff Islands in Behring Sea*. Cd. 8703; White Paper, *United States. No. 1 (1900)*. *Convention between Her Majesty and the United States of America Supplementary to the Convention of April 19, 1850, Relative to the Establishment of a Communication by Ship-Canal between the Atlantic and Pacific Oceans. Signed at Washington, February 5, 1900*. Cd. 30; Blue Book, *China. No. 1 (1900)*. *Further Correspondence Respecting the Affairs of China*. Cd. 93; White Paper, *China.

369

No. 2 (1900). Correspondence with the United States' Government Respecting Foreign Trade in China. Cd. 94; White Paper, *United States. No. 1 (1901). Correspondence Respecting the Convention Signed at Washington, February 5, 1900, Relative to the Establishment of a Communication by Ship Canal between the Atlantic and Pacific Oceans.* Cd. 438; Blue Book, *Venezuela. No. 1 (1903). Correspondence Respecting the Affairs of Venezuela.* Cd. 1399; White Paper, *United States. No. 1 (1904). Correspondence Respecting the Alaska Boundary.* Cd. 1877; White Paper, *United States. No. 2 (1904). Map to Accompany Correspondence Respecting the Alaska Boundary.* Cd. 1878.

As for the State Department documents, particularly useful are the Instructions to, and the Despatches from, the American embassy in London. The Notes, consisting of correspondence with the British embassy in Washington, and the Miscellaneous Letters also contain considerable information. Among the State Department's archives are Reciprocity Treaties, 1898-1907, Canada, John A. Kasson papers. As the Department's expert on reciprocity, Kasson played a prominent part in commercial negotiations with Britain and Canada. The State Department's papers on the Alaskan Boundary Convention and its Miscellaneous Archives, Alaskan Boundary, 1899-1903, and Miscellaneous Archives, Boer War, 1900-1902, are important sources. Some of the American archival material has been published in: the annual series, *Foreign Relations of the United States*; 58th Congress, 2nd session, Senate document 162, *Proceedings of the Alaskan Boundary Tribunal, Convened at London, under the Treaty between the United States of America and Great Britain, Concluded at Washington January 24, 1903, for the Settlement of Questions between the Two Countries with respect to the Boundary Line between the Territory of Alaska and the British Possessions in North America* (7 vols., Washington, 1903); 63rd Congress, 2nd session, Senate document 474, *Diplomatic History of the Panama Canal.*

Other relevant diplomatic correspondence may be found in *Die Grosse Politik der Europäischen Kabinette, 1871-1914* (40 vols., Berlin, 1924-1927); E. T. S. Dugdale, ed., *German Diplomatic Documents, 1871-1914* (4 vols., London, 1928-1931); *Amtliche Aktenstücke zur Geschichte der Europäischen Politik, 1885-1914* (*Die Belgischen Dokumente zur Vorgeschichte des Weltkrieges*) (5 vols., Berlin, 1925). The *Congressional Record, Parliamentary Debates,* and *Debates of the House of Commons,* Canada, though not especially important for this present book, are occasionally useful.

In the Library of Congress's Manuscript Division I used particularly the papers of John Hay, Joseph Choate, and Henry White. The papers of William McKinley and Theodore Roosevelt were also helpful. Many of the Roosevelt papers have been published in *Selections from the Correspondence of Theodore Roosevelt and Henry Cabot Lodge, 1884-*

1918 (2 vols., New York and London, 1925) and E. E. Morison, ed., *The Letters of Theodore Roosevelt* (8 vols., Cambridge, Mass., 1951-1954). The papers of G. W. Smalley, also in the Library of Congress, are very occasionally of use. The papers of F. W. Holls, in the Butler Library, Columbia University, contain much of interest, especially in connection with the negotiation of the Hay-Pauncefote Treaty. W. W. Rockhill's papers, in the Harvard University Library, are of significance for the present study only in connection with the Open Door Policy. Christ Church Library, Oxford University, has recently acquired and started to classify the papers of Prime Minister Lord Salisbury. Though the bulk of Salisbury's correspondence concerned European affairs, there are several volumes relating to America, and these, hitherto not available to the scholar, are of great importance for the study of Anglo-American relations. Many of the letters between Salisbury and Paunce-fote are in this collection rather than in the Public Record Office. The papers of Sir Wilfred Laurier, in the Public Archives of Canada, are very extensive, but those I used contain little pertinent material beyond that available in the Colonial Office records.

There would be little point in listing the newspapers that I used. *The Times* of London occupies a special place because of its occasional prompting by the government but even more because its American correspondent, G. W. Smalley, had an extraordinary influence upon Anglo-American relations through his friendship with leaders in both countries and through his many influential articles in *The Times*, often more in the nature of exhortations to the British government and people than of factual reports.

There are many books with material about Anglo-American relations around 1900; I shall mention only those most closely connected with the present book. The only general survey of diplomatic relations between Britain and America at that time is L. M. Gelber, *The Rise of Anglo-American Friendship: a Study in World Politics, 1898-1906* (London, 1938); as the title suggests, it deals almost as much with world politics as with the rise of friendly relations. Gelber used only published material; although excellent for its overall picture and especially for its account of the international setting, the book is incomplete and defective in places when measured against information available in British and American archives.

The best source of information about the Canadian side is C. C. Tansill's *Canadian-American Relations, 1875-1911* (New Haven, 1943). Whatever doubts may be entertained about some of Tansill's interpretations, one must be grateful for this painstaking digest of a mass of archival material, a digest that saves much time and effort for anyone working in the field.

No study of American diplomacy around 1900 can avoid reference to A. Vagt's exhaustive *Deutschland und die Vereinigten Staaten in der Weltpolitik* (2 vols., New York, 1935). An older, but still useful study is A. L. P. Dennis, *Adventures in American Diplomacy, 1896-1906* (New York, 1928).

Adequate accounts exist of most of the statesmen and other leaders who played prominent parts in Anglo-American relations around the turn of the century. T. Dennett, *John Hay, from Poetry to Politics* (New York, 1933), portrays the Secretary of State sympathetically and deals perspicaciously with several topics concerning Britain and America. W. R. Thayer's *The Life and Letters of John Hay* (2 vols., Boston and New York, 1915) cannot stand up to critical analysis but contains a good many of Hay's letters. Hay's wife, C. S. Hay, edited *Letters of John Hay and Extracts from Diary* (3 vols., Washington, 1908). A. Nevins, *Henry White, Thirty Years of American Diplomacy* (New York and London, 1930), is informative both about an influential figure in British-American affairs and about many episodes of the time. Hay's successor at the London embassy was Joseph Choate. Little of value has been published about this outstanding ambassador; but some general information can be found in E. S. Martin, *The Life of Joseph Hodges Choate as Gathered Chiefly from His Letters* (2 vols., London, 1920). The two American Presidents during the period 1898-1903 were William McKinley and Theodore Roosevelt. Unfortunately their biographies throw little light upon Anglo-American relations. The best biography of McKinley is C. S. Olcott, *The Life of William McKinley* (2 vols., Boston and New York, 1916); a more recent one is W. C. Spielman, *William McKinley, Stalwart Republican* (New York, 1954). J. B. Bishop's sympathetic study, *Theodore Roosevelt and His Time, Shown in His Own Letters* (2 vols., New York, 1920), and H. F. Pringle's better but more hostile *Theodore Roosevelt, a Biography* (New York, 1931) are useful for their portrayals of a curious personality rather than for their slight information about the United States and Great Britain. A good short account is J. M. Blum, *The Republican Roosevelt* (Cambridge, Mass., 1954). Using the Lodge papers, J. A. Garraty wrote an illuminating and sympathetic study of a major figure: *Henry Cabot Lodge, a Biography* (New York, 1953). P. C. Jessup, *Elihu Root* (2 vols., New York, 1938), is excellent on Root and has some material on the Alaska boundary controversy. G. W. Smalley's *Anglo-American Memories, Second Series* (New York and London, 1912) is of significance because written by the prominent American correspondent of the London *Times.* J. W. Foster, *Diplomatic Memoirs* (2 vols., Boston and New York, 1909), has chapters on the Bering Sea troubles, the Alaska boundary dispute, and other Canadian affairs; though not especially revealing, they show the opinions of one of the principal participants. H. K. Beale, *Theodore Roosevelt and the Rise of America to World Power* (Baltimore, 1956), has some material on Roosevelt and Anglo-American relations.

Lady Gwendolen Cecil's notable biography of her father, *Life of Robert, Marquis of Salisbury* (4 vols., London, 1921-1932), stops short of the period covered in my book but gives a remarkable picture of the Prime Minister. However, neither it nor A. L. Kennedy's *Salisbury, 1830-1903, Portrait of a Statesman* (London, 1953), a good short study that carries the story to Salisbury's death, has any direct bearing on Anglo-American relations between 1898 and 1903. B. E. C. Dugdale's *Arthur James Balfour, First Earl of Balfour, K. G., O. M., F. R. S., Etc.* (2 vols., New York, 1937) and J. L. Garvin's *The Life of Joseph Chamberlain* (3 vols., London, 1932-1934), completed by J. Amery, *The Life of Joseph Chamberlain* (London, 1951), are excellent biographies with a fair amount of information about Anglo-American relations, as one would expect in studies of two such staunch advocates of close ties between the two countries. A competent biography of the opposition leader is A. G. Gardiner, *The Life of Sir William Harcourt* (2 vols., London, 1923). Not so good a book, but touching more upon Anglo-American relations, is Lord Newton, *Lord Lansdowne, a Biography* (London, 1929). The only biography of the great British ambassador is R. B. Mowat, *The Life of Lord Pauncefote, First Ambassador to the United States* (Boston and New York, 1929); though not outstanding, it needs to be consulted occasionally.

There are two biographies of the Canadian Prime Minister: O. D. Skelton, *Life and Letters of Sir Wilfrid Laurier* (2 vols., New York, 1922), has some pertinent material as well as a general portrayal of Laurier; J. S. Willison, *Sir Wilfrid Laurier and the Liberal Party* (2 vols., London, 1903), is of use only for background information. A helpful book particularly as regards the Alaska boundary controversy is J. W. Dafoe, *Clifford Sifton in Relation to His Times* (Toronto, 1931). The opposition leader, Sir Charles Tupper, wrote his *Recollections of Sixty Years* (London, 1914), and E. M. Saunders edited *The Life and Letters of the Rt. Hon. Sir Charles Tupper, Bart., K. C. M. G.* (2 vols., London, 1916), but neither has any material directly relevant to Britain and America, 1898-1903. John Buchan, *Lord Minto, a Memoir* (London and New York, 1924), is a study of the Governor-General useful only for background information.

Other books and magazine articles concern the topics of particular chapters. B. A. Reuter, *Anglo-American Relations During the Spanish-American War* (New York, 1924), is a helpful but rather sketchy introduction dealing mainly with the war months. A good study of the European mediation moves is R. G. Neale, "British-American Relations During the Spanish-American War: Some Problems," *Historical Studies, Australia and New Zealand*, vol. 6 (1953), pp. 72-89. D. C. Miner, *The Fight for the Panama Route: the Story of the Spooner Act and the Hay-Herrán Treaty* (New York, 1940), gives the best account of the political maneuverings to abrogate the Clayton-Bulwer treaty.

J. A. S. Grenville, "Great Britain and the Isthmian Canal, 1898-1901," *American Historical Review*, vol. 61 (1955), pp. 48-69, deals with certain aspects of the negotiation of the Hay-Pauncefote treaty. A detailed account of the struggle for Samoa is given by G. H. Ryden, *The Foreign Policy of the United States in Relation to Samoa* (New Haven, 1933). My own *Special Business Interests and the Open Door Policy* (New Haven, 1951) deals with some of the matters important to British and American Far Eastern policy. J. H. Ferguson, *American Diplomacy and the Boer War* (Philadelphia, 1939), describes John Hay's pro-British conduct of foreign policy during that war. D. Perkins, *The Monroe Doctrine, 1867-1907* (Baltimore, 1937), has an excellent chapter on the Venezuelan intervention. J. A. Garraty, "Henry Cabot Lodge and the Alaskan Boundary Tribunal," *New England Quarterly*, vol. 24 (1951), pp. 469-494, quotes a number of letters written by Lodge while serving on the Alaska Boundary Tribunal. J. S. Ewart, *The Kingdom of Canada, Imperial Preference, the Colonial Conferences, the Alaska Boundary, and Other Essays* (Toronto, 1908), though not a scholarly work, has a section on the boundary settlement which should be read, partly because it reflects an extreme Canadian reaction. Viscount Alverstone, *Recollections of Bar and Bench* (New York and London, 1914), defends the Chief Justice's verdict in the boundary case.

Index